Animals and Ourselves

Animals and Ourselves

*Essays on Connections
and Blurred Boundaries*

Edited by KATHY MERLOCK JACKSON,
KATHY SHEPHERD STOLLEY *and* LISA LYON PAYNE

McFarland & Company, Inc., Publishers
Jefferson, North Carolina

LIBRARY OF CONGRESS CATALOGUING-IN-PUBLICATION DATA

Names: Jackson, Kathy Merlock, 1955– editor. | Stolley, Kathy Shepherd, editor. | Payne, Lisa Lyon, editor.
Title: Animals and ourselves : essays on connections and blurred boundaries / edited by Kathy Merlock Jackson, Kathy Shepherd Stolley, and Lisa Lyon Payne.
Description: Jefferson, NC : McFarland & Company, Inc., Publishers, 2020 | Includes bibliographical references and index.
Identifiers: LCCN 2020037801 | ISBN 9781476671734 (paperback) ∞|
ISBN 9781476640143 (ebook)
Subjects: LCSH: Human-animal relationships. | Human-animal relationships in mass media. | Animals in mass media.
Classification: LCC QL85 .A5365 2020 | DDC 590—dc23
LC record available at https://lccn.loc.gov/2020037801

BRITISH LIBRARY CATALOGUING DATA ARE AVAILABLE

ISBN (print)978-1-4766-7173-4
ISBN (ebook) 978-1-4766-4014-3

Front cover image © 2020 Shutterstock

Printed in the United States of America

*McFarland & Company, Inc., Publishers
Box 611, Jefferson, North Carolina 28640
www.mcfarlandpub.com*

One's study of the blurred line between humans and animals often begins with a personal experience with a beloved pet. The authors represented here share the types and names of the significant animals of their lives: forty dogs, forty-two cats, five guinea pigs, two baby chicks, two birds, a goat, a horse, a cow, a rabbit, a bobcat, a rat, some sheep, some monkeys, and lots of fish (tropical and goldfish). We dedicate this book to these remarkable animals, who teach us humanity and deeply enrich our lives:

Akimoto-san
K.C., Spider, Elsa
Shnitzel, Pashoshit, Aslan, Tultul, Anna
Buddy
Star, Mimi
Runt and Izzie; Love Bug and Impala; the monkeys of St. Kitts
Julius
Thomas, Gizmo Minkette, Robert Palmer "Bob" Gamble
Matsu, P.J., Gatsby, Grendel, Heidi
Olympia, Patches, Precious, Lynnie, Maisy, Gomez
Pepper, Heidi, Gypsy, Noodle, Rosebud
Anne Shirley, Winter, Asia, Nefertiti, Azriel, Anthony
Jasper
St. Jerome, Morgan Danger, Kara, Maggie, Bela
Eleanor, Annabelle, Charlotte, Mini, Lucy, Vera
Henry and Penelope; Bonnie and Clyde
Penelope, Daisy, Splotch, Liesl, and Twyla; Blueberry
Snickers, Gobie
Jessica, Patches, Perky, Jake, Roger, Kelly, Shaki
Otis, Poly, Mei-Mei, Row, Gerry, Tang
Benjamin Bunny, Buster, Chester, D.W., Lamentations
Molly, Sassy Devil Kitty, Miss Scarlett
Maggie, Sterling, Sally
Andre, Elvis
Sabre, Leon, B.C., Ernest T.
Olive, Tallulah, Winston
Bluebell

Acknowledgments

In the course of preparing this book, we encountered many individuals intrigued by the idea of human/nonhuman animal blurring, and we appreciate the tales they shared and their enthusiasm for our work. We especially thank our colleagues at Virginia Wesleyan University for their encouragement and insights and to Amy Dudley for her administrative assistance. Without Carl Sederholm at Brigham Young University, this book might still be a bunch of files on our computers; he led us to Harmony Donnelly, also at Brigham Young University, who did an extraordinary job of preparing the final manuscript. We value their time, expertise, and commitment. Susan Kilby and the editors at McFarland championed this project, and we are grateful. Finally, we thank our families—Joe, Nick and Lucie; Bill; John, Jack, and Charlie—for their love and support and for always inspiring us to do our best.

Table of Contents

Introduction

KATHY MERLOCK JACKSON, LISA LYON PAYNE
and KATHY SHEPHERD STOLLEY

The sign shown on the next page stands at the foot of a neighborhood beach access to the Chesapeake Bay in Virginia Beach, Virginia, where the editors of this volume live. We knew neither Chip the dog nor the person who wrote these words and erected the monument, but we understand the accuracy of the sentiment and how widely it is shared. Two things are certain: the qualities of human and nonhuman animals merge, and people and animals of all kinds, domesticated and nondomesticated, share important symbiotic relationships. This book offers reflections on these points.

When editors set out to collect submissions for a book, they have no idea what—if anything—they will receive. Is the topic timely? Are others interested? Does the approach elicit engagement? For this volume on the blurred line between humans and nonhuman animals, we received a much greater response than we anticipated, making for a bigger book, and the range of the topics far exceeded the parameters we had initially outlined. This project began with some quirky news stories that piqued our interest: plastic surgery for dogs, luxury accommodations for horses, animals whose YouTube sites drew millions of views. The evolving idea of anthropomorphism primarily through a Westernized popular culture lens, which lies at the center of this book, became a starting point for exploring how nonhuman animals are likened to humans and its opposite, how humans are likened to nonhuman animals. Anthropomorphization permeates modern popular culture in examples as familiar as Disney's depiction of animals to moral lessons from children's literature to our cultural preoccupations with Internet cats. Increasingly, however, forms and adaptations of anthropomorphization are extending how this concept is expressed and blurring the lines between human and nonhuman in significant ways. As proposals for the book poured in, it was apparent that scholars' interests were also wide-reaching and were just as focused on fictional animals as real ones and on historical treatments as contemporary ones.

Writers have always recognized the characteristics that humans and animals share. The first stories that parents read to their children—familiar fare such as Aesop's fables, "The Fox and the Hare," "The Ugly Duckling," "The Three Little Pigs," "The Frog Princess," "Three Billy Goats Gruff," *Charlotte's Web*, and *The Wind and the Willows*—feature anthropomorphized animals. Children learn about different personalities and ways to navigate the world through tales about animals, both written and on-screen. Animated classics, such as the Disney Studio's *Silly Symphonies*, *Bambi*, *Dumbo*, *Lady and the Tramp*, *101 Dal-*

NEAR THIS SPOT
ARE DEPOSITED THE REMAINS OF ONE
WHO POSSESSED BEAUTY WITHOUT VANITY,
STRENGTH WITHOUT INSOLENCE,
COURAGE WITHOUT FEROCITY,
AND ALL THE VIRTUES OF MAN WITHOUT HIS VICES.

THIS PRAISE, WHICH WOULD BE UNMEANING
FLATTERY
IF INSCRIBED OVER HUMAN ASHES,
IS BUT A JUST TRIBUTE TO THE MEMORY OF
CHIP, A DOG,
WHO WAS BORN IN VIRGINIA IN 2000
AND DIED AT CHICKS BEACH MAY 28TH, 2015

Pet memorial at beach access to Chesapeake Bay on Jefferson Avenue in Virginia Beach, Virginia.

matians, *The Jungle Book*, *The Fox and the Hound*, and *The Aristocats*, and live-action features, such as *Homeward Bound*, *The Adventures of Milo and Otis*, and *Babe*, become childhood favorites. Animal characters illustrate human virtues and foibles. The first section of the book, "Representations: Images of Animals in Media," examines how these blurred lines between human and nonhuman animals entertain and teach moral lessons and thus occupy integral roles in the world's narratives.

The blurring of the line between human and nonhuman animals in contemporary culture is driven by many factors. Rights advocacy—be it for women, LGBTQ individuals, the elderly, children, and immigrants—defines our culture, and many believe that animals should have more rights than have been previously accorded them. Innovations in health and wellness care have skyrocketed, making procedures for pets and other animals possible and desirable. Marketers, always interested in developing new products and audiences, are moving into the animal realm to the tune of billions of dollars annually. Increasingly, pets are identified as full family members. Finally, social media, with their emphasis on fast celebrity and standing out, have drawn attention to animals and fueled new perceptions. In the second section of the book, "Relationships: Interactions Between Humans and Animals," authors explore how and why, while humans and nonhuman animals have always co-existed, the relationship is changing, moving in new directions.

The third section of the book, "Reflections: Cultural Analysis of Human/Animal Blurring," examines the significance of these social constructs across popular culture and the complexities of the human-animal relationship. Contributions address how and why the traits and characteristics humans ascribe to nonhuman animals have significant consequences by shaping our relationships with those animals and other humans, our understandings of ourselves and what it means to be human, and the consequences of those representations for the nonhuman animals who share this world. As behaviors, roles, and expectations that used to be reserved for humans increasingly apply to animals, authors in this section address such questions as: how are lines between human and animal being obfuscated? How are animals becoming, and being treated, more like humans, and to a lesser degree, how are humans becoming more like animals? How are animals becoming extensions of people's identities?

In many ways, this is not so much a book about animals, and the way we as humans regard, define, and (de)construct animals, but a book about the boundaries of humanness. Most simply put, it is a book about us.

PART I

Representations
Images of Animals in Media

Animal/Human Relations in Two Prairie Tales by L. Frank Baum

MARK I. WEST

L. Frank Baum spent his early years in the state of New York and his final years in California, but he lived in the Midwest during his most productive years as a writer. In September 1888, Baum left Syracuse, New York, and moved to the town of Aberdeen in what was then the Dakota Territory. While in Aberdeen, he briefly ran a general store called Baum's Bazaar and tried his hand at operating a weekly newspaper called the *Aberdeen Saturday Pioneer*. Both businesses failed, and in 1891 he and his family moved to Chicago where he stayed until 1910 when he relocated to Hollywood, California, where he lived until his death in 1919. *The Wonderful Wizard of Oz* and most of his other important books date from the years he lived in Chicago, but he often drew on his experiences living on the Dakota prairie in the stories he wrote while living in Chicago (Koupal 203). Such was the case with his Twinkle Tales, a series of fantasy stories he wrote for young children. In two of these stories, Baum explores the relationship between the farmers who settled the prairie and the native animals, and in the process, he blurred the line between humans and animals.

Baum's interest in writing about the lives of animals can be traced back to the days of his youth when he raised and exhibited exotic chickens or "fancy fowls" as he called them (Loncraine 61–62). His favorite breed of chickens was the Hamburg. In fact, he wrote about his breed of chickens in his first published book, *The Book of the Hamburgs: A Brief Treatise upon the Mating, Rearing and Management of the Different Varieties of Hamburgs*. This short book came out in 1886, fourteen years before the publication of *The Wonderful Wizard of Oz*. In writing about this breed of chickens, Baum not only went into considerable detail about lives and characteristics of these birds, but he also advocated that they be treated in a humane way. "Hamburgs," he wrote, "should have free range" (*Hamburgs* 11).

Animals make appearances in many of Baum's fantasy stories. The dog Toto, for example, is Dorothy's boon companion in *The Wonderful Wizard of Oz*, and a hen named Billina figures prominently in *Ozma of Oz*. Baum also wrote a series of animal fairy tales that appeared in a magazine called the *Delineator* in 1905, and two of these animal fairy tales are set on the Dakota prairie. One of them is titled "The Enchanted Buffalo," and the other is titled "The Discontented Gopher" (West 134–154). In these two animal fairy tales, the focus is on the animals' relationships with each other. Animals also take center stage in Baum's *Twinkle and Chubbins: Their Astonishing Adventures in Nature-Fairyland.* Published in 1911 and reprinted in 1987 by the International Wizard of Oz Club, this book is actually a compilation of a series of six little books that originally appeared separately in 1906 and were initially known collectively as the Twinkle Tales.

Most of the stories in *Twinkle and Chubbins* are light-hearted fantasy stories featuring anthropomorphic animals, but in two of them Baum addresses the changing relationship between animals and humans when people move into areas that had previously been occupied by only animals. In these two stories, Baum anticipates the positions that contemporary literary critics in the field of ecocriticism have taken related to animal rights and the destruction of natural ecosystems and native habitats.

The Twinkle Tales are similar in tone to the Oz books. However, because Baum intended these tales for beginning readers, they are written on a somewhat simpler level than his stories set in Oz. The fact that he originally published the Twinkle Tales under the pseudonym of Laura Bancroft suggests that Baum may have seen these stories as appealing primarily to girl readers. He often used female pseudonyms when he was writing specifically for girls. He used the name Edith Van Dyne, for example, when he wrote the girls' story titled *Aunt Jane's Nieces.*

Most of the Twinkle Tales feature a girl who lives on a farm in the middle of the Dakota prairie. The girl in these stories is named Twinkle, and she lives with her parents near the tiny town of Edgeley, North Dakota. Edgeley is a real town that is located about sixty miles north of Aberdeen, South Dakota, where Baum lived from 1888 until the middle of 1891. Baum was familiar with the town of Edgeley because he had gone there a number of times to visit relatives. His wife's sister and sister's family moved to Edgeley in 1882 as homesteaders and struggled to support themselves through farming (Artz 17). Twinkle's parents also work at farming, but these fictional characters are more successful at this occupation than Baum's relatives ever were.

Baum introduces the reader to the wildlife of the Dakota prairie in the tale titled "Prairie-Dog Town." This tale opens with an amusing description of the town of Edgeley:

> On the great western prairies of Dakota is a little town called Edgeley, because it is on the edge of civilization—a very big word which means some folks have found a better way to live than other folks. The Edgeley people have a good way to live, for there are almost seventeen wooden houses there, and among them are a schoolhouse, a church, a store and a blacksmith-shop. If people walked out of their front door they were upon the little street; if they walked out the back doors they were on the broad prairies. That was why Twinkle, who was a farmer's little girl, lived so near the town that she could easily walk to school [*Twinkle* 137–138].

As the story progresses, Twinkle and her friend Chubbins, the son of the local schoolteacher, go on a community picnic. While everyone else is eating and relaxing, Twinkle and Chubbins leave the town of Edgeley and wander across the prairie where they discover a prairie dog town. They are intrigued by the mounds of earth and wonder about the animals that live under these mounds. They decide to lie quietly nearby and wait for the prairie dogs to "stick their heads up" (149). Until this point, the story is completely realistic, but the rest of the tale is full of fantasy elements.

While Twinkle and Chubbins are waiting, a prairie dog emerges from one of the mounds and begins to talk with the children. He informs the children that there is an entire subterranean town beneath their feet. Twinkle and Chubbins want to visit the town, but they are far too large to enter. A wizard-like prairie dog named Presto Digi solves this problem by magically shrinking the children down to the size of prairie dogs. The children then explore the Lilliputian world of the prairie dogs, where they learn that the prairie dogs have their own society quite apart from the human society associated with the town of Edgeley.

The children's underground adventures culminate with a zany luncheon sponsored by the mayor of the prairie dogs. Although the participants in the luncheon behave much like humans, the food that is served is associated with the natural setting of the story:

> Neither Twinkle nor Chubbins was very hungry, but they were curious to know what kind of food the prairie-dogs ate, so they watched carefully when the different dishes were passed around. Only grains and vegetables were used, for prairie-dogs do not eat meat. There was a milk-weed soup at first; and then yellow corn, boiled and sliced thin. Afterward they had a salad of thistle leaves, and some bread made of barley. The dessert was a dish of sweet dark honey made by prairie-bees, and some cakes flavored with some sweet and spicy roots that only prairie-dogs know how to find [*Twinkle* 185–186].

The story concludes with the children returning to the surface after which Presto Digi turns them back to their normal size. Twinkle thanks their hosts for introducing them to the underground world of the prairie dogs and calls out good-bye. The prairie dogs gather aboveground to say good-bye to their child visitors, and "then all of the prairie dogs popped into their holes and quickly disappeared" (*Twinkle* 193).

By the end of "Prairie-Dog Town," Twinkle and Chubbins realize that Edgeley is not the only town on the prairie and that the humans are not the only residents who call the prairie home. Edgeley might be the edge of human "civilization," but Baum makes it clear that there are animal societies that extend beyond edge of human habitation. Although Baum's prairie dog characters are anthropomorphic in nature, Baum presents these animal characters as being equal to the human characters. As portrayed in Baum's tale, the prairie dogs' underground community is every bit as civilized as the humans' aboveground community. By presenting the prairie dogs in such a positive and sympathetic light, Baum implies that humans should treat these animals with respect. This theme is even more pronounced in the Twinkle Tale titled "Mr. Woodchuck."

Like "Prairie-Dog Town," "Mr. Woodchuck" makes extensive use of the Dakota prairie setting. In the beginning of "Mr. Woodchuck," Twinkle's father decides to trap a woodchuck that has been eating his vegetables and other crops. Twinkle accompanies her father while he sets the deadly steel trap near the entrance to the woodchuck's hole. She lingers near the woodchuck's hole, hoping to catch a glimpse of the woodchuck. While she is waiting for the creature to appear, she falls asleep in the grass. What follows is a dream sequence that combines the sort of fantasy elements found in Lewis Carroll's *Alice's Adventures in Wonderland* with a pointed message about the importance of treating animals with kindness and respect.

The dream sequence begins with Twinkle observing a jackrabbit dressed in a messenger-boy's uniform delivering a telegram to Mr. Woodchuck. Like Carroll's White Rabbit, this rabbit is in a hurry. He thrusts the telegram in Mr. Woodchuck's paws and dashes off. Mr. Woodchuck reads the telegram, and from it he learns about the trap. He then notices Twinkle and takes her into a beautiful garden, much like the garden in *Alice*. Once in the garden, Mr. Woodchuck and Twinkle have a memorable conversation, which causes Twinkle to see her world from a different point of view:

> "It's very pleasant in this garden," said Twinkle. "I don't mind being here a bit."
> "But you can't stay here," replied Mister Woodchuck, "as you ought to be very uncomfortable in my

presence. You see, you are one of the deadliest enemies of my race. All you human beings live for or think of is how to torture and destroy woodchucks."

"Oh, no!" she answered. "We have many more important things than that to think of. But when a woodchuck gets eating our clover and the vegetables, and spoils a lot, we just have to do something to stop it. That's why my papa set the trap."

"You're selfish," said Mister Woodchuck, "and you're cruel to the poor little animals that can't help themselves, and have to eat what they can find, or starve. There's enough for all of us growing in the broad fields. … The land belonged to the wild creatures long before you people came here and began to farm. And really, there is no reason why you should be so cruel. It hurts dreadfully to be caught in a trap" [*Twinkle* 30–31].

Like *Alice's Adventures in Wonderland*, "Mr. Woodchuck" concludes with a surreal court proceeding. Twinkle is put on trial for her role in setting the trap. Presiding over this trial is Judge Stoneyheart, an old and wise woodchuck who realizes that Twinkle is dreaming. Nonetheless, he condemns her as an enemy of the peaceful woodchucks. He argues that Twinkle must remember her dream. He is of the opinion that "people don't remember their dreams unless the dreams are unusually horrible" (*Twinkle* 62). In order to make sure that she does not forget the lessons that she has learned in this dream, he sentences her to step on the same trap that her father had set. Just as she is about to step on the trap, Twinkle wakes up.

That evening she remembers her dream, and she decides to speak to her father on behalf of the woodchucks. In the process, Baum suggests that children have a special connection to animals. The conversation that Twinkle has with her father shows how a child's empathy with animals can translate into action:

"Papa," said Twinkle, when supper was over and she was nestled snugly in his lap, "I wish you wouldn't set any more traps for the woodchucks."

"Why not, my darling?" He asked in surprise.

"They're cruel," she answered. "It must hurt the poor animals dreadfully to be caught in them."

"I suppose it does," said her father, thoughtfully. "But if I don't trap the woodchucks they eat our clover and vegetables."

"Never mind that," said Twinkle, earnestly; "Let's divide with them. God made the woodchucks, you know, just as He made us, and they can't plant and grow things as we do; so they have to take what they can get, or starve to death. And surely, papa, there's enough to eat in this big and beautiful world, for all of God's creatures."

Papa whistled softly, although his face was grave; and then he bent down and kissed his little girl's forehead.

"I won't set any more traps, dear," he said.

And that evening, after Twinkle had been tucked snugly away in bed, her father walked slowly through the sweet-smelling fields to the woodchuck's hole; there lay the trap, showing plainly in the bright moonlight. He picked it up and carried it back to the barn. It was never used again [*Twinkle* 68].

"Prairie-Dog Town" and "Mr. Woodchuck" have many points in common. Both are set on the Dakota prairie, both feature anthropomorphic animals that are native to the prairie, and both deal with the interactions between humans and animals. However, the stories differ in tone and theme. "Prairie-Dog Town" is a breezy and fanciful tale that ends without imparting a moral message. "Mr. Woodchuck" is a more focused and serious story that clearly is intended to cause children to question some of society's prevailing practices concerning the treatment of animals. However, both of these stories deal with the interactions between animals and humans, and both encourage child readers to feel empathy for the animals as they try to live alongside the more powerful humans.

Baum's portrayal of human/animal relationships in *Twinkle and Chubbins* speaks to many of the issues that are covered in contemporary scholarly works that look at children's literature through the critical lens of ecocriticism. These scholarly works include *Wild Things: Children's Culture and Ecocriticism,* co-edited by Sidney I. Dobrin and Kenneth B. Kidd, and *Animality and Children's Literature and Film* by Amy Ratelle.

As Dobrin and Kidd point out in the introduction to their collection, children's literature and other forms of children's culture can play an important role in providing children with a "deeper—or at least different—awareness" of the "natural world" (Dobrin and Kidd 7). This point relates directly to Baum's approach to writing about nature. In *Twinkle and Chubbins,* Baum clearly sets out to encourage children to take a different and perhaps more appreciative view of the natural world. By subtitling the book *Their Astonishing Adventures in Nature-Fairyland,* Baum equates nature with fantasy and suggests that interacting with the natural world can be a source of "astonishment." Through his word choices, Baum signals to his child readers that these stories deal with the natural world but not in a didactic way.

In *Animality and Children's Literature and Film,* Ratelle argues that children's literature has the potential of "encouraging child readers to identify … closely with animals" (Ratelle 141). She discusses several children's books that argue for animal rights, including *Memoirs of Dick, the Little Poney,* published anonymously in 1799, Anna Sewell's *Black Beauty,* published in 1877, and Enid Bagnold's *National Velvet,* published in 1935. She argues that these children's books "resituate human/animal interaction in mutual respect and equality, subverting the traditional Western view of humans as an exceptional species" (Ratelle 141). Although Ratelle does not cover any of Baum's stories in her book, the tales in *Twinkle and Chubbins* provide additional examples of children's stories in which animal/human interactions move toward "mutual respect and equality." This is theme is especially evident in "Mr. Woodchuck."

Katharine Rogers, in her biography *L. Frank Baum: Creator of Oz,* discusses several of the stories in Baum's *Twinkle and Chubbins.* She argues that through these stories, "Baum makes a powerful case for animal rights and against human self-centeredness" (Rogers 138). Baum has long been recognized as a pioneering figure in the area of American fantasy literature and as an early advocate for women's rights, but the stories in *Twinkle and Chubbins* suggest that he should also be recognized as an early advocate for animal rights.

WORKS CITED

Artz, Don. *A Tour of L. Frank Baum's Aberdeen.* Aberdeen, SD: Memories Incorporated, 1967.

Baum, L. Frank. *The Book of the Hamburgs: A Brief Treatise upon the Mating Rearing and Management of the Different Varieties of Hamburgs.* Hartford, CT: H.H. Stoddard, 1886.

_____, *Twinkle and Chubbins: Their Astonishing Adventures in Nature Fairyland.* Chicago: Reilly & Britton, 1911.

Dobrin, Sidney I., and Kenneth B. Kidd, eds. *Wild Things: Children's Culture and Ecocriticism.* Detroit: Wayne State University Press, 2004.

Koupal, Nancy Tystad. "The Wonderful Wizard of the West: L. Frank Baum in South Dakota, 1888–91." *Great Plains Quarterly* 9 (1989): 203–215.

Loncraine, Rebecca. *The Real Wizard of Oz: The Life and Times of L. Frank Baum.* New York: Gotham Books, 2009.

Ratelle, Amy. *Animality and Children's Literature and Film.* London: Palgrave Macmillan, 2015.

Rogers, Katharine M. *L. Frank Baum: Creator of Oz.* New York: Macmillan, 2007.

West, Mark I. "The Dakota Fairy Tales of L. Frank Baum." *Baum's Road to Oz: The Dakota Years.* Ed. Nancy Tystad Koupal. Pierre, SD: South Dakota State Historical Press, 2000. 134–154.

Cultivating Conservation

Childhood and Animalhood in the Fiction of Ernest Thompson Seton

MARTIN WOODSIDE

Best known as one of the founders of the Boy Scouts of America, Ernest Thompson Seton was also renowned in his time as an author, illustrator, and naturalist. His main interests were childhood and the natural world, and most of his work brought these twin interests together. As an author, Seton helped create an innovative type of animal story that proved popular with child readers. Featuring eight such stories, Seton's 1898 collection *Wild Animals I Have Known* established his reputation as an author of animal stories— even as it ignited controversy about his credentials as a true man of science. Seton was certainly not the first author to explore the relationship between childhood and animalhood in fiction, but his stories intentionally drew striking comparisons between animals and humans that were unusual and provocative in late nineteenth century America. In fact, *Wild Animals I Have Known* played a powerful role in shaping the relationship between childhood and animalhood in the Western world during the century to come.[1]

Seton's descriptions of the animal characters in *Wild Animals I Have Known* frequently assume a strong human element. Indeed, one of Seton's principal aims in these stories is to demonstrate to his readers that these animal characters are more like humans than is commonly presumed. He gives his animal protagonists names and ascribes emotions, characteristics and desires to them that readers can readily identify with. "How many of us have ever got to know a wild animal?" (47), Seton asks, in "Silverspot: The Story of a Crow," before introducing us to the protagonist, "a wise old crow" (48). In many instances, Seton describes animal abilities and behaviors as complex and even superior to similar human behavior. The crows, he notes, boast "a language and a social system that is wonderfully human in many of its chief points, and in some is better carried out than our own" (51). In "Wully, The Story of a Yaller Dog," Seton describes how Wully is casually abandoned by his master, a thoughtless brute the author describes as "addle-pated Robin." Wully, in comparison, is "a very bright little dog" (227). Night after night, the dog faithfully seeks Robin, "his heart true to his worthless master" (232). Finally, these stories all stay close to the animals' point of view and, as frequently is the case, focus on the ill treatment they receive at the hands of humans. As Debra Mitts-Smith writes, describing Seton's wolf stories, while "the wolves do not tell their stories, the authors give voice, albeit a human voice to the wolves' perspective" (52).

The element of the tragic plays an important role in Seton's animal stories. In the "Note to the Reader" introducing *Wild Animals I Have Known*, Seton notes that the "life of a wild animal *always has a tragic end*" (11). In these stories, fiction, the wild animal is doomed, his/her vaunted wildness relegating them to the vanishing past. Childhood, in the early twentieth century, was increasingly imagined through notions of futurity. However, one of the chief appeals of Seton's fiction is how it ties these two threads together through the lens of nostalgia. As a conservation text, which it surely is, *Wild Animals I Have Known* speaks directly to child readers, while asking readers of all ages to imagine notions of childhood and animalhood through one another, to imagine a world where wild animals can, like children, be protected, their endangered wildness preserved.

As one looks back, the interweaving of childhood and animalhood in *Wild Animals I Have Known* is not all that surprising. The history of the modern animals' rights movement features strong parallels to the history of children's rights in Britain and America. Harold Guither describes an ad-hoc animal rights movement at work in the early eighteenth century, when writers began exploring how animals felt pain and calling attention to the "cruel treatment of animals raised and slaughtered for food, and the religious teachings that influenced humane treatment of both humans and animals" (1). The first society for the prevention of cruelty to animals was founded in Britain in 1821, and the first British law concerning cruelty to animals, the "Ill-treatment of Cattle Bill," was passed into law in June of 1822. The American Society for the Prevention of Cruelty to Animals was formed in 1866, eight years before the New York Society for the Prevention of Cruelty to Children, which was founded in 1874.[2]

In 1894, British crusader Henry Stephens Salt published *Animals' Rights,* which would become a seminal text for animals' rights campaigners. Looking beyond the issue of animal welfare, Salt argues that animals are entitled to some of the same rights as humans. In the first chapter of his book, "The Principle of Animals' Rights," he traces a rhetoric of animals' rights reminiscent of the conception of human rights articulated by Thomas Paine a hundred years earlier in his *Rights of Man.* Referring to the Britain's "Ill-treatment of Cattle Bill," Salt notes that this was the first time that the idea of jus animalium "was recognized, however partially and tentatively at first, by English law, and the animals included in the Act ceased to be the mere property of their owners" (6).

Salt maintains that bill did not go far enough, considering, as it does, animals as property, and he calls for laws that recognize that animals are "possessed of a distinctive individuality" and entitled to certain freedoms. Those freedoms, he writes, include the opportunity to " live one's own life—to realize one's true self." This, Salt maintains, "is the highest moral purpose of man and animal alike; and that animals possess their due measure of this sense of individuality is scarcely open to doubt" (12). Interestingly, Salt compares the fight for animals' rights both to the fights against the slave trade and child labor (167) and invokes John Stuart Mill, who argues the "reasons for legal intervention in favour of children ... apply not any less strongly to the case of those unfortunate slaves and victims of the most brutal part of mankind, the lower animals" (qtd. in Salt 100).

Again, these comparisons are not so unusual. At the same time Salt was advocating for animals' rights, increasing attention was given to children as a group in need of protection. In early twentieth-century America, Progressive Era reformers invested considerable energy in children's rights through a raft of initiatives, including the fight to end child labor and efforts to establish a juvenile justice system. In 1912, The U.S. Children's Bureau became the world's first national body devoted solely to children's welfare. As

Kriste Lindenmeyer points out, the bureau's founders, Lillian Wald and Florence Kelly, perceived childhood as a time that called for protection and dependence and clearly saw children's rights through the lens of futurity and progress. In order to be successful future citizens, they argued, American children needed to live—child mortality was an early focus of the bureau—and be protected (10).

Momentum for forming the Children's Bureau was also driven by the argument that America "was progressing at the expense of many of its youngest members," and children were helpless victims subject to exploitation—in the labor market—and abuse—at the hands of unworthy adults (11). Early Progressive Era arguments for children's rights drew on the incipient science of child development and, as Lindenmeyer puts it, the "new emphasis by physicians, sociologists, and psychologists on childhood as a special period of life with specific needs" (12). Interestingly, she notes, this sentiment gained cultural currency precisely at the time when "the proportions of young people in the total population diminished" (12). As with certain endangered animals, the increasing scarcity of children seems to have influenced how they were valued. By the turn of the century, child and wild animal alike were seen by many as precious resources that required protection from human adults. Teddy Roosevelt was a powerful supporter of Wald's early efforts at child welfare at the Henry Street Settlement. For Roosevelt, Lindenmeyer argues, the idea of a federal children's bureau promised to "act as a conservator of children as a natural resource, preserved for the future in much the same way as the regulation of wilderness and wildlife" (16).[3]

Progressive Era visions of the future were strongly wedded to new ideas about biological development. The emerging twentieth-century science of child development was steeped in late nineteenth-century notions of evolutionary theory, fueling the Child-Study movement, a precursor to modern child psychology. The Child-Study movement included a wide range of educators and researchers dedicated to the scientific observation of children. Many leading voices in the field, including Charles Darwin, understood the child as a literal primitive, a wild creature who could be developed into a civilized adult. For Darwin and others, children became objects of study, and the child became an invaluable tool for understanding the past and plotting a better future. As Scottish psychologist James Crichton Browne explained, in 1883, it was critical to understand that children, in their primitive states, "are not little nineteenth-century men and women, but diamond editions of very remote ancestors, full of savage whims and impulses, and savage rudiments of virtue" (379).[4]

As an educator, Seton was clearly influenced by the Child-Study movement, especially the work of G. Stanley Hall, whose two-volume tome, *Adolescence,* was published in 1904 and provided the dominant framework for this life stage for decades to come. Seton's ideas of child development were steeped in his reverence for the natural world and, like Hall, he saw the essential wildness of boys as a vital resource for ushering in a new generation of men more attuned to nature. In March of 1902, Seton led a group of forty-two boys on a camping exhibition, a trip that led to the founding of the Woodcraft Indians. Seton's vision of the group was published in installments of "Ernest Seton's Boys," a guide to activities for boys, in the *Ladies' Home Journal,* from May to November of that year. These writings were collected and augmented in 1907 for *The Birch-Bark Roll of the Woodcraft Indians,* which spelled out Seton's theory of Woodcraft and became a template for the first Boy Scouts of America handbook a few years later. In his work with boys, the idea of Woodcraft is mostly expressed in terms of the Indian, a type of Indian that, according to Seton, "whether he existed or not, stands for the highest type of the primitive life." This ideal Indian, he notes, "was a master of Woodcraft" and presents a model the boys of the Woodcraft Indians should aspire to (3).[5]

For Seton, animals are masters of woodcraft too, an idea that plays a central role in *Wild Animals I Have Known*. In "Ragglyug, The Story of a Cottontail Rabbit," the young Rag learns which water is safe to drink, and Seton notes that, "thus, he began the study of woodcraft, the oldest of sciences" (82). In "Redruff, The Story of the Don Valley Partridge," the young Redruff "is deep in woodcraft," allowing him to defy hunters and predators, while becoming "famous up and down the valley" (291). Of course, predators learn woodcraft as well. In "The Springfield Fox," the young foxes learn the "earliest lesson in woodcraft" through their introduction to a grassy hollow suitable for hunting mice (161). In each of these instances, the focus is on education. Through woodcraft, the young animal learns how to harness its inner wildness in order to develop properly, just as the young camper in the Woodcraft Indians would learn to harness his inner wildness. Through this "oldest of sciences," the young can be properly developed, young human and animal alike, into successful adults.

Of course, the animals in Seton's stories face a stark imperative to learn their woodcraft well; their very survival depends on it. The stories of Rag and Redruff are particularly poignant in this regard, documenting the daunting challenges smaller, more vulnerable creatures such as rabbits and partridges face simply to survive. Both of these stories are notable for their domestic focus, with loving mothers who school their children carefully in woodcraft before making great sacrifices on their behalf. In Rag's story, Molly, the mother, and Rag live anxiously from day to day avoiding a series of predators, including dogs, owls, weasels, foxes and, most frighteningly, men. For the young Rag, the most sustained threat actually comes from another rabbit, a large male who overpowers him and his mother. Rag challenges the strange rabbit and is beaten badly. From that point, Seton writes, "began a reign of terror for Rag." Neither mother nor son can escape the bigger rabbit. Rather than kill the mother, "the stranger made love to her, and because she hated him and tried to get away, he treated her shamefully" (102).

Seton's attention to the emotional damage of this encounter stands out. He dwells on Molly's shame and on Rag's helplessness. "How maddening," he writes, for Rag "to see his little mother daily beaten and torn, as well as to see all his favorite feeding-grounds, the cosy nook, and the pathways he had made with such labor forced from him by this hateful brute" (103). Seton invests these rabbit characters with emotions his readers can readily identify with, allowing them to feel kinship and empathy for the beleaguered rabbits. In addition, Seton graphically portrays scenes of abuse that may well have struck a chord with child readers, who could relate to Rag's sense of powerless and, perhaps, be all too familiar with the sadistic figure of the powerful male rabbit who punishes the young Rag and his mother repeatedly.

A deep sense of hopelessness pervades Redruff's story. The young partridge is born with eleven siblings. In the story's very first scene, the day-old chicks are attacked by a fox, which their mother cleverly distracts, allowing all the chicks to survive. For the young partridges, though, the fight for survival is constant and the odds are long. They cling to their mother, and Seton explains that instinct "taught them to hide at the word from their mother," while it was "reason which made them keep under the shadow of her tail when the sun was smiting down, and from that day reason entered more and more into their expanding lives" (259). Seton's reader thus learns that the young partridges, like themselves, are creatures of reason, and follow along as these vulnerable creatures are killed off one by one. Born in the spring, only three partridges survive with their mother through September. Striking off on his own, Redruff takes a mate and becomes the head of his own family. For a while, this family lives happily at high ground, behind the high fence of an old castle with Redruff taking charge of the brood and "caring for them as his father never had for him" (279).

Seton highlights the human characteristics of the partridge. For instance, when Redruff finds Brownie, his mate, Seton describes how the male partridge's "whole nature was swamped by a new feeling—burnt up with thirst—a cooling spring in sight" (277). While the infant partridges developed a sense of reason, the mature Redruff is overcome by love. Capable of both rational thought and deep emotion, the birds become easily identifiable to Seton's readers—and instantly sympathetic. If Seton paints Redruff and his family in sympathetic terms, this stands in stark opposition to his depiction of the story's principal human character. Cuddy is an old man who, as Seton describes it "lived in a wretched shanty near the Don, north of Toronto" (265). The vagrant hunter squats on someone else's land and demonstrates a flagrant disregard for gaming laws. Through the course of the story, he harbors a desperate desire to kill Redruff and his family. Eventually, most of the partridge family has been killed, though not all by Cuddy's hand. When Redruff's last living daughter is shot by the hunter, Seton notes that "one by one the deadly cruel gun had stricken his near ones down, till now, once more, he was alone" (294).

Still, Cuddy's cruelty only intensifies. Unable to hunt Redruff in the winter, the old man sets out traps for him. Before long, the partridge is caught, and Seton describes his death in detail: "All that day, with growing, racking pains, poor Redruff hung and beat his great, strong wings in helpless struggles to be free. All day, all night with growing torture, until he longed for death" (295). This comes near the end of the story, as Cuddy transforms from immoral hunter to reprehensible torturer. These final pages mark the end of *Wild Animals I Have Known* as well, and Seton closes this final story with pointed questions for the reader. "Have the wild things no moral or legal rights?" he wonders, "what right has a man to inflict such long and fearful agony on a fellow-creature simply because that creature does not speak his language?" (295).

These questions call openly back to Seton's reader's note, reminding readers of his plea to reconsider animals as thinking, feeling creatures. As these animals "are creatures with wants and feelings, differing in degree only from our own," Seton writes in that introductory note, "they surely have their rights" (12). Seton means for his reader to consider those feelings and think about the question of animals' rights, just as Henry Salt implores his readers to in his *Animals' Rights*, published just a few years earlier.

The graphic suffering of these animals is a potent tool for Seton in his advocacy for animals' rights. In many of these stories, and notably the stories of Rag and Redruff, he shines a spotlight on the relative powerlessness of these animals and the capricious nature of the humans who torment them. As Jon T. Coleman puts it, Seton may "have sentimentalized animals but Seton did not sentimentalize people." In these stories, Coleman argues, "animals burst with feelings while hunters operated in an emotional void" (207). The grave suffering Seton associates with these animals echoes longstanding pleas for the public to consider the suffering of animals more seriously. In 1780, Jeremy Bentham offered one of the most powerful articulations of this line of reasoning. Supposing, Bentham muses, a full-grown horse is "a more rational as well as more conversable animal than an infant of a day or a week or even a month old." Why, he asks, should this matter? The question is not whether animals can reason, Bentham maintains, but "can they talk? but can they suffer?" (qtd. in Salt 14).

Seton's sentimentalized characterizations of wild animals and their suffering corresponds to the long tradition of representing childhood through suffering in various American rhetorical projects, most notably, perhaps, Harriet Beecher Stowe's *Uncle Tom's Cabin*. As Anna Mae Duane argues, Stowe's novel drew on well-established symbolic uses of American childhood "as a site of vulnerability, suffering, and victimhood" (3). Through representations of children like Stowe's Little Eva, Duane maintains, "the vulnerability, suffering, and victimization that occupied the forefront of these accounts became integral to many definitions of childhood itself" (5).

In Seton's time, Progressive Era reformers frequently drew on the symbolic vocabulary of the suffering child. From Lewis Hine's photos of children at work in factories, coal mines, and farms to Jacob Riis's harrowing account of derelict children on the streets of New York, these reformers sentimentalized children as innocent victims in need of protection from unscrupulous adults. Much like Seton's valiant but oppressed partridge Redruff, these children were presented as vital resources going to waste. For advocates of children's rights and animals' rights alike, then, descriptions of suffering frequently employed by reformers denote a process that comments on the increasingly blurred line between children and animals in twentieth-century America.

While all the animal characters in *Wild Animals I Have Known* suffer to some degree, the stories vary in focus on the suffering of stronger and weaker characters. While Rag and Redruff may be Seton's most pitiable characters, the wolf Lobo suffers in ways that clearly touched Seton deeply and seem to have resonated most powerfully with his readers. Seton wrote a number of wolf stories over the years, but Lobo's story, "The King of Currumpaw: A Wolf Story," is the most well-known of the bunch. First published in *Scribner's Magazine* in November of 1894, the story leads off *Wild Animals I Have Known*, introducing the reader to Lobo, "the gigantic leader of a remarkable pack of gray wolves that had ravaged the Currumpaw Valley for a number of years" (15). Described as a despot by Seton, Lobo rules over the valley with impunity, so that "terror reigned supreme among the cattle, and wrath and despair among their owners" (16). Lobo and his pack kill as they please, with the local ranchers, cowboys, and hunters helpless to stop them. Unlike Rag and Redruff, Lobo is not a wholly sympathetic character. He and his pack often kill for sport, as when they wipe out "two hundred and fifty sheep, apparently for the fun of it" (18). Nonetheless, Seton's admiration for the giant wolf stands out. Called on to hunt the wolf himself, Seton recounts being outwitted again and again, with Lobo scrupulously avoiding his traps and foiling his schemes. Lobo's "sagacity seemed never at fault," Seton concedes, adding he may never have caught the wolf save for one fatal weakness (32).[6]

This weakness marks Lobo's tragic flaw, accentuating the human traits of this remarkable animal. Unable to catch Lobo, Seton manages to catch and kill his mate Blanca. The night of Blanca's death, the mighty wolf searches fruitlessly for his mate. After realizing what has happened to her, Lobo is stricken by grief. Listening to the wolf's howls, Seton detects an "unmistakable note of sorrow in it now. It was no longer the loud, defiant howl, but a long plaintive wail." This "heart-broken wailing was piteous to hear," Seton notes, "sadder than I could possibly have believed" (37).

Lobo's heartbreak sparks an awakening in Seton, who goes on to give up hunting wolves and killing animals for sport. Mitt-Smith argues this marks the beginning of a trend in Seton's wolf stories, which pit "the heartless actions of the humans against the generous nature" of his wolves (54). Lobo is not quite as generous as the protagonists of Seton's other wolf stories, but his nobility is unmistakable. Seton impresses that nobility upon the reader, emphasizing Lobo's capacity for heartbreak and, critically, his desire to be free. As Mitts-Smith discerns, for wolves like Lobo "the desire to remain free is paramount, and their struggle to survive embodies an idealization of liberty." Through this idealization, "killing the wolf is taming the land, and the remaining wolves are reminders of a disappearing wilderness" (122).

The wild animal then, like the child, becomes immersed in nostalgia. By the end of the nineteenth century, naturalists like Seton and Roosevelt feared the prospect of wild animals disappearing from the American landscape. Pedagogues such as Hall perceived a similar danger confronting American children, whose inner wildness was threatened by the trappings of modernity. As Seton writes in the introduction to *The Birch-bark Roll*, the outdoor life is a kind of "physical regeneration so needful for continued national existence" (1). The nation, or more specifically the white race, has become "strained and broken by the over-busy world," and Seton envisioned the Woodcraft Indians as a remedy to the threat of overcivilization, restoring young people to nature and cultivating—rather than suppressing—their inner wildness (2).

In *Wild Animals I Have Known*, Seton trains a similar focus on the tragic fates of noble—but doomed—animals such as Lobo. These stories bring together Seton's work as a naturalist and boy worker, establishing wildness as a cherished and endangered part of both childhood and animalhood. As Gail Melson writes in 2001, "for at least the last hundred years, American cultural images weave together child and animal into the same cloth." Child and animal alike "represent the wild and unsocialized in the midst of the 'civilized' family" (18). Seton's animal stories play a pivotal role in the history of representation Melson describes, enshrining childhood and animalhood as objects of nostalgia, signifiers of the wild and its value in an increasingly modernized world.

Seton's wolf stories, in particular, traffic in a strikingly American brand of nostalgia, one that contributes to late nineteenth and early twentieth-century national identity projects. Coleman describes Seton as the father of a distinctive genre of animal story he calls the "last-wolf" story. Marked by strong emotional evocations of "grief, anger, vengeance, and love," these stories, Coleman argues, were "intended to cultivate feelings of loss and longing" and "preyed on sentiments of nostalgia" (213). The last wolf-story, Coleman contends, marks a pivot in cultural attitudes and beliefs toward wolves in America. Early American settlers considered wolves to be devious predators and hated them fiercely. They decimated livestock and threatened the very survival of ranchers. The last wolf-story helped shift these perceptions. "By portraying remnant wolves as doomed-yet-heroic outlaws," Coleman writes, these stories redeemed wolves and "placed wolf-killers at the cutting edge of history." These killers were pivotal to American nation-building, "improving vast landscapes" and "securing them for commercial agriculture." In this way, wolf-killers, like Seton in his younger days, "were the executioners of American progress" (210).

At the same time, the last-wolf story interrogated the costs of this process. Coleman traces a line between Seton's wolf stories and Aldo Leopold's *Thinking Like a Mountain*, published in 1974. Leopold, Coleman argues, uses Seton's template to make wolves the "poster beasts for an environmental movement." Combining nostalgia and ecology, Leopold suggested "the wolf was not a renegade hopelessly out of place in human landscapes." Rather, "wolf hunters were the outsiders, disrupting ecological systems in which predators played a vital role" (220). These shifting valuations of the American wolf hinge on changing ideas about the value and availability of wildness itself. In 1898, the wolf was seen as a threat to civilization, and Seton's sympathetic portrayal of this wild beast was unusual. By 1974, wolves had been placed on the Endangered Species List, and their wildness was seen as a vital resource to be protected.

Changing ideas of American childhood mirror shifting attitudes toward wolves during roughly the same time span. In 1890, Hall published an autobiographical account of his youth, "Boy Life in a Massachusetts Country Town Thirty Years Ago." As Kenneth Kidd puts it, Hall's "memoir of boy life participates in a larger late-nineteenth century narrative closing of the frontier farm" (36). In this memoir, Hall suggests "farm life and therefore farm boys are going extinct" and that both need to be preserved in some fashion to maintain and draw on "the residual savagery of boyhood" (34). For both wolf and boy, Hall suggests, American civilization is paradoxical; it represents the progress of the young nation while threatening to snuff out the vital wildness of the nation's young. At the dawn of the twentieth century, then, ideas of animalhood and childhood were increasingly framed through questions of futurity and loss, and children, like wild animals began to be seen as dependent populations in dire need of protection. In *Wild Animals I Have Known*, Ernest Seton made significant contributions to this ideological braiding, inviting readers to establish links between children and wild animals that have only become stronger in the twentieth and twenty-first centuries.

NOTES

1. Seton's animal stories came under fire from some critics, drawing Seton, very much against his will, into the early twentieth century's "Nature Fakers" controversy. John Burroughs ignited the controversy via his public denouncements of Seton and, more directly, William Long for offering animal fiction that masqueraded as science. Ralph Lutts covers this controversy in full detail in his *The Nature Fakers: Wildlife, Science & Sentiment*.

2. The case of Mary Ellen Wilson made sensational headlines in 1874, in large part because it highlighted the lack of any clear legal recourse for American victims of child abuse. Often referred to as the first recorded case of child abuse in the United States, the case was brought to court by the American Society for the Prevention of Cruelty for Animals because no similar institution existed for children. The New York Society for the Prevention of Cruelty to Children was founded that same year, in response to the Wilson case.

3. Viviana Zelizer uses the categories of the "Useful Child" and the "Useless Child" to frame a sustained analysis of competing discourses of childhood in late nineteenth and early twentieth century America (the "Useless Child" being the precursor for contemporary Western notions of sacralized childhood). For more, see Zelizer's *Pricing the Priceless Child*.

4. For more on Darwin's work in this field, see his "A Biographical Sketch of an Infant," published in 1877 and based on Darwin's firsthand observation of his own infant son.

5. See Ben Jordan's *Modern Manhood and the Boy Scouts of America* for more on Seton and his early involvement with—and subsequent bitter separation from—the Boy Scouts of America. See Chapter Four in Kent Baxter's *The Modern Age* for a thorough examination of Seton and the founding of the Woodcraft Indians.

6. The BBC documentary *Lobo, the Wolf That Changed America* documents how Seton's story helped change American ideas about wolves and spark the modern environmental conservation movement. The wolf, and conservation plans to protect wolf species, remain controversial to this day. See "Why We're So Divided Over Saving Wolves," an interview with writer Brenda Peterson, for more on that.

WORKS CITED

Baxter, Kent. *The Modern Age: Turn-of-the-Century American Culture and the Invention of Adolescence.* Tuscaloosa: University of Alabama Press, 2011.
Browne, J. Crichton. "Education and the Nervous System," *The Book of Health*, Ed. by Malcolm Morris, London, Paris, and New York Cassell and Co., 1883.
Coleman, Jon T. *Vicious: Wolves and Men in America.* New Haven: Yale University Press, 2004.

Darwin, Charles. "A Biographical Sketch of an Infant," *Mind*, Volume 2, Number 7, 1877, 285–294.

Duane, Anna Mae. *Suffering Childhood in Early America: Violence, Race, and the Making of the Child Victim*, Athens: University of Georgia Press, 2010.

Guither, Harold. *Animal Rights: History and Scope of a Radial Social Movement*, Carbondale: Southern Illinois University Press. 1998.

Jordan, Benjamin René. *Modern Manhood and the Boy Scouts of America: Citizenship, Race, and the Environment*, 1910–1930. Chapel Hill: The University of North Carolina Press, 2016.

Kidd, Kenneth. *Making American Boys: Boyology and the Feral Tale.* Minneapolis: University of Minnesota Press, 2004.

Lindenmeyer, Kriste. *A Right to Childhood: The U.S. Children's Bureau and Child Welfare, 1912–46*, Champaign: University of Illinois Press, 1997.

Lobo, the Wolf That Changed America. Directed by Steve Gooder, narration by David Attenborough. BBC Natural World, 2007.

Lutts, Ralph H. *The Nature Fakers: Wildlife, Science & Sentiment.* Charlottesville and London: University of Virginia Press, 1990.

Melson, Gail. *Why the Wild Things Are: Animals in the Lives of Children.* Cambridge: Harvard University Press, 2001.

Mitts-Smith, Debra. *Picturing the Wolf in Children's Literature.* Abingdon, UK: Routledge, 2010.

Salt, Henry Stephens. *Animals' Rights: Considered in Relation to Social Progress.* New York and London: Macmillan and Company, 1894.

Seton, Ernest Thompson. *The Birch-bark Roll of the Woodcraft Indians: Containing Their Constitution, Laws, Games, and Deeds.* New York: Doubleday, Page and Company, 1907.

_____. *Wild Animals I Have Known.* Mineola, NY: Dover Publications, 2000.

Worrall, Simon. "Why We're so Divided Over Saving Wolves." National Geographic.com, 11 June 2017.

Zelizer, Viviana. *Pricing the Priceless Child: The Changing Social Value of Children.* Princeton: Princeton University Press, 1994.

Mister Ed, 1960s Television and the Horse Who Was Not Just a Horse

Kathy Merlock Jackson

In his foreword to *Mister Ed and Me*, actor Alan Young recounts a story about the show's then sponsor, Mitsubishi, inviting the cast to Japan to film for six weeks and the producers finding out that the show's equine star, Mister Ed, had to be quarantined for one month before being brought into the country. "But this isn't an animal," the producers argued. "This is Mister Ed—an actor" (Young xii). Apparently Japanese immigration authorities agreed: the quarantine was reduced to two weeks. Thus, Mister Ed—the horse with the human voice—has always defied categorization.

When the television situation comedy *Mister Ed* debuted on the CBS prime-time line-up on October 1, 1961, the horse named in its title won immediate fame. Previous horses in early live-action screen media had accomplished remarkable feats and shared close relationships with humans, as evidenced by Trigger with Roy Rogers, Champion with Gene Autry, Silver with the Lone Ranger, and National Velvet with Velvet Brown. However, the high-concept series *Mister Ed* featured a horse even more extraordinary than any of his predecessors: he talked. The show, while not a huge ratings booster and award winner, was quirky enough to find an enthusiastic audience composed of both adults and children, and it became a television classic, in part due to its catchy, unforgettable theme song composed by Ray Evans and Jay Livingston and sung by Livingston.

Mister Ed, though, was not the first live-action talking animal to appear on screen. One of the show's directors, Arthur Lubin, had previously done a movie series titled *Francis the Talking Mule* and tried initially to bring that character to television. When producers showed no interest, Lubin's assistant, Sonia Chernus, suggested that he consider the short stories of Walter L. Brooks, the first of which was published as "The Talking Horse" in the September 18, 1937, issue of *Liberty* magazine and later ones in *The Saturday Evening Post*. Brooks, who also wrote the Freddy the Pig series for children with various talking animals, had created a talking horse named Mister Ed, who spoke only to his drunkard owner (suggesting that the conversations *could* be in his owner's imagination).

Like Francis the talking mule, Mister Ed talked only to one person, thus creating the narrative and comedic hook for a new television series. The original pilot for the series was not picked up, but after a total overhaul with new actors, it found a buyer in

CBS and became one of the few television shows to go first into syndication and then to network prime time, where its 143 black-and-white episodes ran for five-and-a-half seasons until February 6, 1966. In *Mister Ed*, the horse talks face to face only to his owner, self-employed architect Wilbur Post, played by veteran actor Alan Young. Producer and comedian George Burns tapped Young for the role of Wilbur during casting, telling his staff, "Get Alan Young. He looks like the kind of guy a horse would talk to'" (Chilton). In the series, Mister Ed and Wilbur become best friends, confidantes, and ideological reflections of one another, blurring the line between animal and human and providing commentary on the consumer lifestyle of the 1960s. The dynamic of forging a personal relationship amid a growing consumer culture propels the show and foretells the future of pets in America, the industries that support them, and their role in celebrity culture.

In the 1960s, as more people were leaving American cities, the television industry was trying to build viewership, especially in rural and suburban areas that were the last to adopt the new medium, so as to expand the audience and increase advertising revenue. It offered many shows featuring animals and bucolic settings designed to lure in the non-urban audience, among them *The Beverly Hillbillies, Petticoat Junction, The Andy Griffith Show*, and *Green Acres*. It also experimented with high-concept, enticing shows too unusual to pass up. As Ed Gross reflects of the 1960s, "[W]e had seven stranded castaways (*Gilligan's Island*), bumbling space spies somehow managing to save the world despite themselves (*Get Smart*), starships exploring the final frontier or getting lost in it (*Star Trek, Lost in Space*), and witches marrying mortals (*Bewitched*), so why *not* a talking horse?" (Gross). In a particularly high-concept strategy to draw in viewers, television toyed with what David Marc in *Comic Visions* calls "magicoms," shows that inserted into a realistic story a magical character whose identity is known to only one character, including such iconic shows as *Bewitched, I Dream of Jeannie*, and *My Mother the Car* (Marc 129). *Mister Ed* was a forerunner of all three of these important trends.

Originally sponsored by car-manufacturer Studebaker (and later Ford and Mitsubishi) and capturing modern American life in the 1960s, the show featured Alan Young, along with Connie Hines, as a young newlywed couple, Wilbur and Carol Post, and their older next-door neighbors, Roger and Kay Addison, played by Larry Keating and Edna Skinner; many of the show's storylines revolve around consumer goods that Carol and Kay covet but their husbands say they cannot afford. Later, following the death of Larry Keating, the Addisons were replaced by Gordon and Winnie Kirkwood, played by Leon Ames and Florence MacMichael. Other supporting roles included Jack Albertson as Kay's brother Paul Fenton and Barry Kelly as Carol's father Mr. Higgins. The show also hosted many guest celebrities, including Mae West, Clint Eastwood, George Burns, Zsa Zsa Gabor, Leo Durocher, Jon Provost, and Sebastian Cabot. However, the real star of the show was the wise-cracking golden palomino stallion named Mister Ed, listed in the show's credits as simply "Himself." In reality, though, the character was played by Bamboo Harvester, a champion show and parade horse foaled in 1949 near El Monte, California, and his deep, sonorous voice was supplied by Allan "Rocky" Lane, a low-budget Western movie actor from the 1930s through the 1950s who was best known for Republic Pictures' Red Ryder series. Mister Ed was unquestionably the key element in the success of the series. Without the horse, there would be no show, just another version of *The Honeymooners* or *I Love Lucy* with two couples playing out the battle of the sexes.

Mister Ed traverses the line between animal and human in many ways, most notably because he talks. Trained by Les Hilton, who, according to Alan Young, "was recognized as one of the finest large animal trainers, if not *the* finest, in Hollywood" (qtd. in Beck 208), Mister Ed appeared on screen to move his mouth and speak, a feat many children believed, and the show's producers found no reason to dispel. Rocky Lane had taken the vocal role solely for the money and asked that he not be listed in the credits because, according to his biographer Linda Alexander, he feared "he would become *Mister Ed* [*sic*] in the eyes of Hollywood, and that truly embarrassed him" (Alexander 248). For decades after the sitcom ended, Alan Young was repeatedly asked how the horse's lips were made to move so that he looked like he was talking, and he invented a story that peanut butter was put in Mister Ed's mouth (Chilton). Young disclosed the reason for this fabrication years later in an interview:

> Al Simon and Arthur Lubin, the producers, suggested we keep the method [of making the horse appear to talk] a secret because they thought kids would be disappointed if they found out the technical details of how it was done …. So I made up the peanut butter story, and everyone bought it [Thomas, "Mister Ed's"].

The real strategy was more complicated. According to Young, trainer Les Hilton used the same technique for *Mister Ed* as he had used for Lubin's *Francis the Talking Mule* series: "It was initially done by putting a piece of nylon thread in his mouth. But Ed actually learned to move his lips on cue when the trainer touched his hoof. In fact, he soon learned to do it when I stopped talking during a scene! Ed was very smart!" (Thomas, "Mister Ed's"). Rocky Lane would stand to the side and mouth his words.

Ed's moving mouth, as distinctive as it was, comprises a very small part of the story. More important in the animal-human blurring are the horse's relationship to Wilbur, his thoughts and words, and his embrace of a modern postwar lifestyle enhanced by new gadgets, conveniences, luxuries, and media celebrities. The first episode sets the tone for the series. In it, Wilbur and Carol Post cross the threshold into their middle-class suburban home at 17230 Valley Spring Road in the San Fernando Valley of Los Angeles and find out that they have a horse in the barn in their backyard. Next-door-neighbor Roger Addison explains that the previous owners "had to leave in a hurry and they said you can keep him, you can sell him, do anything you want with him" ("First Meeting"). Carol sees no need to keep this seemingly ordinary, abandoned horse at their home in the suburbs of southern California and wants to sell him; however, Wilbur is enchanted. He goes out to the barn and reminisces that he has wanted a horse since boyhood, recalling, "It's been a long time since I was a little boy." To his surprise, the horse replies, "It's been a long time since I was a pony" ("First Meeting"). Ann Shellinglaw, in her article "Mister Ed Was a Sexist Pig" in *The Journal of Popular Culture*, points out the significance of this dialogue: "Mirroring occurs between the two characters even as they speak their first words together" (Shellinglaw 250). More examples of this occur, as when Wilbur asks, "What kind of a name is Ed for a horse?" and Ed counters with "What kind of name is Wilbur for a man?" ("First Meeting"). The series gives no good answers as to how and when Ed learned to talk, whether he talked to anyone before, or why he chooses to speak only to Wilbur. When Wilbur attempts to understand, Ed's only response is "Don't try. It's bigger than both of us" ("First Meeting"). Thus, Wilbur adopts the horse left behind. Ed becomes his rescue pet and fast friend, their shared relationship bringing energy and contentment to both of them. Wilbur sets up his architectural home office in Ed's stable, sharing the horse's space and providing much opportunity for conversation between horse and human.

Their relationship, though, continues to blur until, as Carmel Dagan writes, "just who owned whom could occasionally be a matter of debate" (Dagan). Kind, indecisive, and mild-mannered, Wilbur is milquetoast compared to the outspoken, outrageous, and opinionated Mister Ed, his title of "mister" establishing his status. The horse becomes the man's mouthpiece, his double, and his alter-ego, and often gets Wilbur in trouble or leads people to think he's crazy. His wife Carol cannot quite understand his attachment to Ed (a constant tension in the series), and one of Wilbur's acquaintances voices what everyone around him wonders: "What happens when you're near that horse? You lose whatever intelligence you ever had" ("Wilbur Sells Ed"). Ed says and does what Wilbur cannot, acts as his consultant and life coach, and pushes him to be more assertive for his own good. As Ann Shellinglaw observes, "Ed serves as Wilbur's outlet for feelings he cannot otherwise express [and] … the similarity between the name Ed and the word 'id' cannot be unintentional in a show which, in a variety of episodes, presents Wilbur consulting with psychologists to solve problem with his Ed" (251). In some cases, Ed does Wilbur's thinking for him, such as in "Busy Wife," when Carol gets so involved with a women's group that Wilbur feels neglected and with Ed's help finds a way to bring her back. At other times, Wilbur must put himself in Ed's shoes, as when Ed has amnesia or fear of heights and Wilbur pretends that he has the ailment so that he can find a cure. In "Like Father, Like Horse," Ed even says that Wilbur has begun to look like him, that they have the same chin, and when Wilbur checks his image in the mirror, he sees Ed's face superimposed over his own. Just as Ed speaks for Wilbur, so too does Wilbur speak for Ed, as in "Ed's Mother," when at an auction Ed must stop bidding on the old plow horse that is his mother so as to maintain the secret of his ability to talk from Carol when she appears, and Wilbur steps up to make the winning bid for him. As Wilbur and Ed's bond develops, they become equals, sharing a symbiotic relationship. As Ann Shellinglaw observes, "While Carol's relationship to Wilbur never changes, Ed alters between relating to Wilbur like a son, a pet, and a buddy" (248). At the onset of the series, Ed seems crotchety and brash but then morphs into a spoiled brat who insists on getting what he wants, a role he plays for the rest of the series (Canote), but all the while showing glimmers of knowledge and compassion.

Just as Ed functions as a construction of Wilbur, so too does he represent humanity, with all of its inherent virtues and foibles. Ann Shellinglaw characterizes Ed as "a complex character, veering from fear to bravery, innocence to wisdom, selfishness to generosity" (248). Ed can be kind-hearted. In "Little Boy," he helps a new child in town who is being "bullied by the other boys," and in "The Contest" he acts benevolently to an elderly couple who need to return to their homeland to see family by ensuring that they, not Wilbur, win a European trip. In another episode, "Be Kind to Humans," he feels sorry for some hobos he sees in the park and invites them to the Posts' home for a good meal and sleepover. He can also be gentle and needy. When Wilbur and Carol go off on a vacation in the episode "Pine Lake Lodge," Ed tells Wilbur to drive carefully, saying, "You're all I have." He wants comfort from Wilbur when he has "a tummy ache." In "Wilbur Sells Ed," when Ed thinks he wants to be sold to be near the filly of his dreams and then changes his mind, he speaks from the heart to Wilbur, telling him, "You really missed me, huh?" and adding, "Wilbur, we're just a pair of sentimental slobs."

Despite displaying warmth and sentimentality, Ed can also be, as Stefan L. Brandt describes him in "Horsing Around: Carnivalesque Humor and the Aesthetics of Dehierarchization in *Mister Ed*," "unruly and nonconformist, rejecting traditional norms and challenging expectations" (12). In "Kiddy Park," Ed runs away when Wilbur tells him he wants to take a trip alone with Carol. Constantly in competition with Carol for Wilbur's attention, he eats up all the vegetables in her garden in "Stable for Three." In "The Pageant Show," he tries to sabotage Carol and Kay's plans to have their husbands dress in costumes for the community pageant. Brandt further pegs Ed as "marked by a strong sense of misanthropy" (13), a view shared by Marc Hirsh in "A Jerk Is a Jerk, Of Course, Of Course: The Psychosocial Complexities of 'Mr. Ed'" (Hirsh). Hirsh writes, "Nearly every word out of Mister Ed's mouth is either sarcastic or self-pitying. He does whatever he wants and doesn't care that the only human he trusts enough to speak to is constantly covering for him. After drinking Wilbur's lemonade, he complains 'Not enough sugar' to the very person he just stole from (insulting his wife in the process)!" (Hirsh). Although Ed once suggests that he talks to no one but Wilbur because he does not want to end up in a circus, a more probable explanation is that he really does not like anyone else, and that no one else would put up with him. Rocky Lane may well have contributed to the horse's irascible nature. In the foreword to Linda Alexander's biography of Lane, his niece, Pat Grayson-DeJong, writes that her uncle exhibited characteristics of what is today classified as Asperger Syndrome, saying, "He could be rude, abrupt, angry, and sometimes unpredictable. He was inflexible in his thinking and according to some, had no sense of humor. While his acting talent was impeccable, he had little tolerance for stupidity or for people who did not take the job of acting seriously" (Grayson-DeJong).

The complexity of Ed's character becomes particularly apparent in his feelings about and behavior toward other animals. In "Ed the Stool Pigeon," Wilbur and Carol rescue a poodle, and Ed gets so jealous that he tries to get the dog in trouble because he resents having to share Wilbur's attention with another pet. Wilbur's aunt arrives in town for a surprise visit with her talking parrot in "The Aunt," and Ed dislikes the bird (and its limited, irritating vocabulary of "stick 'em up") so much that he takes steps to get it out of his barn but has a change of heart when he realizes how much the bird and the old woman need each other. Ed, although curmudgeonly, proves that he can be outspoken in his call for more humane treatment of animals ("Television's New Frontier"). When he finds out that his mother is being used as a plow horse on a farm in "Ed's Mother," he is horrified and, despite Carol's objections, wants Wilbur to buy her at auction and rescue her. In "Ed Agrees to Talk," he calls the SPCA when Carol hitches him up to a carriage to go into town in a ploy to get Wilbur to buy her a car after he has refused. He defends animals that have to carry heavy loads, including himself when he works on a movie set in "Ed the Lover" and a corpulent cowboy is designated to jump on his back for a quick getaway from a bank robbery; he is not a fan of Westerns because of what the horses have to go through. He even starts a campaign to bar people from riding horses in "Never Ride Horses." Finally, in "Ol' Swayback," he befriends an old swayback horse that others ridicule and convinces Wilbur to keep him. Throughout the series, Ed serves as an advocate for animal rights and comes to the defense of all those without power, such as children, the elderly, and the poor, sometimes tearing up when he sees suffering or injustice. He uses his abilities to solve problems, saying, as he does in the episode "Ed the Desert Rat," "Never send a man to do a horse's job." Ed questions any belief in the superiority of humans over animals.

Ed's multifaceted personality and witty barbs drive the show, but as Ed Gross notes, these alone are not enough to sustain it. Gross poses this question: "One day, out of the blue, a horse starts talking to his owner. Amazing, right? But how do you prove to other people that you're *not* losing your mind when the horse refuses to speak to anyone else? *That* was part of the premise of behind Mister Ed ... offering viewers 143 episodes in total that continued to explore that dynamic, the horse proving himself to be just as needy, petty, and selfish as any human being could be—while at the same time having those moments where he reveals himself to be a true best friend. So how do you get five and a half years out of *that* idea?" (Gross). What made *Mister Ed* work was not just the relationship between Ed and Wilbur but Ed's commentary on modern life, in particular his embrace of niceties generally relegated to those of the aspiring class in America, further blurring the line between animal and human.

Throughout the course of the series, Mister Ed adopts a comfortable middle-class lifestyle. He puts on his oversized eyeglasses and reads the newspaper, staying abreast of current events. He listens to phonograph records (especially classical music) and the radio, and on "The Contest" even competes for a prize on a radio quiz show. He reads books, enabling him to quote Shakespeare and the classics. He watches television, enjoying Jack Lalanne's exercise show and doctor dramas. Once, when Wilbur is surprised to see Ed watching a Western because he knows he does not like them, Ed replies, "I'm waiting for Leonard Bernstein" (Dancis). Ed uses the telephone to make and answer phone calls (because those on the other end neither see him nor know he is a horse), and he especially likes listening to and commenting on the gossip on the party line. He is concerned about his appearance, wearing hats (a French beret, Tyrolean cap, Spanish matador's hat, or straw sun hat, depending on the occasion) and other accessories (especially to look attractive to the fillies), and he wants to get contact lenses after he is seen wearing his big glasses in public. In "Ed's New Shoes," he insists that Wilbur get him new, more comfortable and stylish footwear, and in "Bald Horse," he wants expensive tonics and treatments when he thinks he is losing his hair. In "Saddles and Gowns," he asserts that his request for a new saddle takes precedence over Carol's for a new dress. He enjoys good food, especially warm brownies and pies he steals from Carol's kitchen window. In "A Man for Velma," he strives to keep the cook the Posts hire because he likes her gourmet meals. He picks up the phone and orders his own hay when he feels his daily allotment is not sufficient, and he savors lemonade (with ample sugar) and iced tea. He enjoys many forms of recreation: playing baseball and checkers, surfing, playing music, dancing, placing bets on horse races (especially those involving his niece in her first running season), and even taking flying lessons. When Carol and Wilbur plan a vacation, he believes he should go too, whether to Mexico, Hawaii, or Pine Lake Lodge. Finally, he sides with Wilbur against Carol when she wants to spend money on her own car, a statue, or a new dress but insists on upgrades for his own living quarters, such as a new cozy bed, an indoor shower to give him relief from the heat, a heater from the cold, and in "Ed the Redecorator," a total makeover for the barn. Ed wants to be places that humans are, do what humans do, and have what humans have, crossing the boundary between animal and human. As Ann Shillinglaw notes, Mister Ed "transgresses space, action, realism, and logic, moving into living rooms, neighbors' homes, the desert, lines at the bank.... Ed is barrierless, even fitting into physically impossible spaces such as the cockpit of an airplane" (248). Ed wants to partake in the good life as a full member of post–World War II American society and, in so doing, offers both praise for and criticism of that life. In the words of *Slate* writer Nathan Heller, the joke of the series is not that Mister Ed "acts human; it's the implication that the better part of early '60s home life could be managed, quite adeptly, by a horse with a vocabulary" (Heller).

The episodes in which Ed expresses his entitlement to the luxuries and conveniences of modern life offer some of the funniest and most memorable moments of the series, as Ed not only talks but also *acts* like a human, becoming a true comic figure. These sequences, such as Ed surfing in "Ed the Beachcomber" or hitting a home run and sliding into home base in "Leo Durocher Meets Mister Ed," were the most challenging for the horse and Les Hilton, his trainer. An animal lover who never struck his horses, Hilton practiced kindness when preparing Ed for his scenes, using whips only as "a means of showing the horse whether to go right or left" (Griffith). According to Terence Towles Canote, although Bamboo Harvester, who played Ed, was trained as a show and parade horse and looked especially regal in Pasadena's Rose Bowl Parade, he was not a trick horse; nevertheless, "he learned swiftly. Mr. Hilton could teach Bamboo Harvester what he had to do in only fifteen minutes, and the horse almost always did it in one take" (Canote). In fact, Hilton told Alan Young that the greatest challenge was not teaching Ed how to do things but making him know when *not* to do them (Young 27). A perfectionist, Ed would act forlorn and seek comfort from Alan Young if Hilton corrected him for a mistake as he was learning to use new props or practicing a difficult routine. One producer was recorded as saying that the horse "was the easiest one to work with—it was the humans who were always messing up the shots" (Griffith). On the set, if a scene had to be reshot because another actor made a mistake, Ed would become agitated, thinking it was his fault. In *Mister Ed and Me*, Young relates a time when he asked director Arthur Lubin if he could reshoot a scene because he thought he could do it better, and Lubin answered, "Sorry, Alan, I wasn't looking at you. The horse was perfect" (Young 31). Young also recalls an uninterrupted take in which Ed had to cross from his horse stall to Wilbur's letter file, open the drawer, remove a bunch of carrots (which he loved to eat) and drop them on his desk, return to his stall, and shut the door—and he did it in one take (31). Although Ed had a stunt double named Pumpkin (also called "Punkin"), the crew had to use her only once in all five-and-a-half-seasons of the series. Ed also mastered the technique of breaking the fourth wall and making asides directly to the audience. As Terence Towles Canote observes of his performance, "Sometimes Ed simply shares his opinion with the audience, other times he reveals his motives for some particular scheme, and yet other times he appears to be all knowing. Indeed, Mister Ed appears to know that he is on a sitcom!" (Canote). The perfect gentleman, Ed never relieved himself on the set: he would roll his eyes, and his trainer would take him out behind to the bushes to urinate or defecate. Although *Mister Ed* never won an Emmy Award, Ed was acknowledged for his professionalism: he received the Performing Animal Top Star of the Year (PATSY) Award for best animal performance for four years in a row. Ed won Alan Young's admiration. As Young writes in *Mister Ed and Me*, "This feeling of Ed as a fellow actor rather than a horse was becoming very strong in my thoughts" (Young 28). The sentiment continued, as Young later said that children thought Mister Ed talked because the credits said "Mister Ed played by himself," but "I felt he talked because he was so intelligent that when I was acting with him I felt I was acting with another actor. You get carried away, you know" (qtd. in Beck 210).

Not only was Ed (or perhaps Bamboo Harvester) an actor, he was also a celebrity, especially among children, and he influenced merchandising. By 1962, his image graced a Gold Key comic book line, a Whitman coloring book, Halloween costumes, record albums, a hand puppet, and a Little Golden Book; the original Mister Ed stories by Walter Brooks were reprinted in an anthology in 1963 (Canote). Ed seemed to sense he was a star, enjoying the spotlight, performing his phone dialing skills the moment he saw visitors, and becoming sullen if people paid attention to other horses in the stable. He made guest appearances, and when children got Alan Young's autograph, they wanted Ed's hoof print as well; he happily complied. Ed could, according to horse trainer Loretta Kemsley, exhibit diva-like behavior, demanding "to be first in all things: the meals of alfalfa hay at sunrise and sunset, cleaning his stall, the mid-morning grooming, the noon ration of oats and barley, and even the afternoon training sessions. If Les [Hilton] brought new toys, Ed insisted on playing with them first" (qtd. in Beck 207).

It makes sense, then, that the horse who was part of celebrity culture himself interacted with celebrities on the show. Clint Eastwood joined Ed in a Season 2 episode titled "Clint Eastwood Meets Mister Ed," in which Ed becomes jealous of his horse for attracting all the fillies. In Season 4's "Leo Durocher Meets Mister Ed," Ed, a big Dodgers fan, meets his sports hero, offers tips on how to play the game, and makes a home run when he smashes a ball thrown by Sandy Koufax. During the same season, in "Mae West Meets Mister Ed," Wilbur designs an upscale stable for Mae West, and Ed sees the chance to move in. The following season, in "Ed Writes Dear Abby," Ed hobnobs with Abigail Van Buren, after asking her advice on setting up his bachelor pad. He also meets Lassie's best friend in "Jon Provost Meets Mister Ed." Ed's connection with human celebrities raised his own stature, placing him in their stellar orbits.

By the middle 1960s, *Mister Ed* had made its mark on American television, and the cultural climate changed. Studebaker, *Mister Ed*'s original sponsor, was going out of business, Lyndon Johnson was in the White House and ramping up the war in Vietnam, Bob Dylan was recording *Blonde on Blonde*, and long hair and long skirts were emblematic of a new hippie era far removed from the domestic tranquility of suburban life when *Mister Ed* first hit the air waves (Heller). According to Nathan Heller, Mister Ed served as a transitional figure in that change. In "Trojan Horse: Prime[-]Time's First Countercultural Hero Was a Palomino Named Mr. Ed," Heller, who calls Ed "more Greenwich Village than Greater L.A.," writes, "Ed is not actually a swinger, or an agitator, or folk musician, of course. He's a horse. But he serves as a repository for signs of social unrest— disenchantment with postwar domesticity, educated profligacy, arcane tastes, vindictiveness. His role, as a comedian, was to neutralize those signs in prime time. He makes the first stirrings of cultural upheaval laughable by keeping them contained, quite literally, in a small suburban barn" (Heller). His glory days, though, were drawing to a close.

While never a smash hit, *Mister Ed* for several years had maintained a solid fan base and done well, enough so that even Rocky Lane wanted top billing as Ed's voice, but producers opted to keep the secret and offered him a big raise instead; he accepted the bargain. However, *Mister Ed*'s ratings began falling, and the show was canceled in the middle of its sixth season when new management, sensing change and no longer wanting CBS to be knowns as the hillbilly network, also suspended shows like *The Beverly Hillbillies* and *Petticoat Junction* (Thomas, "'Mister Ed' and Beyond"). The last episode, "Ed Goes to College," aired on February 6, 1966, and Mister Ed retired, returning to his life as Bamboo Harvester. Many conflicting stories have circulated regarding his death, not unlike those of other celebrities, but the most plausible is that he suffered from arthritis and died of old age at a stable in Burbank in 1970; his death was not reported to the press because *Mister Ed* was still being shown in syndication, and its distributor, Filmways, feared children would be distraught if they learned the famous horse had died (Canote).

Reflecting on his role as Wilbur, Alan Young published *Mister Ed and Me*, recounting his role as straight man to the horse, in 1994. He died in 2016 at the age of 96.

Following its cancellation, *Mister Ed* moved into the realm of classic television. It immediately entered syndication as a rerun and has since been seen in fifty-two countries and heard in eight languages (Canote). It began running in 1985 on Nick at Nite, accompanied by a new surge in *Mister Ed* merchandise, including a *Mister Ed* glue stick, post cards, coasters, and a T-shirt with the slogan "I want cable in my stable." Nick at Nite also showed parodies for fictional products and services—such as Mister Ed's After Shave, Mister Ed's Salad Bar, and Mister Ed's Hoof-Shaped Slippers—to promote the show and accentuate Mister Ed as a die-hard consumer. *Mister Ed* reruns also appeared on the Hallmark Movie Channel, and Shout Factory released the entire five-and-a-half seasons of the series in DVD boxed-sets. Given the accessibility of *Mister Ed* episodes, the series has reached the attention of popular culture writers and scholars, where it has not fared well, particularly due to its gender stereotypes, misogynistic attitudes, and emphasis on the importance of masculinity, all typical of 1960s television. The character of Ed—iconoclastic, brash, childish—has also, for some, become tedious. In a more positive vein, Terence Towles Canote considers *Mister Ed*'s legacy to American television:

> While at a cursory glance *Mister Ed* may not appear that important to television history, it actually was. It was among the first in a number of escapist shows that came to dominate television in the Sixties. It was also the first fantasy sitcom of the decade. Finally, it is arguably the same type of sitcom as *My Favourite* [*sic*] *Martian* and *Bewitched*, a sitcom in which an unusual individual turns the life of an ordinary individual upside down. While the premise of a talking horse might have seemed bizarre in 1961, it would not seem so for long [Canote].

Looking back at *Mister Ed* today through the lens of our digital world, one can see how prescient the show was. No longer is it novel to see a live-action talking animal. Innovations in computer-generated imagery have made talking live-action animals a common part of the screen experience, as seen in films such as *Babe* (1995), *Stuart Little* (1999), and *The Jungle Book* (2016). While it may have seemed funny and odd in the 1960s to see Mister Ed dressed in flamboyant hats, riding a surfboard, or playing a harmonica, today images of pets doing remarkable things proliferate on YouTube, social media, and news and entertainment shows. Many animals have become bone fide actors, possessing their own YouTube sites, racking up clicks and followers, and becoming just as much a part of celebrity culture as Mister Ed was. Finally, and most importantly, the line between animal and human, which stands at the center of the *Mister Ed* series, has shifted. Ann Shellinglaw writes that "[t]he talking horse represents a construction of Wilbur Post's own self" and adds, "[t]heir identities blur" (250–251). Stefan L. Brandt offers another interpretation of the horse's status: "Mister Ed proves bold and confident. Yet, Ed is never fully marked as either horse or human, but rather inhabits a liminal space 'in between' these two subject positons" (Brandt). *Mister Ed* stood at the vanguard of changing cultural attitudes toward animals, their roles in our lives, and their involvement in a consumer culture. Products and services for animals designed to evoke humor in the 1960s—gourmet foods, television programming, formal attire, vacations, climate-controlled environments, musical instruments, contact lenses, exercise gear, skateboards, and surf boards—now have become common. Further, while Ed may have traversed social barriers for comic effect, fewer places exist today where pets are not welcomed and cannot go. Mister Ed, as a character in a fantasy sitcom, an actor in his own right, and a media celebrity, reached the airwaves at a pivotal cultural moment and functioned as a harbinger of times to come. "A horse is a horse, of course, of course" went his stuck-in-your-head theme song, but the truth is far less clear.

WORKS CITED

Alexander, Linda. *I Am Mister Ed … Allan "Rocky" Lane Revealed*. BearManor Media, 2014.
"The Aunt" (Season 1: Episode 9). *Mister Ed*. CBS. 2 March 1961.
"Bald Horse" (Season 2: Episode 21). *Mister Ed*. CBS. 18 March 1962.
"Be Kind to Humans" (Season 4: Episode 6). *Mister Ed*. CBS. 27 Oct. 1963.
Beck, Ken, and Jim Clark. "Mister Ed." *The Encyclopedia of TV Pets: A Complete History of Television's Greatest Animal Stars*. Rutledge Hill Press, 2002: 204–214.
Brandt, Stefan L. "Horsing Around: Carnivalesque Humor and the Aesthetics of Dehierarchization in Mister Ed." *European Journal of American Studies* [Online], 13:1, 2018, online since 16 May 2018. http://journals.openedition.org/ejas/12474;DOI:10.4000/ejas.12474.
"Busy Wife" (Season 1: Episode 3). *Mister Ed*. CBS. 19 Jan. 1961.
Canote, Terence Towles. "The Famous Mister Ed." A Shroud for Your Thoughts: Dedicated to Pop Culture in All of Its Forms. 8 June 2013. http://mercurie.blogspot.com/2013/06/the-famous-mister-ed.html.
Chilton, Martin. "Mister Ed Star Alan Young, Friend of Talking Horse, Dies Aged 96." *The Telegraph*. 21 May 2016. https://www.telegraph.co.uk/tv/2016/05/21/mister-ed-star-alan-young-friend-of-the-talking-horse-dies-aged/.
"Clint Eastwood Meets Mister Ed" (Season 2: Episode 25). *Mister Ed*. CBS. 22 April 1962.
"The Contest" (Season 1: Episode 24). *Mister Ed*. CBS. 18 June 1961.
Dagan, Carmel. "Alan Young, 'Mister Ed' Star, Dies at 96." *Variety* 20 May 2016. https://variety.com/2016/tv/news/alan-young-dead-dies-mister-ed-1201779957/.
Dancis, Bruce. "Mister Ed: The Complete First Season." *Pop Matters* 6 Oct. 2009. https://www.popmatters.com/112717-mister-ed-the-complete-first-season-2496094434.html.
"Ed Agrees to Talk" (Season 1: Episode 20). *Mister Ed*. CBS. 16 May 1961.
"Ed Goes to College" (Season 6: Episode 9). *Mister Ed*. CBS. 6 Feb. 1966.
"Ed the Beachcomber" (Season 2: Episode 23). *Mister Ed*. CBS. 1 April 1962.
"Ed the Desert Rat" (Season 4: Episode 12). *Mister Ed*. CBS. 16 Feb. 1964.
"Ed the Lover" (Season 1: Episode 7). *Mister Ed*. CBS. 16 Feb. 1961.
"Ed the Redecorator" (Season 2: Episode 4). *Mister Ed*. CBS. 22 Oct. 1962.
"Ed the Stool Pigeon" (Season 1: Episode 15). *Mister Ed*. CBS. 13 April 1961.
"Ed Writes Dear Abby" (Season 5: Episode 2). *Mister Ed*. CBS. 18 Oct. 1964.
"Ed's Mother" (Season 1: Episode 12). *Mister Ed*. CBS. 23 March 1961.
"Ed's New Shoes" (Season 1: Episode 18). *Mister Ed*. CBS. 4 May 1961.
"First Meeting" (Season 1: Episode 13). *Mister Ed*. CBS. 5 Jan. 1961.
Grayson-DeJong, Pat, M.Ed. Foreword. *I Am Mister Ed: Allan "Rocky" Lane Revealed*, by Linda Alexander. BearManor Media, 2014, pp. 13–15.
Griffith, Cynthia. "The Inexplicably Strange History of Mr. Ed the Horse." Ranker.com n.d. https://www.ranker.com/list/history-of-mr-ed-horse-bamboo-harvester/cynthia-griffith.
Gross, Ed. "The World of 'Mr. Ed'—What You Didn't Know About the Talking Horse (Of Course)." *Closer Weekly* 24 April 2018. https://www.closerweekly.com/posts/mister-ed-158684/photos/mister-ed-short-stories-281532.
Heller, Nathan. "Trojan Horse: Prime[-]Time's First Countercultural Hero Was a Palomino Named Mr. Ed." *Slate* 16 Dec. 2009. http://www.slate.com/articles/arts/dvdextras/2009/12/trojan_horse.html.
Hirsh, Marc. "A Jerk Is a Jerk, Of Course, Of Course: The Psychosocial Complexities of 'Mr. Ed.'" *NPR Monkey See Newscast* 6 Oct. 2009. https://www.npr.org/sections/monkeysee/2009/10/a_jerk_is_a_jerk_of_course_of.html.
"Jon Provost Meets Mister Ed" (Season 5: Episode 5). *Mister Ed*. CBS. 9 June 1965.
"Kiddy Park" (Season 1: Episode 4). *Mister Ed*. CBS. 26 Jan.1961.
"Leo Durocher Meets Mister Ed" (Season 4: Episode 3). *Mister Ed*. CBS. 29 Sept. 1963.
"Like Father, Like Horse" (Season 5: Episode 6). *Mister Ed*. CBS. 10 Feb. 1965.
"Little Boy" (Season 1: Episode 19). *Mister Ed*. CBS. 11 May 1961.
"Mae West Meets Mister Ed" (Season 4: Episode 24). *Mister Ed*. CBS. 22 March 1964.
"A Man for Velma" (Season 1: Episode 17). *Mister Ed*. CBS. 27 April 1961.
Marc, David. *Comic Visions*: Routledge, 1989.
"Never Ride Horses" (Season 5: Episode 16). *Mister Ed*. CBS. 24 Feb. 1965.
"Ol' Swayback" (Season 4: Episode 22). *Mister Ed*. CBS. 8 March 1964.
"The Pageant Show" (Season 1: Episode 8). *Mister Ed*. CBS. 23 Feb. 1961.
"Pine Lake Lodge" (Season 1: Episode 25). *Mister Ed*. CBS. 25 June 1961.
"Saddles and Gowns" (Season 4: Episode 25). *Mister Ed*. CBS. 3 May 1964.

Shellinglaw, Ann. "Mister Ed Was a Sexist Pig." *The Journal of Popular Culture* 30:4 (1997): 245–254.

"Stable for Three" (Season 1: Episode 5). *Mister Ed.* CBS. 2 Feb. 1961.

Thomas, Nick. "'Mister Ed' and Beyond: An Interview." *Cinemaretro* 2016. http://www.cinemaretro.com/index.php?/archives/3909-MISTER-ED-AND-BEYONDAN-INTERVIEW-WITH-ALAN-YOUNG.html.

Thomas, Nick. "*Mister Ed*'s Alan Young Talks About the Talking Horse and Hollywood Lore." *My Daily Find* 1 Dec. 2009. http://www.mydailyfind.com/2009/12/01/mister-eds-alan-young-talks-about-the-talking-horse-and-hollywood-lore/.

"Wilbur Sells Ed" (Season 1: Episode 26). *Mister Ed.* CBS. 2 July 1961.

Young, Alan. *Mister Ed and Me.* St. Martin's Press, 1994.

Blurred Laughter

How Disney and Pixar Animated Films
Teach Children to Laugh Like Animals

TERRY LINDVALL

Animated feature films allow for greater liberties in exploring the phenomenon of anthropomorphic connections between viewers and texts. For example, in *Zootopia* (Jared Bush, Byron Howard, 2016) when Nick Wild the Fox tells Flash the Sloth, who works in the DMV, Department of Mammal Vehicles, a joke ("What do you call a three-humped camel?" "Pregnant"), it takes more than seven seconds for the joke to register with the languorous mammal; however, when it does, Flash laughs long and heartily, beginning with a full Duchenne zygomatic smile and ending up exercising his frontal/platysma muscles and emitting a runaway titter. The audience laughs watching a sloth slowly evolving into hysteria, a moment that invites the question of what the laughter of cartoon animals can teach children about laughter. The humor in *Zootopia* was clearly intended for adults, but children attending the animated feature found themselves laughing as well, even without understanding the jokes. What struck the children was the performance of laughter itself, especially with the idea of a very slow sloth laughing very slowly.

How and what does animal laughter in animated films teach children about laughter? One finds an inherent blurring conception in children learning a universal human trait from animals who are unlikely to experience that trait. Animated films offer one of the most fruitful fields for studying anthropomorphic representations, particularly in bridging that seemingly most human of activities: laughter. Children learn about laughter (when and how to laugh and what is funny) from animated creatures demonstrating such behaviors.

Stemming from the Greek words, *anthro* for human and *morph* for form, the processes of attribution to and identification of animals with human beings function as an enduring trope in animated film comedy. The nature of pictorial anthropomorphic imagery of "laughing" animals is grounded in the popular [mis]conceptions regarding human and animal laughter. Yet in the animated features and short cartoons of Disney and Pixar, a clear range of risible behaviors evident in the cartoon animals stems from human expressions. As these fictional depictions of laughing animals mirror human behaviors, they also serve as both exemplary and revelatory notions of what children should and should not laugh at.[1]

One preliminary caveat must be mentioned. Anthropomorphizing animal behaviors, basically ascribing human qualities to them, carries its own problematic challenges. For such an act assumes that the cognitive processes of animals mirror the arguably much more complex human activities of perception and analysis. These species seem to respond more in terms of stimulus/response behaviors than complicated mental procedures. Dogs just do not perceive the world as their humans do, particularly as their sensory input extends beyond sight and hearing. Nevertheless, one can read into their behaviors a sort of familiarity. The human imagination enables children to interpret certain acts as human related. Canadian psychologist Patricia Ganea and her colleagues argue that while attributing human-like intentions and beliefs is a "very natural way to explain certain animal behaviors, anthropomorphism can lead to an inaccurate understanding of biological processes in the natural world ... [as] Common depictions of animals in children's entertainment are likely to amplify this message." She continues, "Jiminy Cricket is the voice of conscience and not an accurate description of what insects behave like; but, yes, the human-like animal representations in the media are likely to increase the tendency to anthropomorphize the natural world" (Ganea, "Young" 1421). Her research with three-to-five-year-old children suggests that they read more fantastical emotions into anthropomorphic representations in the media.

Other scholars have researched the effects of narrative cues on infants' imitation of mediated behaviors, demonstrating that infants, from eighteen to twenty-four months, imitated novel actions more from television than from picture books as their cognitive flexibility and symbolic understanding matured.[2] Investigating whether anthropomorphism in children's books affected their learning, Ganea and her colleagues studied two-to-five-year-old children and found that when a bird was depicted wearing clothes, reading a book, or talking with human motives, the presentations influenced children's conceptual understanding of the animals, with the result that "anthropomorphic storybooks affect younger children's learning of novel facts about animals" (Ganea, "Do Cavies" 283).

Extending that research, N.E. Larsen, K. Lee and Ganea examined whether "storybooks with anthropomorphized animal characters promote prosocial behaviors in young children" (Larsen). Based on the assumption that children learn moral or prosocial behaviors from anthropomorphized animals as effectively as with human characters, researchers found with preschoolers that human characters increased their "altruistic giving" more than the animal characters, suggesting that "realistic stories, not anthropomorphic ones, are better for promoting young children's prosocial behavior" (Larsen). However, scholar Megan Geerdts argues how recent research in anthropomorphic depictions of animals still supports early learning among children (Geerdts 10).

For example, scholars have found *Daniel Tiger's Neighborhood*—a show founded on the principles and characters of *Mister Rogers' Neighborhood*—to be an effective tool at teaching valuable social skills (politely playing with others or trying new foods) to children with autism. Children may also benefit from animated entertainment that encourages emotional regulation, befriending others who are different, and collaborating to solve problems. Even early exposure to age-appropriate programming can enhance cognitive and academic achievement, particularly if the parents get involved and discuss the content and themes with their children.[3]

However, the question is what lessons might be communicated to children about themselves by watching the emotions and behaviors of mediated animals, particularly in modeling laughter. Carl Safina argues that "sneering at anthropomorphism risks eroding our empathy with other species" (Safina 281). Thus, what do anthropomorphic animals in animated feature films and cartoon shorts from Disney and Pixar Studios laugh at and what might that teach children about laughter? What lessons about laughing may be imprinted upon the imaginations of children that teach them about laughter?[4] In what ways do these films serve as exemplary or revelatory models for children's laughter? According to children literary expert Michael Cart, the oldest and most universal type of humorous books for children is that of "talking animal humor" (Cart 15). And it is often those animals that show what is funny.

One can distinguish among various definitions of laughter, noting that only a few types are shared with the animal kingdom. However, in the context of humor studies, most are not. Yet, as anthropomorphic animals exhibit various forms of laughter, both appropriate and inappropriate, benign and malignant, one can distinguish among them in demonstrating what children see. There is a difference between those laughing behaviors that are exemplary, basically those that set out pro-social models of laughter and those that are revelatory, essentially those that reveal something about the anthropomorphic characters that function as cautionary parables.

Several typologies exist to classify and unpack variables regarding anthropomorphic laughing behaviors.[5] A useful heuristic for studying Disney and Pixar films derives from British children's literature author, C.S. Lewis. Not only did Lewis endow his animal characters in his Narnian Chronicles with sundry varieties of laughter, he also divided the causes of laughter into four overlapping categories. First, he identified the laughter of the spirit as Joy, one marked by reunions and shalom. The second erupted out of Fun, or Play, easily recognized as a shared physical sensation with the animal kingdom, such as in tickling. The third was the Joke Proper, a cognitive play on words and ideas, a celebration of incongruity. The final was Flippancy, a taunting, arrogant humor toward others, including *Schadenfreude*, where one laughs at the misfortune of others with sneering contempt (Lewis, "Letter XI" 49).

As an example, while some scientists may interpret the giggling of rats as joy, it appears to fit more appropriately in Lewis' designation of fun or play, as do most physical pleasures. Actual animals do not use the Joke Proper, but a sense of superiority over others, a form of Flippancy, may occur, especially in hyenas fleeing from their pack with a delicious carcass to eat. As Lewis' first and third categories suggest, although nonhuman primates laugh, human humor seems also to involve more specialized cognitive networks not shared with other species.

Lewis' first two categories of Joy and Play abound in the classic Disney animated feature films.[6] The most sublime moment of joy occurs in *Finding Dory* (2016) when the baby fish Dory, with short-term memory loss, laughs and says "hi, Daddy." Trying to understand WWDD ("What Would Dory Do?"), Dory follows the shells set up by her parents (paralleling how the Hebrews set up memorable stones to mark their way home to Jerusalem from Babylon). A final reunion of parents and child creates a deep heartfelt laughter of joy, with the biblical theme of "you found us" punctuating Louis Armstrong's evocative "What a Wonderful World." The laughter of joy is the celestial music of the heavens for the family. The quiet laughter offers an infectious bonding, of children connecting to parents and of simple, heartfelt laughter. The laughter of an anthropomorphic handicapped fish expresses one of the more powerful (and poignant) forms of affiliative laughter in its ability to tap into overcoming fears of parental separation with a reunion of joy.

The laughter of Play, however, dominates the models in the feature films. In Disney's 1941 feature, *Bambi*, Faline and Bambi meet for the first time as fawns. Their reactions differ; whereas Bambi is apprehensive, the young doe Faline giggles and laughs almost hysterically as she chases, licks, and plays with him. Though spirited, her laugher is also affiliative and filled with delight as she meets the life-long friend who will eventually become her mate.

Likewise, when Tod and Vixie meet for the first time in *The Fox and the Hound* (1981), their introduction is marked by bonding and joyous laughter after their attempts to exchange names goes awry. Taken together, the two movies are important in that they show how a childlike sense of wonder and delight can pervade any relationship, with partners of any age. According to Marc Bekoff, University of Colorado, Boulder, professor of biology and expert in canine play behaviors, dogs also can spur other canines to play with their own distinct sounds, sounds that can also reduce stress levels in kennels.

Examining both spontaneous and volitional forms of that universally produced vocal signal called laughter, Gregory Bryant and Athena Aktipis argue that "participants can distinguish between spontaneous and volitional laughter, that when laugh speed was increased, laughs were judged as more real; and when laughs were slowed down, participants could not distinguish spontaneous laughs from nonhuman vocalizations but could identify volitional laughs as human made" (Bryant 327). Their findings suggest that spontaneous laughter, rather than volitional laughter, might share features with nonhuman animal vocalizations. D.A. Leavens argues that the analyses of acoustic behaviors in the calls of great apes in response to tickling hint at possible evolutionary history of laughter in simians.

Playful tickling dominates a film like *The Jungle Book* (1967) with various characters like the laid-back bear Baloo and his human cub Mowgli engaging each other in jolly fun. Even King Louie the orangutan is not immune from ticklish laughter. Such behaviors are some of the most natural for the animal kingdom. The inhalations and exhalations of chimpanzee laughter are unrecognizable to humans, sounding like screeching. Wrestling, tickling (in armpits and bellies), and play chasing evoke mammal vocalizations. Even dolphins emit short bursts of pulse sounds and whistling that are expressed primarily during play-fighting, suggesting that such noises are the dolphin's equivalent to human laughter.[7]

The ultrasonic calls of rats when tickled or tumbled sound like chirping, but they suggest positive affective states. Remy the rat, in *Ratatouille* (2007), tickles and nibbles under the shirt of Linguini, evoking the laughter of a shared secret. Jesse Bering proposes that "rats laugh, but not like humans." He asks,

> Do animals other than humans have a sense of humor? Perhaps in some ways, yes. But in other ways there are likely uniquely human properties to such emotions. Aside from anecdotes, very little about nonhuman primate laughter and humor is known, but some of the most significant findings to emerge in comparative science over the past decade come from pioneering neuroscientist Jaak Panksepp, of Bowling Green State University, that involved the unexpected discovery that rats—particularly juvenile rats—laugh [Bering].

That is right: rats laugh, a sort of primordial form of laughter. Panksepp would be the first to acknowledge that his findings do not imply that rats have a "'sense of humor,' only that there appear to be evolutionary contiguities between laughter in human children during rough-and-tumble play and the expression of similar vocalizations in young rats. A sense of humor—especially adult humor—requires cognitive mechanisms that may or may not be present in other species" (Panksepp, "Beyond" 62).

It appears that one can tickle rats to make them "chirp with joy" (similar vocalizations occur before having sex or receiving morphine) and rough-housing with chimpanzees will educe "pants of excitement, a sort of ha-ha-ha" limited only by "their anatomy and lack of breath-control." All this stems from Panksepp's investigation of rat laughter and animal emotions triggered by tickling. His research extends into examination of the psychological processes of laughter "Beyond a Joke" and seeks to trace a line from animal laughter to human joy (Panksepp, "Neuroevolutionary" 231). Panksepp argues that neural circuits for laughter exist in "ancient regions of the brain" as dopamine reward circuits in the brain light up during human laughter. Such findings came from ticking rats gently around the nape of their necks. It was like having Remy, from Pixar's *Ratatouille*, under your research cloak. Panksepp speculates that "young rats, in particular, have a marvelous sense of fun" with a prime component being slapstick comedy (Panksepp, "Laughing Rats" 546). Mickey Mouse meets Jim Carey.

So, too, neuroscientist Robert Provine and author of *Laughter: A Scientific Investigation*, played with chimps emitting some unique panting sounds with some rough-and-tumble play. He proposed that a tickle and laughter comprise one of the earliest forms of communication. For Provine, such behaviors seem connected.

Ontologically, the Joke Proper cannot occur in the animal kingdom. The cognitive ability to recognize incongruity has not yet been demonstrated to occur. However, in animated feature films, the simple Joke Proper functions as self-effacing humor for identification with spectators. When Louis the trumpet-playing alligator laughs, he explains his backwards navigation to Tiana and Navene in *The Princess and the Frog* (2009): "I was confused by the topography … and geography … and choreography…." Here, the Joke Proper reveals itself in a sly play on words, which also breaks the fourth wall in a small manner by addressing a previous song and pointing out its incongruity within the world of the film.

In *A Bug's Life* (1998), numerous insects laugh at their own jokes: "there's a waiter in my soup." When the Queen Ant philosophizes about the circle of life things, she sighs, "but that's our lot in life—not a lot, haha." The Black Widow titters when she remembers how her twelfth husband died. A stick bug complains that people "always laugh at me," and it takes the flea circus manager to remind him, shouting, "that's because you a clown!" The best self-effacing humor of the bugs occurs in the outtakes, where the Grasshopper looks at the Princess and growls, "are you saying I'm stupid?" and she laughs, even on the fifteenth take.

Self-effacing humor often comes across as self-protective. When Judy addresses Chief Bogo in *Zootopia* (2016) and claims she's "not just some token bunny," her laugher is self-enhancing and largely defensive; the humor seems uncomfortable, almost forced. It suggests what Rod Martin would term as a means of coping with stress or as a social signal of friendliness. A more ironic sense of identity comes as Judy protests too much: her discomfort comes from being just what she claims she isn't, technically speaking. She is just a little female bunny, and by all odds shouldn't be in the police force. Her being the first "prey" animal cop brings in another aspect of the Joke Proper, which molds humor into more controversial topics such as gender and race.

From the trickster in the old African American folk tales, Br'er Rabbit hoodwinks Fox and Bear into letting him visit his "laughing place" just before they barbeque him in *Song of the South* (1946). His laughter is joyous in that he escapes their clutches, but also marked by a touch of *Schadenfreude*, as when they stumble into a hive of bees. When

Fox laughs at Bear getting stung, Bear pounds him on his head. Br'er Rabbit doesn't run away, but enjoys himself and laughs the boffo, tumbling down, rolling over, and convulsing with mirth, telling his victims, "I said this was *my* laughing place, not yours." The canny Rabbit echoes Will Rogers' observation that "everything is funny as long as it is happening to someone else."

Like Lewis' sense of flippancy, Rod Martin's category of aggressive humor occurs in Alpha, a fierce Doberman pinscher, in *Up* (2009). His snarling, teeth-baring growls harken back to the "roar of the jungle." The pack of dogs cowers before his insulting put downs and psychological threats. However, in a fight with Dug, a most friendly and affectionate golden retriever, he gets his comic comeuppance when Dug accidently places the "Cone of Shame" on Alpha's head stuck in a steering wheel, and Alpha's voice goes squeaky as his voice control box is altered. All the other dogs, once bullied by him, now yelp with hilarity at his high-pitched voice.[8]

Research from evolutionary biology and animal laughter corresponds to and complements these revelatory representations. Various studies have shown that the spotted hyena's laugh, like that of the Doberman in *Up*, encodes information about age, dominant/subordinate status, and individual identity, playing a role during social interactions and pointing to the social position of the animal emitting the sounds. The results show that the hyena's laugh encodes such information, giving receivers cues to assess the social position of an emitting individual. As such, the hyenas are not "laughing" because there is something funny to share, but they use certain acoustical sounds to indicate social relations (Mathevon, "The Hyenas" n.p.). Dr. Frederic Theunissen from the University of California at Berkeley suggests that scavenger hyenas do use a "laughing language" to communicate with each other, with their manic giggling, especially around a kill. But it is more than humor; the laughing sounds signal other social status, need messages, and even "frustration." "Giggles" could even recruit allies against a lion when competing for a dead prey. Arriving at a kill, spotted hyenas with bristled tails and many loud "whoop" vocalizations suggested a form of "laughter" (Mathevon, "What the Hyena's Laugh" n.p.).[9] Summarizing the research, journalist Kay Holekamp concludes that "hyenas are most likely to giggle after being attacked and while being chased around by another hyena who wants the carcass part the giggler is carrying around in its mouth. The giggling hyena seems to be signaling that it wants its social partner to desist and leave it alone. Unfortunately, giggling by a hyena carrying food tends to attract other hyenas to it and actually often results in even more harassment directed at the caller" (Holekamp n.p.).

Aggressive humor is fairly self-explanatory and parallels Lewis' definition of mean-spirited wit. However, examples of such laughter are less frequent in Disney's animated features. *The Lion King* (1994) is one such rare movie that does utilize these two particular forms of humor. Showing off a façade of courage before a skull in an elephant graveyard, Simba laughs with bluster. However, three jeering hyenas appear, marked by the distinctive comedic voices of the matriarch Shenzi, the aggressive Banzai, and the idiot Ed. They ridicule lions as pushy, hairy, stinky, and "u-u-u-gly." These three provide comic relief as mad clown minions of Scar, sniggering as they taunt and prepare to attack and eat Simba and Nala. When Simba attempts a ferocious roar, it comes out feebly, and the hyenas laugh with ridicule. *Schadenfreude* characterizes the not-too-bright, goose-stepping scavengers; when one falls into brambles and is covered with thorns, his sidekick mocks, "there ain't no way I am going in there; what you want me to come out looking like you … *cactus butt*?"

Perhaps no animated film packs as robust a set of textbook examples of laughter as Pixar's Ralph Eggleston's economical, Oscar-winning *For the Birds* (2001). A flock of small birds chatter and mutter against one another until they see a large, goofy-looking bird squawking. They imitate him with aggressive, ridiculing guffaws. The group joins in both in the imitation and in the flippant laughter.

Landing on the wire with the smaller birds, the large bird chortles with fun and delight, seeking to bond with the others. However, they resent his presence, and when he hangs upside down on the wire, they meanly unwind his claws from holding on, tittering all the while—until they realize that releasing him will unbind them and send the wire back toward an explosive equilibrium. As they soar into the air and then crash brutally on the ground, now without feathers, the large bird engages in his own reciprocal, aggressive laughter at the embarrassingly naked little birds, with a boffo and tremendous sense of *Schaudenfreude*. Pixar's short models a remarkably revelatory parable for all to see. He who laughs last laughs best.

While no evidence exists that birds laugh, Raoul Schwing of the Messerli Research Institute identifies the New Zealand parrot kea, with apologies to the "laughing kookaburra," as the first case of infectious laughter in a non-mammal. Its warbling sound actually puts other parrots in a "good mood," even a frisky one (Bates n.p.). "Although it is important not to anthropomorphize animal behavior, it is very clear to anyone working or living with kea that they are intelligent, social, and take pleasure in playing with each other—much like we see in other cognizant species, including ourselves," concluded Tamsin Orr-Walker, chair of the Kea Conservation Trust (Bates).

What one observes is that birds seemingly engage in activities that parallel the human sense of play. The scene in which a murder of crows is introduced to *Dumbo* (1941) is an interesting one. Like the huge-eared baby elephant, the crows share a role as outsiders and underdogs; yet they engage and teach the marginalized elephant. In their first encounter with Dumbo, they respond with aggressive, uproarious belly laughs ("the ninth wonder of the universe, the world's only flying elephant"). However, they simultaneously express a fun and playful sense of shared humor among themselves. As oppressed creatures, they empathize with Dumbo, teaching him both how to fly and how to laugh, culminating in the song "When I See an Elephant Fly." Their group laughter is contagious and teaches one how to laugh at oneself, especially when one is different.

Hyenas, dogs, rats, and fish may do something that, perhaps, could be imaginatively construed as laughter. But, as John Donovan sees it,

> taking that seemingly simple leap is tricky. Any attempt to ascribe a human trait to something that isn't human—it's called *anthropomorphizing*—is inherently risky. The more difficult question is whether animals—even those happy-go-lucky chimps and rats—are advanced enough to actually have a "sense" of humor. Whether they can laugh at something that doesn't include physical stimuli. That's been harder to determine. Still, the simple idea that animals can laugh should bring a smile to any grump's face [Donovan n.p.].

The laughter of animated anthropomorphic characters mirrors human behaviors and reflects contexts in which laughter may be affiliative and benign, or mean and aggressive. As such, the animated film shares qualities with the parable and, with its use of cartoon animal figures, even more with the fabulous form, such as the beast fable of Aesop and la Fontaine, and serves as cartoon hieroglyphs in unveiling ways in which laughter functions. In his poem "Impenitence," Lewis observed,

> Why! [Animals] all cry out to be used as symbols,
> Masks for man, cartoons, parodies by Nature
> Formed to reveal us
> Each to each, not fiercely but in her gentlest
> Vein of household laughter... [Lewis, "Impenitence" 3].

Even anthropomorphic cartoon figures carry significance in their existence. They may teach that children are brother and sister to jackals, hyenas, and rats, but even more they teach children about their own laughing behaviors, of both the glorious joys as well as the sinful *Schadenfreude*. These animal caricatures of silly rabbits and wily coyotes serve as hieroglyphs in unveiling human nature, including its vices as well as its virtues.[10]

Various styles of laughter appear throughout Disney and Pixar feature films and shorts, as anthropomorphic animated characters exhibit various forms of affiliative humor, self-enhancing and self-defeating humor, and aggressive humor. While their laughter provides examples of what is permissible to laugh at, it also suggests, as with the Doberman, the birds, and the hyenas, what is more malignant. These animated films teach lessons that children should not imitate the bullying or mocking laughter, but should foster habits of joyous, fun, and incongruous hilarity with others who may seem different. One can laugh slowly like the Flash the Sloth and cherish each guffaw with delight. Yet, all the laughter, as Rod Martin notes, is contagious and contributes to strong feelings of group identity, even if it is with crows and fish (Martin, "The Situational" 270). For viewers, young and old, the opportunity to identify with laughing cartoon animals also creates a moment to review their own styles and practices of laughter, both animal and human.

NOTES

1. Both Disney and Pixar animators wrote books on what is funny. See Frank Thomas and Ollie Johnston's *Too Funny for Words* (Abbeville Press, 1987) and Jason Katz and John Lasseter's *Funny!:Twenty-Five Years of Laughter from the Pixar Story Room* (Chronicle, 2015). The phenomenon of blurred laughter occurs in adult literature/animated films as well. The horrific ending of George Orwell's classic *Animal Farm* culminates in a disturbing scene where "loud laughter and singing come from the farmhouse" as men and pigs meet in terms of equality. When other animals gaze in at the window, however, some queer things happen, as the faces of the two species begin to melt and blend: "pig to man; man to pig; pig to man again" and it is "impossible to say which was which." The blurring of the two species of human and porcine in laughter suggests a merging of the lines of demarcation that typically distinguish them from each other. And it is the face of laughter that brings them strangely together to raise issues about the asymptote of shared connections.

2. See Gabrielle Simcock, Kara Garrity, and Rachel Barr. "The Effect of Narrative Cues on Infants' Imitation from Television and Picture Books." *Child Development* 82:5 (2011): 1607–1619.

3. See Dotson, Wesley H., et al. "Evaluating the Ability of the PBS Children's Show *Daniel Tiger's Neighborhood* to Teach Skills to Two Young Children with Autism Spectrum Disorder." \ *Behavior Analysis in Practice* 10.1 (2017): 67–71 and Christensen, C.G. "Effects of Prosocial Television on Children's Social and Emotional Competencies: A Systematic Review." Paper presentation in a symposium at the annual meeting of the Midwest Psychological Association, Chicago, IL (May 2013).

4. Humans' history with domesticated animals is complex, but no animal is more beloved in the United States than the dog. As the first species to be domesticated, dogs inhabit more households than cats, fish, birds, and other pets. See Diamond, J.M. *Guns, Germs, and Steel: The Fates of Human Societies* (W.H. Norton & Company, 1999). In her pilot study *Tails of Laughter*, Robin Maria Valeri found people who owned dogs and people who owned cats and dogs all laughed more frequently than people who owned just cats. Even people with no pets reported laughing more than cat owners. The most frequent source of laughter was spontaneous laughter resulting from a situation, which implies that, all other factors being equal, people who spend time with the absurd and joyful creatures that inspired Proverbs 26:11 are more probably more willing to recognizing their own folly and laugh at themselves and the world all around. See Valeri, Robin Maria. "Tails of Laughter: A Pilot Study Examining the Relationship between Companion Animal Guardianship (Pet Ownership) and Laughter." *Society & Animals* 14.3 (2006): 275–293.

5. Through his HSQ (Humor Styles Questionnaire) Canadian psychologist Rod Martin outlined four distinct kinds of laughter that mark human behavior with a particular valence: affiliative (a humor that creates fellowship and well-being, a sort of bonding laughter that finds shared humor in everyday life); aggressive (humor that insults or disparages others, used to put down or shame others, even a form of bullying); self-enhancing (humor that is self-deprecating, able to laugh at oneself in a good-natured way, and a means of coping with stress); and self-defeating (humor which demeans the self rather than others, of putting oneself down as the butt of jokes). See Martin, Rod, Patricia Puhlik-Doris, Gwen Larsen, Jeanette Gray, Kelly Weir. "Individual Differences in Uses of Humor and Their Relation to Psychological Well-Being: Development of the Humor Styles Questionnaire." *Journal of Research in Personality* 37:1 (February 2003): 48–75.

6. Frank Thomas and Ollie Johnson's compendium of gags showcase animated creatures laughing, from the three little pigs to Donald Duck in *Too Funny for Words: Disney's Greatest Sight Gags* (Abbeville Publishers, 1987); various animators at Disney such as Ken Anderson would teach others how to "see the funny side of particular characters" (22). Each character would possess a certain kind of humor brought to life with "funny drawings." The Nine Old Men gave children who were taunted because of their physical appearance a character with whom to identify in *Elmer Elephant* (1936). From the laughter of derision, literally de-rising another, emerged an affiliative laughter of bonding, showing how difference, not deficits, are important and the basis for healthy humor. Pixar revealed the senses of humor of its animators as well in *Funny!: Twenty-Five Years of Laughter from the Pixar Story Room* (Chronicle Books, 2015), showing how animators like John Lasseter and Pete Docter would experiment with a character's sense of humor, "trying to get a handle on who he was before we wrote the script" (130).

7. See David Cox's "Ticking Rats and Giggling Dolphins: Do Animals Have a Sense of Humor?" *The Guardian* 17 November 2015. https://www.theguardian.com/science/blog/2015/nov/17/tickling-rats-giggling-dolphins-do-animals-sense-humour. Accessed June 23, 2017. With regard to the laughter of play, the body and its peculiar functions, especially dealing with light taboos on excretion, evoke much laughter. Children watching comic moments of bathroom humor learn an invaluable comedy lesson: fart jokes always are funny. For example, in *Finding Nemo* (2003), two seagulls are floating on the ocean water. An underwater explosion takes place under them. When a bubble pops behind one of them, the other sarcastically says, "nice." The enthymeme of flatulence always works.

8. Researcher Patricia Simonet of the University of Nevada, Reno, chased down dog laughter, finding a "breathy, pronounced, forced exhalation" that spectrographs revealed as frequencies beyond human hearing. She recommended inviting your dog to play with you using the "hee-hee-hee" sound without the "ee" sound, as in a Heimlich maneuver. http://www.animalliberationfront.com/Philosophy/Morality/Speciesism/Animal Laughter.html. Accessed June 23, 2017.

9. Also see von Radowitz, John."Hyenas Use a 'Laughing Language' to Communicate." *Independent* 30 March 2010. http://www.independent.co.uk/environment/nature/hyenas-use-a-laughing-language-to-commu nicate-1930995.html. Accessed June 21, 2017. Also see McGhee, Paul "Chimpanzee and Gorilla Humor: Progressive Emergence from Origins in the Wild to Captivity to Sign Language Learning." *Humor: International Journal of Humor Research* 31:2 (De Gruyter, 2018): 405.

10. One must also acknowledge in closing that one can observe, as satirist Jonathan Swift quipped, "beasts may degenerate into men," recognizing the inversion of human and animal, not only in the animated film, but in literary fictions such as George Orwell's *Animal Farm* and Kafka's *Metamorphosis*, not to mention Gary Larson's *The Far Side* (and are we authors like his naive scientists trying to "test whether or not animals kiss?"). See Simon Critchley's *On Humour* (Routledge, 2002), 31.

The author would like to thank research students Mickella Rast and Hayley Heath for their insightful and substantial contributions.

WORKS CITED

Amidi, Amid. *The Art of Pixar Short Films*. Chronicle Books, 2009.

Bates, Mary. "These Parrots Can Make Other Parrots 'Laugh.'" *National Geographic* 20 March 2017. https://www.theguardian.com/science/blog/2015/nov/17/tickling-rats-giggling-dolphins-do-animals-sense-humour. Accessed June 23, 2017.

Bering, Jesse. "Do Animals Other Than Humans Have a Sense of Humor? Maybe So." *Scientific American* 1 July 2012. https://www.scientificamerican.com/article/rats-laugh-but-not-like-human/. Accessed June 21, 2017.

Bryant, Gregory A. and C. Athena Aktipis. "The Animal Nature of Spontaneous Human Laughter." *Evolution & Human Behavior* 35:4 (July 2014): 327–335.

Cart, Michael. *What's So Funny? Wit and Humor in American Children's Literature*. HarperCollins, 1995.

Donovan, John. "No Joke: We Aren't the Only Animals That Laugh." *Mother Nature Network* 5 August 2015. https://www.mnn.com/earth-matters/animals/stories/no-joke-we-arent-only-animals-laugh. Accessed June 21, 2017.

Ganea, Patricia, Lili Ma, and Judy DeLoache. "Young Children's Learning and Transfer of Biological Information from Picture Books to Real Animals." *Child Development* 82:5 (September/October 2011): 1421–1433.

Ganea, Patricia A., Caitlin F. Canfield, Kadria Simons-Ghafari, and Tommy Chou. "Do Cavies Talk? The Effect of Anthropomorphic Picture Books on Children's Knowledge about Animals." *Frontiers in Psychology* 5 (2014): 283.

Geerdts, Megan S. "(Un)Real Animals: Anthropomorphism and Early Learning About Animals" *Child Development Perspectives* 10: 1 (March 2016): 10–14.

Holekamp, Kay E. "Why Do Hyenas Laugh?" *The New York Times* 11 July 2011. https://scientistatwork.blogs. nytimes.com/2011/07/11/why-do-hyenas-laugh/. Accessed June 21, 2017.

Larsen, N.E., K. Lee and Patricia Ganea. "Do Storybooks with Anthropomorphized Animal Characters Promote Prosocial Behaviors in Young Children?" *Developmental Science* 2 (August 2, 2017).

Lewis, C.S. "Impenitence." *Poems.* Geoffrey Bles, 1964.

Lewis, C.S. "Letter XI." *The Screwtape Letters.* Macmillan, 1968.

Martin, Rod A. "The Situational Humor Response Questionnaire (SHRQ) and Coping Humor Scale (CHS): A Decade of Research Findings." *Humor: International Journal of Humor Research* 9 (1996): 251–272.

Mathevon, Nicolas, Aaron Koralek, Mary Weldele, Stephen E Glickman and Frédéric E Theunissen "What the Hyena's Laugh Tells: Sex, Age, Dominance and Individual Signature in the GigglingCcall of *Crocuta Crocutai.*" *BioMedical Central Ecology* (https://bmcecol.biomedcentral.com/articles/10.1186/1472–6785–10–9). Accessed August 7, 2017.

Mathevon, Nicolas, Aaron Koralek, Steve Glickman, and Frederic Theunissen. "The Hyena's Laugh as a Multi-Informative Signal." *The Journal of the Acoustical Society of America* 125: 2709 (2009).

Owren, M.J. and Zimmermann, E. "The Evolution of Laughter in Great Apes and Humans" *Communication of Integrated Biology* 3:2 (March 2010): 191–4.

Panksepp, J. "Beyond a Joke: From Animal Laughter to Human Joy?" *Science* 308: 5718 (April 1, 2005): 62–63.

Panksepp, J. "Neuroevolutionary Sources of Laughter and Social Joy: Modeling Primal Human Laughter in Laboratory Rats." *Behavior Brain Research* 182:2 (September 4, 2007): 231–44.

Panksepp, J., and J. Burgdorf. "'Laughing' Rats and the Evolutionary Antecedents of Human Joy?" *Physiological Behavior* 79:3 (August 1979): 533–47.

Safina, Carl. *Beyond Words: What Animals Think and Feel.* Henry Holt and Company, 2015.

Surprisingly Human

Producing Nonhuman Selves for Human Entertainment

Candace Korasick

The expansion of cable offerings, not to mention of online programming, has resulted in the need of television networks to carve out niches for themselves. When it debuted in 1996, Animal Planet was the place to go for nature documentaries, host-driven shows like Steve Irwin's *The Crocodile Hunter* and later *The Jeff Corwin Experience*, and pet-education shows such as *Dogs 101*. In 2010, Animal Planet rebranded itself with the tagline "Surprisingly Human." There was a subsequent shift in programming, much of which was less about animals and more about humans who interact with animals: *Pitbulls and Parolees, River Monsters, Call of the Wildman, Gator Boys, My Cat from Hell*, etc. (Indeed, except for the series *Too Cute* and the annual *Puppy Bowl*, the preponderance of animal-themed shows seemed to focus on "problem" animals.) For a while, Animal Planet aired several shows that were not even about animals: *Wild Alaska*, about men who run a gun store; *Ice Cold Gold*, about prospectors in Greenland; reruns of *Dirty Jobs*, in which Mike Rowe did some of the filthiest jobs in the U.S., and *Rocky Mountain Bounty Hunters*, which was exactly what the title implies. For a network that calls itself Animal Planet, it was, indeed, surprisingly human.

It is worth noting that Animal Planet's lineup has changed again, eliminating most (but not all) of the human-only programming in favor of those in which humans interact with animals. *Pitbulls and Parolees* and *River Monsters* still air, but now there are more shows about animal caretakers such as *Dr. Jeff: Rocky Mountain Vet, The Vet Life*, and *Vet Gone Wild*, all about veterinarians and their patients; *The Zoo*, which gives viewers a look behind the scenes at the Bronx Zoo; and *Dodo Heroes*, which tells "inspiring stories of animals in need … and the humans who go to unimaginable lengths to give them hope" (*Animal Planet* n.p.).

Animal Planet aired *Meerkat Manor* and *Big Cat Diary* in the mid–2010s, and despite the fact that both shows had been out of production for more than five years, they were staples of Animal Planet's 2013–2014 morning lineup. Two episodes of each program were shown weekday mornings. Although neither show is regularly on Animal Planet in 2018, they occasionally re-air. *Big Cat Diary* was being shown on Animal Planet as recently as April of 2018, and *Meerkat Manor* was shown on Discovery Family for several afternoons in June of 2018. Although *Big Cat Diary* did not win any significant awards, it was to have been a one-season series for BBC One and Animal Planet, but its popularity lead to eight more seasons (Richards 329), and in 2018, Animal Planet announced production of a follow-up to *Big Cat Diary*, titled *Big Cat Legacy* (Maglio n.p.). *Meerkat Manor* was nominated for three prime-time Emmy Awards during its original run ("Meerkat Manor—Awards") and won a Gold Medal in the Nature and Wildlife division of the 2006 New York Film Festival ("Meerkat Manor"). In 2007, it was Animal Planet's most watched program (Bellafante n.p.).

Something about these two programs continues to appeal to viewers. (Fans of *Meerkat Manor* can—and do—continue to follow the day-to-day struggles of meerkats via The Friends of the Kalahari Meerkats website, even though the last season of the show was produced in 2008.) Unlike most of the contemporary Animal Planet shows, these two programs contain no direct human-animal interactions. Nonetheless, their continued appeal is tied to the fact that both big cats and meerkats are "surprisingly human."

Overview of Programs

Unlike more traditional nature documentaries, these shows focus on the day-to-day activities of *specific* wild animals. The animal "stars" of both shows are named, and viewers can recognize individuals by both appearance and behavior. The narrators present biographies of the major characters, sometimes insinuating motives beyond instinct and survival to the animals' behaviors. As such, they go beyond anthropomorphism to the production of selves for the animals filmed. This is not problematic in and of itself. There is ample evidence for nonhuman animal selfhood. The issue at hand is the creation of selfhood as a consumable product and concerns that are raised depending on how we do so.

"Welcome to the Maasai Mara"

These are the words that welcome the viewer to the very first episode of *Big Cat Diary*, which was filmed in the Maasai Mara National Reserve in Kenya. It premiered on BBC One in 1996 and was occasionally still being shown on Animal Planet in 2018. The hosts and narrators for the first two seasons, Simon King and Jonathan Scott, are veteran wildlife filmmakers, specializing in African wildlife. They were later joined by Saba Douglas-Hamilton, a Kenyan wildlife conservationist. What made Big Cat Diary a departure from previous wildlife documentaries is that each season it followed particular animals, some of them over multiple seasons, creating what King referred to as "a diary, if you will" during the premier episode. Season 1 introduced us to the Marsh pride and the Ridge pride of lions (most of whom were never given individual names on-air), cheetah Kidogo and her cubs, and Half-Tail the leopard, about whom Scott said, "I've known this cat for six or seven years" ("The Hunt Begins").

Big Cat Diary could well be viewed as being as much about the process of filming wildlife as it is about the cats themselves. King, Scott, and Douglas-Hamilton all spoke directly to the camera about what they were observing … or not observing. In an episode of Season 2, King mentions that a lot of their time is spent just sitting and waiting, after which there is a montage of him reading a book, eating lunch, even working out with dumbbells while the Marsh pride slept in the distance ("From Dawn Till Dusk"). Their personal excitement and worries over the animals they were filming was part of the program.

"Meet the Whiskers"

The focus of *Meerkat Manor* is a gang of meerkats that are part of the Kalahari Meerkat Project in the Kuruman River Reserve in South Africa. The project is a long-term study of several troupes by Cambridge University, one of which is "the Whiskers." When it premiered on Animal Planet in 2005, key members of the gang were introduced to the audience by name. Some, like "brave little Shakespeare" and "the naughty kids," were assigned personalities as well. Unlike *Big Cat Diary*, in *Meerkat Manor* the filmmakers are not part of the show, nor are they part of the research project. There is no talking to the camera. Like most nature documentaries before it, *Meerkat Manor* has a narrator who is performing a script. For the United States, that narrator was Sean Astin for the first three seasons and Stockard Channing in the last. While the scripts are factual in most regards, they are also embellished, suggesting a sort of drama to the life of meerkats in the Kalahari. To facilitate this perception, a lot of the day-to-day activities of foraging and grooming are edited out ("Meerkat Manor-Backstage" n.p.).

Animal Selfhood

The literature on selfhood in sociology, psychology, and philosophy is quite extensive. The nature of self has been of significant interest to social psychologists at least since the heyday of the American pragmatists in the late nineteenth and early twentieth centuries (Gecas and Burke 41; Holstein and Gubrium 18). The dominant models in sociology have relied heavily on interaction, language, and reflexive thought. It is through our interactions with others, including the ways that we use language to define and "speak" ourselves to others, and the ability to be the subjects of our own thoughts, to evaluate our behaviors, that we are told that our selves come into being.

The notion that animals don't think at all, a position forwarded years ago by Rene Descartes, who argued that they are mere machines (61), is out of favor. We have ample evidence from scholars in sociology, psychology, and biology to prove otherwise (Bekoff 489; Irvine, *If You Tame Me* 149, Shapiro 34), and we've known for some time that some nonhuman animals—elephants, dolphins, orcas, and all of the great apes—pass the rouge test, indicating self-recognition in a mirror (Coren n.p.). But whether or not nonhumans are actually capable of having a self, as sociologists understand it, is still a matter of debate.

For centuries, humans—at least Westerners—have maintained that there is something unique about humans that sets us above other animals. This position, the doctrine of human dignity, has two core components. First, human life is special, sacred even, and is to be protected. Second, nonhuman life does not warrant the same moral protections. This position is in no small degree bound to Judeo-Christian religious tradition (Kowalski 5; Linzey 111; Rachels 88), but secular philosophy, going back at least as far as Aristotle (5), posits that humankind is morally superior based on our capacity for rationality

(Rachels 178). Even Immanuel Kant's arguments in favor of the humane treatment of nonhuman animals were based on protection of human moral integrity; treating animals poorly diminishes humankind's moral standing (Rachels 90).

In his book, *The Bonobo and the Atheist*, Frans de Waal stops short of claiming that other species are moral beings in the same sense that humans are. However, he does assert that our belief in our superior intelligence is due to a bias in how scientists construct experiments (de Waal 22). We construct tests of both intelligence and morality that work for humans. De Waal contends throughout the book that some other species are definitely moral, but to demonstrate this, we have to give up our understanding of morality as derived from religion (23) and embrace "bottom-up" morality embedded in "the importance of social relationships" (228).

So what? Some species of nonhuman animals are rational, possibly even moral. But are they reflexive thinkers? While some theorists contend that they are (Haraway 206; Shapiro 48), Leslie Irvine argues that they need not be to be in possession of selfhood (*If You Tame Me* 120). Irvine contends that sociologists from Mead forward rely too heavily on language as a requirement for communication and, therefore, for thought. We do not need to speak with animals. We merely need to perceive them to have a mind (Irvine, *If You Tame Me* 121). Clearly this is typical of pet owners, as evidenced most clearly by Clinton Sanders' research on how people speak for their nonhuman companions when at the veterinary clinic (Arluke and Sanders 72).

Building on Daniel Stern's research on infants and Jaber Gubrium's research on Alzheimer's patients, Irvine asserts that selfhood rests on four conditions previously identified by Stern: agency, coherence, affectivity, and self-history (*If You Tame Me* 128). In addition, Following Irvine's example, it becomes clear that the makers of both *Meerkat Manor* and *Big Cat Diary* are producing genuine nonhuman selves for their audiences and not just falling back on uncritical anthropomorphism for the sake of entertainment.

Agency

Agency is simple enough to explain and accept; it is the capacity for self-willed action (Irvine, *If You Tame Me* 128). This rules out plants (as far as I can tell, anyway), but includes nonhuman animals. When I call my dogs, they come to me … usually. Although I may have precipitated the movement, they decide whether or not answering my call is worth their while.

In *Meerkat Manor*, the Whiskers gang goes about foraging and fighting at the direction of the dominant female. It is she who leads them out of the burrow each morning to search for food. It is she who decides where they will forage and when they will change dens. When the pups are too young to accompany the adults on foraging expeditions, young adults stay behind to babysit. Part of the drama on *Meerkat Manor* comes from these babysitters' decisions to either defend or move the pups when threats arise.

Likewise, the cheetahs, leopards, and lions in *Big Cat Diary* move about in response to hunger and threat. These larger predators, in particular, make clear decisions about which prey to target during a hunt and when to introduce their young to meat. In an episode titled, "They Are Cheetahs," King draws viewers' attention to the way a cheetah named Honey has started bringing her cubs live fawns so they can practice tripping and suffocating prey.

There is little room to argue against the agency of both meerkats and big cats within the context of these shows. Certainly, their behaviors are shaped by their environments, but not in ways that are absolutely deterministic. Although each animal behaves in more or less predictable ways according to species, the structure of the shows, showing the same animals day-in and day-out, allows viewers to witness the extent to which each animal decides for itself its own activities for the day.

Coherence

Coherence refers to the recognition of the boundaries of self and the ability to recognize others as distinct entities (Irvine, *If You Tame Me* 133). It requires one to know that others are "not me." Irvine's research in shelters and dog parks revealed that not only do guardians treat their companion animals as distinct others, but that canines are capable of distinguishing between different people. This is of no surprise to anyone with a companion animal (*If You Tame Me* 106). My dogs act differently toward me than they act toward my spouse or to other human beings. As Irvine concluded, canines (and probably other companion animals) interact with different humans in different ways, just as we do.

The standard practice in wildlife research is to interfere as little as possible with the animals' daily lives. By limiting their contact with the animals, the researchers behind each program provide little to no opportunity for viewers to learn if the individual animals respond differently to individual human beings. But just as our companion animals have particular relationships with specific animals they encounter, the subjects of both *Meerkat Manor* and *Big Cat Diary* seem to treat animal others as unique animal others.

In Season 1 and the first half of Season 2 of *Meerkat Manor*, all of the Whiskers seek the approval of dominant female Flower, at least to her face. She has the strength, cunning, and experience to expel any member who displeases her. At various times, she has alternately punished or tolerated the presence of adult females who return to the burrow after mating with a roving male, a strict no-no for meerkat families. Every member of the gang behaves toward Flower as if she is unique.

There is also evidence, however, that an individual meerkat's "identity" is of no importance. Throughout all four seasons, regardless of who is dominant, the Whiskers engage in battles with neighboring meerkat families—sometimes to the death of one or more meerkats. But when one of the nondominant females goes into estrus, there is no evidence of bad blood having arisen out of a prior skirmish. The little mammals will fight one day and mate the next. This does have a corollary in human behavior. We also respond to people according to their roles in a situation, treating anonymous individuals according to their apparent status within the social structure.

There is clearer evidence for some wild animals distinguishing between various animal others in *Big Cat Diary*. In most cases, these recognizable significant others seem to be blood relatives. A case in point is that of a grizzled pride male named Scar. In Season 3, Scar is routed by two younger males. A male who loses such a fight rarely survives long without the pride females, who do the vast majority of the hunting. Even if the male's wounds and age do not impact his ability to hunt, his conspicuous mane is easily spotted by prey. Scar, however, beat the odds because two of his adult sons, who left the pride upon reaching sexual maturity, accept his companionship and allowed him to share their kills. If they had been acting purely on instinct, they would have chased off another adult male.

Affectivity

Animal guardians can readily describe the moods and personalities of their companion animals. Affectivity is the demonstration of both emotions (categorical affects) and ways of being (vitality affects) (Irvine, *If You Tame Me* 137). Some animal researchers have recently confirmed that dogs, at the very least, do experience emotions as humans understand them (Andics et al. 1031; Nagasawa et al. 213). It is through affectivity that companion animals make their core selves available to humans (Irvine, If *You Tame Me* 158; Shapiro 40).

The attribution of affectivity to wild animals is often suspect. We can easily identify the emotions of our nonhuman housemates because we live with them. We have day-to-day experience with the ways our companion animals respond to a variety of events, especially our own behaviors. The departure from traditional documentary style is what allows *Big Cat Diary* and *Meerkat Manor* to forward the possibility of affectivity to their audiences. The episodic formatting and the focus on the mundane conjures for viewers a sense of familiarity with the animals. They feel as if they *know* these animals.

Flower, the above-mentioned dominant female of the Whiskers, often behaves in ways that appear to be cruel. At the end of the episode titled "The Godmother," she moves the entire troupe on her young pups' first foraging trip, abandoning female Mozart and her newborn litter. The narration implies that this was a calculated move, meant to both punish Mozart and improve the odds of survival for Flower's litter. Flower, quite honestly, comes across as cold, in part because Mozart is also Flower's offspring. There is no maternal affection. But it is actually quite unfair to attribute human sensibilities to nonhuman animals, especially human codes of morality. In the first episode of Season 2 of *Big Cat Diary*, King stresses to the audience that behavior that would appear to "callous" by human standards is not cruel, but a necessary step in raising young cheetahs ("Meeting the Big Cats").

That is not to say that we should never anthropomorphize animal behaviors, some of which may well be better understood in human terms. As Irvine explains in *My Dog Always Eats First*, describing animal behaviors and emotional states in anthropomorphic terms is often the correct choice (15). For one thing, humans are our frame of reference, ergo it is pretty much impossible to completely avoid it. But it is often the most efficient way to communicate what has been observed. All the presenters in *Big Cat Diary* have at one time or another described the behavior of a female in estrus as "flirtatious." Clearly, it would be a mistake to attribute the mating behaviors of wild predators to human dating sensibilities, but "flirtatious" serves as an easy shorthand for explaining to the audience why a female, especially one of a solitary nature as a leopard or cheetah, is suddenly behaving as if an interloping male is not a threat to her. (It also demonstrates our own gender stereotypes around heteronormative courtship, but that is a discussion for a different venue.) In the same vein, when cheetah Amber finally abandons her adult cubs, it is most efficient to explain the young cheetahs' behaviors in terms of loss and sadness. They appear to be sad and confused, and remain in the area in which they last saw Amber for quite some time. When they do encounter their mother again, they engage in playful behaviors, seeming to be happy to be reunited. Amber's behaviors, if we were to assign the closest human emotion to them, demonstrate resignation ("Stealing from Baboons").

Much as we each know our own companion animals, and perhaps even some of the individual wildlife near our homes, the makers of *Big Cat Diary* and *Meerkat Manor* do know the animals they are presenting to us. Both programs are based on several years of ongoing study of the same groups of animals in a specified geographic area. Although the length of the study is not expressly stated in *Big Cat Diary*, both King and Scott make references throughout the program to how long they have "known" specific cats. Furthermore, in their commentary, they often reference a particular animal's history—how many litters a female has raised successfully, what battles have been fought to what effect, and what precipitated an apparent falling-out between related animals.

Self-History

It is clear that affectivity is intricately tied to self-history. Nonhuman animals cannot narrate their own lives as humans do, but they do remember; and memory provides continuity for the self (Irvine, *If You Tame Me* 140). Nonhuman memory may not operate in the same ways as human memory, but there is little doubt that dogs and cats remember places, things, and people. How else do we account for the nonhuman companion who is relaxed at home but a terror at the clinic, who knows what games are played with a ball, who recognizes the smells and sounds of distinct humans (Haraway 70; Irvine, *If You Tame Me* 140).

Because both *Meerkat Manor* and *Big Cat Diary* are founded on long-standing research and conservation projects, the creators can give us insight into these animals' histories. Each group of animals has been studied for more than a decade, allowing us to discern distinctions between similar animals and attribute personalities to them.

For example, "Rebellious Mozart," as one meerkat is described during opening credits of Season 2, is derived from her frequent slipping away from the family group when she is in estrus. During her mother's tenure as the dominant female of the gang, Mozart conceived several times. Sometimes her pregnancy was carried to term within the group; other times Flower drove her out of the family. It is her *history* of running off in search of an unrelated male that allows humans to perceive her as rebellious. The audience watches as Mozart sneaks off again and again, despite never raising a litter successfully. Because we know her history, and perhaps because we expect her to learn from her past, the creators of *Meerkat Manor* can conjure family drama on par with some prime-time, network fare.

In a much less dramatic example, we see that self-history includes intergenerational history. The researchers for *Big Cat Diary* often speak of Kike, a cheetah with an affinity for field vehicles. Most of the animals in both programs are habituated to human presence and human tools. Several episodes of *Meerkat Manor* show meerkats being weighed and measured in exchange for treats, and lions and leopards often stroll past the cameras and vehicles in *Big Cat Diary*, paying them no mind. Kike makes use of vehicles as part of her daily routine. Once Kike is identified as the cheetah on screen, viewers know they are likely to see her on or under a vehicle. She uses them to escape threats, scout for prey, and to rest. She often marks them as her own with urine and feces, and viewers know that if researchers are too slow closing a sunroof, they will get doused. But this behavior is not seen as willful or defiant, but adaptive. Kike makes use of the vehicles because they are part of her environment and because her mother, Amber, also mounted the vehicles to survey the area, although Amber did not use them as extensively as Kike. Likewise, one expects that Kike's cubs will eventually use the vehicles in similar ways, especially as they are seen playing on and around them while Kike lounges on the hood. It is the duration of the presenters' experiences with these particular animals that allows us to see clearly how a particular animal's biography contributes to individual identity.

Conclusion: Collaborative Construction or Contrivance?

In both *If You Tame Me* and *My Dog Always Eats First,* Irvine makes a strong case for the way "animals confirm and enrich that sense [of self] in us" (*If You Tame Me* 119, *My Dog* 133). Her intention, in part, was to demonstrate that in contributing to the self-hood of the humans with whom they interact, companion animals *must* have a subjective selfhood of their own, something beyond run-of-the-mill anthropomorphism. It is not difficult for people to accept the premise that our companion animals—dogs, cats, and horses in particular—have selves. We know them so well—their preferences and their peccadilloes, their talents and their temperaments. Furthermore, even if they are not reflexive thinkers, they give the appearance of being able to take on the role of the significant other, maybe even the generalized other. Attributing selfhood to our companion animals, whether we truly believe it is there or not, allows us to bond more securely to the animals that are a part of our daily lives (Arluke and Sanders 81). But we do not conjure these selves for them out of thin air; they are collaborative works between us and our nonhuman companions. Donna Haraway extends this argument to wild animals, noting that even though they do not share our homes, they are part of our everyday lives: "[W]e are in a knot of species coshaping one another in layers of reciprocating complexity all the way down" (42). In other words, we collaboratively co-construct selves for ourselves, other humans, and the animals we encounter.

As domesticated animals have transitioned from economic assets to cherished companions, it makes sense that we would include them in our ruminations about selfhood. Several researchers have made persuasive arguments for this. Once we have done that, extending the same considerations to wildlife is hardly farfetched, but it is not easy for the average person to evaluate the selfhood of wild animals beyond their own yards. Explorations of selfhood in nonhumans other than primates is possible in *Meerkat Manor* and *Big Cat Diary* because both are premised on existing, longitudinal research projects. The film crews are not gathering footage of just any animal of the appropriate species, but specific, known animals. This allows the viewer to assess the animals' behaviors over time.

Neither the big cats nor the meerkats have reflexive selves. However, when we hold *Big Cat Diary* and *Meerkat Manor* up to the standard Irvine presents, we can see that the stars of both programs do display *elements* of individual selfhood. There is no denying that all of the animals in both have agency; they do not rely on air or water currents to take them where they need to be. But the issues of coherence, affectivity, and self-history require closer inspection. There is some more support for the idea that the nonhuman stars of *Big Cat Diary* meet all of Irvine's criteria. The hosts speak for the cats in a way that is very similar to how the average person speaks for her companion animals (Arluke and Sanders 67). Coherence and self-history seem evident, and the case for affectivity can be made. These cats are, indeed, surprisingly human.

The meerkats, on the other hand, seem to fall short on both self-history and affectivity. *Meerkat Manor* is sometimes guilty of overdramatized interpretations; creator Caroline

Hawkins acknowledges that the television shows *Dallas* and *Desperate Housewives* influenced her (*Meerkat Manor: The Official Website* n.p.). As such, the program plays up mating and fighting over foraging ("Meerkat Manor—Backstage" n.p.). This difference between *Meerkat Manor* and *Big Cat Diary* makes sense from a ratings standpoint. Several hours of footage of meerkats digging in sand for scorpions and centipedes is not as compelling or engrossing as a pride of lions taking down a zebra. The soap-opera style has unquestionable entertainment value, but it limits the viewers' ability to evaluate the potential for selfhood in meerkats as compared to our access to the selves of the animals in *Big Cat Diary*.

If we extend Haraway's argument, we see that the discrete aspects of animal selfhood are themselves complex and collaborative. As such, even if the meerkat selves presented to us are more contrived than the selves of the big cats, *Meerkat Manor* blurs the lines between human and animal in some ways that are, indeed, authentic. But beyond the mental exercise of trying to determine if other species—species that are not that close to us and that do not share our homes—have selves, why should we care? Can't we leave this issue to philosophers and ethologists? Simply put, when we poke holes in the barriers, we chip away at the "psychological distance necessary to exploit animals ruthlessly" (Arluke and Sanders 81).

Big Cat Diary and *Meerkat Manor* are hardly the first programs to indulge in anthropomorphism. In my youth, I was particularly fond of *Charlie, the Lonesome Cougar*, which occasionally aired on *The Wonderful World of Disney* on Sunday nights. But this film was a work of fiction and not meant to be a representative of the lives, much less the selfhood, of wild cougars. Increased competition for viewers means wildlife documentaries are pressed to innovate in order to attract a larger audience share. *Big Cat Diary* is acknowledged to be the first wildlife "docusoap" (Richards 322), a label *Meerkat Manor*'s creator embraces (*Meerkat Manor: The Official Website* n.p.). In an interview, *Big Cat Diary* creator Robin Hellier said he wanted to create a "natural history soap opera" to compete with primetime soaps (Richards 326). Similarly, *Meerkat Manor* was explicitly built on the scaffolding of both television dramas and reality television (*Meerkat Manor: The Official Website* n.p.). These programs' influence can be seen in current programs such as National Geographic Channel's *Savage Kingdom*. Instead of presenting large African predators as inhabitants of a shared ecosystem, each episode focuses on the matriarch in a clan. Her behaviors are presented as calculated, an attempt to become "queen" of the savannah, rather than as the product of generations of instinct an evolution (Hoppin n.p.). The parallels to *Game of Thrones* are unmistakable, especially as the program is narrated by Charles Dance, one of the stars of the HBO drama.

The late philosopher James Rachels credits Charles Darwin for making possible, if not directly causing, the undermining of the doctrine of human dignity by making both the God thesis and the rationality thesis suspect (5). *On the Origin of the Species by Natural Selection* in particular challenged the doctrine of human dignity by suggesting that the difference in rationality between humans and nonhuman animals is a matter of degree rather than of kind (Rachels 133). While Darwin did not consider the behaviors he observed to be of the same order as human morality (Kowalski 56; Rachels 147), Rachels contends that this is evidence of morality in animals, a position that is supported by the research of ethologist Marc Bekoff (492) and sociologist Donna Haraway (27). But while many, if not most, people are willing to accept that animals are sentient and intelligent, human beings have a vested interest in not perceiving them as moral (Kowalski

58). As Gary Kowalski put it, "By denying that animals possess a moral sense we tell ourselves that human beings are of a fundamentally higher order. We can therefore colonize and enslave with impunity those who are 'lower'" (58). Nonetheless, we must be careful not to overly, uncritically anthropomorphize animal behaviors, lest we hold animals to human standards of morality.

WORKS CITED

Andics, Attila, et al. "Neural Mechanisms for Lexical Processing in Dogs." *Science*, vol. 353, no. 6303, 2016. pp. 1030–1032.

Animal Planet. www.animalplanet.com/schuedule. Accessed 01 Jun 2018.

Aristotle. "This History of Animals." *The Animals Reader: The Essential Classic and Contemporary Writings*, edited by Linda Kalof and Amy J. Fitzgerald, Berg Publishers, 2007. pp. 5–7.

Arluke, Arnold. and Clinton R. Sanders. *Regarding Animals*. Temple University Press, 1996.

Bekoff, Marc. "Wild Justice and Fair Play: Cooperation, Forgiveness, and Morality in Animals." *Biology and Philosophy*, vol. 19, no. 4, 2004. pp. 489–520.

Bellafante, Ginia. "'The Desert Has Lost Its Favorite Rose': Death Comes to the Whiskers Family." *The New York Times*. 10 Oct 2007, www.nytimes.com/2007/10/10/arts/television/10bell.html?_r=1&oref=slogin. Accessed 02 Oct 2018.

"Challenge on the Marsh." *Big Cat Diary*, Season 3, Episode 7, BBC Two, original air date 04 Feb 2001.

Charlie, the Lonesome Cougar. Directed by Winston Hibler, Walt Disney Productions, 1967.

Coren, Stanley. "Does My Dog Recognize Himself in a Mirror?" *Psychology Today Online*, 07 July 2011, www.psychologytoday.com/blog/canine-corner/201107/does-my-dog-recognize-himself-in-mirror.

Descartes, Rene. "From the Letters of 1646 and 1649." *The Animals Reader: The Essential Classic and Contemporary Writings*, edited by Linda Kalof and Amy J. Fitzgerald. Berg Publishers, 2007. pp. 59–62.

de Waal, Frans. *The Bonobo and the Atheist: In Search of Humanism Among Primates*. W.W. Norton and Company, 2013.

"From Dawn Till Dusk." *Big Cat Diary*. Season 3, Episode 8, *BBC Two*, original air date 18 Feb 2001.

Gecas, Viktor, and Peter J. Burke. "Self and Identity." *Sociological Perspectives on Social Psychology*, edited Karen S. Cook, et al., Allyn and Bacon. 1997. pp. 41–67.

"The Godmother." *Meerkat Manor*, Season 2, Episode 12, *Animal Planet*, original air date 10 Nov 2006.

Haraway, Donna J. *When Species Meet*. University of Minnesota Press, 2008.

Hawkins, Caroline, creator. *Meerkat Manor*, Oxford Scientific Films, 2005.

Hellier, Robin, creator. *Big Cat Diary*, BBC One, 1996.

"History of Meerkat Manor." *Meerkat Manor Official Website*. www.meerkatmanor.co.uk/how-it-all-started.htm. Accessed 01 Feb 2014.

Holstein, James A., and Jaber F. Gubrium. *The Self We Live By: Narrative Identity in a Postmodern World*. Oxford University Press, 2000.

Hoppin, Ashley, creator. *Savage Kingdom*. National Geographic Channels, 2014.

"The Hunt Begins." *Big Cat Diary*, Season 1, Episode 1. BBC One, original air date, 11 Sep 1996.

Irvine, Leslie. *If You Tame Me: Understanding Our Connection with Animals*. Temple University Press, 2004.

_____. *My Dog Always Eats First: Homeless People and Their Animals*. Lynne Reinner Publications, 2015.

Kowalski, Gary. *The Souls of Animals*. Stillpoint Publishing, 1991.

Linzey, Andrew. "Animal Rights as Religious Vision." *Social Creatures: A Human and Animal Studies Reader*, edited by Clifton P. Flynn. New York: Lantern Books, 2008. pp. 107–116.

Maglio, Tony. "Animal Planet Orders 'Big Cat Diary' Follow-Up Series 'Big Cat Legacy.'" *The Wrap*. www.thewrap.com/big-cat-diary-legacy-animal-planet-marsh-pride/. Accessed 30 Sept 2018.

"Meerkat Manor." *Oxford Scientific Films*. www.oxfordscientificfilms.tv/portfolio-item/meerkat-manor/. Accessed 02 Oct 2018.

"Meerkat Manor—Awards." IMDb. www.imdb.com/title/tt0765725/awards?ref_=tt_awd. Accessed 02 Oct 2018.

"Meerkat Manor—Backstage." *Friends of the Kalahari Meerkat Project*. friends.kalahari-meerkats.com/index.php?id=mm_background. Accessed 20 Mar 2014 and 27 Mar 2018.

Meerkat Manor: The Official Website from the Makers of Meerkat Manor. www.meerkatmanor.co.uk, accessed 08 June 2018.

"Meeting the Big Cats." *Big Cat Diary*, Season 2, Episode 1, *BBC Two*, original air date 11 Oct 1998.

Nagasawa, Miho, et al. "Attachment Between Humans and Dogs." *Japanese Psychological Research*, vol. 51, no. 3, 2009. pp. 209–221.

Rachels, James. *Created from Animals: The Moral Implications of Darwinism*. Oxford University Press, 1990.

Richards, Morgan. "The Wildlife Docusoap: A New Ethical Practice for Wildlife Documentary?" *Television and News Media*, vol. 14, no. 4, 2014. pp. 321–335.

Scholey, Keith, and Robin Heiller. *Big Cat Diary*. BBC Natural History Unit, 1996.

Shapiro, Kenneth J. "Understanding Dogs through Kinesthetic Empathy, Social Construction, and History." *Social Creatures: A Human and Animal Studies Reader,* edited by Clifton P. Flynn, Lantern Books, 1996. pp. 31–48.

"Stealing from Baboons." *Big Cat Diary,* Season 2, Episode 9, *BBC Two,* original air date 06 Dec 1998.

"They Are Cheetahs." *Big Cat Diary,* Season 4, Episode 5, *BBC Two,* original air date 24 Nov 2002.

Fargo

Morality in the "Animal" Kingdom

LYNNETTE PORTER

"We used to be gorillas. All we had was what we could take.... If you don't stand up [to anyone who bullies or oppresses you] and show them you're still an ape, deep down where it counts, you're just going to get washed away" in the "red tide" of modern life ("The Crocodile's Dilemma"). This philosophy of Lorne Malvo (Billy Bob Thornton), the first "animal" protagonist in the FX television series *Fargo* (2014–present), represents the mindset of human "animals" who prey on other characters and possibly summarizes the point of the entire series. The first three seasons' episodes blur the line between what is human (e.g., moral and society building) and what the series defines as "animal" (e.g., disruptive, brutal, and immoral).

Based loosely on Joel and Ethan Coen's Oscar-winning film *Fargo* (1996), the Emmy-nominated or -winning anthology television series focuses each season on strange, tragic, and unusually violent deaths occurring in a frozen community in Minnesota, although characters in Fargo, North Dakota, are featured at some point in the story. At least one character connects one season to the next [e.g., Season 1's fatherly Lou Solverson (Keith Carradine), an eighteen-year state trooper who retires after being shot during a traffic stop, is seen as the young officer (played by Patrick Wilson) featured in Season 2]; however, the crimes take place in different time frames. During the first story, drifter hit man Lorne Malvo corrupts average insurance agent Lester Nygaard (Martin Freeman) in Bemidji, Minnesota, in 2006. The next season's episodes take place in Luverne, Minnesota, as well as in Fargo, in 1979, when the Gerhardt family's criminal activities invite a turf war that spills over onto the lives of innocent citizens. Season 3, set in St. Cloud, Minnesota, in 2010, is the most political to date, as mastermind businessman V.M. Varga (David Thewlis) infiltrates and consumes the lives of Stussy brothers Emmit and Ray (both played by Ewan McGregor).

Despite the plots ping-ponging across decades, the one constant is the presence of human "animals" that seem to be a hybrid between humans and nonhuman animals. These characters may be highly intelligent and look human, but they also display characteristics that viewers and the moral center of the series—law enforcement officers—consider animal-like, either because of a misinformed concept about the typical nature of animals or the pop culture influence of children's stories like *Little Red Riding Hood* and *Peter and the Wolf*. In *Fargo*, for example, animals are perceived as vicious; as in

53

Malvo's gorilla story, animals look out for themselves and can brutally destroy whatever gets in their way—an extreme generalization across species and situations that often portrays animals as little more than immoral killing machines. The series illustrates how the hybrid "animals" who blur the line between what we think of as being human (e.g., moral) or being animal (e.g., immoral—or lacking the capacity to determine morality) are increasingly nefarious in finding ways to influence and destroy formerly innocent humans as they struggle to move up the economic food chain.

The "animals" who influence or prey upon others often masquerade as friendly travelers just passing through town, owners of Mom and Pop companies, the neighbors next door, or business partners. Not only do they display crude or vicious "animal" instincts or behaviors, but they either delight in helping civilized people shed their humanity or simply do not care what happens to others who interact with them. In *Fargo*, "animals" primarily envision life as an economic food chain that they must top and are perceived by other characters (and likely the audience) as not only immoral but downright evil because they will do anything in order to help themselves.

Throughout the first three seasons, the characters who give in to their (popularly perceived) animal instincts and break the law, often in horrendous ways, are equated with a lack of morality. However, *Fargo* paradoxically shows inhumane, immoral "animals" as succeeding economically despite their lack of human decency; the television trope of Good triumphing over Evil is not always a given as the series progresses. Although "animal" characters evade the law for their crimes and financially benefit for illegal or immoral activities for a time during Seasons 1 and 2, by the end of the season they get their "reckoning"—such as a violent death—which restores viewers' faith in law and order and the morality needed to avoid social chaos. Yet, Season 3 implies that, because of an imbalanced socioeconomic and political environment, "animals" are far more likely to become and remain wealthy, no matter how evil their crimes or how widespread their destruction. The correlation between illegal, immoral, or simply socially inappropriate "animal behavior" (at least as defined in *Fargo*) and legal or moral justice is portrayed as becoming increasingly tenuous.

Through characters' dialogue and, especially, the camera's focus on animal-themed images, audiences are reminded of the slippery moral slope requiring characters to decide how far they will shift from human toward "animal" behavior. Series creator, executive producer, and frequent script writer Noah Hawley loads episodes with animal symbolism to compare humans and animals as one way of underscoring hybrid "animals'" socially aberrant behavior and mindset. Episode titles, such as "The Crocodile's Dilemma," "The Rooster Prince," "Buridan's Ass," "A Fox, a Rabbit, and a Cabbage," and "Rhinoceros," remind viewers of the "animal" connection, and even a few "animal" character names (Kitty Nygaard, Bear Gerhardt, and Running Bear) are interspersed across seasons. Additionally, the way humans are treated, while alive or dead, becomes another comparison with animals. A human body in a meat grinder or a limb caught in a bear trap or impaled with a hunter's arrow also dehumanizes characters, turning them into mere "meat."

During an early interview, Hawley admitted, "[w]e have a lot of animal imagery throughout the [first] season" (VanDerWerff), a trend that continues in subsequent seasons. The visuals—including close-ups of animals, stuffed toys, animal-like headpieces or clothing, or cultural icons like Paul Bunyan and Babe, the Blue Ox—especially help viewers identify "animals," as well as humans having a moral crisis, possibly on their way to turning into an "animal" throughout the series' first three seasons.

The Prevalence of "Animals" Identified as Wolves

In *Fargo*, real animals—a term loosely referring not only to mammals but birds, reptiles, amphibians, fish, and insects—usually suffer in a comparison with humans. Instead of focusing on animals' positive, nurturing traits, *Fargo* emphasizes violence and barbarity. Humans are frequently compared with wolves, and, in Seasons 1 and 3, the protagonist "animal" is overtly symbolized by a wolf. Although wolves in the wild work together to protect and nurture their young, groom each other, socialize, and play (Feddersen-Petersen), for example, *Fargo* characters portrayed as "wolves" are different in important ways. Often they are lone wolves looking out only for themselves (such as Malvo or Varga) and are thus more antisocial than social. More significantly, they viciously and indiscriminately kill others of their kind.

Instead of realistically displaying animal traits, wolves as symbolized in *Fargo* may often remind viewers of childhood stories like *Little Red Riding Hood*, in which the hungry wolf dresses in human clothing to fool Little Red Riding Hood and is only discovered when the child notices the wolf's inhumanly large eyes and sharp teeth. Similarly, throughout Season 1, Malvo wears different disguises and takes new names in order to blend in with the innocents he wants to deceive. This "wolf in sheep's clothing" most notably dresses and acts like a dentist in order to win the confidence of the people he befriends—all so that he can learn the location of the man under witness protection he has been hired to kill ("A Fox, a Rabbit, and a Cabbage"). Although he appears human, Malvo acts more like a *Little Red Riding Hood*–style wolf: he "fakes" normal human behavior (e.g., making friends, getting engaged, working as a dentist) to lure prey into confiding in him; he disguises himself with a new hairstyle, wardrobe, name, and even catchphrase ("Aces!") so that he can achieve his purpose (i.e., kill); and he thinks of himself as different from—and superior to—the people around him. Like the wolf in *Little Red Riding Hood*, Malvo cannot completely hide his "animal" nature, which surfaces in violent ways.

Although wolf symbolism is largely missing from Season 2, one television critic summarized the first two seasons' "animal" characters with specific wolf imagery that resonates with *Little Red Riding Hood*: "The consistent theme through … *Fargo* is the wolf at the door, but in Season 2, there's the wolf (the encroaching violence) and then there's the wolf in sheep's clothing. The latter is represented by the women who, in a world of violence and chaos, might just be the true threat" (George). Season 2's primary "animals" are the Gerhardt crime family, epitomized by matriarch Floyd (Jean Smart), who ably takes over as head of the family business when her husband is incapacitated by a stroke. Floyd can be vicious and defines her fierceness in terms of motherhood—she might be considered an alpha wolf backed in a corner to defend her rowdy pups against outside dangers. During her reign as head of the crime family, Floyd feels attacked on two fronts: Her missing (and later found dead) son massacred everyone in a diner, which invites the unwelcome attention of law enforcement; even more threatening is an out-of-state crime syndicate attempting to take over her family's business. Like Malvo, she can disguise her wolf-like attributes when she pretends to be a sheep. In public, Floyd may seem like any grieving wife who faces the difficulties of her husband's incapacitation or mother who has just lost a son, but, in private, she efficiently issues deadly orders that ensnare local citizens and result in mass carnage.

In Season 3, animal imagery is prominent in several episodes, none more so than in "The Narrow Escape Problem," which revolves around Sergei Prokofiev's *Peter and the*

Wolf. Not only does the musical theme become a key part of the episode's soundtrack, but the familiar music is backed up by the story's voiceover narrator, Billy Bob Thornton (Season 1's Malvo). Having "the wolf of Season 1" (O'Keeffe) explain which *Fargo* character is represented by each *Peter and the Wolf* character further highlights the significance of Season 3's wolf, Varga. In *Fargo*'s version of *Peter and the Wolf*, Emmit Stussy is the bird; his brother Ray, the duck; and Ray's girlfriend Nikki Swango (Mary Elizabeth Winstead), the cat who gets away.

Just as the bird and duck in the original story bicker about who can swim or fly and thus is better, so do brothers Emmit and Ray bicker and compare themselves to each other. Neither seems aware that they are stalked by cat Nikki. Whereas Nikki's stalking of Emmit involves criminal activities designed to deprive him of wealth—in particular, a rare stamp that Ray believes his brother cheated him out of—she more benignly ensnares Ray with her sensuality and sexual prowess. Ray follows parolee Nikki's lead in a series of schemes designed for Ray to get what he believes is owed him. Alas, the duck/Ray is devoured by the wolf, albeit indirectly. Having suffered wolf Varga's takeover of his lucrative parking lot business, Emmit reconsiders his feud with his brother and decides to make amends by bringing him the valuable framed stamp. However, the brothers argue and, in a struggle over the stamp, the frame breaks, and a glass shard fatally stabs Ray ("The Lord of No Mercy"). The wolf's influence casts a shadow over the murder scene when Emmit, afraid to be seen leaving his dead brother's home, enlists Varga to clean up the mess. Emmit renounces a little more of his humanity and morality when he fears to go to the authorities and instead seeks the assistance of the "animal" who has systematically gone about destroying his life but can clean up the bloody mess and dispose of the body.

A more direct connection can be made between Nikki and the cat, because, until the final episode, she seems to have nine lives. When wolf Varga tries to capture Nikki, in *Peter and the Wolf* terms she quickly "climbs a tree" (i.e., escapes his henchmen). Although she suffers near-death experiences, such as a cruel beating, a vehicular accident, and an arrow through the leg, she so often survives being hunted by Varga's men that she seems unreasonably lucky. Nikki is like a feral cat who is trying to become domesticated; she understands life on the streets but wants to establish a domestic life with Ray, one in which the couple can compete in professional bridge tournaments. She is far from being a wild, ruthless animal, although she turns vigilante in her attempt to destroy Varga after Ray's death. Nikki frequently wears a jacket made from squares of faux fur; she is not as "animal" as Varga or his henchmen, who often don animal masks. The lead henchman frequently wears a headpiece made from a snarling wolf's head—a further connection to being wolf Varga's number one employee—and is unapologetically brutal in beating or hunting Nikki, who is a pussycat compared to Varga's men. A final allusion to cats further cements Nikki's connection to her *Peter and the Wolf* character. After Ray's death and yet another of Nikki's escapes from Varga's men, she stumbles into a bowling alley's bar. There she meets a godlike character who tells her that "Ray is the cat," suggesting Ray's reincarnation, and lets her hold the kitten. Nikki melts as she gingerly pets it and, after looking in its eyes, is convinced that it is indeed Ray. Perhaps, in a quirky series referencing everything from alien encounters to children's stories, it is possible that Nikki's feline-like influence on and association with Ray would render him a kitten in the afterlife. Given Ray's moral slide from parole officer to criminal before his death, another reading of "Ray is the cat" can suggest that his essence is no longer human, but animal, even if the once-timid Ray is cuddly and vulnerable in this form.

Peter and the Wolf is not a perfect mirroring of the season's characters or ongoing plot points, but it underscores the importance of the human character, Peter, in contrast to the season's many "animals." Peter's distinctive musical theme begins when police officer Gloria Burgle (Carrie Coon) is first shown in the episode. She, like Peter, is not afraid of wolves. In the children's story, Peter is instrumental in capturing the wolf and having him placed behind bars in a zoo ("The Story of Peter and the Wolf"). Burgle likely sees herself as Peter—the hero who can vanquish wolf Varga and put him behind prison bars. This episode seems to foreshadow the "Good wins, and Evil is thwarted" finales of the previous two seasons and sets up audience expectations that, by the end of Season 3, Peter/Burgle will incarcerate wolf/Varga. However, in *Fargo*, unlike in *Peter and the Wolf*, the human character who captures the wolf may not be victorious by the end of the story.

Varga's wolf-like influence is so pervasive throughout the season that the *Fargo: Season 3* DVD set's character introduction emphasizes only his wolfish difference from other characters. In the first introductory clip, Varga is shown "wolfing" a huge breakfast. The camera zooms in as he voraciously stuffs his mouth with food from a variety of plates before him. After Varga cleans his mouth following a bulimic episode, the camera's extreme close-ups highlight his blackened, broken teeth as the "animal" opens his mouth widely in front of a mirror. In addition to being *Peter and the Wolf*'s villainous animal, Varga reminds viewers of the scene when Little Red Riding Hood exclaims, "what a terrible big mouth you have" (Grimm Brothers). In many popularized versions of the story, Little Red Riding Hood says, "My, what big teeth you have!" ("Red Riding Hood")—an image highlighted by the camera's lingering focus on Varga's open mouth and, because of the close up, very big teeth. Varga of the voracious appetite, for wealth as well as food, has big metaphoric teeth that he sinks into his hapless victims.

Marking Territory: Animal Behavior Mimicked by "Animals"

Whereas a fictionalized children's version of wolves, in particular, might offer entertaining or cute pop culture comparisons to animals, *Fargo*'s "animal" protagonists often mimic real animals' behavior to display dominance. They more explicitly blur the line between human and animal behavior by acting as animals really do. Marking one's territory with waste (e.g., urine, feces) illustrates "animal" characters' base nature and their unabashed, unapologetic claim to letting other predators know they are staking a claim on a territory.

Varga marks territory most often. Shortly after he takes over the company formerly run by now-figurehead-only partners Emmit Stussy and Sy Feltz (Michael Stuhlbarg), he urinates in Sy's prized World's Best Dad coffee mug. To add to the humiliation, Varga's men force Sy to drink their boss's urine in a primal display of Varga's power over former executives ("The House of Special Purpose").

Furthermore, bulimic Varga not only purges a gluttonous breakfast during a lengthy scene early in "The Narrow Escape Problem" but, after inviting himself to dinner at Emmit Stussy's home, interrupts discussing the expansion of his and Emmit's business to vomit into the downstairs bathroom's toilet. As the camera closes in on the closed bathroom door, Varga's loud retching consumes the soundtrack as he yet again marks his territory (the Stussy home he has invaded as thoroughly as the business). Although

Varga is most often compared with a wolf, actor David Thewlis envisions his character as a cold-blooded reptile, and his bulimia could be compared to "the regurgitation of snakes." Thinking of the characters he embodies as "animalistic" is familiar to Thewlis, "going back to my bloody drama-school days, in terms of equating [characters] with creatures. And it's very much there as a theme of all the seasons of *Fargo* as well: the predator and the prey" (Cohen). To assert his dominance especially over his now-figurehead business partners, Varga chooses crude, "animalistic" ways to foul their possessions and territory.

Both urinating in Sy's mug and loudly purging his dinner at Emmit's home go beyond a lack of manners. These scenes show that, even in small ways, Varga grossly flaunts societal conventions and leaves his scent to display dominance. He is unashamed to mark his territory and appease his appetite for power. That the brief DVD character summary includes "animal" scenes of vomiting and urination from among the hundreds of Varga scenes available in Season 3 illustrates to the series' fans who buy DVD sets that Varga is more "animal" than human—even without considering his directives that lead to others' deaths.

Although Season 3 episodes explore in greater detail than in previous seasons the power of wealth and the greedy "animals" who prey on less technically savvy businessmen, characters' baser animal traits still are emphasized as an inherent part of their personality. Although wealthy humans typically demonstrate cultured manners and may exude poshness, wealthy "animals" like Varga prefer to "disappear," as he says, so that the hordes who may one day revolt against the rich cannot identify him. Varga not only consciously dissociates himself from cultural etiquette and social markers of affluence, as well as isolating himself from the wealthy, but expresses his dominance through crude "animal" behavior.

He is not the only character in Season 3 to enjoy marking territory. When Ray Stussy and Nikki decide to steal the valuable stamp, Nikki stealthfully enters Emmit's home office, where the stamp at one time had been framed on a wall. Unable to find where the stamp has been moved, a frustrated, angry Nikki marks the room with a used tampon. She claims the heart of Emmit's home and empire as her own territory (on behalf of Ray) and indicates her intention of eventually taking the stamp from Emmit ("The Principle of Restricted Choice"). When Varga later visits Emmit at home, he comments on the lingering "unflushed toilet" odor, a potent reference to Nikki's scent marker alerting others to her territorial claim (as well as disgusting humans who come in the office).

During Season 1, when territorial marking is first introduced, Malvo uses this behavior both to warn away a competitor and to have some fun by dehumanizing other characters. He delightedly encourages people to indulge their baser instincts. When Malvo observes a motel clerk berate her employee by comparing his intelligence to that of a clam, the "animal" sees a humorous opportunity to help the young man get back at his employer in an animalistic way. He explains how urinating in a car's gas tank can mess up the vehicle and points out that being labeled clam-like is offensive. A few minutes later, Malvo watches the young man follow his "advice" by urinating in the gas tank of his employer's car. However, Malvo is not finished causing mayhem. He calls the motel clerk to let her know what is going on ("The Crocodile's Dilemma"). The act of "lowering" a young man of questionable intelligence to the status of an animal belligerently marking his territory is yet another success story in Malvo's quest to dehumanize civilized people.

Of course, Malvo also likes to disgust a competitor by refusing to abide by social norms. When a new client's security guard visits Malvo in his hotel room to tell him that his services to find and dispose of a blackmailer are unnecessary, the "animal" assesses his rival and chooses a crude way of showing how unconcerned he is with this potential threat to his job. During the conversation, Malvo leaves the bathroom door open, casually drops his trousers, and sits on the toilet, presumably to defecate ("The Rooster Prince"). The act reviles the security guard, but Malvo has marked his territory in a very basic way and has no qualms about ignoring propriety to make his point that he is indifferent to a rival.

Scent marking territory is one way that "animals" perform an animal behavior and blur the line between animals and humans. However, this act is benign when compared with the vicious behaviors assumed by characters and viewers to be animalistic.

Destroying Threats by Being Worse Than Animals

As Lou Solverson explains near the end of Season 1, some immoral people are lower than animals. He recalls a case "back in '79" that was pure "madness," a gruesome crime scene in which the bodies were stacked "one after another. If you stacked them high, they could've climbed to the second floor. I saw something that year that I've never seen before or since. I'd call it animal, except animals only kill for food" ("A Fox, a Rabbit, and a Cabbage"). [The carnage is later shown as it happens in Season 2's showdown when the Gerhardt family and many of their rivals are massacred in a Sioux Falls, South Dakota, parking lot ("The Castle").]

"Animals" in *Fargo* display barbarity that is worse than anything animals (who, by most definitions, have no sense of morality, although that could be argued) might do. "Animals" cross lines separating them both from normal (presumably moral) humans and animals when they believe they need to destroy perceived threats not only to their life but to their freedom, success, or happiness. They have no morality; they act in response to a perceived threat and do not care about consequences to others. They often choose a violent response instead of retreating or avoiding a potentially deadly situation.

In a 2014 interview, Billy Bob Thornton described his predatory character Malvo as a variety of nonhuman creatures. Malvo is "like an alligator" because he is focused on a goal and has a specific job to do. More generally, Thornton explained that Malvo literally lives like an animal; he is "part of the animal kingdom" and, just like an animal, can "lure prey." He lives in the moment and does not consider the morality of killing. "To say he's right or wrong, it would be like saying a polar bear's wrong" (Gennis).

Hawley, in contrast, believes Malvo has more motivation than Thornton gives him credit for; he "just has this fascination with taking a civilized person and turning them [*sic*] into an animal" (VanDerWerff). Whereas Thornton makes a case that Malvo is merely an "animal," Hawley's comment suggests that, considering the way he wrote the character, Malvo truly blurs the line popularly defining what is considered human and animal. The hit man not only kills to thrive economically or survive as a free man, but he enjoys manipulating others into behaving like "animals." His cognitive abilities mark him as human, but his lack of morality more closely (and far more negatively) associates him with animal stereotypes.

Although other civilized characters across the series' first three seasons find themselves under the increasingly pervasive influence of "animals," Lester Nygaard's story is emphasized as a cautionary tale at the heart of Season 1. It warns viewers that losing one's footing on that slippery moral slope can lead to one's descent into "animal" (or, according to Lou Solverson, worse than animal) behavior and, as fitting in the morality tale of Season 1, death. In the first episode, Nygaard, his nose bloodied by an encounter with bully Sam Hess (Kevin O'Grady), who tormented Lester throughout and after high school, meets Malvo in the emergency room. When a wide-eyed, sincere Malvo asks Nygaard if he should take care of (i.e., kill) the bully, Lester wrinkles his forehead and seeks clarification. However, the ER nurse suddenly calls him for treatment, and, in trying to participate in two conversations at once, Nygaard inadvertently answers "yes" to Malvo's question. The bully ends up dead, and a horrified Nygaard confronts Malvo. The soft-spoken insurance agent becomes defensive when Malvo insists that Nygaard told him to kill Hess. However, he listens as Malvo explains that Nygaard is "more of a man today than you were yesterday" because of Hess's murder. Although Nygaard does not picture himself as the type of man who would order another's death, he nonetheless becomes a murderer soon after his discussion with this "animal" in human guise. Frustrated by his wife's continuing verbal abuse and enraged by her latest criticism as he tries yet again to fix their battered washing machine, Nygaard bludgeons his wife to death. However, he is still "civilized" enough to recognize that this is bad behavior and that the police likely will find out. In desperation, Nygaard phones Malvo to ask for help. With an undercurrent of glee, Malvo asks Nygaard if he has been a "bad boy." Malvo has succeeded in turning the small-town milquetoast into a murderer who just might get away with his crime.

The visual foreshadowing of Nygaard murdering his wife subtly illustrates the prevalence of animal symbolism. Earlier in the day Nygaard listens to Malvo explain one's inner gorilla and need to stand up for oneself. When Nygaard's wife walks through the living room on her way to check Lester's progress in fixing the washing machine, she passes an interesting prop. A stuffed gorilla sits in a chair next to the sofa. The toy's unexplained presence in the home of a childless couple seems to be just another quirk of *Fargo*. After all, the series also inexplicably introduces UFOs in later episodes. However, the gorilla plushy becomes a symbol of Lester's dormant "inner gorilla" and foreshadows the shift from a cuddly, peaceful, civilized man to an awakened gorilla about to violently destroy a threat to his well-being. Such visual elements not only serve as ironically playful symbols to entertain detail-oriented viewers but also emphasize the theme of humans embracing their inner animal instincts.

Months later, when Nygaard attends a Las Vegas sales convention where he celebrates his newfound success resulting from a shift to "animal" behavior, he coincidentally sees Malvo, who is using a different name and disguising himself with a new look as part of a long con. After badgering his former "mentor" and literally backing him into a corner in a crowded elevator, Nygaard is nonetheless stunned when Malvo pulls out a gun and murders his three marks, who might have begun to question what they know about him in light of Nygaard's comments. Of course, Malvo blames Nygaard for "forcing" him to commit murder. Whereas Nygaard once thought of himself as a successful "animal" predator moving up the economic food chain, he quickly becomes the enraged Malvo's prey.

Just as a toy gorilla foreshadows the blurring between Nygaard's human and animal natures moments before the on-screen death of his first wife, a huge Paul Bunyan and Babe, the Blue Ox, statue indicates far more than local color or a prominent landmark; it foreshadows another moral dilemma for Lester right before the likely death of his second wife. As he parks in the shadows near his office, where he has stashed passports and plane tickets, the statue comes into focus in back of the car. It begs the question whether Nygaard will be a man and thus willing to sacrifice himself to possibly keep his wife safe—or, if he chooses to drive away, keeping his spouse away from Malvo for at least a little longer. He could turn himself into the police officer who thinks he witnessed the Las Vegas murders and make sure his wife is protected. In short, Lester Nygaard could be "Paul Bunyan"—a man, with the morality ascribed to humans in *Fargo*. On the other hand, Nygaard could cement his change to an "animal" by acting immorally—becoming the "Ox" option in the visual metaphor—and stubbornly protecting himself from a dangerous situation while sending his wife to what could be her death.

The scene is set to emphasize the way Nygaard insincerely portrays concern for his wife, simply to ensure that she will not only don his parka but pull up the hood to conceal her face, all, according to Lester, to keep her warm. His faked husbandly concern is a poor imitation of his wife's real concern when Lester explains that he has pulled his back and asks her to retrieve the tickets while he remains in the car. Like Malvo, Nygaard chooses to show human concern while predatorily using others' real human emotions against them so that they willingly do what he says. The audience watches from Nygaard's viewpoint as Malvo shoots and kills the person in the orange parka ("A Fox, a Rabbit, and a Cabbage"). Nygaard once again has chosen to look human but act "animalistically." Through the visual metaphor of Paul Bunyan and the Ox, *Fargo* illustrates how Nygaard has blurred the line between human and animal and become a true series "animal."

After his wife is murdered, Nygaard knows that Malvo will not stop hunting him like an animal until he, too, is dead. He sets an old bear trap that he finds in the basement and hides in his bedroom. The trap indeed breaks Malvo's leg after the predator breaks into the house, and the severe injury allows Nygaard to escape. Wolf imagery again comes into play. Before the wounded Malvo is gunned down by former police officer/now rural mail carrier Gus Grimly (Colin Hanks), he glimpses a wolf outside the window ("Morton's Fork"), one of Hawley's favorite moments from the first season. Malvo then realizes that he is "not the predator anymore. He's the prey now" (VanDerWerff). Nygaard suffers a similar fate. By the end of Season 1, both Malvo and Nygaard have lived as "animals" but ultimately succumbed to their roles as prey. Malvo is shot to death by Grimly, and Nygaard falls through a lake's thin ice as he attempts to allude pursuing law enforcement officers.

Throughout Season 1, Malvo's aim is to subvert law-abiding citizens, not only to commit mischief or crimes but to abandon their concept of morality. Grimly, for example, would not normally take a life, especially in a brutal manner, even to protect his community. He was a reluctant police officer who would rather have what he perceives as a safer job as a postman; however, because he has become a postman with a rural route, he nonetheless faces a moral dilemma when he encounters Malvo far from town and has the opportunity to undo an earlier run-in with the "animal." When he was a police officer, Grimly pulled over Malvo for a traffic violation. The "animal" calmly rolled down his window and explained that people sometimes know when it is in their best interest to walk away from a situation. He implied that, if Grimly continued to detain him, something very bad would happen. Cowed, Grimly let Malvo go, only later learning of his many crimes ("The Crocodile's Dilemma"). However, the level of violence Malvo instigates leads Grimly to believe that Evil, as represented by Malvo, must be destroyed—not arrested and tried in a court of law. By the end of the series, Grimly becomes an inadvertent vigilante who stumbles across Malvo's hiding place. When he finally can capture the badly wounded Malvo, Grimly does not treat the criminal as a human and give him a chance to go to jail but simply puts him down like a rabid animal ("Morton's Fork"). Although Malvo dies, he has accomplished his mission—turning another good, civilized person into a morally ambiguous one.

Society "wins" because a murdering con man "animal" is no longer around to destroy others. However, the manner of Malvo's death provides him with a type of victory, as evidenced by the "chilling smile on Malvo's bullet-pocked face," which "drain[s] the act of any sense of chest-thumping vindication" (Adams). Although the most important "animal" characters die by the end of the season, the moral victory of Good besting Evil is largely absent.

The Rise of "Animals" and the Fall of Morality

For a series that poses sometimes difficult questions about what it means to be human or "animal," and thus moral or immoral, *Fargo* provides few religious images or scenes. Although Gloria Burgle and her son exchange Christmas presents, the celebration is secular. Law enforcement officers do not reference the Bible or participate in religious activities. Instead, the characters who refer to the Bible, such as Malvo's passing reference when he says he has not had pie that good "since the Garden of Eden" ("A Fox, a Rabbit, and a Cabbage"), underscore the fact that the struggle between Good/Moral and Evil/Immoral—or, as *Fargo* depicts it, Human/"Animal"—goes back to the dawn of humankind. When religion is specifically mentioned, it seems to be a traditional balm that the wicked appreciate rather than being representative of the faith of the just (e.g., law enforcement). For example, during Season 2, "animal" Bear Gerhardt tries to comfort his mother about the family's many losses by telling her that the family will be reunited "on high." Bear has been taught at some point along the way that loved ones always go to heaven. Because the Gerhardts have directly killed or indirectly had others killed through their machinations, his sense of morality seems skewed (Hill).

Morality in *Fargo* may have surprisingly little religious basis beyond what might be expected from the series' Midwestern setting. Without a religious imperative, what determines whether one is human or not is therefore based on a personal sense of what is right or wrong that goes beyond the law. Such characters as Lou or Molly Solverson or Gloria Burgle—all law enforcement officers—do not rely on a Christian God's blessing or a heavenly reward for doing what is just. The threat to their morality, as illustrated by the increasing power of "animals," suggests a threat to the heart of a human society. The line between human and "animal" may be blurred by many pivotal characters each season, but the implication of who will win in the ongoing battle between Good/Human and Evil/"Animal" has changed between Seasons 2 and 3.

Throughout the first three seasons, the dramatic focus shifts across time from a lone wolf assassin in 2006 to a violent local crime syndicate in 1979 to a slippery businessman in 2010. Despite the shifts in setting, the series suggests that human "animals" are more likely to survive and thrive than their law-abiding, humane counterparts as society devolves into a morally bankrupt culture. At the beginning of Season 1, most viewers and *Fargo* characters would agree that morality holds society together and establishes people as "better" than true animals. However, by Season 3, the certainty that immoral law breakers will get their comeuppance in the legal system—or even through ruthless vigilante justice—is greatly diminished. The most humane humans, often represented by the police officers striving to bring murderers or organized crime bosses to justice, begin to find themselves unable to wring a moral victory from their work. Who ultimately will win this battle between Good and Evil, Human or "Animal," Morality or Immorality is debated throughout three seasons' episodes, with the answer that Good/Human/Morality will triumph becoming increasingly uncertain.

In an article attempting to analyze whether morality is biologically or culturally determined, biologist Francisco J. Ayala informally defined *morality* as one's beliefs of what is right or wrong, good or evil, and one's behavior based on those beliefs. More specifically, individual societies support the notion that the "particular norms by which moral actions are judged vary to some extent from individual to individual and from culture to culture (although some norms, such as not to kill, not to steal, and to honor one's parents, are widespread and perhaps universal), but value judgments concerning human behavior are passed in all cultures" (Ayala). Whereas most *Fargo* viewers may agree with this statement, the series' "animals" do not buy into these "universal" beliefs. Murder is prevalent in all three seasons, either commissioned by the lead "animal" or committed by him or her. Greed is a common motive that often leads characters down that slippery slope toward murder or becomes an acceptable part of a criminal lifestyle. Even common frustration with spouses, children, or employers can lead to a momentary burst of anger that has devastating personal and legal consequences. To the "animals" of *Fargo*, human life (other than one's own) is not special; survival of the fittest often means killing a potential threat before it can materialize into something real; and, in particular, "real men" (a phrase used frequently, especially in Season 1) are not afraid to let their primal, animal instincts ensure their superiority to others fighting for a higher place on the economic food chain. "Animals" have no remorse about actions that viewers likely see as immoral.

A high level of intelligence without morality, as previously defined, is paramount to the success of *Fargo*'s "animal" characters. Season 1's Malvo is the most obvious "animal" within the first three seasons, and the symbolism surrounding him makes him seem far less human than later seasons' predators or the people he influences who begin a moral slide away from compassionate humanity. Floyd Gerhardt must, throughout Season 3, manage her familial roles as wife, mother, and grandmother, but she also must shrewdly plan dealings with the police and business rivals. Season 3 is dominated by businessman Varga, who efficiently takes over the company and life of Minnesota's "parking lot king," Emmit Stussy, because of his ability to use technology and gather information. He manipulates others' perception of "truth" just as he physically manipulates the lives of Emmit and Sy. To be "animal" in *Fargo* requires a great deal of skill and intelligence, but cleverness and shrewdness usually are used to plot others' downfall and to secure advantages only for oneself.

The Human Element: Law Enforcement Officers and Their Moral Imperative

The concept that morality cannot be legislated is not absolute, as laws protecting citizens against discrimination in employment or housing, for example, illustrate. Nonetheless, an individual's moral compass cannot be so easily dictated or regulated by the existence of laws, as *Fargo* illustrates. Whereas Thornton has stated that Malvo does only what comes naturally to him, just as animals kill to stay alive, without a thought whether such an act is immoral, the comparison is not as clear cut as the actor or creator Hawley suggests. Lead villains plot carefully in order to succeed, and only spur-of-the-moment reactions or miscalculations get them killed (as Malvo and Floyd find out). Humans are distinguished from animals by the capacity for logical, rational thought and can fathom long-term cause-effect relationships. For the majority of episodes within their respective season, Malvo, Floyd Gerhardt, and Varga illustrate confident, intelligent planning and a deep understanding of human nature. Malvo, in particular, is coolly logical in explaining potential consequences, and Varga understands how to manipulate technology and the law to ensure he can escape entrapment. "Animals" excel in long-term planning and deception.

Although differences in cognitive ability may separate humans from animals, the level of morality separates *Fargo*'s moral humans from the immoral "animals" that blur the line between true animal behavior and human actions. Law enforcement officers consistently are portrayed as the defenders of society and the moral backbone of the series. In particular, Molly Solverson (Allison Tolman), as well as Gus Grimly (Season 1), Lou Solverson (Season 2), and Gloria Burgle (Season 3) represent humanity and morality, and they often must overcome increasingly difficult challenges to their employment, integrity, and survival. Yet, even these defenders of both the law and morality recognize the slippery slope of extenuating circumstances.

During Season 1, for example, Grimly explains gray areas of morality to his daughter during a conversation about confronting bullies. Whereas the girl is adamant that one should always stand up against a bully and thus protect others, Gus disagrees. He notes that he has two jobs—as an officer and as a father—but fatherhood is his priority. If standing up to a "bully" (or, worse, an "animal" like Malvo) might get him severely hurt or killed, he will not risk orphaning his daughter, even if the Evil person then can continue to hurt others. Grimly's morality, reflected in scenes when he first confronts Malvo during a traffic stop, as well as later gunning him down, is situational and pragmatically focused on protecting his family first. *Fargo* succeeds in showing that even the most moral characters may rely on situational ethics, rather than absolute moral imperatives, in order to allow what they determine is justice to prevail. However, their moral standards are far higher than those of most citizens and are oppositional to those of the immoral "animals."

Although lip service, at least, to the universal values assumed to be important to a moral, human society continues throughout three seasons, the third season's finale can make viewers question where society is heading. In the final scene, Varga (going by a different name five years after events from previous episodes) faces off against former police officer/current Homeland Security agent Burgle. Confident that this criminal would one day be captured and imprisoned for his many offenses, Burgle smugly interrogates Varga, who calmly assures her that he is only awaiting someone with greater authority than Gloria to release him. The season ambiguously ends with the camera slowly focusing on the interrogation room's door and the ticking clock—but viewers do not learn whether Varga is released or incarcerated ("Somebody to Love").

Even if the majority of viewers still ascribe to universal values represented by Good characters like Burgle, Evil or morally bankrupt characters like Varga are increasingly portrayed as protagonists on television (e.g., *Breaking Bad*, *The Americans*). By *Fargo*'s third season finale, Charles Darwin's "survival of the fittest," not the presence of morality, ultimately determines a character's fate. Although many episodes within the first two seasons emphasize Darwin's belief that "of all the differences between man and the lower animals[,] the moral sense or conscience is by far the most important," morality is a social construct that, as Ayala explains in his study, can change rapidly, even within a generation. When an action once deemed immoral or illegal becomes accepted by a majority of voters, laws change. Ayala cites behaviors as diverse as smoking cigarettes or marijuana and legalizing homosexuality or same-sex marriage as examples of moral evolution during the past century. Whereas most citizens may see these changes as positive, *Fargo* suggests that society may be becoming more accepting of "animal" behavior as the likeliest way to economic success.

The third season's morally ambiguous finale only states overtly what Malvo says in Season 1: "Your problem is that you spent your whole life thinking there are rules. There aren't" ("The Crocodile's Dilemma"). Thewlis's Varga would agree with that assessment; the actor described his character as having "no scruples.... He doesn't care. He is absolutely and irredeemably predatory" (Gilbey). Through the words and deeds of "animal" characters and the interviews of the actors who portray them, viewers might be tempted to feel overly cynical about the fate of humanity.

Nevertheless, Hawley insists that he is an optimist, no matter how frequently he lets his audience grapple with moral issues and consider the divisions created by economic imbalances. He has also written scenes in which Lou Solverson reminds his daughter Molly that, as a police officer, she cannot become too jaded by the crimes she has seen and must instead believe in the existence of something good. Gloria Burgle tells her young son that they must stick together in order to deal with everyday life. In a 2017 interview, the series creator explained that characters and viewers alike "can really be overwhelmed by how complicated the universe seems," but there is "a simple answer and that's, 'Treat people well and listen and respect' ... I like that at the end of the day, there's a very simple morality to a very complicated moral universe" (Fienberg).

Not all viewers may be satisfied with Hawley's conclusion about morality. What is certain is that *Fargo* illustrates uncertainty whether a moral (i.e., human) life can be a successful life. In its most enlightening episodes, *Fargo* provides a series of characters who are faced with moral dilemmas and opportunities to express their humanity or encourage their animal instincts. The struggle is what makes *Fargo* provocative entertainment that is relevant to viewers on their own moral journeys. Whether people are going to be more "animal" or more human is, according to Hawley, "something we have to decide every day" (Holloway). What interests Hawley is the escalation of the struggle that forces both *Fargo* characters and viewers to continually test their moral boundaries as they answer a central question: "You'll do this, but will you do that?" All the series' "animals" to date have insistently, immediately answered "yes."

Works Cited

Adams, Sam. "Why 'Fargo's Unsatisfying Ending Is One of the Series' Best Moments." *Indiewire*, 18 June 2014, www.indiewire.com/2014/06/why-fargos-unsatisfying-ending-is-one-of-the-series-best-moments-126386/. Accessed 2 Jan. 2018.

Ayala, Francisco J. "The Difference of Being Human: Morality." *Proceedings of the National Academy of Sciences of the United States of America*, 107 (Supplement 2) 9015–9022, May 2010. doi.org/10.1073/pnas.0914616107. Accessed 12 Feb. 2018.

"Buridan's Ass." *Fargo: Season 1,* written by Noah Hawley, directed by Colin Bucksey, 20th Century Fox, 2014.

"The Castle." *Fargo: Season 2,* written by Noah Hawley and Steve Blackman, directed by Adam Arkin, 20th Century Fox, 2015.

Cohen, Finn. "Actor David Thewlis on the 'Fargo' Season Finale, V.M. Varga, and Greed." *New York Times,* 21 June 2017, www.nytimes.com/2017/06/21/arts/television/actor-david-thewlis-on-the-fargo-season-finale-vm-varga-and-greed.html. Accessed 6 June 2018.

"The Crocodile's Dilemma." *Fargo: Season 1,* written by Noah Hawley, directed by Adam Bernstein, 20th Century Fox, 2014.

Darwin, Charles R. *The Descent of Man, and Selection in Relation to Sex. Appleton and Company,* 1871. Google Scholar.

Feddersen-Petersen, Dorit U. "Chapter 7: Social Behavior of Dogs and Related Canids." *The Behavioural Biology of Dogs* (ed. Per Jensen). 105–125. CABI, 2007.

Fienberg, Daniel. "'Fargo' Creator Goes Inside Season 3 Finale and Offers Hope for Franchise's Future." *The Hollywood Reporter,* 21 June 2017, www.hollywoodreporter.com/fien-print/fargo-season-3-finale-explained-1015844. Accessed 5 June 2018.

"A Fox, a Rabbit, and a Cabbage." *Fargo: Season 1,* written by Noah Hawley, directed by Matt Shakman, 20th Century Fox, 2014.

Gennis, Sadie. "*Fargo*: 10 Things Malvo Is Like, According to Billy Bob Thornton." *TV Guide.* 28 Apr. 2014, www.tvguide.com/news/fargo-lorne-malvo-billy-bob-thorton-1080995/. Accessed 2 Jan. 2018.

George, Kat. "'Fargo' Season 2 Set a Bold, New Standard for Female Heroes and Anti-Heroes." *Decider,* 17 Dec. 2015, decider.com/2015/12/17/the-women-of-fargo-season-2/. Accessed 2 Jan. 2018.

Gilbey, Ryan. "'My brain was on fire': David Thewlis on Naked, Fargo, and creeping out the Coens." *Guardian,* 29 May 2017, www.theguardian.com/tv-and-radio/2017/may/29/david-thewlis-fargo-coen-brothers-interview. Accessed 6 June 2018.

Grimm Brothers. "Little Red Riding Hood." Virginia Commonwealth University, germanstories.vcu.edu/grimm/redridinghood.html. Accessed 23 June 2018.

Hill, Libbie. "'Fargo' Recap: Massacre at Sioux Falls." *Los Angeles Times,* 8 Dec. 2015, www.latimes.com/entertainment/tv/showtracker/la-et-st-fargo-recap-20151208-story.html. Accessed 24 June 2018.

Holloway, Daniel. "'Fargo' Finale: Noah Hawley Talks Season 3." *Variety,* 21 June 2017, variety.com/2017/tv/news/fargo-finale-noah-hawley-1202475323/. Accessed 2 Jan. 2018.

"The Lord of No Mercy." *Fargo: Season 3,* written by Noah Hawley, directed by Dearbhla Walsh, 20th Century Fox, 2017.

"Morton's Fork." *Fargo: Season 1,* written by Noah Hawley, directed by Matt Shakman, 20th Century Fox, 2014.

"The Narrow Escape Problem." *Fargo: Season 3,* written by Monica Beletsky and Noah Hawley, directed by Michael Uppendahl, 20th Century Fox, 2017.

O'Keeffe, Jack. "Who's the Narrator on 'Fargo'? A Star Returns in a Very Important Cameo." *Bustle,* 10 May 2017, www.bustle.com/p/whos-the-narrator-on-fargo-a-star-returns-in-a-very-important-cameo-56424. Accessed 2 Jan. 2018.

"The Principle of Restricted Choice." *Fargo: Season 3,* written by Noah Hawley, directed by Michael Uppendahl, 20th Century Fox, 2017.

"Red Riding Hood." Red Riding Hood Wikia, http://redridinghood.wikia.com/wiki/Little_Red_Riding_Hood. Accessed 12 July 2018.

"Rhinoceros." *Fargo: Season 2,* written by Noah Hawley, directed by Jeffrey Reiner, 20th Century Fox, 2016.

"The Rooster Prince." *Fargo: Season 1,* written by Noah Hawley, directed by Adam Bernstein, 20th Century Fox, 2014.

"Somebody to Love." *Fargo: Season 3,* written by Noah Hawley, directed by Keith Gordon, 20th Century Fox, 2017.

"The Story of Peter and the Wolf." *Patma Music,* http://www.patmamusic.org.au/files/PW%20story.pdf. Accessed 12 July 2018.

VanDerWerff, Todd. "Fargo showrunner Noah Hawley takes us through the show's first season." *TVAVClub,* 18 June 2014, tv.avclub.com/fargo-showrunner-noah-hawley-takes-us-through-the-show-1798269551. Accessed 2 Jan. 2018.

"Varga." *Fargo: Season 3.* 20th Century Fox, 2017.

Beautiful Cockroaches
and Featherless Birds

*Anthropomorphism in Books
for Latinx Children*

STACY HOULT-SAROS

Subtitled "A bilingual celebration of friendship and ecological wisdom" (2), Carmen Tafolla's *Baby Coyote and the Old Woman/El Coyotito y la Viejita*, with illustrations by Matt Novak, tells a didactic tale of symbiotic relationships between desert-dwelling humans and nonhumans. The book opens with an image of a smiling coyote surveying "his desert" as an equally pleased-looking toad hops into the scene (2–3). While the young mammal's favorite activities appear typical of his species (chasing tumbleweeds, watching cactus flowers bloom and toads scamper), he is drawn repeatedly to the home of an old woman, whom he watches as she goes about her daily tasks. The two coexist in harmony as she leaves him water and scraps, and he chases nuisance species (rabbits and prairie dogs) from her garden. The soft gray of her hair and apron match the young animal's fur, and while she never sees him, they are shown in close proximity as he watches her work from behind a saguaro (4–5).

Like Tafolla, many writers and illustrators of books for Latinx[1] children deploy anthropomorphized animal characters in service to a range of narrative and lyric strategies. While sympathetic nonhuman characters may reinforce connections between Latinx human protagonists and the natural world and bolster images of happy, harmonious family and community life, reworkings of familiar tales and rhymes (drawn from English- and Spanish-language traditions) call attention to difference even as they strive to unite diverse experiences and audiences across linguistic and cultural divides. Finally, harsh depictions of migration, poverty, isolation and discrimination feature animals whose emotions, actions and reactions reflect those of humans facing similar challenges, inviting child readers of divergent backgrounds to identify and empathize with human victims of injustice. Mirroring the complexity of the issues explored in this last category, the domestic, farmed and free-ranging animals that embody these lived experiences for young readers blur the lines between humans and disparate animal species, displaying a combination of human and nonhuman characteristics; some of these texts' most powerful moments involve unexpected breaks with the animals' mostly humanlike personalities and ways of being. Latinx animal characters thus occupy a uniquely liminal space

67

between humanity and animality even as they represent the in-betweenness of Latinx culture.

Connectedness with Nature

The plot of *Baby Coyote* turns on the eponymous youngster's decision to take action against the accumulation of garbage behind his human benefactor's home. His slumping posture and hangdog facial expression clearly demonstrate his dismay at her surprisingly destructive act of maintaining a trash pile (8–9). When he begins returning discarded items to her door, she wisely finds uses for them, until her discovery one morning of a pile of papers, cans and a bottle of cleaning fluid (along with a set of tiny coyote tracks) leads her to think deeply about what the animal is trying to tell her. He visibly perks up, smiling with ears and tail pointed upward, as he watches her reaction to the items he has left for her (14–15). Enlightenment arrives in a rare moment in which she spots the coyote, who has chosen to reveal himself by sitting near her, and the two share a knowing gaze (16–17); her pointing finger indicates that she credits him with a plan she conceives to sort and recycle her refuse, which she takes to town in the bed of her truck. A conversation with a man in town reinforces the importance of recycling, linked to natural processes:

> "So these things will have a new life?" asked the woman.
> "Exactly!" said the man.
> "Like when the sun comes up again for another day?" asked the woman.
> "Yes, exactly," said the man [20].

The story ends with the old woman and the coyote looking happily out over the desert: "Its air was clean and its skies were many colors. The cactus flowers bloomed. The toads scampered across the dust. And the sun went down in peace" (22). The closing illustration brings the story full circle as it repeats the initial image with subtle changes: the toad now looks up admiringly at the coyote, while the latter gazes directly out at the readers, as if to challenge them to follow in the old woman's environmentally responsible footsteps (24). The artist's use of the same bright green for the coyote's eyes, the toad's skin and the cacti in the background links these elements to each other, as the green blossoms on the woman's dress connect her to the nature surrounding her solitary home (23). At the same time, the animal's cognitive process, moving from negative emotions at the sight of a trash heap to a multiphase, ecologically sound action plan, is surprising in a story that departs from a realistic scenario of mutual dependence. Tafolla's development of an appealing animal character with strong capacities for problem solving and persuasion provides a new twist on indigenous wisdom linked to deep connections with nature.

The author of *Animal Poems of the Iguazú/Animalario del Iguazú*, Francisco X. Alarcón, is open about his objective in creating this bilingual collection: as he states in his "Introduction," "I hope these poems will motivate all of us to take action to protect the wild animals and plants of the Iguazú area and of the entire world" (2). His frequent collaborator, illustrator Maya Christina Gonzalez, provides vibrant portraits of creatures who speak directly to the reader in short first-person poems set in Argentina's Iguazú National Park, allowing them to teach young readers about their species' characteristics and behaviors. Some of the tropical denizens peer directly out at the reader, and a few are even credited with an ability to think figuratively: a toucan boasts, "for a beak / I have two / papaya slices" ("Toucan" 6). Manuel M. Martín-Rodríguez comments on the functions of the short poetic lines characteristic of Alarcón's work: "In the case of Alarcón's poetry for children ... the combination of textual blanks, undetermined imagery, and short, memorable lines becomes essential for creating empowering literary spaces for young readers..." (78).

One animal simultaneously exhibits humanlike personality traits and reveals a basic truth about its own species' relationship with humans: the coati owns up to pride in its outsize tail, curiosity and omnivorous nature, "sniffing out / the food I know / you all carry" ("Coatí" 14). Like the hungry mammal, a small lizard takes pride in its tail, which has been lost, "but as a lizard / I can still / grow it back" ("Lizard" 14). A few of the creatures even use the opportunity to make critical comments about human visitors to the area. A jaguar challenges the human perception that its species is nearing extinction, as the apex predator will continue to embody the "untamed / living spirit / of this jungle" ("Jaguareté [Jaguar]" 19). A nest of smiling baby birds compares helicopters "carrying humans / who can't fly / by themselves!" to natural pests, referring to them as "these big mosquitos / with noisy motors" ("What a Pest!" 20), while the collective poetic voice of a group of ants describes human tourists as "giant ants":

> holding digital cameras
> taking lots of photos
> of each other
> ignoring the great
> and tiny wonders
> all around them ["Giant Ants" 21]

Following these musings on the shortcomings of the park's human visitors, the final poem, "Same Green Fate," accompanied by an Edenic scene of animals lovingly interacting with each other as they contemplate the natural majesty of the falls, takes on a gentler tone as it encourages readers to listen to and learn from the rainforest and its diverse species: "*protect all of us / for the Earth's fate / for your own sake*" (31). The illustrator's technique enhances the message about interconnectedness, not merely blurring, but rather eliminating the line, as she explains in a note to readers: "I decided to honor the animals by painting them in a very detailed way, and to use cut paper for the rainforest background and for the people, to show that we are all made up of the same materials" (32). Connected as they are by the shared cutout backgrounds, the poems, like their corresponding paintings, give voice to animals who demonstrate myriad motivations for speaking out. Readers are invited to ponder unique physical features, abilities and habitats that separate the Iguazú natives from their human poetic objects, but the nonhumans' acts of describing, explaining and critiquing aspects of their ecosystem and its components paradoxically bring them closer to young readers who share their use of language. Martín-Rodríguez finds a deep counteracting impulse in these deceptively simple poetic creations: "Alarcón celebrates native knowledge, myths, and languages in a way that exposes children readers to scenarios that go beyond their own immediate social contexts. For U.S. Latina/o children, who may have faced racism and linguistic-based forms of discrimination in their daily lives, *Animal Poems* provides a vindication of non-dominant languages and beliefs that such readers may find empowering" (86).

Latinx Communities

Another Alarcón/Gonzalez collaboration incorporates anthropomorphized animals that do not speak aloud for themselves; they rather reflect human emotions or illustrate qualities subject to the human poetic subject's judgment. The title of *Iguanas in the Snow*, part of a cycle of four seasonal poetry collections, reflects the experiences, familiar to many young Latinx readers, of relocation to radically different climates and the accompanying culture shock. Set in San Francisco, the book features text and illustrations that are graced by a diverse range of pets and free-ranging animals associated with the city. Most of the nonhuman characters fulfill decorative or affective functions: stylized iguanas wearing colorful caps evoke Mexico as they crawl through a variety of scenes populated by multicolored children and their families, and pets (often pictured wearing unmistakable smiles) add to the book's joyful tone of celebration of happy life in a multicultural city. The poetic voice's appreciation for and identification with nonhuman creatures is communicated in a poem named for the city, in which he expresses pride in the connection with "Saint Francis—/ the patron saint / of all animals" (10).

A curious instance of projected anthropomorphism provides a different spin on relationships between San Franciscans and animals both literal and figurative. "Los más grandes de San Francisco," translated as "The Biggest San Franciscans" (all poems are presented in both languages, but not always in the same order), describes with pride the famous sea lions that have long been one of the city's principal tourist draws. After a series of unusually ambivalent and even critical statements about these animals that "pay / no attention / to tourists"; are "noisy" and "smelly"; are fond of "long naps"; and "came uninvited / from the sea" to take over the marina, the poetic voice attributes an extraordinary level of awareness to the creatures, asserting that they "must know" that "this shore was / theirs long before / there was a city here" (14). The illustration jarringly contradicts the initial statement about tourists as four of the six sea lions pictured are looking directly at five human characters who point, wave and otherwise appear delighted to observe them (15). The animals' expressions are mild and inscrutable, but human and nonhuman gazes clearly meet, and the skin tones of the human figures harmonize with the soft browns of the sea lions' coats, visually blurring the line between the two species. In highlighting their imposing size and less appealing (to humans) characteristics as well as their legitimate claim to the shore, the poetic voice reinscribes their value from tourist attractions to autonomous beings whose right to a peaceful coexistence with human city dwellers (whether or not the latter find their presence pleasing) is unquestioned. The speaker's musings on the animals' origins also serve to link their mythical return to repressed memories of decimated native populations; their direct gaze may be read as silently incriminating by humans whose treatment of nonhumans and cultural others has left much to be questioned.

Also set in California, Gary Soto's series of books about the low-riding, mambo-loving Chato humorously depicts life in the barrio for an anthropomorphic cat and other clothed, Spanglish-speaking animals. In *Chato's Kitchen*, which finds the feline hoping to eat his neighbors (a family of mice), Susan Guevara's illustrations are rife with cultural references, from food products to the cross dangling from the neck of Chato's friend Novio Boy and the shawl worn by the mouse family matriarch. While the title character's elongated body, shorts and tank top ensemble, and backward-facing cap paint him as more human than cat, his actions are distinctly catlike: upon the first appearance of the mice carrying tiny sacks of groceries, baseball equipment and other miniature items, "His whiskers vibrated with pleasure and he leaped onto the fence for a closer view."

When the new neighbors unwisely accept his invitation to dinner, he pulls out ingredients for fajitas, enchiladas and other typical foods, enlisting Novio Boy's assistance with the homemade tortillas. The dinner guests arrive with their contribution, freshly made quesadillas, riding atop a friend they had asked permission to bring: a dog named Chorizo, whose presence strikes terror into the hearts of the would-be assassins. As they rush for cover, framed family portraits and a shrine with candles and religious figures further humanize the cats as their primal fear of dogs impedes them from expressing normal cat aggression: "They didn't hiss or swat the air. They ran and cowered under the dining table." Though clad in a multicolored vest and beret, the dog is less anthropomorphized than the other animals: "Chorizo wagged into the house, his belly bumping over the threshold. He click-clicked on paw-nails into the kitchen, his nose picking up the smells of simmering food." In naming the unwelcome but unfailingly polite guest after a meat product, Soto draws a sharp contrast between Chorizo and the cats, depicted as crafty, creative, and considerably more verbal than the laid-back canine. The happy ending, in which all the characters enjoy a bountiful feast, celebrates Latinx culinary traditions that enable the hapless partners to enjoy the meal even though no guests are consumed.

If, as Jamie Campbell Naidoo affirms in *Celebrating Cuentos*, "[t]he potency of the visual image and its effects on a child's construction of reality can assist or prevent a child's ethnic development" (19), the funny and loveable Chato, with his expressive face and strokeable, textured fur, offers Chicanx children a hero whose neighborhood, speech patterns and cultural practices are reassuringly familiar. In her Foreword to *Celebrating Cuentos: Promoting Latino Children's Literature and Literacy in Classrooms and Libraries*, Yuyi Morales writes warmly of the value of Latinx stories for readers both familiar and unfamiliar with the cultures portrayed: "The Latino child recognizes himself or herself in the stories, finds in the illustrations things that he has at home, sees foods that she eats with her family, cherishes celebrations that his loved ones taught him about, understands habits that exist within her community. The non–Latino children, the ones not yet familiar with the culture, open the book and encounter surprises, those that we like all other ethnic groups, have to offer from the most precious gifts of our culture" (xi).

New Twists on Anglo Classics

Books that reframe familiar Anglo stories with characters and settings recognizable to Latinx children feature animals that occupy a liminal space between one culture's well-worn rhymes and tales and the lived experiences of a bicultural target audience. Characterized by the author/illustrator, Angela Dominguez, in an interview as "a Peruvian indigenous twist on *Mary Had a Little Lamb*" (Aldama 81), *María Had a Little Llama* is graced with a cover image of the eponymous child and her prized pet hugging and smiling directly at the reader. The title is easily recognized as a riff on the familiar English-language rhyme about pet ownership, but the Hispanicized version of the protagonist's name (in the title and Spanish lines from the bilingual text) and the transformation of the creature to a domestic animal associated with Andean populations locate the simple, minimalist verses in a geographic and cultural context unfamiliar to most child readers.

The llama in question, set apart from others of her species by her white coat and apparent autonomy to wander unrestrained by fences or enclosures, demonstrates her closeness with Maria through humanlike facial expressions and a penchant for dancing to the music of her owner's pan flute. The Andean setting is reinforced by Inca-like stone structures and a background map of the Inca trail, which the creature appears to consult along the way.

Great merriment ensues when the llama (oddly identified as male in the English text, though feminine pronouns corresponding to the feminine noun "llama" are used in the Spanish) follows her beloved Maria to school, passing by other llamas and a sheep being driven in the opposite direction by a dog. She clearly enjoys the attention of several delighted children seen surrounding and petting her. Both owner and pet wear identical mischievous expressions while considering a sign indicating that llama attendance is against school rules. The "moral" tacked on unexpectedly at the end (the teacher explains that the llama loves Maria because Maria loves her) testifies to a mutually fulfilling relationship between members of different species, but the final illustration again depicts a huddled group of darker-coated, less joyful-looking llamas behind a fence watching the white llama's playful interactions with Maria and a band of human musicians. Significantly, Maria is the only child shown sporting traditional Andean headgear, suggesting a stronger connection with a domesticated animal as characteristic of a more traditional lifestyle. More troubling is the likelihood that readers will relate the llama's elevated status in the community to the whiteness of her coat. While the snowy whiteness of Mary's little lamb is unremarkable for its species, Dominguez risks sending an uncomfortable message about the racial hierarchy by preserving that detail from the original tune.

Little Roja Riding Hood, Susan Middleton Elya's retelling of a childhood favorite with a contemporary twist, contains a liberal sprinkling of Spanish words along with bicultural references in Susan Guevara's illustrations. As young Roja's multitasking mother prepares a soup for the ailing Abuela while watching telenovelas, the family cat makes frightening faces as tiny blind mice cavort through the scenes. The traditional storybook villain, who first appears leaning against a tree next to Roja's path, inevitably blurs the line, wearing a bandanna and a skull pendant as he talks in rhymes to her and her ever-present pet. The carnivore's subsequent exchange with Roja's sickly grandmother proceeds predictably, beneath the benevolent gaze of the older woman's household saint, and as the granddaughter arrives on the scene, her faithful feline companion reacts with arched back and fanned-out tail to the unnatural sight of the caped wolf as a pair of birds use Spanish ("¡Mira!)" to call Roja's attention to the impending disaster. As in more traditional versions of Red Riding Hood's tale, the predator is anthropomorphized to exaggerate the threat posed to the grandmother: he represents the intersection of cartoonish, depraved animality with humanlike cunning and duplicity. Only the combined protection of the saint and her daughter's repurposed hot soup can save the wolf's intended victim from an untimely demise. The coexistence of multiple forms and levels of anthropomorphism (the birds' speech, the ubiquitous mice with their dark glasses, and the cat's exaggerated facial expressions) allows Guevara to engage multiple folkloric tropes to heighten both the drama and the humor of Middleton Elya's reimagined tale of an imperiled child saved by her own resourcefulness and mental quickness.

Bobbi Salinas's Mexicanized version of *Los Tres Cerdos/The Three Pigs: Nacho, Tito y Miguel* transforms the familiar porcine siblings of the childhood tale through a steady stream of visual references to border cultures. The opening page shows the three piglets counting their savings in their mother's house, adorned with family and religious portraits and traditional candles (1). As the well-known plot advances, with each pig constructing a home from materials bought from anthropomorphized animal vendors, Salinas's images situate them in border spaces: between a desert, complete with cacti and geographically correct reptiles, and rolling farmland that provides bountiful crops under the watchful eyes of a personified sun (3); between a rocky, arid strip and a wooded area (9); and between a cactus fence and a dry, agave-dotted field graced with colorful farmed creatures (14). Following the expected victory of the third, sharpest brother, Miguel, over the glowering, shorts-wearing wolf, José, the three celebrate with green chile stew and tortillas before beginning construction on a full adobe compound where they will all live happily ever after.

The author explains her intended message in a brief "Summary": "Miguel, the cleverest and darkest of the pigs, sees through the wolf's artificially sugared tricks, and ultimately destroys the wolf's power to deceive others. The story exposes how those in positions of power are often less strong and frightening than we are sometimes led to believe." Miguel's strength appears to derive from the knowledge gleaned from books that line his adobe dwelling: Sor Juana and Pablo Neruda share shelf space with Thurgood Marshall, Wilma Mankiller and other multicultural trailblazers (16). The other pigs' interior décor decisions (musical instruments for Nacho [4] and art, including portraits of Frida Kahlo and Cantinflas [11], for Tito) suggest creativity over intellect, but Miguel combines both with his reading material and vocation (he is seen writing at a computer when José makes his first appearance through a window [16]). Salinas's equation of dark skin with cleverness subverts racist assumptions about skin color and intelligence, just as the pigs' dedication to cultural and intellectual pursuits challenges negative associations of a commonly consumed animal with gluttony and messiness.

If these reimagined tales from the English-language children's canon allow for fruitful cross-cultural exchanges, it should be noted that attempts by non–Latinx writers to cross cultural borders have not always been felicitous. Among other critical voices, Mary Pat Brady has summarized the problematic use of superficial and stereotypical references to Mexican culture in the popular *Skippyjon Jones* series: "Breathing new life into the stereotype of the *frito bandito*, Skippyjon Jones is a mischievous Siamese cat who fantasizes a Chihuahua alter ego, while the text itself engages many of the tropes of Latino/a children's writing (including the mix of languages, symbolic locales, and typical foods). In other words when a brand becomes fungible, its appropriation and rejuvenation as stereotype becomes far easier to manage" (380–381). *Skippyjon Jones in the Doghouse*, for example, finds Judy Schachner's diminutive creation imaginatively transformed into a Chihuahua named Skippito after being placed in time out by his mother. The roots of his trans-species identity go unexplained as he rhymes a response, asserting that he is, in fact, "[a] Chihuahua to my bones."

While his species dysphoria and identification with the iconic Mexican dogs appear sincere, Skippy's anthropomorphic use of his "very best Spanish accent" is grating. His shaky Spanish ("*poco perrito*") and the equally inauthentic Spanglish spoken by Los Chimichangos, the gang of Chihuahuas that join him in his adventures, uncomfortably blur the line, detracting from an already muddled plot involving a bobblehead in an attic and a dénouement that requires the transcultural hero to be rolled into a bean burrito. Non-Latinx children are certain to be engaged by the book's humorous rhymes and quirky, action-packed illustrations, but the combination of mock Spanglish and the stock features of the cinematic Mexican bandit will be offensive to cultural insiders. Oralia Garza de Cortés and Jennifer Battle warn of the harmful effects of recycling such negative images: "Such misguided, stereotypical depictions in children's literature only serve to further distort and negatively impact Latino children's own self-image, identity, and literacy development during their formative years" (65).

Traditional Tales Retold

Another category of texts features versions of well-known Latin American tales for a young Latinx readership. Lucía M. González's retelling of the traditional Cuban tale *The Bossy Gallito* (in Spanish, *El gallo de bodas*, "The Wedding Rooster") combines with Lulu Delacre's intricate illustrations of scenes based on Miami's Little Havana to update a well-known folktale about a rooster's efforts to appear elegant at a family wedding, despite his inability to resist the temptation of two shiny corn kernels in the mud. Throughout the text and illustrations, nonhuman characters engage in humanlike activities (decorating cakes, playing dominoes, putting out fires and, of course, marrying each other) and are credited with human attributes like bossiness (and rebelliousness upon being bossed). Ironically, after the hapless protagonist is unsuccessful in ordering a decidedly non-anthropomorphic goat and various inanimate elements to clean his beak, it is his close connection with friend the sun that saves him by agreeing to help: "The sun was his good friend. The little Gallito always sang to him first thing in the morning to wake him up." The sun's compliance sets in motion a chain reaction of helpfulness that leads to a break with anthropomorphic character, as the rooster crows with gratitude. In the illustrations, which (unlike the text) portray the mingling of diverse types of birds, no one appears bothered by the interspecies union of the rooster's Uncle Perico, a parakeet, to a heron several times his size; hence, a tale about bossiness and friends helping each other also becomes a powerful statement on love and harmony across difference.

An insider cultural perspective on the rooster's bossy personality emerges from the author's note entitled "About the Bossy Rooster" at the end, in which she explains that roosters naturally fight each other for dominance in the poultry yard and that cockfighting is popular in Caribbean cultures, where the men "pride themselves on the bravery of these roosters." While the Gallito is never shown in physical combat with another creature, the impulse to dominate others can be seen in his assumptions that other animals, grass, water and fire will carry out his instructions. The happy ending, in which the rooster makes it to the wedding and is even seen leaving in the honeymoon car with the bridal couple, portrays a joyful outcome born of friendship and gratitude; while his elegant appearance is consistent with González's characterization of cockfighting champions as "the aristocrats of their breed," this version of the tale presents the child reader with a positive, if fanciful, alternative to the tragic outcomes of real-life animal fights.

Roosters and chickens are among the more popular nonhuman protagonists in Latin American and Latinx narratives, with competing versions of the Gallito's story sharing shelf space with different retellings of the Spanish tale of *Medio Pollito* (Half-Chick), a similarly episodic narrative traditionally recounted to explain the origins of weather vanes. In Eric A. Kimmel's version, as in others, the chick protagonist's life is off to a rough start when he hatches from a half egg, emerging with one eye, wing and leg, and only half a comb and half a beak. These obvious challenges are not enough to curb the youngster's ambition to travel solo to Madrid to meet the king, even as skeptical barnyard denizens mock his decision. His journey and the mother hen's empowering message ("You can do anything if you put your mind to it") may be seen as inspirational by young readers with different abilities, and the youngster, outfitted with a tiny bag and walking stick, proves himself a worthy role model by coming to the rescue of a body of water, a fire, and the wind, all of whom cry out for his help along the way.

The chick's arrival in the city leads to a deeply disturbing series of events as the royal cook overhears him using human speech, promises to introduce him to the monarch, and immediately sets about cooking him in a pot. Valeria Docampo's dark illustrations mirror the horror of the young hero's situation: "The cook slammed the heavy lid down on the pot and left. Medio Pollito was trapped. The water grew warmer. Soon it would begin to boil. That would be the end of him." As the terrified bird struggles to escape, he is saved by the friendly elements he assisted during his trip: the water and fire refuse to cook him, and the wind carries him to the top of a cathedral, where he still stands, showing the human inhabitants of Madrid the direction of the wind. In Kimmel's short message to readers, "A Note about the Tale," he explains the differences between older versions and his contemporary take on the familiar story: "Traditional versions of this story reflect the rigid, repressive society of Old Spain. Medio Pollito is rude, selfish, and tries to rise above his station. He is drowned, burned, and set on top of the cathedral as a warning to others." He affirms that he "chose to celebrate the half-chick's spirit of adventure"; child readers may also discern lessons about karma and the benefits of helping others with no immediate reward in sight. Kimmel's decision to eliminate the more violent actions of the Spanish original will make the story more palatable to an audience that will find much to admire in the chick's selflessness and refusal to be defined by what others see as physical limitations.

A traditional Cuban story that continues to be reinterpreted for a child audience is the romantic tale of Martina and El Ratón Pérez. In *Martina the Beautiful Cockroach*, retold by Carmen Agra Deedy with illustrations by Michael Austin, the comely protagonist is anthropomorphized, through both common fairy-tale motifs and culturally specific devices, but also unmistakably an animal other. She is first seen preparing to present herself to a series of suitors in her family home in Old Havana. The text foregrounds her animality with nods to the cockroach lifestyle as well as negative stereotypes associated with the species: "Now that Martina was 21 days old, she was ready to give her leg in marriage. The Cucaracha household was crawling with excitement!" Austin's glowing illustrations seek to make a historically reviled insect loveable while Cubanizing the family with cigar boxes, food products and musical instruments evocative of Martina's island homeland. In the hallowed tradition of Cuban resourcefulness, the family uses a stamp of national hero José Martí as a painting in Martina's dressing room. When her wise grandmother suggests a plan for using another well-known national product, coffee, to weed out unsuitable candidates for Martina's groom, the young bride-to-be wisely follows her advice, rejecting an elegant rooster, an ill-mannered pig and an "oily" (and hungry) lizard when their reactions to a spilled beverage reveal less-than-ideal personality traits.

Martina is beginning to despair when she spots a small mouse in the garden below. Armed with her Abuela's comb and shawl, she approaches little Pérez, only to find herself with coffee on her feet as he, too, has followed his Cuban grandmother's suggestion about the Coffee Test. The story ends with the two wise elders toasting with cups of *café cubano* as the lovers marry under a garland of pink flowers. The sweet ending, with the happy couple bathed in a ring of light from a streetlamp, reinforces the gently nostalgic tone of the paintings, filled with colonial buildings, vintage cars and tropical vegetation. Agra Deedy's bilingual version of this interspecies love story calls attention to the multicultural and multiracial roots of Cuban culture as it seeks to rescue two oft-maligned creatures from the negative characteristics attributed to them by the humans whose spaces they co-inhabit.

Señor Cat's Romance and Other Favorite Stories from Latin America is a collection of popular tales, including alternate versions of Martina's and Medio Pollito's stories, retold by Lucía M. González and Lulu Delacre. Delacre's visual interpretation of the titular Spanish ballad about feline nuptials has the hero dressed up in peninsular period finery, blurring the line with historical accuracy as he prepares to wed a captivating Moorish cat. Both are depicted with cat heads atop humanlike bodies, and the wedding party enjoys typical treats including nougats, Spanish wines and fine meats (42–44). Ironically, a stereotypically tomcat-like behavior, singing atop a roof, leads to disaster as Señor Cat falls and is presumed dead. As the kittens of the community weep in kitten language ("*Miau-miau, miau-miau*" [45]), the protagonist is awakened from a coma by the scent of sardines in another quintessentially feline moment. That the humble fish (and not the finer offerings from the wedding celebration) are identified as the hero's favorite dish is surprising given his status in the community, as evidenced by the open mourning and solemn finery of his funeral procession (45). Non-Latinx children will be interested to hear, in the rhyme and in a brief addition from the author, that cats in Spanish-speaking countries have only seven lives ("Something about the Story" 46). At the same time, these enduring stories address experiences common to all cultures. As the author notes in her "Foreword," "The dominant themes of these stories are universal to the childhood experience. Their characters learn the power of sharing, they learn to overcome grief, they learn the value of wit and cleverness" (7). Through the costumes and other textual and graphic references to Spanish customs, readers of this ballad learn bits of historical reality wrapped up in a cautionary tale about the dangers of reckless behavior.

Gloria Anzaldúa imagines an empowering variation on traditional tales of La Llorona in *Prietita and the Ghost Woman/Prietita y La Llorona*, with illustrations by Christina Gonzalez. Motivated by the need to find a healing plant to cure her mother of an unnamed illness, the child protagonist follows a traditional healer's advice and ventures into the forbidding woods of the King Ranch. In her quest for the elusive rue, Prietita has a series of encounters with ambiguously anthropomorphized animals that appear to help her to locate the plant. The first meeting, with a white-tail deer, is the most mysterious as the animal seems to lead her intentionally: "The deer lifted her head and stared at Prietita. She made a soft sound and began to move into the woods. Prietita thought she heard her say, 'Follow me,' so she started after her." Subsequently guided by a salamander, a dove, a jaguarundi and a group of fireflies, she is led directly to the natural remedy by La Llorona herself, who bears a strong physical resemblance to the young heroine even as she glows with golden light like the lightning bugs glimpsed before. Anzaldúa explains in a note at the end that the story is based on her own childhood near the real-life King Ranch, and that her intent is "to encourage children to look beneath the surface of what things seem to be in order to discover the truths that may be hidden." Prietita's mystical communication with nonhumans and their apparent ability and willingness to help her may seem as improbable to non–Latinx readers as the appearance of the floating, ghostly woman, but nature's undeniable healing powers are highlighted in the context of a parent's illness, a threatening situation with which children of all cultures can identify.

The Lizard and the Sun/La Lagartija y El Sol, an Alma Flor Ada offering illustrated by Felipe Dávalos, builds on a short reading, encountered by the author as a child, that honors indigenous Americans' respect for the sun ("Author's Note"). The narrative is set in a pre–Columbian past characterized by open communication between humans, non-human animals, and other natural elements. When the sun, depicted as a glowing human face, disappears, all members of the sentient community share the same reactions: "All of the plants, the animals, and the people were waiting anxiously for the sun to appear. … The people were cold. The birds had stopped singing, and the children had stopped playing." The animals collectively decide to search for the sun, but the lizard is left to continue her search alone after others, from toads and frogs to eagles and jaguars, have given up.

The reptilian protagonist is a curious mix of anthropomorphism with species-specific traits: her face and body are not modified to look human, and she climbs rocks, scurries up tree trunks, and reflects on the uniqueness of an oddly glowing rock she encounters, demonstrating familiarity with a range of specific rock types. No one in the pre–Hispanic metropolis is surprised when the small lizard secures an audience with the emperor and seeks his counsel about the unusual stone, gesturing expressively with her tiny feet to underscore its uniqueness. When she is unsuccessful in moving the rock as he has commanded, he responds by undertaking the journey himself, calling on the lizard and a woodpecker to accompany him. A stunning image of the three of them gazing at the rediscovered sun asleep under the glowing rock reinforces close connections between humans and animals: the greens of the lizard and the bird harmonize with the ruler's headdress, and the lizard's tale curls around the emperor's arm as he rests on the ground, placing himself at the same level as his companions.

The wise leader recognizes what is at stake when the sun indicates a desire to continue sleeping: "Without the sun, the children could not go out to play, the birds could not come out to sing, and the flowers would not bloom." The situation is resolved when musicians and dancers clad in feathers and other animal-like costumes wake up the sun with their festive performance. The emperor lifts up his two animal friends to thank them for their contributions, and the story concludes with a moral based not on lessons for human children, but rather on typical animal behaviors: "And since that day, all lizards love to lie in the sun. They like to remember the day when one of their own found the sun's hiding place and helped bring him back to give lights and warmth to everyone." Along with her courage, perseverance and ability to speak, the projection of human emotions and collective memory contribute to a partial anthropomorphism of the lizard that serves mainly to elevate a seemingly insignificant animal as a being worthy of respect and recognition.

The cultural in-betweenness of Latinx children is manifested in battling folk heroes in René Colato Laínez's *The Tooth Fairy Meets El Ratón Pérez*, illustrated by Tom Lintern. When little Miguelito loses a tooth, signals are beamed both to the Tooth Fairy in her castle and to the legendary Latinx rodent (last seen marrying Martina the cockroach) in his cave, and both spring into action to capture the coveted tooth. The dialogue between the competing would-be collectors highlights the two heritages united in a child who sleeps peacefully, oblivious to the culture wars playing out in his bedroom:

"Eeeeek, a mouse!"
"*¡Guau, una señorita bonita!*"

When the tooth is lost in the struggle, the fairy and the mouse race to locate it against a backdrop of bicultural books, toys and posters. Lintern's illuminated illustrations clearly present the Tooth Fairy as thoroughly humanized with the enhancements of wings and a wand, while Pérez is both humanized (through clothing, speech and use of human technologies) and unmistakably animal: he annoys his adversary by shoving his whiskers in her face and sniffs around the boy's room for the lost tooth. In the end, the blonde, fair-skinned Anglo icon and the Spanglish-speaking Pérez agree that the tooth is sufficiently precious to warrant a collaborative effort:

> "It is a beautiful tooth!" the Tooth Fairy said with tears rolling down her face.
> "*Es un bello diente*," El Ratón Pérez agreed with tears in his whiskers. "I can squeeze into small places, but I cannot crawl up that high."
> "Wait a minute," the Tooth Fairy said. "Let's rescue our tooth together! I'll carry you up."

After hatching a plan to use the tooth to help Pérez build a rocket ship to visit the moon before incorporating it into the Tooth Fairy's castle construction, the unlikely duo is last seen dancing around their prized possession. Oblivious to their conflict and subsequent reconciliation, Miguelito awakes to find a double reward: two coins with a note that reads, "From your amigos forever, the Tooth Fairy and El Ratón Pérez." An explanatory author's note at the end ("Who are the Tooth Fairy and El Ratón Pérez?") reveals the cultural origins of the two icons in England and Spain, along with the Spanish expressions used by the mouse, presuming an Anglo readership likely unfamiliar with Pérez and his language. As Frederick Luis Aldama has observed, "Deep immersion in storyworlds by and about Latinos can lead to greater plasticity in the reader's cognitive schemas about the world. … It can show non–Latino readers other ways of existing and can hold at bay rigid ways of thinking about race, gender, and sexuality" (Aldama 13). The ever-popular Pérez further provides a more positive image of mice than is customary in English-language stories, approximating humanity by combining ingenuity and a vocation for rocket science with bilingual language skills that allow him to navigate new situations with flexibility and resourcefulness.

Loosely based on the storied childhood of a celebrated cultural icon, Monica Brown's *Frida Kahlo and her Animalitos* sheds light on the close bond between the iconic Mexican artist, depicted as a young girl in John Parra's lively illustrations, and her menagerie of pets. The opening scene shows her intent on drawing a range of animals, including, but not limited to, the pets named in the text: "two monkeys, a parrot, three dogs, two turkeys, an eagle, a black cat, and a fawn." While some of her creations resemble their living counterparts, a cat and a caterpillar are clearly smiling, and one dog sports an unrealistic bright blue coat. Throughout the book, Brown draws attention to features the young Frida shares with her pets: the parrot is colorful like Frida's house and traditional clothing; the fawn has "beautiful, watchful eyes" like the artist's; the cat is playful and independent and has shiny black hair like Frida's; and the monkeys are mischievous like their human companion.

Parra's animal figures further blur the line between the human artist and her frequent models through anthropomorphic facial expressions and postures. Burros ridden by Frida and her friends smile as they pass through the halls of her school, and a tiny hairless dog mimics her contented face, eyes closed with a peaceful smile, tilting its head in the same direction in which she leans. Monkeys wield human-made objects, are rocked like babies, and have humanoid faces that appear enhanced with cosmetics like those used by Frida, now growing into young womanhood. A series of images of the artist painting her animals is introduced with a summary explanation: "Frida's animals were her children, her friends, and her inspiration." The creatures' inconsistent anthropomorphism may be interpreted as part of the author's narrative decision to situate her tribute in the style of many famous Latin American novels, as she shares in her "Author's Note": "I chose to write about Frida's animalitos as a way of highlighting Frida's magical creativity—her strength, her sense of adventure, her indomitable spirit—throughout her life. What insights do her beloved animals tells us about the young Frida? It was an honor to use *lo real maravilloso* (the marvelous real) to imagine just that." Brown has revealed another, more personal reason for her focus on animals in an interview with Frederick Luis Aldama: "I decided, as a person who has given my children a house full of animals and pets like guinea pigs, dogs, and fish, that I would write from the perspective of her muses and the animals the surrounded her and comforted her" (Aldama 45). The animals' important role in sustaining Frida through a series of traumatic experiences is emphasized in scene after scene of physical closeness, as when the parrot, Bonito, snuggles in bed with Frida at nap time. Interestingly, the monkeys in Parra's illustrations are considerably more anthropomorphic in appearance than those included in some of the artist's most famous self-portraits, which capture interspecies affection while preserving the primates' enigmatic otherness.

Harsh Realities

As in other narrative traditions, Latinx stories sometimes recur to animal characters and images to make harsh realities understandable to child readers. In Duncan Tonatiuh's *Pancho Rabbit and the Coyote: A Migrant's Tale*, cuddly creatures are deployed to soften the harsh realities of a story about border crossings, violence and exploitation. As the author has acknowledged in an interview, he was advised by an editor to make his protagonists children or animals to facilitate identification. He elaborated that this text "is a fable like the Little Red Riding Hood story, but it is also an allegory of the journey that undocumented immigrants go through to reach the U.S. When the book first came out, there were a few negative reviews—some even thought it was liberal propaganda—but for the most part the response was very positive" (Aldama 243). Accompanied by narrative drawings reminiscent of indigenous codices, the text portrays a family of rabbits and their animal friends wearing clothes, speaking in English and engaging in culturally specific activities like decorating with *papel picado* and eating *mole*. While all the animal characters are anthropomorphic, the rabbits' humanlike hands and feet further strengthen their identification with humans.

The story is set in motion when Papá Rabbit and other male animals head North "to find work in the great carrot and lettuce fields." A rooster and a ram are pictured bent under the weight of their backpacks as Papá waves good-bye to the family he must leave behind to support. The sad expressions of the family and their neighbors when Papá fails to return from the North as expected accompany a conversation in which characters comfort themselves by imagining possible excuses for his delay. When his son Pancho sets out to find his father, his journey brings him into contact with the stock figures of every immigration tale: a literal coyote who demands his *mole*, rice, beans and *aguamiel*; and snake border agents who require his tortillas as a bribe. Throughout the treacherous journey to the North, the rabbit and the coyote are the only animate beings in the nearly all the illustrations, reinforcing the isolation and vulnerability of migrant populations. After the horrors of train travel, river and desert crossings, and a long crawl through a tunnel, the most violent moment occurs when the bandanna-clad coyote breaks with human moral tradition and threatens to roast and eat an innocent character to whom he has been speaking. The terrified youngster cowers under the enormous, jagged shadow of the murderous coyote: "He was the fastest animal back on the rancho, and normally he could outrun the coyote. But he was tired from the long journey. He could not reach the door. He could not reach the window. All he could do was huddle in a corner as the coyote slowly approached." Pancho's reduction to a meal for a hungry predator dramatizes the victimization of immigrants forced to rely on treacherous strangers to reach their destinations.

As if by magic, Pancho is rescued by his father and his friends, who were returning after being robbed of their money and gifts by a gang of crows, sadly paralleling the reality of many migrant workers. The jubilation of the fiesta held upon the homecoming of Papá, Pancho and the other breadwinners is dampened by an ambiguous ending: after Papá projects more trips to the North in case of future droughts, the children express a wish to accompany him, while Mamá simply hopes it rains. As Tonatiuh affirms in an "Author's Note" filled with facts about immigration to the U.S., "We seldom see the dangerous journey immigrants go through to reach the U.S. and the longing that their families feel for them back at home. It is my desire that [this book] captures some of that sentiment; ironically, the animals convey the *human* emotions and side of the story." Unflinching narratives like Tonatiuh's challenge the perception that, as Mary Pat Brady has observed, "…in general, the stories that enfold Latino/a children into the ambit of representability emphasize extended, heteronormative, happy families and the broad-spirited facility of Spanglish—which is to say quotidian pleasures rather than equally quotidian dangers" (380). While Pancho's family is depicted as lovingly united throughout the trials of separation, their allegorical tale depicts an all-too-common set of experiences, blurring the line in a way that will be recognizable to children of immigrant parents and understandable to readers unfamiliar with the challenges they face.

A good number of books feature parrots, drawing on both their associations with different areas of the Spanish-speaking world and their more humanlike features and abilities. The unusual pet in Juan Felipe Herrera's *Featherless/Desplumado* is depicted by illustrator Ernesto Cuevas, Jr., as strikingly similar to Tomasito, the boy to whom the young parrot is gifted by his father in the opening scene. The child, who uses a wheelchair due to spina bifida, quickly notes the bird's disabled foot and leg and his lack of feathers, observing that this latter distinction makes it impossible for him to fly (4–5). Initially resistant to bonding with his new roommate despite the physical challenges they share, Tomasito is too wrapped up in his own concerns about making friends at a new school and his desire to play soccer to attend to Desplumado; his dismissal of the bird echoes his own experience of being excluded from the other children's play.

As the child warms up to his new classmates and is invited to participate in his favorite sport using his wheelchair as "wings" (12), he finds compassion for his pet, warming him up with a feather from his own pillow. After a successful soccer performance, Tomasito finds himself dreaming about flying alongside the parrot, both magically free of the physical limitations of their waking lives. When the child awakes and injures his back attempting to stand, while Desplumado stretches his wings sympathetically, his response to his concerned father reveals the true meaning of the dream: "'I want Desplumado to fly, to feel the edges of the sky!' I say. 'You mean, *you* want to fly, *hijo*,' Papi says" (26). The parrot's semi-anthropomorphic response goes undepicted in an illustration focused on the bond between father and son: "Desplumado nods his little naked head and shakes his smooth wings" (26). After scoring another goal on the soccer field, the protagonist cannot wait to share the news with his pet, who jumps onto his hand, clearly acknowledging a trusting relationship with his new owner. The boy's final words to Desplumado ("'You can be a flyer too, Desplumado. There's more than one way to fly!'" [30]) are accompanied by a close-up image of the two staring into each other's dark eyes, the earthy tones of the parrot's featherless body blending seamlessly with the child's skin and shirt (31). While Herrera's note at the end aims to raise awareness about spina bifida and its causes (32), the text sends a positive, inclusive message about different abilities and about the formation of loving human/animal relationships.

A pet parrot helps a human character with another set of challenges in *Mango, Abuela and Me*. Meg Medina tells the story of a Spanish-speaking grandmother who struggles to adjust to life in a city after leaving behind her island home. As the young narrator relates in first person her initial attempts to communicate with her older relative, an Angela Dominguez illustration reveals a clear separation of species. While Abuela and Mia cuddle together to look at a book, a teddy bear rests against a pillow to the right, while Mia's pet hamster, Edmund, plays on a hamster wheel inside a cage with thick bars. Abuela's connection to wild parrots is evident in one of only two keepsakes she has brought from home: a red parrot feather found in her suitcase along with a photograph of Mia's grandfather. Mia and Abuela struggle valiantly to learn each other's primary languages, but when one day their practice is interrupted by Mia's trip to a pet store to purchase seeds for Edmund, the girl spots the answer to their communicative challenges: a parrot sporting red wings evocative of her grandmother's treasured feather.

The new pet's presence provides a golden opportunity for language teaching and learning as they teach him to speak in both languages and to dance to traditional songs. While he is caged in most illustrations, one side of the cage is invariably kept open, suggesting a level of freedom denied the hamster, who is never seen outside some sort of enclosure (a cage or hamster ball). Soon Mango is outside with Abuela visiting with the neighbors, who find it increasingly easy to converse with the bird's owner as, with his help, her English grows more sophisticated. The story ends with Mia drawing a picture of Mango, who smiles from his open-sided cage as if posing for his human companions. Below the dedications and other end matter appears an image of a free-ranging Mango pushing Edmund in his little ball, reinforcing the bird's elevated position in the household hierarchy. The parrot's capacity to interact with the family and broader community through bilingual speech locates him in a privileged but liminal space between two species, as he simultaneously mirrors Abuela's position as a tropical transplant adjusting to a new geographic and cultural context.

Finally, a book about a real-life Latin American hero relies on a selective anthropomorphism to bolster its message about literacy. *Waiting for the Biblioburro*, by the same duo (Monica Brown and John Parra) who created *Frida Kahlo and her Animalitos*, features images of animals throughout its simple story of an extraordinary intervention into the life of a country family. Pets, farmed animals, free-ranging birds and monkeys establish the rural Colombian setting in which young Ana longs for an education as she does her chores. Most of the nonhuman beings are depicted with reasonably realistic forms, colors and behaviors, though two goats appear to smile, and a butterfly can be seen atop a tree, leaning over as if to enjoy a book Ana is reading. More fantastic creatures appear as Ana spins bedtime stories for her younger brother: the illustration shows hybrid-looking beasts cavorting in a natural space with trees, flowers, volcanoes and a waterfall.

Ana's and the other local children's lives are turned upside down by the appearance of the Biblioburro operation: two smiling burros carrying books through the country-side, along with a depiction of Luis Soriano Bohórquez, the librarian who initiated the program. The two laboring animals smile contentedly, eyes closed, through a series of illustrations, apparently happy to be serving the cause of children's library services. Counter-intuitively, increased access to books brings the community of young readers into a closer relationship with nature. In the earlier scene in which Ana reads the only book she owns, she ignores both the inquisitive butterfly and a larger-than-life ladybug crawling towards her; the new stories she discovers open a new world filled with performing animals (a trumpet-playing monkey and a pink dolphin balancing a ball on his or her nose), a smiling lion, and the ever-present burros, who continue to smile while feeding on the grass nearby. Parra's inclusion of happy, eager-to-please creatures imparts a positive tone to a story that has the potential to open discussions about human uses of animals, and the "Author's Note" at the end erases their contributions completely: "This book is a cel-ebration of Luis and all the teachers and librarians who bring books to children every-where—across deserts, fields, mountains and water." The warm, reassuring illustrations put to rest any concerns about the care and treatment of beasts of burden forced to work for the betterment of human characters, and readers from outside the culture portrayed are encouraged to focus on the uplifting message about empowerment through educa-tion.

As protagonists or in supporting roles, in bilingual or monolingual texts, animal characters add depth, complexity and considerable appeal to books written for and about Latinx children. These texts play a crucial role in children's education and development, by recreating familiar experiences for children who recognize their own cultures, and by opening up new worlds to those looking at the characters' experiences from the outside. As Belinda J. Acosta has observed, "All young people need to see themselves, but they need to see that world, whether it's on the other side of the planet or in that house on Mango Street. To see something of themselves reflected in other children … helps us see each other's humanity and inspires us to make room at the table instead of building fences, and perhaps—just perhaps—draws us closer to embracing instead of vilifying those unlike ourselves" (Aldama 255). Further, referring to the Latinx authors whom he interviewed for *Latino/a Children's and Young Adult Writers on the Art of Storytelling*, Frederick Luis Aldama points out that "[t]hey all talk about creating literature that seeks to open up multiple spaces of culture and of geographic and linguistic experience to enrich the lives of all other readers that make up the nation as a whole" (14). The animal characters in these books do more than open windows onto other human cultures: they invite readers to respect and to learn from their animality as they literally and figuratively bridge the gaps and blur the lines between species. The in-between condition of anthro-pomorphic animals allows for rich explorations of the double cultural identity of Latinx children, their families and their literary heroes.

NOTE

1. The inclusive term "Latinx" is used throughout this article as a gender-neutral alternative to "Latino(s)" or "Latina(s)." The use of this newer term is increasingly common in academic writing and in educational settings.

WORKS CITED

Acosta, Belinda J. "Afterword: We All Need Chocolate Factories and Casitas on Mango Street." *Latino/a Children's and Young Adult Writers on the Art of Storytelling*, by Frederick Luis Aldama, U Pittsburgh P, 2018. 253–255.

Ada, Alma Flor. "Author's Note." *The Lizard and the Sun/La lagartija y el sol*, by Ada, illustrated by Felipe Dávalos, translated by Rosalma Zubizarreta, Bantam Doubleday Dell, 1997.

_____. *The Lizard and the Sun/La lagartija y el sol*. Illustrated by Felipe Dávalos, translated by Rosalma Zubizarreta, Bantam Doubleday Dell, 1997.

Agra Deedy, Carmen. *Martina the Beautiful Cockroach: A Cuban Folktale*. Illustrated by Michael Austin, Peachtree, 2013.

Alarcón, Francisco. *Animal Poems of the Iguaza/Animalario del Iguazu*. Illustrated by Maya Christina Gonzalez, Children's Book Press, 2008.

_____. *Iguanas in the Snow and Other Winter Poems/Iguanas en la nieve y otros poemas de invierno*. Illustrated by Maya Christina Gonzalez, Children's Book Press/Editorial Libros para Niños, 2001.

_____. "Introduction." *Animal Poems of the Iguaza/Animalario del Iguazu*, by Alarcón, illustrated by Maya Christina Gonzalez, Children's Book Press, 2008.

Aldama, Frederick Luis. "Duncan Tonatiuh." Aldama. 241–246.

_____. *Latino/a Children's and Young Adult Writers on the Art of Storytelling*. University of Pittsburgh Press, 2018.

_____. "Monica Brown." Aldama. 41–48.

Anzaldúa, Gloria. *Prietita and the Ghost Woman/Prietita y la Llorona*. Illustrated by Christina Gonzalez, Children's Book Press/Libros para Niños, 1995.

_____. "When I was a little girl…" *Prietita and the Ghost Woman/Prietita y la Llorona*, by Anzaldúa, illustrated by Christina Gonzalez, Children's Book Press/Libros para Niños, 1995.

Brady, Mary Pat. "Children's Literature." *The Routledge Companion o Latino/a Literature*. Routledge, 2012. 375–382.

Brown, Monica. "Author's Note." *Frida Kahlo and Her Animalitos*, by Brown, illustrated by John Parra, North-South, 2017.

_____. "Author's Note." *Waiting for the Biblioburro*, by Brown, illustrated by John Parra, Tricycle Press, 2011.

_____. *Frida Kahlo and Her Animalitos*. Illustrated by John Parra, NorthSouth, 2017.

_____. *Waiting for the Biblioburro*. Illustrated by John Parra, Tricycle Press, 2011.

Campbell Naidoo, Jamie, editor. *Celebrating Cuentos: Promoting Latino Children's Literature and Literacy in Classrooms and Libraries*. Libraries Unlimited, 2011.

Colato Laínez, René. *The Tooth Fairy Meets El Ratón Pérez*. Illustrated by Tom Lintern, Tricycle Press, 2010.

_____. *Maria Had a Little Llama/María tenía una llamita*. Henry Holt and Company, 2013.

_____. "Who Are the Tooth Fairy and El Ratón Pérez?" *The Tooth Fairy Meets El Ratón Pérez*, by Colato Laínez, illustrated by Tom Lintern, Tricycle Press, 2010.

Garza de Cortes, Oralia, and Jennifer Battle. "Sliding Door 1: The Politics of Publishing Latino Children's Books." Campbell Naidoo and Park Dahlen. 63–66.

González, Lucía M. *The Bossy Gallito/El gallo de bodas: A Traditional Cuban Folktale*. Illustrated by Lulu Delacre, Scholastic, 1994.

_____. "About the Bossy Rooster." *The Bossy Gallito/El gallo de bodas: A Traditional Cuban Folktale*, by González, illustrated by Lulu Delacre, Scholastic, 1994.

_____. "Foreword." *Señor Cat's Romance and Other Favorite Stories from Latin America*, by González, illustrated by Lulu Delacre, Scholastic, 1997.

_____. *Señor Cat's Romance and Other Favorite Stories from Latin America*. Illustrated by Lulu Delacre, Scholastic, 1997.

Gonzalez, Maya Christina. "A note about the artwork," *Animal Poems of the Iguazú/Animalario del Iguazú*, by Francisco X. Alarcón, illustrated by Maya Christina Gonzalez, Children's Book Press, 2008. 32.

Herrera, Juan Felipe. "Everyone Asks Tomasito…" *Featherless/Desplumado*, by Herrera, illustrated by Ernesto Cuevas, Jr., Children's Book Press/Editorial Libros para Niños, 2004. 32.

_____. *Featherless/Desplumado*. Illustrated by Ernesto Cuevas, Jr., Children's Book Press/Editorial Libros para Niños, 2004.

Kimmel, Eric A. *Medio Pollito/Half Chick*. Illustrated by Valeria Docampo, Marshall Cavendish Children, 2010.

_____. "A Note about the Tale." *Medio Pollito/Half Chick*, by Kimmel, illustrated by Valeria Docampo, Marshall Cavendish Children, 2010.

Martín-Rodríguez, Manuel M. "Children's Literature sin Fronteras: *Mesticismo* and Ecopoetics in Francisco X. Alarcón's *Animal Poems of the Iguazú*. *The Bilingual Review/La Revista Bilingüe*, vol. XXXIII, no. 5, 2017. 76–90.

Medina, Meg. *Mango, Abuela and Me*. Illustrated by Angela Dominguez, Candlewick, 2015.

Middleton Elya, Susan. *Little Roja Riding Hood*. Illustrated by Susan Guevara, G.P. Putnam's Sons, 2014.

Morales, Yuyi. "Foreword: Splendid Treasures of *Mi Corazón*." Campbell Naidoo. ix–xi.

Salinas, Bobbi. "Summary." *Los tres cerdos/The Three Pigs: Nacho, Tito y Miguel*, by Salinas, Spanish version by Amapola Franzen and Marcos Guerrero, Piñata, 1998.

_____. *Los tres cerdos/The Three Pigs: Nacho, Tito y Miguel*. Spanish version by Amapola Franzen and Marcos Guerrero, Piñata, 1998.

Schachner, Judy. *Skippyjon Jones in the Doghouse*. Puffin, 2005.

Soto, Gary. *Chato's Kitchen*. Illustrated by Susan Guevara, G.P. Putnam's Sons, 1995.

Tafolla, Carmen. *Baby Coyote and the Old Woman/El Coyotito y la VIejita*. Illustrated by Matt Novak, Wings, 2000.

Tonatiuh, Duncan. "Author's Note." *Pancho Rabbit and the Coyote: A Migrant's Tale*, by Tonatiuh, Abrams Books for Young Readers, 2013.

_____. *Pancho Rabbit and the Coyote: A Migrant's Tale*. Abrams Books for Young Readers, 2013.

Friend or Food?

The Limits of Anthropomorphism at Disney

Kristi Maxwell

In Coral Reef, a seafood restaurant situated alongside a *Finding Nemo*–inspired ride in Epcot, the official Walt Disney World website encourages guests to "watch fish, sharks, turtles and rays swim in the Seas with Nemo & Friends aquarium while you enjoy seafood, steak and chicken." A server approaches a family of four that includes two young boys and asks them if they've had a chance to look over the menu. One of the young boys points to the fish swirling around in the panoramic aquarium and asks, "Are we going to eat *them*?" The server, with a speed that suggests he has engaged this question before, responds, "No, those are Mickey's friends."

The answer itself recalls the vegetarian sharks and their support meeting in Disney's Pixar film *Finding Nemo* (2003). Not eating fish acts as a type of sobriety in the film— the structure of the meeting borrows from the structure of Alcoholics Anonymous— suggesting that meat-eating is an addiction or choice (rather than a biological imperative). The meeting begins with a pledge: "I am a nice shark, not a mindless eating machine. If I am to change this image [of myself as a mindless eating machine], I must first change myself. Fish are friends, not food" (*Finding Nemo*). Here, meat-eating is tied to the rote, iterating how the habitual becomes naturalized through repetition. Though Coral Reef incorporates Nemo and Friends into the restaurant experience, it does so without taking any meaningful notes from the film in which those characters appear, reversing the mantra "Fish are friends, not food" to "Fish are food, not friends." In the film, the trio of vegetarian sharks works to hold each other accountable and intervene when interven-tion is needed (for instance, after the smell of the forgetful blue tang Dory's blood awakens the shark Bruce's appetite for fish). The vegetarian sharks—carnivores *by nature*—are used to play on popular arguments regarding humans and eating habits: "but humans are omnivores *by nature*." The sharks prevail in changing their nature; the film's ending implies they're still "on the wagon," as Dory is seen leaving one of their meetings after returning to the reef with Marlin and Nemo.

The disjunction between filmic message and Disney park menus is not isolated to *Finding Nemo* and Coral Reef. Magic Kingdom visitors encounter and giddily hug Piglet then pose for a picture with Donald Duck before they saunter on to Belle and the Beast's banquet hall for their reservation at Be Our Guest, whose menu includes *coq au vin*-style braised pork and Croque Monsieur, an open-faced ham sandwich topped with cheeses and a fried egg—and, if these options do not satisfy, one need only hop on the monorail to arrive at Chefs de France in Epcot for *canard aux cerises* (duck breast with cherries). Interestingly, "the gray stuff" that Lumière encourages Belle to try during her first feast at the Beast's castle in the Disney-animated film *Beauty and the Beast* (1991)— presumably *pâté de foie gras,* given the aristocratic French setting—is imagined as a mousse dessert at Be Our Guest, which suggests that imaginative food interventions are not impossibilities within the Disney parks' structure. The phrase "the gray stuff" itself reinforces the significance that naming plays in eating practices, where animals are routinely erased from the foods they become, e.g., "calf" becomes "veal." In *The Sexual Politics of Meat*, feminist-vegetarian scholar Carol J. Adams explores practices of naming, marketing, and erasure:

> Behind every meal of meat is an absence: the death of the animal whose place the meat takes. The "absent referent" is that which separates the meat eater from the animal and the animals from the end product. The function of the absent referent is to keep our "meat" separated from any idea that she or he was once an animal, to keep the "moo" or "cluck" or "baa" away from the meat, to keep some*thing* from being seen as some*one*. [14].

The paradigm of animals-as-food is used to create scenes of horror and dramatic conflict in the Disney films versus an ostensibly gourmand experience in the parks. For instance, one goes from rooting for the crab in crab vs. chef in Disney's *The Little Mermaid* (1989) to praising the chef for his crab dish in any of the upscale dining options in the parks: humans, as it turns out, are fickle fans. In *Some We Love, Some We Hate, Some We Eat*, anthrozoologist Hal Herzog examines humans' complicated and inconsistent relationships with nonhuman animals. He writes,

> The moral psychologist Jonathan Haidt says, when push comes to shove, we are all hypocrites. [...] [T]he vast majority of us are inconsistent, often wildly so, in our attitudes and behaviors toward other species. What are we to make of this?
> In the 1950s, the social psychologist Leon Festinger proposed one of the most influential theories in psychology—that when our beliefs, behaviors, and attitudes are at odds, we experience a state that he called cognitive dissonance. Because dissonance is uncomfortable, people should be motivated to reduce these psychic conflicts caused by inconsistency. We might, for example, change our beliefs or our behaviors, or we might distort or deny the evidence [Herzog 261].

This moral inconsistency is satirized in Disney's *Moana* (2016), in which Moana, the daughter of the island's chief, samples pork in front of her friend Pua, a pig whose very name translates to "pig" *and* "pork" (Bush), redressing the tendency to erase the animal from the meat, but doing so in translation, suggesting the English-speaking world's relationship to food necessitates repression. Moana comments on the tastiness of the pork, exclaiming, "Mmm! That is good pork!" and causing Pua to give her a confused, sad look, to which she fumbles to respond, "Oh! I didn't mean ... no, I wasn't.... What? They're calling me, so I gotta.... Bye!" (*Moana*). It is perhaps the shame Moana experiences in this moment that leads her to consider the ways in which certain bodies are valued and thus treated as expendable or nonexpendable in a later scene when a member of her community suggests they eat her rooster friend HeiHei. After observing HeiHei pecking at a rock, the villager questions the intelligence of the bird, suggesting that a lack of intelligence justifies killing. He asks Moana, "Can we just ... cook him?" Moana replies, "Well, some of our strengths lie beneath the surface, while others ... far beneath. But I'm pretty sure there's a lot more to HeiHei than meets the eye," a reply that revolves around claims of interiority, imagining an inner life for the rooster friend. Later, HeiHei is reduced to a "boat snack" when he first encounters the demigod Maui; by the end of their time together, when HeiHei has successfully transitioned from food to friend, Maui affectionately calls him "Drumstick," a reminder that the rooster's protection is tenuous: he is safe … for now.[1]

While Alan Tudyk voices HeiHei, Pua is *voiced* by real pigs (Flaherty), adding an additional layer of complexity to the intersection of human and animal that is typically represented in the animated animal figures. Here, the nonhuman animal communicates with the human animal through a means other than language, unconsciously evoking philosopher and posthumanist theorist Donna Haraway's concept of "response-ability." For Haraway, response-ability is not only the ability to respond to one another, but also a responsibility to promote multispecies flourishing and a call to recognize multifarious modes of communication.

Lines Drawn and Blurred

The cognitive dissonance one experiences in Disney parks, where one ricochets between encounters with the animals one loves and animals one eats, highlights the blurred line between animal and human. The dissonance is arguably worth examining because of an animal rights ethos at work in so many Disney films. Etymologically, *animation*, "the action of imparting life," stems from *animāre*, "to give breath to, to enliven with a particular spirit." Eating animals requires animation's opposite: the action of taking life. Animation raises questions about connection. To what extent do viewers love the animal on screen and to what extent do viewers love the human deposited inside the animal, the voice actor—the coin in the piggy bank, a metaphor that brings issues of worth and value to the fore? The animated animal characters in the films and the fur characters in the Disney parks exemplify the powers and limits of anthropomorphism: the fact that identification processes can engender love for an individual, but not care for a group or species. To love because one sees oneself in another—here, the human in the animal—is ultimately to love oneself, not to love the other.

Even so, films can have real effects, and their lessons can aid those who, negotiating cognitive dissonance, seek to "change [their] beliefs or [their] behaviors" (Herzog 261). In fact, viewers' relationships to animals in films *have* influenced changes in behaviors, as moral philosopher Nathan Nobis argues in his elucidation of "the Babe effect," the film *Babe*'s documented influence on vegetarianism in young people, especially preteen and teenage girls. While some dismiss the film's effect as merely sentimental and emotional, Nobis argues that the film's birth of new vegetarians is bound to its moral reasoning, claiming "there is a strong, inspiring, case for vegetarianism found in the film" (n.p.). Nobis writes, "Thus, I argue that *Babe* helps us get the facts right about animal minds," going on to explain,

What are animals like, according to *Babe*? Of course, in the film animals can *talk*—that's false—but what does the film present that is true? Many things. At a most basic level, the film presents animals having minds: they have beliefs and desires: they want things and have beliefs about how to get them. Animals are not mindless, preference¬less beings: what happens to them matters to them, even if it doesn't matter to anyone else. It shows animals having emotions: they can be sad and lonely, happy and content. Most importantly, it shows that animals can feel pleasure and pain: they can *suffer* [n.p.].

Disney films time and again depict animals in distress, and films' arcs are often organized around eliminating this distress. To return to *Finding Nemo*, shortly after Nemo is deposited in the dentist's aquarium, Gill, another tropical fish in the tank who once made his home in the ocean, laments to Nemo, "Fish aren't meant to be in a box, kid. It does things to you." Later, after the tank gang's escape plan has failed, Nemo and his new allies improvise, working to ensure that Nemo does not go home with the dentist's niece, Darla "the fish killer," who reflects the ways ostensible "innocence" masks and excuses real violence. During the uproarious scene, pelican Nigel flaps around the dentist's office, and Gill is launched from the tank, causing the dentist to exclaim, "Crikey! All the animals have gone mad!" Of course, the dentist's reading of this scene implicitly revolves around an argument of definition: one (human) animal's "madness" is another (nonhuman) animal's liberation, cheekily recalling Australian philosopher Peter Singer's seminal text *Animal Liberation: A New Ethics for Treating Animals* (1975), which popularized the concept of *speciesism*. The tank gang challenges speciesism, wherein humans are determined superior as a species and thus get to decide the fates of other animals.

The dentist believes that his capture of Nemo is philanthropic, announcing, upon depositing Nemo in the office tank, "I found that little guy struggling for life out on the reef, and I saved him."[2] However, just as Marlin does not "read human" and is thus unable to make sense of the writing on the diving mask recovered at Nemo's abduction site, the dentist is unable to "read fish" and thus misinterprets the ocean encounter. The aquarium, here, is a site of conflict and imprisonment, the latter of which is reinforced by Gill's black-and-white stripes recast as prison wear. Viewers root for Nemo and his tank mates to escape, to get back to the ocean.

Animal-Human Hierarchies

Moana and Disney's *The Princess and the Frog* (2009) both thematize the blurred line between (nonhuman) animal and human. In fact, blurring the line is part of both films. In *Moana*, not only does the demigod Maui have the ability to shape-shift, becoming an insect, hawk, shark, and so on, but also Moana's grandmother reincarnates as a stingray. Similarly to the Beast in *Beauty and the Beast*, in *The Princess and the Frog*, both the protagonist Tiana and her eventual love interest Prince Naveen are turned into frogs (before turning back into humans). This transmogrification is heightened in light of Tiana's ambition to open a Cajun restaurant where frog, one presumes, given its ubiquity on menus throughout New Orleans, is likely to be part of the menu. In fact, one of the dramatic arcs revolves around Tiana and Naveen's escape from the clutches of a small boatful of poor white frog hunters.[3] Tiana and Naveen's animal ally, the trumpet-playing alligator Louis, is no less vulnerable, given the number of Cajun recipes that call for gator. Mardi Gras provides Louis with an opportunity to perform with a jazz band whose members are dressed up as various animals, which allows them to "see" Louis as an equal (which is to say, as one of them: a human), inviting him to sit in with them, a scene that contrasts with Louis' memory of an attempt to play jazz "with the big boys" hired to play on a riverboat; in the flashback, as Louis begins to jam, the riverboat passengers scream and scatter.

The Princess and the Frog is framed around reimagining human and nonhuman-animal hierarchies. An early song in the film, "When We're Human," finds Tiana, Naveen, and Louis describing what their lives as humans will look like. For Louis, being human is being given permission—to exist, to play music—to be human is to be celebrated. For Naveen, being human is pursuing pleasure. Tiana chastises Naveen's hedonism with her work ethic and sense of accountability. She sings, "When I'm a human being/ At least I'll act like one" (*The Princess and the Frog*). She punctuates the song's thesis that being human is a privilege (and complicates this idea by alluding to socioeconomic barriers certain humans have to encounter and overcome, singing, "I've worked hard for everything I've got"). If "When We're Human" suggests that being human is the ideal, then one of the final songs, "Dig a Little Deeper," challenges this claim, suggesting that uncritical valorization of the human is short-sighted. Voodoo priestess Mama Odie asks Tiana and Naveen what they need, to which Tiana answers, "We need to be human." Mama Odie responds, "Y'all wanna be human, but you're blind to what you need." Mama Odie's dismissal of the *need* to be human is perhaps unsurprising; she has enmeshed herself in the world of nonhuman animals, living in the swamp with a coterie of birds and snakes. Playing on the familiar trope of the blind prophet who *sees* differently (and thus with more insight), Mama Odie's lesson helps Tiana and Naveen embrace their animal-selves, singing, "Don't matter what you look like / […] Don't even matter what you are / A dog, a pig, a cow, a goat / Got 'em all in here / We got them all in here." She highlights the human connection to the larger animal world, in our very make-up ("We got them all in here"). After Tiana and Naveen miss the opportunity to be kissed and thus transformed back into humans, they affirmatively claim their identities as nonhuman animals: "We're staying frogs, and we're staying together."

Similarly to the knife-wielding chef in *The Little Mermaid* and fur-loving Cruella de Vil in *101 Dalmatians*, Louis identifies "trappers and hunters with guns" as a threat to the film's protagonists. Humans who see the lives of animals as expendable—as theirs to extinguish—are framed as antagonists: the bad guys.

Remy the rat, star of the Disney's Pixar film *Ratatouille* (2007), finds ways around his nonhuman form in order to cook in the kitchen of Chef Gusteau's famed restaurant and acts as a triumphant example of the late chef's axiom "Anyone can cook." The fact that Remy occupies the space of "anyone" rather than "anything" is also a subtle gesture toward questions of subjectivity. In the film, after a 2-D cookbook illustration of the chef transforms into a 3-D version who acts as a literal "spirit guide" for Remy, leading him to the restaurant in Paris, Remy finds a co-conspirator in Linguini, garbage boy and son of the late Gusteau.[4] Each has an attribute the other needs to be successful in the contemporary restaurant kitchen: Remy, cooking skills, and Linguini, human form.[5] Remy takes the reins (in this case, Linguini's hair) and steers Linguini toward excellence in cooking. To say it differently, Remy "animates" the young cook, highlighting the animal in the human, a reversal that parallels the spirit guide reversal—conventionally spirit guides are represented as animals aiding the human.

Overall, the relationship Remy and Linguini develop is mutually beneficial: Linguini gets to make not only a name for himself, but a career, and Remy gets to be housed and is given the opportunity to put his skills and passion to use. That said, the film still negotiates issues of exploitation: the morning before Remy and Linguini's first day of work as cooks in the kitchen, Remy gets up early to make them omelets. Linguini scarfs his down and yanks Remy out of the house before he's had time to eat his. Only when Linguini recognizes Remy's lethargy in the restaurant does it dawn on him that Remy is hungry. Throughout the film, the act of taking food is framed as stealing for Remy. The spirit of

Gusteau admonishes Remy on several occasions, telling him not to steal food from the kitchen, and, after their first night as roommates, Linguini wakes up feeling certain that Remy has stolen from him (he hasn't: he has not disappeared, as Linguini suspects, but, instead, he's in the kitchen preparing breakfast). At issue here is compensation and exploitation: at what point has Remy *earned a right* to food, especially inside a system where his labor is invisible (both metaphorically and literally, hidden as he is under Linguini's chef hat)? Remy must depend on Linguini to determine and dispense his meals, a subtle reminder of the human-animal hierarchy that is troubled in the film, but not displaced.

The film grapples with the concept of one's nature through an exploration of innate abilities and questions of inheritance—something presumed to be "in one's blood" and thus "natural." In the film's opening scene, we learn that Remy's longstanding heightened sense of smell and taste has positioned him not only to appreciate food in ways his garbage-loving family cannot, but also to be the poison-detector, saving his colony from extermination. Linguini, on the other hand, may be the son of Gusteau, but cooking is not "in his blood," though he uses the cultural myth of inheritance to explain his ability to cook—despite his lack of formal training—at a press conference late in the film, after "his" dishes have seemingly single-handedly (double-pawedly?) reinvigorated the restaurant's menu and saved its reputation.

Of note, the dish that has everyone clamoring to get a table at Gusteau's is *confit biyaldi*, a refined version of ratatouille, a rustic stewed vegetable dish. This stands in contrast to fine-dining standards represented in Chef Skinner's kitchen upon Remy's arrival to Paris and the restaurant: racks of lamb, salmon, filets, duck, foie gras. In fact, Skinner, who dines at Gusteau's at a table nearby the critic Anton Ego in the penultimate scene scoffs at Remy's signature dish upon its arrival: "Ratatouille? They must be joking." This is perhaps unsurprising, given Skinner's warning to Linguini earlier in the film: "One can get too familiar with vegetables, you know." Skinner's words resonate with depictions of certain high-powered male chefs who treat vegetarianism as anathema.[6] In *The Sexual Politics of Meat*, one of Adams' foundational arguments is that "meat is part of the cultural mythology of maleness" (18):

> It has traditionally been felt that the working man needs meat for strength. A superstition analogous to homeopathic principles operates in this belief: in eating the muscle of strong animals, we will become strong. According to the mythology of patriarchal culture, meat promotes strength; the attributes of masculinity are achieved through eating these masculine foods. Visions of meat-eating football players, wrestlers, and boxers lumber in our brains in this equation. Though vegetarian weight lifters and athletes in other fields have demonstrated the equation to be fallacious, the myth remains: men are strong, men need to be strong, thus men need meat. The literal evocation of male power is found in the concept of meat [43].

One of Disney's most hyperbolic representations of this phenomenon is found in the figure of *Beauty and the Beast*'s antagonist Gaston. In the animated film, the scene for the musical number "Gaston" opens with the entitled Gaston muttering, from his veritable animal throne—a large chair upholstered with animal hide and supported by four large animal horns—in light of Belle's rejection, "Who does she think she is? […] No one says no to Gaston." His sidekick LeFou tries to cheer him by asserting (in song), "Every guy here [at the tavern] would love to be you, Gaston." The song exposes Gaston's superlative male status as superficial, relying on physical attributes such as his thick neck. Somewhat bolstered, Gaston joins the song, flexing his arm muscles and bragging, "As a specimen, yes, I'm intimidating." LeFou pipes in, "Not a bit of him's scraggly or scrawny," to which Gaston replies, "That's right, and every last inch of me's covered with hair," after which he goes on to divulge the secrets to his strength: "When I was a lad, I ate four dozen eggs every morning to help me get large, and, now that I'm grown, I eat five dozen eggs, so I'm roughly the size of a barge." Masculinity, physicality, and protein-consumption are intricately bound together in this image, as is a valuation of nonhuman animals in terms of personal trophy: "I use antlers in all of my decorating," Gaston pronounces, gesturing toward a wall of mounted animal heads from the cradle of his animal-clad chair. Adams stresses to readers the relationship between the oppression of women and the oppression of animals, writing, "Manhood is constructed in our culture, in part, by access to meat eating and control of other bodies" (17). To flaunt animal death—"control of others' bodies"—is to perform the hegemonic ideal of masculinity. However, this version of masculinity, embodied by the film's antagonist and revolving around strength and power, is shown to be weak as the story of Belle and the Beast unfolds.

Compassionate Futures

The resistance toward imagining a more compassionate future is not limited to *Ratatouille*'s Chef Skinner. When trying to convince Remy to rethink his idea that rats and humans could harmoniously exist alongside one another, Remy's father, Django, takes him to look into the window of a pest control store and implores him to recognize that "the world we live in belongs to the enemy [humans]—we must live carefully; we look out for our own kind; when all is said and done, we're all we got" (*Ratatouille*). Remy challenges his father, asking, "You're telling me that the future is—can only be—more of this?" "This" is not only "humans as enemies," but also a capitalist system that invests in animal death over animal life. Django goes on to claim, "This is the way things are. You can't change nature," to which Remy replies, "Change is nature—and it starts when we decide."[7] By inserting the notion of "choice" into a conceptualization of the "natural" (and reinforcing nature as an adaptive system rather than one of rote repetition), Remy complicates ideas of what exactly counts as "natural" and suggests that social constructions of normalcy can supplant "nature": this is especially relevant in food culture, where certain stigmatized eating practices (notably, veganism) are integrated into menu options by way of "allergy-friendly" options, as is the case at the Disney parks, where egg-free and dairy-free options are sequestered to the allergy-friendly menus, launched in 2015 (Brandon). Intentionally or not, this shift in identifiers (from "animal-free" to "allergy-friendly") naturalizes (and thus depoliticizes) choice, making X something one *can't* eat rather than something one *chooses* not to eat, muting analysis of eating practices.

At the D23 Expo, July 14–16, 2017, in Anaheim, California, Walt Disney Parks and Resorts Chairman Bob Chapek and Imagineer Tom Fitzgerald shared information about Epcot updates, including the addition of a *Ratatouille* ride modeled after the one in Disneyland Paris, in which riders "shrink down to the size of Remy and join him on a crazy race throughout the kitchen of Gusteau's restaurant" (Inside the Magic). Upon reviewing the Parisian version of the ride, one sees that the "race" throughout the kitchen would better be characterized as a "chase," as riders in their "ratmobiles" avoid Chef Skinner's clutching hands. Scheduled to be completed in 2021, coinciding with Disney World's fiftieth anniversary, the ride will be a part of the France Pavillion in the World Showcase and is part of a larger project to make Epcot attractions "more timeless, more relevant, more family, and more Disney" (Inside the Magic). The conceit of the ride itself is worth pondering. Here, the act of shrinking down—making oneself small—is the agent for possible self-identity. What are the goals of such identification? What does it mean for park guests to situate themselves inside rat bodies? If the rat is the vehicle, what is the metaphor? The ride organizes itself around a vision of empathy whose banner and method is a celebration of "walking in someone else's shoes"—a call for one to be mobilized, which, on its surface, might seem laudable.

In *When Species Meet*, Haraway points out that the "move of claiming to see from the point of view of the other" is "facile and basically imperialist, if well intentioned" (21). The ride promotes a version of empathy that relies on occupying others' positions in order to access their point of view—occupation being the operative word. One's attempt to *see as* does not allow one to *see*—to use Haraway's language, there is no opportunity for an "intersecting gaze," no opportunity for mutual recognition, and thus no avenues for "response-ability."

The casting of humans in animal roles for human purposes and pleasure epitomizes the failures of empathy, why "walking in another's shoes" is an inadequate intervention upon oppression—limited forms of habitation do not lead to happy co-habitation. Here anthropomorphism is a conceit that allows humans to distance themselves from "animals." There is, after all, no line—blurred or otherwise—between human and animal, as the human is animal and that which we demarcate "animal" (to distinguish it from ourselves) really signifies "nonhuman animals." A trip to the Disney theme parks, then, is entangled with questions of how to distinguish the animals one loves from the animals one eats from thriving animals from endangered and/or exploited animals.

Speaking to the ethos of the park, Fitzgerald claims, "Epcot has always been, from day one, an optimistic celebration of the *real* world […] it's really a living showcase of the world we've created and the world we continue to create together." Chapek further elucidated "the DNA of Epcot," highlighting "ideals of optimism, hope and awe and wonder of our world" (Inside the Magic). Both Fitzgerald and Chapek stress optimism. Yet, if we break down claims about Epcot, the place these ideals are missing is in the food, even as consumer demand and investments in plant-based companies and products grow on a national and international level.[8] Haraway opens *When Species Meet* with the question, "How is 'becoming with' a practice of becoming worldly?" and stresses that humans exist "in relation" to multispecies networks and habitats (3). Humans must ask how outdated "top-of-the-food-chain" paradigms can be reimagined to address the need for mutual thriving and eating practices that prioritize sustainability.

Perhaps unsurprisingly, one of the park's most enduring visions of progress, the Magic Kingdom's Carousel of Progress, last updated in 1993, uses meat consumption as a platform for humor and, more subtly, as a site of conflict. Located in Tomorrowland, the Carousel of Progress, mythologized as Walt Disney's most beloved "ride," was first created for the 1964–65 New York World's Fair in collaboration with General Electric and features four "acts," one set in the 1900s, another set in the 1920s, a third set in the 1940s, and a final "contemporary" act. In the last tableau vivant in the Carousel of Progress, set in early twenty-first century U.S.A., the father performs "progress"—he is in the kitchen "fixing" dinner while his wife, daughter, and the grandmother (along with his son, the grandfather, and the pet dog) engage in leisurely activities in the step-down living room.[9] While one might initially be tempted to read this redistribution of domestic tasks as progressive, the father and his automated sous-chef (the voice-programmed oven) manage to reproduce the trope of the incompetent domestic man and reassure the audience that humans will remain superior in the face of artificial intelligence all in the span of two minutes: through a series of voice-programming mishaps (directly tied to a video game being played in the living room in which space has been militarized), the turkey in the oven burns, and everyone laughs that this has happened yet again.

Most interesting here is why a turkey is in the oven to begin with in this future-eyeing vision. Olivia Petter, writer for the *Independent*, synthesizes a new study from researchers at the University of Oxford who completed "one of the most comprehensive analyses to date into the detrimental effects farming can have on the environment and included data on nearly 40,000 farms in 119 countries." She writes,

> Eating a vegan diet could be the "single biggest way" to reduce your environmental impact on earth, a new study suggests. Researchers […] found that cutting meat and dairy products from your diet could reduce an individual's carbon footprint by up to 73 percent. Meanwhile, if everyone stopped eating these foods, they found that global farmland use could be reduced by 75 percent, an area equivalent to the size of the US, China, Australia and the EU combined [Petter n.p.].

The limited imagination when it comes to the future of food directly relates to the unwillingness to make visible and address systems of exploitation that disproportionately benefit white America (the vision of the future promoted by the ride) and speak to the ways the corporate imagination supplants the human imagination in order to sustain the "magic" of Disney.[10]

The ethos of Disney revolves around power of imagination. The films ask viewers to invest in human-animal relations and suggest that emotional and ethical connections with animals can be coextensive. It is possible that a new generation of viewers and consumers can change the food landscape of the parks, finding ways to integrate what is on screen into what is on (and not on) the plate.

NOTES

1. This use of terms of endearment underpinned by endangerment resonates with the first encounter between vegetarian shark Bruce and Dory and Marlin. After Bruce introduces himself to the fish, he inquires, "So, what's a couple of bites like you doing out so late?"

2. The film's quaint scene of capture is worth considering, especially given the global tropical fish trade. According to research conducted by National Geographic's Special Investigations Unit and reported by Rachael Bale, a National Geographic Society wildlife trade investigative reporter, "Up to 90 percent of the 11 million tropical fish that enter the U.S. each year are caught illegally with cyanide, according to a 2008 report from the National Oceanic and Atmospheric Administration" (Bale). Cyanide is squirted onto fish and into coral reefs, temporarily (at best) debilitating the fish and killing the coral (Bale). Bale reports, "Each live fish caught with cyanide destroys about a square yard of coral, according to biologist Sam Mamauag of the International Marinelife Alliance, in the Philippines." Though *Finding Nemo* is set in Australia, not the U.S., its impact on the global tropical fish market has been noted. Travis M. Andrews of the *Washington Post* reports, "Overfishing due to pet demand, along with rising ocean temperatures and ocean acidification, has all led to the Center for Biological Diversity to petition the National Marine Fisheries Service to put clownfish on the Endangered Species List, the Los Angeles Times reported in 2012."

3. When Tiana and Naveen's frog-appetites do kick in, eating animals is depicted as "instinct" rather than "choice." Tiana is unable to control her tongue—a veritable, if unwieldy marionette string—as it goes after a bug, tugging the rest of her to follow. Of course, unlike humans, within biology, frogs are carnivores, so the meat diet of Tiana and Naveen, in their frog states, should not be surprising. However, after the comic "first-bite" scene, the food the two eat is of note: Tiana teaches the prince how to mince vegetables (mushrooms and okra), and they make a variation on a (vegetarian) gumbo, and, later, when the prince, still in frog form, is about to propose, he leads Tiana to a table with a fruit and vegetable platter.

4. That the illustration "comes to life" and serves a pedagogical function is telling in regard to the ethos of Disney animation.

5. There is, of course, precedence for wanting to keep rats away from food meant for human consumption, given our knowledge that rats are carriers of disease. Even so, the film asks us to suspend disbelief in order to prioritize the human-animal relationship and issues of belonging at the film's center.

6. The late Anthony Bourdain's distaste for vegetarians and vegans is especially well documented. In *Kitchen Confidential*, he writes, "Vegetarians, and their Hezbollah-like splinter faction, the vegans, are a persistent irritant to any chef worth a damn. To me, life without veal stock, pork fat, sausage, organ meat, demiglace, or even stinky cheese is a life not worth living. Vegetarians are the enemy of everything good and decent in the human spirit, and an affront to all I stand for, the pure enjoyment of food." Celebrity chef Gordon Ramsey has also been a vocal critic of vegetarianism and veganism, often in Tweet-form; in one such Tweet, in 2016, in response to a fan's question about food allergies, he responded that he is allergic to vegans, and, in another, in 2018, he antagonized vegetarians by claiming to be a member of PETA before going on to note that PETA, here, stands for "people eating tasty animals."

7. *Ratatouille* suggests that the narratives we circulate influence our visions of what is possible or impossible. Early in the film, on Remy's first night as a guest (versus pest) in Linguini's home, a black-and-white movie plays, and viewers hear the snippets of a conversation that includes, "the best kind of dream, the kind that we can share," after which the film invests in a vision of mutual thriving.

8. *Forbes* contributor and host of the Vegan Business Talk podcast Katrina Fox reports, "Sales of plant-based food in the U.S. went up by 8.1% during the past year, topping $3.1 billion, according to research carried out by Nielsen for the Plant Based Foods Association (PBFA) and the Good Food Institute." Dairy and egg markets are not the only ones "to feel the pinch": "Finally, the global meat substitutes market is expected to garner a revenue of $5.2 billion by 2020, registering a compound annual growth rate of 8.4% during the forecast period 2015–2020, according to Allied Market Research" (https://www.forbes.com/sites/katrinafox/2017/12/27/heres-why-you-should-turn-your-business-vegan-in-2018/#742c45d42144).

9. Ironically, this staging still literally places the father "above" the rest of the family, a visual reassertion of hierarchy, be it intentional or not.

10. Recall this ride was initially developed in collaboration with G.E. and used as a means of advertisement through the company's sponsorship of the ride through the '80s.

Works Cited

Adams, Carol J. *The Sexual Politics of Meat: A Feminist-Vegetarian Critical Theory*. Tenth Anniversary Edition. The Continuum Publishing Company, 2000.

Bale, Rachael. "The Horrific Way Fish Are Caught for Your Aquarium—With Cyanide." *National Geographic* 10 March 2016. https://news.nationalgeographic.com/2016/03/160310-aquarium-saltwater-tropical-fish-cyanide-coral-reefs/.

Beauty and the Beast. Directed by Gary Trousdale and Kirk Wise, Walt Disney Pictures, 22 Nov. 1991.

Brandon, Pam. "New Allergy-Friendly Menus at Disneyland, Walt Disney Resorts." Disney Parks Blog 14 April 2015. https://disneyparks.disney.go.com/blog/2015/04/new-allergy-friendly-menus-at-disneyland-walt-disney-world-resorts/.

Bush, Jared (June 15, 2016). "That would be the pig. :) (replay to @TheRock @thejaredbush Is Pua the pig short for Puaka (Common Polynesian word for Pig) or Pua as in Hawaiian for flower? Lol)." (Tweet) *Twitter*. Retrieved on Dec. 5 2018.

Coral Reef Restaurant. *Epcot Dining*. Walt Disney World/Disney.com. https://disneyworld.disney.go.com/dining/epcot/coral-reef-restaurant/.

Finding Nemo. Directed by Andrew Stanton and Lee Unkrich, Walt Disney Pictures/Pixar Animation Studios, 30 May 2003.

Flaherty, Keely. "34 Magical 'Moana' Facts You Probably Don't Know." *Buzzfeed* 26 Nov 2016. https://www.buzzfeed.com/keelyflaherty/magical-moana-facts-you-probably-dont-know?utm_term=.iqdE4w4oy#.qq46535kO.

Haraway, Donna. *When Species Meet*. Posthumanities Series, Vol. 3. University of Minnesota Press, 2008.

Herzog, Hal. *Some We Love, Some We Hate, Some We Eat: Why It's So Hard to Think Straight About Animals*. HarperCollins Publishers, 2010.

Inside the Magic. "Big Epcot Changes Announcement—Ratatouille, Guardians, Future World, Space Restaurant—D23Expo." *YouTube*, commentary by Bob Chapek and Tom Fitzgerald, 14 July 2017, https://www.youtube.com/watch?v=g3TK27DV_EI#action=share.

The Little Mermaid. Directed by Ron Clements and John Musker, Walt Disney Pictures, 7 Dec. 1989.

Moana. Directed by Ron Clements and John Musker, Walt Disney Pictures, 23 Nov. 2016.

Nobis, Nathan. "The 'Babe' Vegetarians: Bioethics, Animal Minds and Moral Methodology." *Bioethics at the Movies*, edited by Sandra Shaphay, Johns Hopkins University Press, 2009, pp. 56–73.

Petter, Olivia. "Veganism Is 'Single Biggest Way' to Reduce Our Impact on Planet, Study Finds." *Independent*, 1 June 2018. https://www.independent.co.uk/life-style/health-and-families/veganism-environmental-impact-planet-reduced-plant-based-diet-humans-study-a8378631.html.

The Princess and the Frog. Directed by John Musker and Ron Clements, Walt Disney Pictures, 11 Dec. 2009.

Ratatouille. Directed by Brad Bird, Walt Disney Pictures/Pixar Animation Studios, 29 June 2007.

Singer, Peter. *Animal Liberation: A New Ethics for Our Treatment of Animals*. New York Review, 1975.

PART II

Relationships

Interactions Between Humans and Animals

From Trauma to Trust

The Convoluted Relationship
Between Jews and Dogs

Hadas Marcus *and* Tammy Bar-Joseph

Apart from the ubiquitous appeal of "man's best friend," contrasting perspectives on dogs are idiosyncratic to cultures, faiths, and ethnic groups worldwide, based on their history and traditional beliefs. Best-selling author and psychologist Stanley Coren describes our long paradoxical relationship with dogs as both friends and foes: "In some times and places, people have viewed dogs as loyal, faithful, noble, intelligent, courageous, and sociable; in other eras and locations, humans have thought dogs cowardly, unclean, disease-ridden, dangerous, and unreliable"(1). This statement sums up in a nutshell the Jewish and Israeli attitude towards canines. For many reasons, Jews have shared an ambivalent, convoluted history with dogs, with many twists and turns along the way, one that has been essentially incompatible until recently.

Because it is a species that is adored and endlessly studied on one hand, and abused and misunderstood on the other, the dog is an appropriate and fascinating subject through which to explore the blurring of human/animal boundaries. Dog-human hybrids are a ubiquitous theme in mythology, literature, cinema, art, and other cultural products. This ancient motif appeared in hieroglyphics, with the Egyptian god Anubis bearing the head of a black jackal or canine. The hybrid remains prevalent even today in popular culture, from movies with talking dogs, to William Wegman's fanciful portraits of dressed-up Weimaraners. For as long as humans have been telling stories, they have told them about animals. Popular culture provides a fertile ground for complicating and blurring the human/animal divide. Erica Fudge, a renowned U.K. scholar in critical animal studies, contends that "the stories told about dogs, we might argue, are never really about dogs at all, they are always about humans" (37). Whether it be state-of-the-art social media, or more conventional genre such as literature and film, this appears to be true.

In *When Species Meet*, Donna Haraway describes the intersection between humans and animals as "entanglement" or "contact zones" in which a process of "becoming with" takes place in "a subject- and object-shaping dance of encounters" (4). Although Haraway deals with connections between many types of beings, the prominent scholar has a particular fascination with canines, and she refers to our multi-layered bonds with them as *relatings*. In response, Birke and Hockenhull explain that "[t]hinking about, or living with, a particular kind of dog, within a particular kind of human world, carries with it a complex and rich history…. Our *relatings* with dogs are never innocent … they are always run through with other histories and other meanings" (20–21). These remarks shed light on the complex encounters between Jews and dogs through the lens of popular culture, especially during and after the Holocaust. While religious dictates in Judaism deemed canines as filthy and untrustworthy animals, in contemporary secular Jewish and Israeli society, dogs have become increasingly popular as cherished companions, and are no longer valued for purely economic, security, or pragmatic reasons. David Rodman sums up the Jewish relationship with dogs throughout history, pointing out how attitudes have slowly improved over generations:

> the image of the dog in the Hebrew Bible is overwhelmingly negative… [it has] remained a less-than-beloved creature in the Jewish imagination, certainly until recent times. With the return … to Eretz Israel, however, the status of the dog …has undergone something of a revolution, at least amongst "secular" Jews [437–438].

Dogs and Jewish Suffering

Where can we find examples of popular culture involving both dogs and Jews that illustrate how their lives have become tightly enmeshed? Upon scratching the surface, one finds that there is no dearth of such material, yet regrettably much of it is unpleasant. Dating back more than a century, one story in which a dog represents Jewish suffering is a woeful tale by the Yiddish author Sholom Aleichem (1859–1916), whose real name was Solomon Naumovich Rabinovich. He is aptly called the "Jewish Mark Twain" for his ironic humor, use of a pseudonym, the natural speech of his characters, and colorful depiction of local folk—in this case, poor Eastern European Jews in the *shtetl* (village). The writer is best known for "Tevye the Dairyman," posthumously adapted to become the widely acclaimed theatrical and cinematic production of *Fiddler on the Roof*. Sholom Aleichem's lesser-known story "Robchik," written in 1901, depicts the injustice of anti-semitism from a canine point-of-view. It unfolds without the dog actually narrating, but through his eyes, a technique known as animal focalization. The protagonist is a meek, forlorn creature who endures persecution and the misfortunes of the stereotypical passive and bookish "Old Jews" of the Diaspora before the state of Israel was born, and is mercilessly subjected to endless torment.

The Yiddish story "Robchik" appeared in English translation in *A Treasury of Sholom Aleichem Children's Stories* edited by Alicia Shevrin. The highly anthropomorphized dog was a gentle soul, one who was constantly bullied and abused by the townspeople who took pleasure in harassing him. Aleichem writes, "To swat Robchik on the rump with a stick or to kick him in the flank with one's heel, to fling a rock at his head, or to pour slops on him was almost an obligation, a great sport" (qtd. in Shevrin 121). Repeatedly uprooted, he nearly starved to death, and was too gentle to defend himself. To depict Robchik's vulnerability, Aleichem continues, "The dog suddenly rolls over on the ground, legs in the air, trembling and staring you in the face, as if to say: 'Here! You want to beat me? Go ahead and beat me!'" (122). Deprived of physical comfort, and feeling hopeless, he could not comprehend the reason for his misery, as he contemplates his plight, which in many ways echoes the adversity of Jews in Eastern Europe before World War I:

Robchik was getting tired of this exile, this wandering from one place to the next ... he walked aimlessly, a lonely dog going in circles as he felt his belly shrink and his intestines shrivel.... And out of great anguish he became a deep thinker, a philosopher: why was he, a dog, being punished more than all the other beasts.... [128].

In both secular and religious Judaism, references to dogs are abundant and in the past were almost always negative. Dogs were instruments of terror used by wealthy estate-owners in the violent *pogroms* (persecution by the Russian Empire) in the nineteenth century, waged by the Russians against the poverty-stricken Jews of Eastern Europe. In the World War II era, large German canine breeds were exploited by the Nazis for brutal purposes. These loyal dogs obeyed their masters' orders to intimidate, deter, hunt down, control, injure, and bite off the breasts or genitals of Jews, which often led to an agonizing death. Members of the Third Reich blurred the boundaries between humans and animals by elevating dogs to a higher rank and dehumanizing, animalizing, and exterminating Jews and other groups. As Arluke and Sanders claim, "Boundary work—the drawing and blurring of lines of demarcation between humans and animals—was essential to the Nazi paradox" (132). The resulting intergenerational traumas and damaging associations are deeply rooted in the Jewish/Israeli cultural mentality and have been extremely difficult to cast off.

In Judaism, historically, this has been a tenuous bond, fraught with a deep sense of ambivalence that has emerged for multi-faceted reasons. These were based on the Bible, later religious teachings, superstition, derogatory and connotative language (mostly Yiddish) and above all, culturally-embedded, intergenerational traumas derived from associations of "malicious" dogs that were trained to pursue and torment Jews in the *pogroms* and Nazi Germany. As Monika Baár explains,

Jewish culture has witnessed ambiguous attitudes to dogs until recent decades, but this was more due to distressing historical experiences than to religious tradition... tragic and horrific experiences in the course of pogroms and later in concentration camps, when dogs were purposefully trained to attack Jews, resulted in them becoming associated with the "enemy." In recent decades however, this aversion has been overcome and pet keeping has become both widely accepted and increasingly popular among (the secular) Israeli population [48–49].

Exploring the human/canine divide in Jewish popular culture, and the breaking down of rigid barriers between the species, leads to many examples of dogs being vilified, particularly in literature and cinema about the Holocaust. Typically, films dealing with this era, such as the epic drama *Schindler's List* (1993), *Life Is Beautiful* (1997), and *Adam Resurrected* (2008), feature monstrous images of heartless Nazis holding on to barking German shepherds as crowds of frightened Jews disembark a train and stand in line during a selection process, or huge and ferocious-looking dogs obeying the ruthless commands of SS men by attacking Jewish prisoners in striped uniforms, or Dobermans standing guard in the concentration camps. Paradoxically, these same breeds of German origin, which evoked fear and were discriminated against in the past, are often idealized today, especially in Israel. This is because they are representative of the self-sacrificing service and military dogs in the much-admired elite *Oketz* (Hebrew for "Sting") unit, who endanger themselves to protect the civilian population. Dogs in the *Oketz* unit are much loved and treated extremely well in every aspect of their care. Once they die, these dogs are honored by a ceremonial military funeral in a beautiful cemetery, next to a monument which reads "Walk softly since here is the resting place of Israeli soldiers" (Katz). Likewise, an annual Memorial Day ceremony is held for the fallen dogs, one that is covered by the Israeli news media.

Jewish/Israeli Cultural Barriers Toward Dogs

The seeds of dog culture emerged in the 1930s in Israel (then Palestine), prior to the establishment of the Jewish State. At that time, canines were used primarily for guarding property and herding, and there was very limited interest in anything else. The authentic breed of the Bedouins, the frail-looking and swift Saluki, was prized for its superb hunting and herding capabilities, and the Canaan dog was highly valued for in its unrivaled aptitude for guarding. Thus, in the early twentieth century in the Middle East, dog ownership was a domain that Bedouins and Westernized elites appreciated but not many Jews engaged in. Until recent decades, Jews generally harbored deep cultural misgivings and anxieties about dogs, largely because in Eastern Europe in the nineteenth and early twentieth centuries, they had been the guardians of the gentry's estates, and had been trained to attack on command. Thus, canines were considered unfit to be counted as members of Jewish families, a trait that distinguished them from prominent non–Jewish landowners and noblemen, who were much attached to their dogs.

Gradually, however, the Zionist dream of building a Jewish state transformed former antipathy towards dogs into varying degrees of tolerance and later even trust. The local pariah of the Middle East, known as the Canaan dog, is one of the world's oldest breeds; it was recognized as "the national dog of Israel" due to the unflagging efforts of two steadfastly Zionist women who had strong pioneering visions. The first was the brilliant Austrian cynologist (expert on dogs), Prof. Rudofina Menzel, who emigrated to Palestine with her husband in 1934. The second is Myrna Shiboleth, a dedicated breeder and authority from the U.S., who spent nearly fifty years running a kennel near Jerusalem raising Canaan dogs until being forced by the government to close down due to land disputes; thus, she relocated to Italy in 2017 (Golan). Both women made valiant attempts to popularize the breed in Israel and abroad, but with limited success, as their rather aloof nature doesn't make them very good pets. As Edward Tenner explains, this breed "turned out to be fiercely territorial as well as intelligent and self-reliant … the dogs of ancient Israel, ready to emerge from centuries of neglect and to defend a land of their own…" (77).

The Menzels were also chiefly responsible for the development of dog culture, for they saw the human/canine bond as essential to the emergence of the "New Jew": a bold, muscular, capable figure who took pride in cultivating the soil, harvesting crops, building communities, and protecting the land, while feeling reverence for the natural world. Through a lifetime of dedication, the Menzels introduced the dog as a valuable asset, not only to the police and the military in Israel, but also to civilians. They also called upon new immigrants to discard the image of traditional Jews in the Diaspora (outside of Israel), particularly from Eastern Europe, who were detached from nature and animals, and were not involved with raising dogs. Historian Binyamin Blum notes a major shift in Jewish attitudes towards dogs:

> In Europe, Jews were widely believed to suffer from an irrational fear of dogs, and dog ownership was generally discouraged…. By the twentieth century, however, Jewish attitudes towards dog were undergoing a conscious refashioning, at least in some circles. Through a stronger bond with the land and with nature—including animals—the Zionist movement sought to forge a new Jewish identity. Dogs were casted to play a key role in the plan for creating a braver, closer to nature, "New Jew" [649].

To date, the most comprehensive and fascinating scholarly work on the relationship between Jews and canines is the anthology of essays titled *A Jew's Best Friend?: The Image of the Dog Throughout Jewish History*, edited by Phillip Ackerman-Lieberman and Rakefet

Zalashik. In an essay on Yiddish proverbs about dogs, Robert Rothstein notes that derogatory phrases were frequently used, as well as proverbs which accentuate the distancing of Jews from canines, for example, "If a Jew has a dog, either the dog is no dog or the Jew is no Jew" (135). The book comprises in-depth studies of a wide range of issues, including how dogs are represented in various works of contemporary popular culture, such as the Israeli cult film *Azit the Paratrooper Dog* and the disturbing novel *Adam Resurrected* by Yoram Kaniuk (and its cinematic adaptation), which illustrates the eradication of human/canine boundaries in a rehabilitation center for mentally ill Holocaust survivors. In the introduction to *A Jew's Best Friend?: The Image of the Dog Throughout Jewish History*, the editors point out how we can erroneously interpret canine behavior, in an attempt to draw parallels that don't actually exist:

> If dogs help us figure out what it means to be fully human, then the line that we draw between humans and dogs establishes the binary opposite: the animal…. Nevertheless, the similarity between dogs and humans has led humans to project human traits and even human motives onto dogs…. Since dogs are both like and unlike humans, we humans impose human traits on dogs and we likewise use dogs to describe human behavior [2].

It would be misleading to claim that up until the Holocaust, canines were readily accepted by Jews, and animosity towards them only began with World War II. Pre-existing negative attitudes towards dogs were pervasive for centuries; however, Jewish feelings of dread and abhorrence of canines were severely aggravated during and after the Holocaust. Prior to that time, religious biases and restrictions, chiefly negative descriptions from the Bible and other ancient texts, labeled dogs as impure and bestial animals that were forbidden as pets, but they were permitted for specific roles only such as guarding.

Judy Brown, author of two controversial novels and numerous magazine articles on Jewish topics, left the cloistered community of the ultra–Orthodox in New York, to delve into subjects that she viewed as irrational and unjust. With a sharp sense of tongue-in-cheek humor, irony, and wit, she described the culturally transmitted, exaggerated prejudices which some Jews still have against all dogs, even if they are obviously harmless. Brown encapsulates many of the reasons that her parents and grandparents were terrified of dogs, and feels relief when her own children demonstrate uninhibited love for animals, thus avoiding intergenerational trauma:

> When I was a little girl, there were things as clear as sunlight…. One of those things was that dogs were despicable creatures. They were scary and dirty, with teeth like knives, and paws with claws, ripping flesh off bone, the way they'd done to Jews in the Holocaust…. Only gentiles liked dogs, taking strange comfort in the animals; good Jews stayed far away…. Our grandparents and relatives taught us about the snarling dogs of Eastern Europe…. Over the years, the fear became lodged in the communal psyche…. A good Jew passes on the fear to his children, lest they shall be led astray…. I remember feeling surprised at how quickly my children took to animals, and at the joy they expressed while playing with them. I was certain that my fear was genetic, an inherent part of my DNA. Yet I quickly discovered that children aren't afraid of animals.

The Holocaust: Dehumanization and Animality

For most people, a loud, barking dog is merely an irritation. If the noise becomes excessive, it can lead to official complaints, which can sour the relationships between otherwise friendly neighbors. However, there are those for whom barking is not only an annoyance, but a source of profound distress, one that is loaded with terrifying associations of German soldiers and torture of Jewish prisoners. For many, it is painful reminder of the Holocaust, when dogs were forcibly trained to be vicious accomplices to Nazi crimes against humanity. Repercussions of this intergenerational transmission of trauma exist to this day, but with time these ripple effects have diminished until something triggers a painful memory. While arranging the festivities for Israel's seventieth Independence Day celebration to be held on April 18, 2018, in Jerusalem, the Israeli Culture and Sport Minister, Miri Regev, decided to add disturbing sound and visual effects to the event. Attendees were stunned by the sounds of rumbling trains and barking dogs that blared from the loudspeakers, as children donning yellow stars crossed the stage carrying suitcases. Regev told the Army radio station, "I'm very pleased with how we nailed the Holocaust." The sound of barking was symbolic of the tragedy, for dogs were a source of constant humiliation and peril for Jews in concentration camps and ghettos ("Regev Adds Holocaust").

Indeed, remnants of this trauma are still everywhere in the realm of popular culture. It is no wonder that many Jews and their offspring in the post–Holocaust era have suffered from what might appear to be an exaggerated attitude of revulsion and fear towards dogs. A twisted Scottish man was recently charged with a hate crime for training his girlfriend's pug to salute Hitler, which he then uploaded as a controversial YouTube clip. Archival photos in books, on the Internet and in museums depict SS men lavishing affection on pampered military dogs, and Hitler with his beloved Blondi. In *The Drowned and the Saved*, Primo Levi wrote about Auschwitz: "Without a spoon, the daily soup could not be consumed in any other way than by lapping it up, as dogs do..." (99). This line echoes the sense of utter dehumanization and blurred boundaries which many Jews experienced during the Holocaust.

One brief scene in *The Pianist* depicts a feeble old man in the Warsaw ghetto, trembling from the bitter cold, who lunges at an old woman carrying a hot can of barley soup. After it spills all over the ground, they glare at each other scornfully, then the man throws himself full length in the slush, lapping up the soup from the cobblestones like a dog. The distraught woman, howling and crying, beats the man for stealing precious food. Another touching scene is in *La Vita è Bella* (*Life Is Beautiful*), in which an innocent boy, reads aloud in Italian from a shop window sign warning in bold letters, "No Jews or Dogs Allowed." Baffled, he turns to his father and asks, "Why aren't Jews and dogs allowed in?" Guido—played by Roberto Benigni, who directed the film and won the Academy Award for Best Actor for this role—fumbles for an answer: "They just don't want Jews or dogs to go in." He consoles his young son by making up a story that in the local hardware store, Spaniards and horses, and in the pharmacy, Chinese and kangaroos, are not permitted in either. The two of them discuss what sign they would hang in their own bookstore blocking entry to people and animals they despise, such as Visigoths and spiders.

In Elie Wiesel's *Night*, a slim novel which is required reading in many American public schools, the author makes frequent allusions to Jews being addressed as dogs by the Nazis at Auschwitz and Buchenwald:

"If anyone goes missing, you will be shot, like dogs" [24].

"He [the SS officer] looked at us as one would a pack of leprous dogs clinging to life" [38].

"The SS made us increase our pace. 'Faster, you tramps, you flea-ridden dogs!' If one of us stopped for a second, a quick shot eliminated the filthy dog" [85].

The Saint Bernard, a breed normally visualized as a massive but gentle animal with a cask of brandy around its neck, trekking through snow-covered terrain to rescue a lost traveler, harbors ties to the Nazis. This happy, familiar image stems from the famous story of a noble, selfless dog named Barry, a national and highly symbolic hero in Switzerland, who saved the lives of around forty mountaineers throughout his lifetime in the early 1800s. Various Swiss tourist attractions, such as the Saint Bernard hospice kennel, commemorate and honor Barry, and the actual dog, preserved by taxidermy, is on display in a museum. Hollywood added new dimensions to this altruistic image with the goofy but loveable Beethoven and the terrifying Cujo. In stark contrast to the legendary Swiss canine idol, however, is another huge dog who first belonged to SS officers Paul Groth in Sobibor, and later to Kurt Franz (nicknamed "Lalke" meaning "doll" in Yiddish—due to his falsely docile appearance) in Treblinka. This notorious mixed Saint Bernard dog, whose name, ironically, was also Barry, was converted into an evil accomplice of the Nazi regime, in one of the most repugnant examples of the blurring of the human/canine divide in all of history.

Numerous heart-wrenching testimonies from the Eichmann trial in 1961 describe this enormous canine that ripped off the genitals or bit the buttocks of naked concentration camp prisoners, and mauled others to death. Franz was one of the most sadistic commanders of the Treblinka extermination camp. Whenever he shouted "*Mensch, schnapp den Hund!*" ("Man, catch that dog!"), Barry would attack people and literally tear off pieces of their flesh. By this command, he was referring to the Jew as the "dog" and addressing the Saint Bernard as "Man." Although sentenced to life imprisonment in 1965, Franz was eventually released in 1993.

Holocaust scholar Daniel Jonah Goldhagen wrote an enraged op-ed in *The New York Times* about the injustice of liberating such a heinous murderer, who fondly remembered the World War II period as "the best years of my life." The article featured a ghastly sketch of Barry by famous illustrator Marshall Arisman, in which the brutish creature has an appalling human-like face with a man's thick arms and hands on a large dog's body. The bones of a severed human leg dangle from his mouth (as shown on the *Holocaust History Channel*). Sadly, as the article and many testimonies confirmed, it was not the fault of the dog that so many prisoners were mutilated and killed by him. Goldhagen explained, "Barry was not by nature vicious. When Franz was not around, Barry permitted prisoners to play with him. It was Franz who transformed the dog into a ferocious beast." Following the war, the dog was adopted by a physician and became as docile as ever, laying peacefully at his owner's feet and never harming anyone until his death in 1947. In "The Best Friend of the Murderers: Guard Dogs and the Nazi Holocaust" Robert Tindol points out that Barry's ostensibly conflicting behavior was studied extensively by Konrad Lorenz, director of the Max Planck Institute for Behavioral Research, and Nobel Laureate for his groundbreaking studies on aggression (111).

Indisputably, cruel acts carried out by dogs who attacked Jewish prisoners, such as the infamous Great Danes named Rolf and Ralf owned by Amon Göth, (played by Ralph Fiennes in *Schindler's List*), were horrendous and unforgivable. Yet one must ask, were the dogs inherently brutal, a human characteristic, or just obediently following instructions given to them by their heartless masters? Tindol reiterates that blame should not be assigned to the dogs. He wrote,

one can only wonder if an utterly vicious and uncontrollable dog would have happily tagged along by a master while wagging its tail without occasionally assaulting a passerby on its own initiative…. The guard dogs may have enforced their masters' desires, but the likelihood is that they were doing so out of loyalty and probably love for their human companions. Therefore, the actions of the dogs indeed reflected the intentions of their masters… [119–120].

Certain canine breeds were assigned overtly political and ethnic traits, particularly the German shepherd during the Third Reich, which represented the purity of the Aryan race. Arluke and Sax wrote an insightful piece in 1992, long before critical animal studies had become a burgeoning field as it has in recent years. The authors explain how the blurring of boundaries between animals and Germans was seen as the "natural order," and this was especially true of certain breeds of dogs, particularly Alsatians. In contrast to the high status that was given to these dogs, Jews were seen as equivalent to contaminating pests that must be annihilated:

Nazi German identity relied on the blurring of boundaries between humans and animals and the constructing of a unique phylogenetic hierarchy that altered conventional human-animal distinctions and imperatives… to kill certain people furthered the Nazi quest for purity … we saw this blurring in the animalization of Germans themselves as well as other humans… "lower animals" or "subhumans," such as the Jews and other victims of the Holocaust, were to be exterminated like vermin [27–28].

Svetlana Filippova, a Russian filmmaker, created the touching animated film *Brutus* (2014) about a dog during the Holocaust. In this illustration, the dog seems concerned about his Jewish owner, a woman who is very despondent due to the war. The dog is later confiscated by the Nazis and forcibly trained to be used against Jewish prisoners. Russia, 2014, color and black and white, 13 minutes (courtesy Svetlana Filippova).

Unfortunately, space here does not permit an in-depth analysis of two rather controversial Israeli Holocaust novels, both tragicomic fantasies, which have both been adapted into American movies. The first is *A Jewish Dog* by Asher Kravitz, a bittersweet, witty "animal autobiography" narrated by a family dog, a mutt, who was confiscated from his loving Jewish home due to the enforcement of Nuremberg Laws, which prohibited Jews from owning pets. The dog was adopted by an SS officer who trained him to become an accomplice to the Nazis. Yet this story comes full circle when the dog is reunited with his previous owner and together they escape. A movie to be released at this writing, *Shepherd: A Jewish Dog*, directed by Lynn Roth, is loosely based on Kravitz's novel, and a Russian short film titled *Brutus* was already made by Konstantin Fam as part of his Holocaust trilogy *Witness*. Both these films feature a German shepherd as the main character, although the novel did not. A profoundly disturbing film, *Adam Resurrected*, with powerful performances by Jeff Goldblum and Daniel DeFoe, encapsulates the human/canine bond and post-traumatic memories of the Holocaust on many levels. Based on the novel by Yoram Kaniuk titled *Adam, Son of a Dog (Adam Ben Kelev)*, the movie unfolds in a non-chronological order, taking place in a mental institution in the Israeli desert, intercut with flashbacks that slowly reveal the details of the past. The protagonist, Adam Stein, a famous comedian and entertainer in Germany, was forced to act like a dog in order to save his own life in a concentration camp, and yet he is unable to let go of this trauma once the war is over. Any one of these works, whether it be the books or the films, deserves a full chapter unto itself to investigate the many parallels and intersections between canine and human boundaries during and after the Holocaust.

Luckily, however, not all popular culture dealing with Jews and dogs is so dismal and harrowing. Transversing history and geography, and moving away from the horrors of the past, a treasure trove of upbeat anecdotes and even laughable examples can be found to illustrate this complicated relationship.

The Lighter Side in the U.S.—From Bark Mitzvahs to Cloned Pups

Dogs in Jewish life also take on a lighter note as the trend-setters of popular sentiment. Professor P. David Marshall, defines the term "celebrity" as a person who, via mass media, enjoys "a greater presence and wider scope of activity and agency than are those who make up the rest of the population" (ix). Thus performers and cultural icons are closely watched and emulated by hordes of admirers, a situation which also holds true in their attitudes towards domesticated animals. In terms of the bonds between contemporary American Jewish celebrities and their pets, many have drawn widespread media attention. In 2011, Seth Rogen tweeted, "This is my dog Zelda. She's Jewish." He uploaded a photo of her next to a Hanukkah menorah and holiday decorations. The ring-bearer at Adam Sandler's wedding was his bulldog Meatball, who wore a tuxedo and a white skullcap (*yarmulke*). When Meatball died, Sandler held a memorial service and later adopted another bulldog, whom he named Matzoball.

The flamboyant fashion designer Isaac Mizrahi, of Syrian origin, was raised in an Orthodox Jewish household in New York City, yet he abandoned his strict background to study performing arts. Mizrahi is admired not only for the striking attire he creates for people, but also for his "luxury dog clothes" which ads claim are "a mix of sophistication, comfort, and personality." Besides his transformation from an observant Jew to a gay secular one, Mizrahi describes another dramatic change he underwent when he adopted a mutt. He humorously accentuates how the lines between human and canine can merge together:

> I needed to get in touch with my inner mutt.... Before Harry, I was merely human. I'm all dog now, an honorary member of the K9 race. All those years before Harry, I had to seek out reasons and opportunities to be nonhuman. Then the K9 thing happened to me, and once it did, I embraced it.... I don't miss being human at all [qtd. in Szabo vii].

A much-publicized case involves Barbra Streisand, often considered a Jewish diva. In 2017, the entertainer cloned her geriatric dog, a Coton de Tuléar, for an astronomical price which she paid to a genetic engineering company to create two puppies named Miss Violet and Miss Scarlett. Streisand was attacked online by a barrage of criticism from animal rights organizations who viewed her actions as selfish and unethical, when she could have spent the same money on homeless dogs in shelters (Coren). Despite this, she is concerned for the welfare of all dogs, not just her own pets. For example, in 2015 she expressed vehement opposition to the Chinese Yulin Dog Meat Festival by writing a petition to have it stopped (Lima).

Jerry Seinfeld, known as the world's most successful living Jewish comedian, seems to run into trouble with dogs, at least on television. A hilarious scenario transpires in the popular sitcom *Seinfeld* which deals with Jerry's contempt of Farfel, a loud, unruly dog who he is forced to watch due to an emergency, in which a fellow airline passenger is suddenly taken very ill. Jerry becomes irritated when he cannot leave home for days on end, and he cannot locate the dog's owner. The supposed "animal" is never shown on camera, yet it creates havoc in the apartment. In actuality, the incessant barking that infuriates Jerry is the voice of a human imitating a dog:

> Let go, Farfel! Let go, gimme that! Gimme the sneaker you stupid idiot! ... I've got a wild animal in the house! ... Bad dog! Bad dog! You go outside! Outside!! What do you want from me? Tell me! Money, you want money? I'll give you money, how much?!

In this episode titled "The Dog," Jerry remarks cynically about the peculiar nature of modern human-canine relationships: "If you see two life forms, one of them is making a poop, and the other one is carrying it for him, who would you assume was in charge?" In real life, however, Seinfeld is fond of his own dachshunds, but things do not always go smoothly there either. One of them, a timid female, was so terrified of him that celebrity dog trainer Cesar Millan was asked to intervene, which became an episode of *Cesar 911*. The program opens with Jerry complaining sarcastically, "I am loved by millions, except for one dog.... The hostility—that I don't deserve."

How to Raise a Jewish Dog is a book which pokes fun at the plethora of self-help manuals for people seeking guidance on how to care for and train their beloved pets. In the introduction, authors Ellis Weiner and Barbara Davilman pose four questions (alluding to the Passover Seder) that define the essence of a "Jewish dog," which are "an exaggerated sense of his own wonderfulness, an exaggerated sense of his own shortcomings, and an extremely close relationship with his master" (5). In a later chapter, the authors parody stereotypical Jewish neuroticism: "When it comes to raising a Jewish dog, remember that it is always better to imagine the worst, and then panic, and then realize you're being silly" (105).

Jokes aside, what about serious Jewish traditions that mark symbolic rites of passage—can dogs be included in these as well? While some might chuckle at the outlandish idea of celebrating a Bark Mitzvah, others, particularly the observant, find the idea not only preposterous, but offensive. Bark Mitzvah ceremonies are becoming a wildly popular, yet controversial coming-of-age ritual in North America that are celebrated in homes, parks, grooming salons and even reform synagogues with dogs wearing a traditional prayer shawl. The ceremony usually begins with the rabbi reciting a prayer or blessing over the dogs and ends with a certificate saying "Muzzle Tov!" (rather than "Mazal Tov"). Some owners take advantage of this occasion as a fundraiser in lieu of gifts, asking guests for donations to animal welfare.

Dogs in Israeli Popular Culture

Jewish American icons (and their fans) who spoil their dogs are not alone in the ways they worship them and incorporate them as family members in every aspect of their daily lives. While Israelis may not be quite as extravagant or quirky as their American counterparts when it comes to dogs, those fortunate enough to have a good home are still showered with abundant love and affection, and lines are continually blurred between the human and canine divide. The Israeli actress-model Gal Gadot, or Wonder Woman, displays affectionate bonds she shares with her dog Lola through social media. Two famous Israelis living in southern California have earned an unmatched status when it comes to dogs. The first is professional trainer and best-selling author Tamar Geller, a former army officer whose methods based on unrestrained love rather than harsh discipline have helped Oprah Winfrey, Ben Affleck, Charlize Theron, Natalie Portman, Reese Witherspoon, and many other celebrities with their dogs. On the other end of the spectrum is Eldad Hagar, who founded the rescue organization "Hope for Paws" with his wife Audrey. Hagar is widely admired for videos of his Houdini-like stunts to save nearly dead dogs, cats, and other animals in extremely precarious situations, and at great risk to himself.

Canine icons in television, cinema and literature were geared for Israeli children and teens, and functioned as powerful agents of cultural and social change which contributed greatly to a positive shift in attitudes towards dogs. A key example of this was the much-admired German shepherd heroine of the series of books *Azit, the Paratrooper Dog* (*Azit, Hakalba Hatzanhanit*) by Lt. Gen. Mordechai "Motta" Gur, an important politician and the 10th Chief of Staff of the Israeli army between 1974 and 1978. Gur is remembered for his courageous military strategy in the 1967 war, and was instrumental in the conquest of the Old City of Jerusalem. These books later became a 1972 cult film with the same title, directed by Boaz Davidson. Arguably the most illustrious celebrity dog in the Israeli cultural mentality, "Azit" was both a mythic character and a fantasy military superhero, the Israeli counterpart of Lassie and Rin Tin Tin in her valor, loyalty, and self-sacrifice. Nonetheless, Azit surpassed them both in her unrealistic abilities to "save the day" by shielding both soldiers and civilians from harm, and defeating the enemy in impossibly hazardous circumstances. It should be noted that all three of these mythological canine heroes were purely fictional, although Rin Tin Tin had the most basis in reality.

Children's educational television programs in Israel in the 1980s featured two dogs that still rouse great nostalgia, Dobi Doberman and Tulip. These television dogs became superstars and are considered emblematic of that generation, many of whom are middle-aged parents themselves. In *Doberman the Good Sport*, the main character was the friendly Dobi who worked for the police by instructing children how to safely cross streets. In one of the endless reruns, "Dobi on Duty," an officer greets the dog in the morning by reminding him of his job to teach youngsters appropriate pedestrian behavior. With his communicative body language and animated barking, the protective Doberman guided children across the street while they chanted the Hebrew theme song that remains stuck in the heads of many Israeli adults today.

The choice of a German shepherd and a Doberman for these roles was significant, due to the intense fear these breeds instilled in many Holocaust survivors and subsequent generations in Israel and abroad. Negative images were exacerbated by popular culture, such as in the science fiction film *The Boys from Brazil* (1978), in which the malevolent cloned Hitler youth ordered three Dobermans to viciously attack on command. German shepherds were vilified to an even greater extent in cinema. One horrific scene in *Escape from Sobibor* (1987) is of a young naked boy, standing in line to the crematorium, who attempts to makes a desperate run for his life moments before a German shepherd gruesomely tears him to pieces (only heard but not shown).

The immensely popular Israeli television show *Somersaults* with Dalik Wollinitz and his famous mixed German shepherd-Collie named Tulip was aired throughout the 1980s. Dalik and Tulip appeared regularly in this program that dealt with difficult issues such as bereavement, serious illness, and war trauma. Tulip did not take an active role in the show, but his presence was therapeutic, enabling children to speak openly about painful situations. Tulip motivated youngsters to want to raise dogs and boosted the popularity of the German shepherd and its acceptance as a family dog, which broke down a sturdily entrenched cultural barrier and discrimination against certain "bad" breeds of dogs. This led to the dramatic transformation of the German shepherd as a fierce military machine—a deeply engrained image in the Israeli collective memory due to the Holocaust—to a peaceful friend. Tulip was pampered; his own personal taxi cab driver chauffeured him to the Educational Television set, where he was served bottled mineral water instead of drinking from the tap. According to Wollinitz, his beloved canine was an inseparable part of his family until he died at the ripe old age of sixteen (Frenkel).

Ironically enough, these television shows starred the kinds of dogs which were most despised by many Jews in Israel and worldwide because of their close association with the Holocaust: the German shepherd and the Doberman. Boria Sax has explored the Nazi/dog binary, in particular, the German shepherd, a breed that was developed as an idealized representation "intended to embody the virtues of the German people, and anticipated the Nazi attempts to breed humans back to primeval Aryan stock" (83). As Linda Kalof and Ramona Fruja Amthor have pointed out, the multidimensional meanings of animals

> are tethered to the historically specific norms and values of the society in which they occur, and it is widely acknowledged that the shaping of the social world is accomplished in large part by cultural representation … specific dog breeds have emerged as dangerous in every decade since the 1950s (in the 1960s the German shepherd was the "bad dog *du jour*" and in the 1970s, it was the Doberman Pinscher) [165–166].

Since the establishment of the state of Israel, there has been a gradual paradigm shift in attitudes, and canines are now represented in popular culture as loving pets, courageous military heroes (especially in books and film) and wonderful service dogs for the disabled. In fact, Tel Aviv has earned a reputation as one of the world's most dog-friendly cities, and this surprising fact has saturated the media. Just as in almost any other Westernized country, vast numbers of dogs in Israel are adored family members able to take full advantage of an endless array of upscale products such as gourmet and special diet dog food, social and obedience clubs in dog parks, Dog TV, and costly, tailor-made grooming and exercise services. The evolving role of the dog in the current Jewish and Israeli mentality is an extension of the development of secular leisure pursuits, and a metaphor of more enlightened perspectives that have accompanied a new awareness of animal welfare. The warmer bonds formed between Jews and dogs in recent years is something of an unexpected turn, a quiet revolution that has occurred bit by bit, reflecting a radical departure from the mostly negative perceptions of canines of the past. Contemporary works of popular Jewish culture reflect this slow but steady surge in acceptance of dogs, after centuries in which they had been largely regarded with fear and loathing. May this positive attitude be here to stay.

WORKS CITED

Ackermann-Lieberman, Phillip, and Zalashik, Rakefet, eds. *A Jew's Best Friend? The Image of the Dog Throughout Jewish History*. Sussex Academic Press, 2013.

Adam Resurrected. Directed by Paul Schrader. Bleiberg Entertainment, 2008.

Arluke, Arnold, and Boria Sax. "Understanding Nazi Animal Protection and the Holocaust" *Anthrozoos: A Multidisciplinary Journal of The Interactions of People & Animals*, 5(1): 1992. pp. 6–31.

Arluke, Arnold, and Clinton R. Sanders. *Regarding Animals*. Temple University Press, 1996.

Baár, Monika. "From Working Animals to Cherished Pets: Canine Histories across the Centuries." *Historisch Tijdschrift Groniek Historical Magazine*, vol. 48, no. 206–207, 2015. pp. 47–59.

Birke, Lynda, and Jo Hockenhull, eds. *Crossing Boundaries: Investigating Human-Animal Relationships*. Brill, 2012.

Blum, Binyamin. "The Hounds of Empire: Forensic Dog Tracking in Britain and Its Colonies 1888–1953," Volume 35, Issue 3, Law and History Review, 2017, pp. 621–665.

Brown, Judy. "An Old Dog's New Tricks—A Gentle Pooch Helps a Hasidic Girl Overcome Her Fear of Dogs." *The Jewish Daily Forward* 4 Feb. 2013. https://forward.com/author/judy-brown-eishes-chayil/.

Coren, Stanley. *The Intelligence of Dogs*. Free Press, 2006 (1993).

_____. "Live, Love, Live Again: Barbra Streisand's Cloned Dogs," *Psychology Today*, March 12, 2018. https://www.psychologytoday.com/us/blog/canine-corner/201803/live-love-live-again-barbra-streisands-cloned-dogs.

"Dobi on Duty." *Doberman the Good Sport*. Israel Educational Television, 1981. https://www.youtube.com/watch?v=u7fkhPLP2wg.

"The Dog." (Season 3: Episode 4). *Seinfeld*. Giggling Goose Productions. NBC. 9 Oct. 1991.

Escape from Sobibor. Directed by Jack Gold. Zenith Productions, 1987.

Frenkel, Billie. "The First Dog of Israeli Television" (Hebrew). *Ma'ariv* 20 March 2007 https://www.makor rishon.co.il/nrg/online/1/ART1/558/769.html.

Fudge, Erica. "The Dog, the Home and the Human, and the Ancestry of Derrida's Cat." *Oxford Literary Review*, vol. 29, no.1–2, 2007. pp. 37–54.

Golan, Patricia. "Canaan Canines: Leaving on a One-Way Ticket to Italy." *Jerusalem Post* 4 Apr. 2018. https://www.jpost.com/Jerusalem-Report/Canaan-canines-Leaving-on-a-one-way-ticket-to-Italy-547863.

Goldhagen, Daniel. "Treblinka's Other Monster." *The New York Times* 21 Aug. 1993, L 19.

"Goldhagen on Kurt Franz and Barry." *Holocaust History Channel* https://holocausthistorychannel.wordpress.com/2013/11/24/goldhagen-on-kurt-franz-and-barry/.

Haraway, Donna. *When Species Meet*. University of Minnesota Press, 2008.

Ivry, Benjamin. "How Dogs Went from Feared Enemy to Jew's Best Friend." *Forward*, 9 July 2013. https://forward.com/culture/179831/how-dogs-went-from-feared-enemy- to-jews-best-frien/.

Kalof, Linda, and Ramona Fruja Amthor. "Cultural Interpretations of Problem Animals in *National Geographic*." *Études rurales*, no. 185, 2010. pp. 165–180.

Kaniuk, Yoram. *Adam Resurrected*. Trans. by Seymour Simckes. Atheneum,1971.

Katz, Yaakov. "The IDF's Best Friend." *Jerusalem Post* 20 Dec. 2007. https://www.jpost.com/Magazine/Features/The-IDFs-best-friend.

Kravitz, Asher. *A Jewish Dog*. Translated by Michal Kessler, Penlight Publications, 2015.

Levi, Primo. *The Drowned and the Saved*. Trans. by Raymond Rosenthal. Simon & Schuster, 2017 (1988).

Life Is Beautiful (La Vita è Bella). Directed by Roberto Benigni. Miramax, 1997.

Lima, Natalia. "Barbra Streisand Joins Fight Against Dog Meat Festival." Ecorazzi, July 7, 2015. http://www.ecorazzi.com/2015/07/07/barbra-streisand-joins-fight-against-dog-meat-festival/.

Marshall, P.D. *Celebrity and Power: Fame in Contemporary Culture*. University of Minnesota Press, 1997.

McKenzie, Lesley. "Meet Hollywood's Top Canine Trainer: 'A Life Coach for Dogs and for People.'" *The Hollywood Reporter*, 18 June 2018. https://www.hollywoodreporter.com/news/meet-tamar-geller-a-life-coach-dogs-people-1119248.

Pfefferman, Naomi. "The Mensch List: Hope for Paws Founder's Dogged Devotion." *Jewish Journal* 2 Jan. 2014. http://jewishjournal.com/tag/eldad-hagar/.

"Regev Adds Holocaust Effects to Independence Day Event, Says She 'Nailed It,'" *Times of Israel*, April 17, 2018. https://www.timesofisrael.com/regev-adds-holocaust-theme-to-independence-day-event-says-she-nailed-it/.

Rodman, David. Book review of "A Jew's Best Friend? The Image of the Dog Throughout Jewish History." *Israel Affairs* 20:3, 2014.

Sax, Boria. *Animals in the Third Reich: Pets, Scapegoats, and the Holocaust*. Continuum, 2000.

"The Seinfeld Episode" (Season 3: Episode 1). *Cesar 911*. Nat Geo WILD. 19 Feb. 2016.

Shevrin, Aliza (ed). *A Treasury of Sholom Aleichem Children's Stories*. Rowman & Littlefield Inc., 1996.

Spiro, Amy. "A Holocaust Film with a Canine Twist." *The Jerusalem Post*, 6 Mar. 2018. https://www.jpost.com/Israel-News/Culture/A-Holocaust-film-with-a-canine-twist-544355.

Szabo, Julia. *The Underdog*. Workman Publishing Co., 2006.

Tenner, Edward. "Citizen Canine." *Wilson Quarterly* 22, no. 3: 1998. pp. 71–79.

Tindol, Robert. "The Best Friend of the Murderers: Guard Dogs and the Nazi Holocaust." In *Animals and War*, edited by Ryan Hediger, Brill, 2013. pp. 105–22.

Weiner, Ellis, and Barbara Davilman. *How to Raise a Jewish Dog*. Little Brown and Co., 2007.

Wiesel, Elie. *Night*. Trans. by Marion Wiesel. Hill & Wang, 2006 (1958).

No Room in the Boat?

Pets vs. People in Disaster Relief Efforts

Amy J. Lantinga

The Human/Pet Bond

Kittens, hamsters, rabbits, and dogs—just a few of the types of animals that Americans have welcomed into their homes with open hearts and wallets. According to the American Veterinary Medical Association, it is estimated that in 2011, nearly 37 percent of American households owned a dog, and nearly 31 percent owned a cat. An American Pet Products Association (APPA) consumer survey put the 2017–18 numbers at over 84.6 million American households that have at least one pet (American Pet Products Association "Owner Survey"). Few can deny the powerful relationship humans have cultivated with their pets. Using social support theory to examine the pet/owner bond, Michael Meehan, Bronwyn Massavelli, and Nancy Pachana studied the relationships of pets and their humans and determined that owners rank their pets high on scales of social attachment, often as high as those attachments to family and good friends. And these animals are often well cared for and considered part of the family. In fact, the APPA reports that in 2017, Americans spent $69.51 billion on the well-being of these pets ("Pet Market and Ownership Stats"). But in spite of the billions spent on pet spas, doggy day cares, dog walking services, pet acupuncture, pet insurance, cat condos, collars, clothing, food, treats, grooming, and veterinarian bills, one thing humans do not spend much on is *time* preparing an emergency or evacuation plan for their pets in the case of a natural or man-made disaster.

While the Red Cross, American Veterinary Association, and Humane Society encourage owners to create a disaster preparedness plan for their pets, rescue efforts in the midst of major disasters still may exclude pets or place them far at the bottom of the list. Knowing that pets provide support, decrease stress, and provide disaster survivors with a sense of purpose and normalcy, disaster preparation and relief efforts have a long way to go to include pets within disaster relief structures and systems.

Within this discussion of animals and disasters, the term "pet" and "companion animal" are used interchangeably, as are "human" and "owner." This essay places attention on more "traditional" pets, mostly cats and dogs, and will not discuss exotic animals like fish or large animals like horses, which many Americans consider pets, but require more extensive forms of rescue and relief. In fact, numbers for losses of fish who suffocated in the New Orleans Aquarium due to power outages during Katrina, or farm animals drowning during floods, are shocking and disturbing, and as Leslie Irvine argues persuasively, are worth examining in the future. This essay will also center mostly upon more recent natural disasters, specifically hurricanes, in the United States. However, as Elena Garde, Guillermo Enrique Pérez, Gerardo Acosta-Jamett, and Barend Mark Bronsvoort remind us, "Eighty-five percent of the disasters and 95 percent of disaster-related deaths occur in the developing world, [and] less than 1 percent of the disaster-related publications are originating from these countries" (1074). Animals worldwide suffer alongside humans, and it is a problem no nation has yet solved.

In the United States, Hurricane Katrina forced an ugly spotlight onto the ways disaster relief efforts simply left pets behind, metaphorically and literally. And although other disasters could easily be examined in as great a depth, Katrina is a particularly useful start in examining the blurred lines that can and have existed between humans and their pets during a disaster.

The Emotional Cost of the Human/Pet Bond

Animals have added companionship, physical assistance, and increasingly, the compassion and comfort needed for humans to get through difficult situations. Developments include studies on dogs reducing stress in homesick college kids (Binfet et al.); funeral dogs offering support for the grieving (Pawlowski); "courthouse dogs" providing comfort to children and victims of violent crime, jurors, and witnesses (McCleery); dogs working with veterans experiencing post-traumatic stress disorder (PTSD) (O'Haire et al.); prisoners working with puppies to promote responsibility, integrity, and pride (ReCHAI); and horses aiding PTSD affected youth (Mueller and McCullough). Some physicians have even gone so far as to call dogs "the new pro-biotics," for the health benefits microbe-laden dogs bring to children building immunities (Schiffman). Psychologists and physicians promote pet ownership for mental and physical health, noting the scientific benefits of pet ownership and relationships with therapy animals.

During disasters, people are often separated from their companion animals. And research has demonstrated that it is the more continuous relationship and contact with animals that provides these mental and physical benefits in humans. For example, if a human no longer has the animal in sight, some of the lasting effects of decreased heart rate and decreased levels of anxiety diminish (Jones et al.). Therefore, one can argue that sustained interaction with companion animals and preserving pet relationships during times of trauma are what aids the human in the mental and physical health so critically needed during and after a disaster. Keeping people with their pets during and post-disaster is critical.

My Pet, Myself

John Berger's classic essay "Why Look at Animals?" explores the lines—delineated, parallel, and blurred—that exist between and among humans and their animals:

> The pet completes him, offering responses to aspects of his character which would otherwise remain unconfirmed.... The pet offers its owner a mirror to a part that is otherwise never reflected..... Since

the autonomy of both parties has been lost (the owner has become the special-man-he-is-only-to-his-pet, and the animals has become dependent on its owner for every physical need), the parallelism of their separate lives has been destroyed [14–15].

A common joke suggests that pet owners seem to bear physical resemblance to their pets, and Roy and Christenfeld (2005) actually argue there is truth to this (at least for dogs). But the line between pet and owner often blurs beyond the physical. Many owners develop relationships with their pets that highlight their beliefs and construction of their own gendered identity, choosing animals and giving them attributes that reinforce their own masculine or feminine presentations. In doing so, these pet owners have not just developed a human/pet bond, they form an intricate construction of "my pet is me, I am my pet," further blurring lines between them, while connecting human and animal even more powerfully emotionally and socially. Ramirez's study of pets and owners finds that "gender norms influenced both the types of pets that owners chose to acquire and, among those who decided to get a dog, its breed, size, and sex" (377). He discovered that women who own dogs often describe them in feminine terms, and men prefer to describe their dogs' level of activity, strength, and physical appearance (381). Veterinarian and author Bruce Fogle reinforces this concept, arguing that "powerful and aggressive dogs such as Rottweilers and German shepherds … not only have a protective function but also reflect their owners' desires to present social selves which are correspondingly aggressive" (qtd. in Sanders). Interestingly, Ramirez found that "owners often remarked that they used their dogs as displays of props to confirm their own gender identities" (382). Humans create relationships with their pets that reinforce gender stereotypes, alternately aligning themselves with the dog's "feminine" or "masculine" qualities, or rejecting them as needed within their own construction and presentation of identity (382–383).

While many humans associate strongly with their pets, during a disaster a fine line has historically been drawn to separate the two, especially in disaster relief work. However, many understand the critical need to save both human and animal during a disaster, and that not doing so jeopardizes both entities. An animal rescue worker post–Katrina acknowledges the dilemma of "humans over animals" that many believe should guide relief work, saying, "It's not a matter of choosing animals over humans. If I were coming across a person and an animal, I'd help both. What I do for animals doesn't diminish my feelings for humans. And I *am* helping humans" (Anderson and Anderson 17). As many have embraced a "pet as self" mindset, this blurred relationship is critical to understand in the lens of a disaster. While the pet and owner may be linked, a hierarchy still exists. The pet's safety and well-being are solely in the hands of its owner. And often in a disaster, the owner's circumstances may be in someone else's hands.

Trusting Those in Charge

When faced with a place in the boat—at the cost of leaving your beloved pet behind—the dilemma is clear. Sadly, countless Katrina victims seeking safety encountered this situation. As rescue workers, often in the form of Coast Guard, National Guard or state and local police, maneuvered boats through flooded neighborhoods, they offered assistance to residents, but most often not to the companion animals. Often owners were told they couldn't bring the animals for safety reasons, as stressed animals are unpredictable, or the presence of the animals might scare other rescued victims. Or they were told this round of rescues didn't have room and the resources for pets. Often they were reassured that pets would later be retrieved and cared for by rescue workers. One bus driver moving evacuees out of New Orleans simply stated he didn't want a "dirty dog" on the bus. Subsequently, the owner of that dog, named Little Bit, was forced to leave the dog in a field before boarding the bus (Scott 172).

For many Katrina victims, this was a wakeup call about trusting those in charge; like their own animals, they found themselves vulnerable and completely in the hands of those meant to protect them. Perhaps one of the best known and compelling disaster narratives focusing on animals is that of Snowball, the small dog who eventually changed the course of companion animals and disaster response. The story begins with Associated Press writer Mary Foster breaking the story of Snowball, a little dog who had been initially evacuated to the area of the Superdome with his owner, a little boy. But when buses arrived, the family was informed by National Guardsmen that no pets were allowed. Foster witnessed the police stripping the little boy of the dog he held in his arms, and the child so distressed that he became ill. Reportedly, Snowball was left to fend for himself as his family was driven away, and he was never found again (Brinkley 516).

Perhaps even more devastating is the separation of Molly, a Seeing Eye dog, from her owner at the hands of the Coast Guard. Denise Okojo, blind and undergoing cancer treatments, was forced into a basket and airlifted away while her companion of six years, a Labrador retriever dog Molly, was forced to stay behind in the flooded house (Brinkley 517). Several individuals reported being bullied, badgered, or even beaten by rescuers when refusing to climb in boats without their pets. A man named William from East New Orleans found himself in a desperate situation, pushing his beloved dog, Miss Morgan, onto a roof and staying in the flood waters himself, knowing if the dog fell in the water, she would be washed away. Fourteen hours later, Coast Guard members approached in a boat and offered William a rope. He told rescuers he would not get in the boat until Miss Morgan was saved. The rescuers assured William the dog would be rescued, but only after William took the rope. William details the betrayal of his rescuers: "But as soon as they pulled me onto the boat, they sped away without Miss Morgan." William claims he could hear Miss Morgan's whining and barking from several blocks away as the boat retreated (Scott 19).

One man who refused rescue reported being Tasered by police, gaining consciousness only to find himself in the boat and his animal left behind. Others reported being held at gunpoint. While the National Guard continued their armed, "Drop your pets or else" policy toward many victims along Interstate 10, the Louisiana SPCA had already found buses and had asked authorities if they could take the animals of the evacuees, shadow the "human" buses, and thus reunite victims with their companion animals. They were told "no" (Brinkley 518). Throughout evacuation efforts, authorities gave mixed messages, and pet owners were often confused about rules. Pets were not officially allowed in boats, helicopters or buses, though a few generous rescue workers did allow them. Some owners were told that if they made their own way with their pets to the Superdome, they would be allowed in, but this was not true. Some owners voluntarily relinquished their pets to shelters not understanding their pets could be sent to a different state or euthanized if not picked up soon enough. Some made the excruciating decision to euthanize their pets on the spot because of a pet's age, condition, or personality around other pets (Anderson and Anderson 86). Many victims left their animals in homes, attics, and rooftops with bowls of food and notes attached to them, giving their names and vital information on how to be reunited. Other owners with good intentions but less foresight locked their animals in crates and cages, thinking the animals would be safer in a contained space while waiting for rescue—rescues that never came.

Many of Hurricane Katrina's victims did not have a choice in evacuating. Many New Orleans' residents were old, infirm, alone, did not have the financial resources, or simply did not own cars. Where should they go? Where would they stay? How would they get there? Would their pets be welcome? Nearly one-third of residents were non-evacuees. Forty percent of these stated they did not want to evacuate due to worries of leaving their pets behind (Fritz Institute). Melissa Hunt, Kelsey Bogue, and Nick Rohrbaugh studied pet ownership and evacuation of pets pre–Hurricane Irene—*six years* after Katrina. Of their sample, nearly a quarter reported not evacuating due to pet-related reasons. However, in spite of owners' desires to evacuate with a pet, an estimated 250,000 stray and owned animals were left behind as a result of Katrina (Anderson and Anderson 71; Scott 54). Of that number, only an estimated 5–12 percent of animals were reunited with their owners (Anderson and Anderson 173).

If there was not this understanding of animals' roles in our lives pre-2005, Hurricane Katrina and subsequent media coverage put it on the map. Desperate pictures of animals swimming in oily water, standing forlorn and frightened on rooftops, and the story of Snowball made clear to many that people were not willing to evacuate without their pets—and being asked or forced to do so is expensive emotionally, physically, and financially. Even the financial costs of relief efforts increase when rescuers must go back to neighborhoods to search for abandoned pets (Anderson and Anderson 8; "Saving Animals Saved Their Humans"). Saving animals *and* humans is the practical choice. Anything else puts the emotional health and physical safety of both pet and owner, and trust in government, at risk.

Saving My Animal, Saving Myself

Leaving a pet behind in a disaster leaves deep emotional scars, similar to those developed when one loses one's home, possessions, and property. Animal recuse workers reported that owners cast adrift from their homes and their lives post–Katrina would enter the shelters and repeat mantras like, "If only I can find my cat, I'll be okay" (Scott 218). Hurricane victims who left a pet behind suffered as much as emotionally, or often more so, as a hurricane victim who lost a house (Hunt, Bogue, and Rohrbaugh). Also, a forced abandonment of the pet adds exponentially to the trauma in terms of strength and duration of depressive and PTSD symptom. (Hunt, Al-Awadi, and Johnson). Anne Culver of the United States Humane Society agrees: "People can lose everything, but as long as they have their pets, they can go on" ("Saving Animals Saves Their Humans" 108). Those familiar with animal rescue efforts agree that saving animals has a direct relationship to how human victims cope post-disaster. Researchers on resiliency also understand the power of keeping things as "normal" as possible post-disaster, and argue that communities that can do this well rebound from trauma more effectively. Daniel Aldrich, professor and director of Security and Resilience Program Northeastern University, states that "Another big key is to engage in their normal activities as soon as possible. What's most disruptive when emerging from a tragedy is not getting back to your routines—their first priority should be to re-establish normalcy as best they can" (qtd.

in Callahan). Keeping pets and owners together allows for the creation of structures and routines, which will help both human and animal. Kirrilly Thompson, Danielle Every, Sophia Rainbird, Victoria Cornell, Bradley Smith, and Joshua Trigg argue in their article "No Pet or Their Person Left Behind: Increasing the Disaster Resilience of Vulnerable Groups through Animal Attachment, Activities and Networks" that "As pets and other animals provide assistance for these challenges in daily life, recovery without pets can lead to their exacerbation in life after a disaster" (229). Further, our relationships with pets may inspire us to save ourselves in future disasters. Especially for more vulnerable populations, "pet and animal-related activities and social networks could be used as conduits for disseminating disaster resilience information and engaging pet and animal owners in disaster resilience building behaviors" (216). Owners' love and feelings of protection for their pets may lead them to crafting disaster plans that will serve both pet *and* owner.

This discussion does not begin to address the number of animals that humans rely upon, not only for companionship and love, but for science, research, food, and labor. While "nearly 1.3 billion of the world's poorest people depend on animals" for their livelihood (Carroll), Leslie Irvine, researcher, Katrina volunteer, and writer of the thorough and compelling text on animals and disasters, *Filling the Ark*, argues powerfully that the United States does not do well protecting its livestock and research animals during disasters. She notes that "Even the U.S. Department of Agriculture ... has no funding or mandate to rescue animals raised for food" (2). Having a stronger disaster response for these types of animals would also allow humans to increase resiliency and strength in families, communities and their economies.

Memorial Hospital: The Blurred Line Between Care and Chaos

One might assume that large facilities in hurricane zones would have systems and protocols in place to reduce harm and loss. Yet many hospitals in the Hurricane Katrina flood zone faced dire circumstances. In spite of routine hurricanes dousing the area for centuries, many electrical systems and generators remained on lower floors, leaving patients and workers to deal with power outages that crippled necessary air conditioning, lighting of stairwells and corridors, and essential medical equipment like respirators. During Katrina, Memorial Hospital became a scene of confusion and fear, leading hospital workers to make painful decisions for both humans and (some) animals alike. And for any New Orleans citizen who did not evacuate before the storm, lack of clear evacuation plans, inconsistent communication, fear of looters and general chaos, and rumors that no one was coming for them led many to make drastic decisions for themselves and for others.

Routinely, essential workers at the hospitals in New Orleans would be accompanied by their families and pets during hurricanes, understanding that they would have long hours and could best manage their lives during the emergency if they brought their lives with them to work. However, nothing about this hurricane was routine. Sheri Fink's *Five Days at Memorial* presents in painstaking detail the ordeal workers and patients faced. Floodwaters rose, generators died, communication from parent company administration faltered, formal evacuations for patients dwindled, and gunshots rang out in the night. Several hospital workers realized—like citizens on the street—that their animals added exceptional burden to an already dire evacuation situation. Katrina hit on a Monday. On Thursday, when Memorial's parent company finally executed an evacuation plan for its workers, the helicopter pilots refused to take animals aboard. Dr. John Thiele at Memorial Hospital followed the wishes of his colleagues and helped some euthanize their pets humanely. One colleague who was able to quickly train her small dog to lie quietly in a duffel bag took her chances, but expressed her guilt at leaving her colleagues behind. Thiele stated, "Don't cry, just go.... An animal's like a child" (6–7).

The skeleton crew at Memorial continued to weigh their options. The hospital had no power, patients languished in sweltering corridors, and medical professionals labored to carry patients' beds up dark stairwells to get them to the roof for some relief. Evacuations for patients was slow, inconsistent, and painful. Hospital workers could not save themselves until the patients were saved. In some minds, a decision—though seemingly impossible—was clear. For a few patients who could not be moved, and not cared for as needed due to lack of power and lack of critical attention, a few medical professionals sought ways to ease their suffering. As New Orleans was described as "an irrational and uncivil environment," post-storm (9), the leap from euthanizing animals to euthanizing people was made. Dr. Anna Pou and two nurses were later charged with multiple counts of homicide, as twenty-three patients were found with elevated levels of morphine, midazolam, and lorazepam in their systems. However, a grand jury would not indict.

If medical professionals believed they were conducting humane euthanasia in the wake of the disaster, they were not the only essential workers doing so. Similarly, this blurred line between rescuer and tormenter became more defined when pet owners discovered their animals left behind purposefully at schools across New Orleans, places they were told were safe to wait for rescue, had been shot and killed by police. After Katrina, hundreds of residents found their ways to three of St. Bernard Parish areas schools, where they waited, with their pets, for assistance. When the police arrived, the deputies told everyone to leave their pets—that a shelter would care for them—and began the human evacuation to dry land across the Mississippi (Scott 184–5). When owners said goodbye to their animals in the school, they attached notes to them, or wrote messages on the classroom walls or chalkboards, informing rescuers of their pets' names, how to care for them, and how they could be contacted when a reunification of owner and pet could occur (Anderson and Anderson 279). However, these animals did not receive the care promised by the police. Dozens of dogs, while tethered to desks, were shot execution style by police. Some animals were found in stairwells, shot in the back or chest, left to die painful deaths due to blood loss. St. Bernard High School was described as "the scene of a bloodbath against pets" (Scott 184). Some police were unapologetic about their role. Sergeant Minton tried to explain, "Really, it's [to] benefit a dog, really, because, you know, where's he gonna find food, where's he gonna find water, you know? So I just looked at it more humane for the dog, you know." He also tried to justify the brutal behavior as self-defense. "They tried to eat us. Four days into it, [a deputy] almost got eat up by a Pit Bull" (Scott 187–88).

Clear understanding of what truly happened at both Memorial Hospital and St. Bernard Parish Schools seems blurred. Doctors at Memorial were prosecuted and then exonerated. Deputy Minton and his colleague, Sgt. Chip Englande, were charged with animal cruelty, but the Louisiana attorney general dismissed the charges (Irvine 25). Some say euthanasia occurred. Some say it was an impossible situation. Some simply say it was murder. In both cases, those whom New Orleans citizens trusted to protect them, who may have done equal harm to humans and animals, have been given a pass, and animals and humans alike paid the ultimate price.

People Helping People, Animals Helping Animals

While there are incidents of poor judgment and brutality, research has shown that disasters generally bring out the good in humanity. Contrary to any belief of disaster survivors behaving badly, Rebecca Solnit's *Paradise in Hell* presents the conflicting view that "The image of the selfish, panicky, or regressively savage human being in times of disasters has little truth to it" (2). Both Wolfenstein's "rise and fall of post-disaster utopia" (in Barton 206) and Fritz's "community of sufferers" (28) posit that humans in disasters generally behave splendidly and work with each other more than against. Some recent disaster relief efforts showcase the building of community created around the safe rescue of humans and animals. The flooding in Baton Rouge, followed by Hurricane Harvey pummeling Houston highlighted the effectiveness of the Cajun Navy, an informal but rather structured group of locals who took rescue efforts into their own hands and began saving their neighbors. On their Facebook page, they proudly and defiantly announce: "We don't wait for the help, We are the help! We the people of Louisiana refuse to stand by and wait for help in the wake of disasters in our state and the country. We rise up to unite and help rescue our neighbors!" (Louisiana Cajun Navy Facebook). Many in the community believe this brave and caring group, and not the "distant forces of government," are responsible for their safety and well-being (Wallace-Wells).

While not an organized force, animals have been seen also putting themselves at risk during a disaster in order to help a fellow animal. Days after the breach of the levees in New Orleans, rescuers on the hunt for abandoned animals combed neighborhoods. One International Fund for Animal Welfare volunteer reported the story of a dog found swimming in the toxic water. When the rescue boat approached, instead of coming to the boat, the dog swam in another direction; the rescuers followed. This dog led them to what rescuers called, "his girlfriend," a female dog trapped inside a house. It was only when the female dog was secured in the boat that the male dog allowed himself to be rescued, too. The volunteer reported that while stroking the male dog's head, the volunteer jerked his hand away from the dog's fur, feeling as if his hand had been burned. The volunteer interpreted that the dog willingly spent more time in the toxic water than he needed to in order to save a fellow animal (Anderson and Anderson xiii).

Animal rescuers post–Katrina working near an apartment building met a dog named Katie and her companion, Bandit, an old Chihuahua. Bandit eagerly jumped in the rescue boat and made himself comfortable after his ordeal, but Katie would not. She led rescuers deeper into the building, finally up to the apartment's attic, where Katie's owner had placed a bird in its cage and a fishbowl on a shelf. Rescuers returned to the boat with all pets in hand, and the owner, thanks to her trusted dog, Katie, reunited with her pet family (Anderson and Anderson 56). At the Jefferson Parish animal shelter, a volunteer witnessed an American pit bull terrier nursing two different litters—her own and that of a different dog (Scott 11).

While thousands of human volunteers flood disaster zones around the United States and place effort on search and rescue of the region's animals, instances exist of animals rescuing humans or leading them from danger, too. After Japan's earthquake and resulting tsunami in 2011, an eighty-three-year-old woman believed herself and her Shih Tzu, Babu, to be safe in her home. But Babu, agitated and distressed, paced until the woman put the leash on the dog and went outside. Babu pulled on his leash, leading his owner up a hill and away from their regular walking path near the water. Babu persisted pulling his owner along until they reached the hilltop, where the woman looked back and saw her home submerged in flood water (Elder). Larger animals are also capable of assisting humans in trouble. During the 2017 Indian floods, (domesticated) elephants were spotted helping humans out of flood waters. These animals are apparently skilled in assessing danger during a natural disaster, and like rescue dogs, "have a good sense of smell and have been known to alert rescuers to people trapped in buildings" (Gibbens). Search and rescue teams around the world have utilized dogs for search and rescue as well as recovery of remains, demonstrating that of course they can be trained, but also that they are natural partners to humans in disaster relief work.

There's an App for That

A pet being recused by a human or another pet is only step one of a long battle. Most pets who have been left behind in a disaster struggle to be reunited with their owners. Using the same ways that humans connect, pets have found success in connecting with their owners through the use of social media. Those who have fallen prey to kitten videos on YouTube are aware of the power that cute animals have to lure viewers to the Internet and social media sites. Disaster relief organizations have taken full advantage of this and have used sites to get needed attention for animal victims of disasters. Similar to the photographs and "have you seen?" posters plastered to lower Manhattan fences, gates and windows after 9/11, Camp Tylertown rescue compound in Mississippi, nicknamed Ellis Island for its ability to shelter and catalogue hundreds of lost and forlorn pets (Scott 38), created binders of mugshots of rescued animals from Katrina, hoping to assist owners who roamed the massive shelter looking for their companions (Scott 160). Animal rescue workers after many disasters establish social media sites and enlist the support of Petfinder to create profiles for rescued animals separated from their families. Profiles are designed to reconnect owners and pets, but since only a fraction of animals are reunited with their families post-disasters, these profiles of reconnection often shift to attract new owners. Pet profiles are modeled after human dating sites, showcasing multiple photos of the pet in as many cute poses as possible, and even writing pet narratives in the first-person, detailing the pet's personality, likes, and requirements for a suitable match.

Petfinder had a daily posting of animals arriving at Best Friends base camp after Katrina. While most companion animals post–Katrina were not reunited with their owners, due to Petfinder's success in using social media and technology as a connective tool, 15 percent of the pets that had been rescued by the Best Friends organization had been reunited with owners by December 2006 (Scott 166). Anderson and Anderson argue that rescue organizations "cannot overemphasize how important it is for animal shelters and animal welfare organizations to have volunteers or staff who specialize in focusing media attention onto pet adoption and publicizing the many ways these organizations serve their communities" (256). Social media sites have demonstrated their importance in connecting and reuniting animals and people just as powerfully as they continue to connect humans every day.

Media Darlings and Disasters

Not only do social media platforms help to get an animal's message disseminated after a disaster, the television and news media are equally powerful in highlighting the plight of animals and soliciting emotional responses from viewers. Borrowing form the success of human-interest stories after a disaster, the media turned several animals' situations into a "pet interest story." As a tragedy can become personalized and more digestible for us when it is on a more intimate scale, media know to create a narrative around a particular victim and showcase that story for greatest emotional impact. Animals have also been the "human interest story" of a disaster, which has served them well. Just as a human with a particularly compelling story is often the face of the disaster and becomes the media's darling, certain pets have leveraged public opinion. Individual animals have also been the focus of post-disaster features in newspapers and television. What may have begun with Snowball at the Superdome continued with journalists' deep dives into the lives of certain animals, thus putting a needed furry face to the tragedy. (Anderson and Anderson 253). Journalist Anderson Cooper performed emotional searches for dogs on camera, with one of his most compelling focusing on Red, a dog who had been hit by a truck post–Katrina and rendered partially paralyzed until rescue workers found and rehabilitated him. CNN's coverage led to Red's finding a permanent home (Scott 121). Actor Matthew McConaughey and Oprah Winfrey combined efforts to film live animal rescues aided by Dr. James Riopelle, who stayed in an empty, darkened Lindy Boggs hospital to single-handedly care for an army of animals left behind by employees (Anderson and Anderson 253). NBC *Dateline* crews also filmed a profile on the Best Friends shelter in Tylertown, Mississippi, and its efforts. Eight animals were later reunited with owners (on camera!) due to being spotted on the profile (Scott 133). The highly-publicized story of poor, abandoned Snowball is reportedly one reason the Pets Evacuation and Transportation Standards (PETS) Act of 2006 was created, as the media attention and strong public response motivated politicians to act to do more for animals and their humans (Irvine 23).

What the media choose to portray in the middle of disaster relief shifts the narrative in a particular direction—for both humans and animals alike. In Katrina, the issue of race lurked beneath many stories—who was evacuated and was not, whose neighborhood was more damaged and whose was not, and who was considered a looter and who was not. While many people bond and help their fellow man, disasters are often the feeding grounds for opportunists—and looters often appear. Many of these individuals may already be criminals, eyeing hardware stores for tools to use to break into valuable places like warehouses, landscaping companies, and industrial facilities. But many are just trying to survive. However, according to the media—depending upon who is caught where— the narrative seems to change. Some members of the media were questioned whether the captions ascribed to photographs of Katrina victims were worded differently based on the race of the victim. One young black man wading through the water with a case of soda was labeled as "looting," while a white man and light-skinned woman in a similar scene were described as "finding" such items (Kinney).

Apparently animals can be looters, too. After Hurricane Harvey in Texas, one animal was spotted on an abandoned street "looting," and its image and surrounding story went viral. A large dog named Otis walked purposefully down the empty street with a large dog food bag clasped in his powerful jaws. A local resident who spotted Otis snapped a photo. "It's like he's on a mission…. I just thought it was so cute," the resident stated (Phillips). But unlike other human victims, this hungry pup-cum-looter was considered resourceful and adorable, showcasing the way the media and the viewers label disaster victims depending upon certain criteria of race, class—and species.

Flood as the Great Equalizer

In a DVD the city of New Orleans created for the 60 percent of residents who sheltered in place during Katrina due to transportation constraints, the local Red Cross executive director informed New Orleanians, "You're responsible for your safety, and you're responsible for the person next to you" (Nolan). This statement, rather ominous in hindsight, reinforces Solnit's premise that in disasters, we are our neighbor's keeper. This common vulnerability and strength create a disaster community in which rescuer, victim, human, animal come together to survive as one. This rare time of special unity was acknowledged by the Baton Rouge community during the 2016 Louisiana floods, in response to the presence of the Cajun Navy. Wallace-Wells reports, "There was a social elegance in the idea that working-class families were rescued by working-class heroes in boats, in episodes that not always, but sometimes, cut across racial lines." And neighbors took pride in the slogan they created, "Floodwaters don't discriminate" (Wallace-Wells). Rescued animals may also have been humbled, as rescuers during Katrina reported that cats, dogs, birds, and spiders all "got along" when rescued. An animal rescue worker named Susie tells the story of a goose who suddenly ran toward her while Susie was scouting an abandoned neighborhood. The goose, willingly netted, sat comfortably in the back of a pickup truck filled with lose dogs and crated cats. Susie interpreted the menagerie: "The animals all got along. They knew they had been saved, and at that moment they all were on equal ground" (Scott 64). Species were not discriminated against in rescue efforts. Dogs, cats, birds, snakes, chickens, ducks, insects, pot-bellied pigs, iguanas, hamsters, exotic fish, ferrets, and one emu were saved (144–153). Disasters can serve as the great equalizer of all creatures. But actually, certain animals—and certain humans—are more vulnerable to the effects of disasters in the first place. And the fate of certain individuals and animals during and post-disaster has a great deal to do with how victims are divided by others in terms of race, class, and species.

Who Gets Saved?

In a disaster, which people, and by extension, which animals, fare better? As Katrina showed us, older, poorer people did not fare as well. The mean age of Katrina victims was sixty-nine years. Approximately 50 percent of the people who died were seventy-five years and older, while fewer than ten percent of victims were younger than forty-five years old (Brunkard et al.). Older animals didn't do much better. Dogs between six months to five years old had the highest survival rate (Scott 207). The statistics are not unique to Katrina. In many disasters, including Katrina, the poor, the disabled, and the elderly, are disproportionately affected (Flanagan et al.). Charles Perrow and Melissa Hunt, Kelsey Bogue, and Nick Rohrbaugh remind us that while the coastal areas of the United States are often enjoyed by those who can afford to own and develop them, it is the poor and minority groups who possess fewer resources to expedite a safe evacuation. Further, this population suffers the greatest during recovery. After Katrina, New Orleans police officer Warren Riley railed against this reality: "I can assure you that if some storm hit Kennebunkport, Maine, it would have been a different story" (Brinkley 509). In an interview, Terry Ebert of Homeland Security later lamented, "We didn't do enough to help earmark the special needs people…. We will next time" (Brinkley 24). There will be a next time. In an area of the country where hurricanes are not surprising, it is this lack of foresight that surprises many. Randy Cohen, the former ethics columnist for the *New York Times Magazine*, wrote a response to Memorial Hospital's Safety and Evacuation Plan for its most vulnerable patients: "Why weren't there plans to cope with these patients when you knew a storm was coming? Sometimes the ethical—the most important ethical question sometimes is the one you ask not at the moment of crisis, but the duty you have to anticipate certain kinds of crises and avoid them" (Fink 275). Further, as race, poverty, and age indicate more marginalized populations in disasters, certain pets may be marginalized, too—and this stigma may, in part, result from the stigma that taints their owners.

Pit bulls are dogs that carry such stigma, and that reputation is magnified during disasters. As was previously presented, New Orleans police officers post–Katrina justified executing these dogs because they claimed to have feared being attacked by them. During Hurricane Harvey in 2017, rumors went viral about the senseless euthanizing of pit bulls, or the transfer of these controversial dogs to high-kill shelters, to make room for more "desirable" dogs. The Houston SPCA refused help from the Best Friends Animal Society, a group that undertook incredible work to rescue animals, shelter them, and organized reunions with the region's displaced owners during Katrina. That added to the suspicion of what may have been happening at the shelter. The Houston SPCA took to Facebook to defend itself, but volunteer workers at the temporary shelter reported being locked out, and the fates of some dogs may remain unknown (Goldman). Whatever may or may not have happened to the pit bulls, decisions are made during a disaster about who is and is not as valued. Pit bulls who were saved at the Lamar-Dixon animal shelter post–Katrina made up 25 percent of the dogs rescued after the hurricane. This high number left them vulnerable to a different kind of abuse—victims of potential dog fighting. Pit bulls became the most stolen dog from shelter, leaving the volunteers no choice but to arrange for twenty-four-hour surveillance and security forces to protect the animals and the volunteers who cared for them (Anderson and Anderson 120–121). The breed that is loved to be hated and loved for its alleged capacity for hate was a significant casualty of Katrina before, during, and after the storm.

Bronwen Dickey, in her text exploring the rich history of pit bulls in American society, expands the lore of the domesticated dog as one that speaks to many: "In the thirty-five thousand years since we entered the interspecies partnership that made civilization possible, the literature of dogs has mostly become a literature of longing: for home, for safety, for acceptance, and probably for some flicker of the wildness we ourselves have lost" (22). This connection between animal (in this case, dog), and human almost bridges the gap between who humans once were and what we have become.

Pit bulls have their own lore, but it is often one of violence and aggression. Pit bulls, often scrutinized in the media, are often blamed for attacks and violence they did not even commit. In a case captured by a CBS news camera, an animal control investigator in California was bitten by a pit bull. After processing this news footage, not only did

Los Angelinos report "seeing loose 'pit bulls' where none existed" (Dickey 161), animal control workers across the country reported increases in pit bull complaints—even when it was clear that twenty-seven different dog breeds had actually been the culprits in the incidences (161). One reason for this may be that pit bulls are often connected with African American street culture, which often seals the identity of both dog and man. As Dickey writes,

> In a pit bull, a young man could see whatever version of himself he wanted, from family defender to resourceful hustler, to unbowed survivor. Never had a generation of African-Americans, especially the urban poor, connected with a specific type of dog they felt represented their collective identity [Dickey 191–192].

Rapper DMX wrote that while growing up in housing projects, his pit bull Boomer was not only protector and companion, but like a "real person." "The dog was more like me than I ever imagined, and I was like my dog" (194).

Just as Dickey presents that culturally and socially pit bulls can be pariahs, the actor Michael B. Jordan, lead in the 2013 *Fruitvale Station*, posits in an Oprah Winfrey interview that African American males are the pit bulls of America: "We're labeled vicious, inhumane and left to die in the street." If one accepts Jordan's argument, it is simple to connect the media's negative portrayal of African American men as aggressors and looters during Katrina to the way pit bulls have been treated during disasters. Whether killed brutally by police in St. Bernard Parish schools or euthanized in Texas to make room for more desirable dogs, certain animals in a disaster are treated similarly to humans. Just as society creates a hierarchy of more valuable humans, it does so for animals, too.

The Future

Hurricane Katrina put a spotlight on the painful decision many survivors had to make to abandon pets to choose safe evacuation. Data collected from Katrina and other natural disasters demonstrate painful, often unnecessary choices humans make for their animal companions in times of disaster. The result is emotional distress for both human and pet, unnecessary death of companion animals, and difficult living conditions for the animals who are left to survive in a post-disaster landscape. While the Pets Evacuation and Transportation Standards (PETS) Act of 2006 improves many things, including allowing federal money to create emergency animal shelters and offering aid to state and local governments who create evacuation plans including pets and service animals, even recent hurricanes show that many are still not clear on these laws, are not capable of following through during an emergency situation, or may simply not treat their own animals with care during a disaster. Daniel Aldrich argues that "[t]hough it's perhaps counterintuitive, getting through multiple traumatic events gives people an inoculation to it. People can use the lessons they've learned from the past to help bounce forward" (qtd. in Callahan). However, data show that not all lessons learned lead to greater outcomes for pets. In spite of the PETS legislation, many pet owners still report not evacuating during Hurricane Irene in 2011, for example, due to pet-related reasons (Hunt, Bogue, and Rohrbaugh). Many owners cited confusion about evacuation or difficulty in the pet-evacuation process. During Hurricane Irma in 2017, animals in the Florida Keys were found left tied to trees and poles, locked up in pens, or simply abandoned outside to face the dangerous conditions in spite of being warned by authorities that such treatment is a felony: "This is a prime example of animal cruelty," says Florida State Attorney Dave Aronberg. "We will find you, and we will prosecute you" (Brinlee). Over a decade since Katrina, there is still work to be done.

Disasters, man-made or natural, are a part of our future. Scientists predict that natural disasters such as hurricanes will not only be more frequent but be stronger and more damaging due to issues of climate change and urbanization (Shuckburgh, et al.). Not only are some types of natural disasters increasing, population trends around the world put millions in the most vulnerable locations (Perrow 29). Many places around the world, especially coastal cities in the United States, are examining not only their infrastructure but their policies and disaster plans, too. The lessons of the past have shown the physical damages of these storms cost millions and billions to communities, but the emotional toll on citizens may be insurmountable. Policies and plans to include companion animals in our own personal disaster plans is a must as jurisdictions and governments work to improve formal evacuations plans that include pets. And this does not even begin to scratch the surface of including and protecting the research animals and agricultural animals humans rely upon for our future (Irvine). Researchers and authors cannot resist the easy reference to the Biblical ark in examining animal rescue, but we cannot wait for one single individual like Noah nor rely on divine intervention to improve rescue efforts.

Instead, we are all responsible for examining our mindset toward disasters in general and shift away from what Karen Cerulo refers to as "positive asymmetry," a way of putting negative scenarios into perspective by denouncing "the worst." In *Filling the Ark*, Leslie Irvine was the first to examine animal treatment and recuse through Cerulo's lens of positive asymmetry. It is human nature and our brain's way of protecting us that we operate from positive asymmetry to believe that the worst cannot happen to us. Positive asymmetry looks similar across disasters. Scott, a landlord from Orleans Parish who did not heed Katrina warnings to evacuate, stated, "[t]here is always the forecast of doom and gloom one or two times every year. We had already evacuated for four hurricanes that didn't hit or were weak. It's such a pain with 1.3 million people trying to take the same highway out of town. We just stopped listening to the warnings" (Anderson and Anderson 80). Even Hurricane Harvey in 2017 left people scrambling, wondering what they would possibly take in an evacuation they had only moments to prepare for. "There were so many things, I couldn't think of one thing. I think I was in a dream it wouldn't happen," Harvey victim Dale Crumbaugh stated (McCrummen 2017). Irvine notes the pervasive presence of positive asymmetry in her analysis of animal disaster responses and the constant utterings of "We never imagined" she heard from animal owners, rescue agencies, and volunteers (120–123).

If we believed that every failure, danger, or disaster could be ours (which would be a form of negative asymmetry, Cerulo explains), we surely would not rise up from our beds each day. But in protecting ourselves from these seemingly unfathomable thoughts— "what's the worst that can happen?"—we are actually endangering our animals, who have no choice but to rely upon human reasoning in the face of a disaster. According to Cerulo, within positive asymmetry, a practice groups and communities utilize is "clouding," which enables the group to keep the worst-case scenario out of focus—intentionally:

> The practice makes the worst fuzzy and incomplete, and encourages groups and communities from pursuing the "correction" that would bring the worst into focus. Thus, clouding adjusts the impact of the worst, making its territory difficult to inhabit. Via clouding, the worst becomes the latent element

of consciousness—present, but at play beneath the surface. Like static on a radio that makes it difficult to draw in certain sounds, clouding encourages us to abandon the worst-case signal, turn the dial, and tune in the clearer, more manifest best-case alternative [95–96].

How could we imagine the physical damage and loss of homes, jobs, and basic infrastructure of our communities? How could we imagine those who protect us each day would turn on us and our animals? How could we imagine making the painful decision to euthanize the helpless, sick, and weak? We may not have the imagination to conjure these scenarios, but these disaster narratives are our reality now. Our disorganization and disbelief prior to and in the midst of that disaster chaos cannot be routine. The best approach to adopt, Cerulo believes, is "best and worst, separate but equal" (Cerulo 241). This means awareness of the pending disaster, acknowledgment of its severity, wide and open dissemination of information, broad communication, and a creation of a plan. Marita, Mike, and Lee argue that it was such thinking and behaviors that contributed to the PETS Act in the first place. These cognitive and behavioral steps seem to be what might save people—and animals—in our future.

Maybe humans should start working more like our animals: rely less on our faulty reasoning and more on the animal instinct of pure survival: spend less time rationalizing and avoiding the worst-case scenario, and spend more time taking lessons from our pets and thinking of preservation first. Perhaps that is the line that needs to be blurred. Animals have no choice of what happens to them in a disaster. While they may move on instinct, they do not have the choice to stay, to evacuate, to trust others to make decisions for them. This is where the line is clear. Humans do have this choice. "Planning means you made a choice," Anderson and Anderson remind us. "You chose to be smart, to be aware, and to know that disasters are possible, even in the illusory safety of your home. Planning means that you are proactive and working to beat the odds" (240). Cats cannot rationalize. Dogs do not weigh their options. But people make many choices to evacuate or not, or to treat potential disasters as annoyances or absolute. It is decision-making that separates humans from animals, yet this faulty decision-making often serves to endanger more humans and animals. It is a cycle—the more resilient we can be during disasters, the better our animals will fare. The more we have our animals with us, the more resilient we will become. The more resilient we become during and post-disaster, the greater chance we can protect our animals and keep them with us, further strengthening our resiliency. As a nation we readily adopt our pets, but until we adopt the mindset and full awareness that we—and our pets—should and must prepare actively for the worst, there will never be enough room in the boat.

Works Cited

American Veterinary Medical Association. "U.S. Pet Ownership Statistics." *AVMA*. www.avma.org/KB/Resources/Statistics/Pages/Market-research-statistics-US-petownership.aspx. Accessed 10 Jul. 2018.

American Pet Products Association. "2017–2018 APPA National Pet Owners Survey." *APPA*. americanpetproducts.org/Uploads/MemServices/GPE2017_NPOS_Seminar.pdf. Accessed 10 Jul. 2018.

American Pet Products Association. "Pet Industry Markets Size and Ownership Statistics." *APPA*. www.americanpetproducts.org/press_industrytrends.asp. Accessed 10 Jul. 2018.

Anderson, Allen, and Linda Anderson. *Rescued: Saving Animals from Disaster*. New World Library, 2006.

Barton, Allen H. *Communities in Disaster: A Sociological Analysis of Collective Stress Situations*. Doubleday and Co., 1979.

Berger, John. *About Looking*. Vintage Books, 1980.

Binfet, John-Tyler, Holli-Anne Passmore, A. Cebry, Kathryn Struik. and C. McKay. "Reducing University Students' Stress Through a Drop-In Canine Therapy Program. *Journal of Mental Health,* vol. 27, no. 3, 17 Dec. 2017, pp. 97–204. DOI: 10.1080/09638237.2017.1417551.

Brinkley, Douglas. *The Great Deluge: Hurricane Katrina, New Orleans, and the Mississippi Gulf Coast.* Harper-Collins, 2006.

Brinlee, Morgan. "Florida Pets Abandoned During Hurricane Irma are Rescued by Animal Control." *Bustle,* Bustle Digital Group, 10 Sept. 2017, www.bustle.com/p/florida-pets-abandoned-during-hurricane-irma-are-rescued-by-animal-control-2307153. Accessed 5 Jun. 2018.

Brunkard, Joan, Gonza Namulanda, and Raoult Ratard. "Hurricane Katrina Deaths, Louisiana, 2005." *Disaster Medicine and Public Health Preparedness.* 28 Aug. 2008, ldh.la.gov/assets/docs/katrina/deceasedreports/KatrinaDeaths_082008.pdf. Accessed 22 Jul. 2018.

Callahan, Molly. "London Fire: How Structures, and People, Can Withstand Trauma." *News@Northeastern,* Northeastern University, 15 June 2017, news.northeastern.edu/2017/06/15/london-fire-how-structures-and-people-can-withstand-trauma/. 5 May 2018.

Carroll, Joshua. "After the Flood: How Saving Animals Is About More Than Just Sentimentality; Providing Assistance and Aid to Humans Is Obviously the Priority in Disaster Situations, but Animals Represent a Financial Lifeline to Many Communities." *Guardian.* Guardian Newspapers Limited. 3 Aug. 2015. Academic OneFile. link.galegroup.com.ezproxy.neu.edu/apps/doc/A424087779/AONE?u=mlin_b_northest&sid=AONE&xid=246a84be. Accessed 30 May 2018.

Cerulo, Karen. *Never Saw It Coming: Cultural Challenges to Envisioning the Worst.* University of Chicago Press, 2008.

Dickey, Bronwen. *Pit Bull: The Battle Over an American Icon.* Alfred A. Knopf, 2016.

Elder, Scott. "Tsunami Heroes: Rescued or Reunited, Animals and People Pull Together After a Huge Natural Disaster." *National Geographic Kids* Nov. 2011, p. 20+. *Gale.* www//link.galegroup.com.ezproxy.neu.edu/apps/doc/A276807948/ITOF?u=mlin_b_nortest&sid=ITOF&xid=b35f851e. Accessed 30 May 2018.

Fink, Sheri. *Five Days at Memorial: Life and Death in a Storm-Ravaged Hospital.* Crown Publishers, 2013.

Flanagan, Barry E., Gregory W. Edward, Elaine J. Hallisey, Janet L. Heitgerd, and Brian Lewis. "A Social Vulnerability Index for Disaster Management." *Journal of Homeland Security and Emergency Management,* vol. 8, no, 1, 5 Jan. 2011, doi: 10.2202/1547-7355.1792.

Fritz, Charles E. "Disasters and Mental Health: Therapeutic Principles Drawn from Disaster Studies. *Historical and Comparative Disaster Series No. 10.* "Disaster Research Center, University of Delaware, 1996, udspace.udel.edu/handle/19716/1325?show=full. Accessed 3 April 2018.

Fritz Institute. *2006 Fritz Institute-Harris Interactive Katrina Survey Reveals Inadequate Immediate Relief Provided to Those Most Vulnerable.* 26 Apr. 2006, www.fritzinstitute.org/prsrmPR-FI-HIKatrinaSurvey.htm. Accessed 7/10/18.

Garde, Elena, Guillermo Enrique Perez, Gerardo Acosta-Jamett, and Barend Mark Bronsvoort. "Challenges Encountered During the Veterinary Disaster Response: An Example from Chile." *Animals,* vol. 3, no. 4, 2013, pp. 1073–1085, doi.org/10.3390/ani3041073.

Gibbens, Sarah. "Elephants Rescue Hundreds of People from Floods." *National Geographic,* 16 Aug. 2017, news.nationalgeographic.com/2017/08/asian-elephants-rescue-people-floods-india-nepal-video-spd/. Accessed 1 Jun. 2018.

Goldman, Laura. "Did the Houston SPCA Euthanize Pit Bulls at a Temporary Shelter?" *Care2.com,* 8 Sept. 2017, www.care2.com/causes/did-the-houston-spca-euthanize-pit-bulls-at-a-temporary-shelter.html. Accessed 23 April 2018.

Hunt, Melissa, Hind Al-Awadi and Megan Johnson. "Psychological Sequelae of Pet Loss Following Hurricane Katrina." *Anthrozoos,* vol. 21, no. 2, 28 April 2015, pp. 109–121, doi.org/10.2752/175303708X305765.

Hunt, Melissa G., Kelsey Bogue, and Nick Rohrbaugh. "Pet Ownership and Evacuation Prior to Hurricane Irene." *Animals,* vol. 2, no. 4, 28 Sept. 2012, pp. 529–539. doi: 10.3390/ani2040529.

Irvine, Leslie. *Filling the Ark: Animal Welfare in Disasters.* Temple University Press, 2009.

Jones, M. Gail, Simon M. Rice and Sue Cotton. "Who Let the Dogs Out? Therapy Dogs in Clinical Practice." *Australasian Psychiatry,* vol. 26 no. 2, Apr. 2018, pp. 196–199, *Sage Journals,* doi.org/10.1177%2F1039856217749056.

Kinney, Aaron. "Looting" or "Finding"?: Bloggers Are Outraged Over the Different Captions on Photos of Blacks and Whites in New Orleans." *Salon,* 2 Sept. 2005, www.salon.com/2005/09/02/photo_controversy/. Accessed 18 Jun. 2018.

Louisiana Cajun Navy. "Post." louisianacn.com/Facebook. Facebook. Accessed 20 Jun. 2018.

Marita, Mike, Rebecca Mike, and Clark J. Lee. "Katrina's Animal Legacy: the PETS Act." *Journal of Animal Law and Ethics,* vol, 4, no. 1, May 2011, pp. 133–160.

McCleery, Kathleen. "Meet the 'Courtroom Dogs' Who Help Child Crime Victims Tell Their Stories." *PBSNewshour,* 27 May 2016, www.pbs.org/newshour/show/meet-the-courtroom-dogs-who-help-child-crime-victims-tell-their-stories. Accessed 4 May 2018.

McCrummen, Stephanie. "With Floodwaters Rising and a Rescue Boat Waiting, the Urgent Question: What to Bring?" *Washington Post,* 31 Aug. 2017, www.washingtonpost.com/national/with-floodwaters-rising-and-a-rescue-boat-waiting-what-to-bring/2017/08/31/429a77c2-8e76-11e7-91d5-ab4e4bb76a3a_story.html?noredirect=on&utm_term=.0092a353de88. Accessed 1 Jul. 2018.

Meehan, Michael, Bronwyn Massavelli, and Nancy Pachana. "Using Attachment Theory and Social Support

Theory to Examine and Measure Pets as Sources of Social Support and Attachment Figures." *Anthrozoös*, vol. 30, no. 2, 16 May 2017, pp. 273–289, doi: 10.1080/08927936.2017.1311050.

"Michael B. Jordan 'Black Males, We Are America's Pit Bulls.'" *Oprah's Next Chapter*. Oprah Winfrey. OWN, 8 Dec. 2013. Oprahwww, www.oprah.com/own-oprahs-next-chapter/whymichael-b-jordan-says-black-males-are-americas-pit-bulls-video. Accessed 17 Jul 2018.

Mueller, Megan, and Leslie McCullough. "Effects of Equine-Facilitated Psychotherapy on Post-Traumatic Stress Symptoms in Youth." *Journal of Child & Family Studies*, vol. 26, no. 4, Apr. 2017, p. 1164–1172. doi: 10.1007/s10826-016-0648-6.

Nolan, Bruce. "In Storm, N.O. Wants No One Left Behind." *Times-Picayune*. 2005 July 24, www.columbia.edu/itc/journalism/cases/katrina/Press/Times-Picayune/2005-07-24%20TP%20Evacuation.pdf. Accessed 30 Jun. 2018.

O'Haire, M.E., and K.E. Rodriguez, "Preliminary Efficacy of Service Dogs as a Complementary Treatment for Posttraumatic Stress Disorder in Military Members and Veterans. *Journal of Consulting and Clinical Psychology*, vol. 86, no. 2, Feb. 2018, pp. 179–188, doi: 10.1037/ccp0000267.

Pawlowski, A. "When Humans Grieve, More Funeral Homes Are Offering Therapy Dogs to Help." 22 Jun. 2017 *TODAY*, Today.com, www.today.com/health/therapy-dogs-funeral-homes-help-mourners-process-grief-t112992. Accessed 25 July 2018.

Perrow, Charles. *The Next Catastrophe: Reducing Our Vulnerabilities to Natural, Industrial, and Terrorist Disasters*. Princeton University Press, 1997.

Phillips, Kristine. "A Photo of a Dog Carrying a Bag of Food After a Storm Hit Texas Went Viral. Here's His Story." *The Washington Post*. 27 August. 2017, www.washingtonpost.com/news/animalia/wp/2017/08/27/a-photo-of-a-dog-carrying-a-bag-of-food-after-a-storm-hit-texas-went-viral-heres-his-story/?noredirect=on&utm_term=.3aacc27d3fdd. Accessed 5 May 2018.

Ramirez, Michael. "'My Dog's Just Like Me': Dog Ownership as a Gender Display." *Symbolic Interaction*, vol. 29, no. 3, Summer 2006, pp. 373–391, *Wiley*, www.jstor.org/stable/10.1525/si.2006.29.3.373. Accessed 6 Jun. 2018.

ReCHAI: Research Center for Human-Animal Interaction. "Current Research." *Research Center for Human-Animal Interaction*, rechai.missouri.edu/current-research/. Accessed 12 Jul. 2018.

Roy, Michael M., and Nicholas J.S. Christenfeld. "Dogs Still Do Resemble Their Owners." *Psychological Science*, vol. 16, no. 9, 2005, pp. 743–44, psy2.ucsd.edu/~nchristenfeld/Publications_files/Dogs-II.pdf. Accessed 4 Sept. 2018.

Sanders, Clinton R. "The Animal 'Other': Self Definition, Social Identity and Companion Animals." *Advances in Consumer Research*, vol. 17, 1990, pp. 662–668, acrwebsite.org/volumes/7082/volumes/v17/NA-17. Accessed 22 May 2018.

"Saving Animals Saves Their Humans, Disaster Expert Advises Responders." *Emergency Preparedness News*, 19 July 2005, p. 108. General OneFile, link.galegroup.com/apps/doc/A134673270/ITOF?u=mlin_b_northest&sid=ITOF&xid=f5ed3945. Accessed 9 Jun. 2018.

Schiffman, Richard. "Are Pets the New Probiotic? Epidemiological Studies Show That Children Who Grow Up in Households with Dogs Have a Lower Risk for Developing Autoimmune Illnesses Like Asthma and Allergies." *New York Times* 6 Jun. 2017, mobile.nytimes.com/2017/06/06/well/family/are-pets-the-new-probiotic.html?smid=fb-nytimes&smtyp=cur&smvar=wkndst&_r=0&referer=https://m.facebook.com./. Accessed 2 Jun. 2018.

Scott, Cathy. *Pawprints of Katrina: Pets Saved and Lessons Learned*. John Wiley & Sons Publishing, 2010.

Shuckburgh, Emily, Dann Mitchell, and Peter Stott. "Hurricanes Harvey, Irma and Maria: How Natural Were These 'Natural Disasters'? *Weather*. vol. 72, 8 November 2017, pp. 353–354, https://doi.org/10.1002/wea.3190.

Solnit, Rebecca. *A Paradise Built in Hell: The Extraordinary Communities That Arise in Disaster*. Penguin, 2009.

Thompson, Kirrilly, Danielle Every, Sophia Rainbird, Victoria Cornell, Bradley Smith, and Joshua Trigg. "No Pet or Their Person Left Behind: Increasing the Disaster Resilience of Vulnerable Groups through Animal Attachment, Activities and Networks." *Animals*, vol. 4, 2014, pp. 214–240, doi:10.3390/ani4020214.

Wallace-Wells, Benjamin. "Why Does America Need the Cajun Navy?" *The New Yorker*, 31 August 2017, www.newyorker.com/news/news-desk/why-does-america-need-the-cajun-navy. Accessed 20 Jun. 2018.

Mirrored Caregiving

Chronic Illness in the Human/Animal Household

Terri Kovach

December 22, 2015. About 2:00 a.m. The rattling noise begins, with a small jostling of the bed. It gets louder, and my first thought is the dog is trying to get at one of the cats under the bed. As my sleep fog clears, I realize that Bela never chases the cats in the night. I flip on the light as my husband rouses from sleep; Bela is at the foot of the bed, trying to stand. She is slipping around on the wooden floor that is covered in urine puddles. The vomiting begins as she struggles to keep her feet beneath her. Trying to keep her sixty-five-pound body from falling, I half-walk, half-drag her into the bathroom. In the dim light, my husband has stepped in a puddle of urine, so his feet and the bottoms of his pajama pants are soaked. He asks about getting her into the car and to the ER vet. Bela's eyes look lost. Now lying on the bathroom floor and trembling, she vomits again and her breathing moves into a slow, long pattern as I sit next to her. Chest heaving, she takes three long, very slow deep breaths over about one minute. My husband and I do a quick calculation of the distance and time to get to the emergency vet and realize Bela is likely dying right here on our bathroom floor. We watch. Shortly her breathing comes back to normal. Still on her side, Bela starts to glance around. When she finds her feet, she acts as though she's going to vomit again. I lead her outside where she jumps briskly off the back porch into the dark yard, squats to urinate, sniffs the freezing air, and prances back to us on the cold porch. She pops into the house and stops to drink a little water from the cat bowl. We clean her up. We clean the floors up. We clean ourselves up.

December 22, 2015. At 2:40 a.m. Bela is back on her bed, quietly snoring. The lights are out, but we're wide awake in our dark bedroom. I think, "Just a seizure. I'll talk to the vet in the morning."

According to the American Veterinary Medical Association (AVMA), there are nearly 150 million cats and dogs living as pets in U.S. households (American Veterinary, "U.S"). Significant research outlines the benefits of pet ownership for humans, for both social relationships and health outcomes. Most research surrounding the care of ill animals revolves around treatment options in the veterinary literature and end-of-life decision making and euthanasia in the social science literature. The long-term care of chronically ill animals has not been so robustly explored. Research by Spitznagel et al. ("Caregiving"; "Predicting") may be the first to use an instrument known as the Zarit Burden Interview that is intended to measure the burden of caregiving to humans on a population that is giving care to animals. A qualitative examination of the experience of living with three chronically ill companion animals in a household that also has long-standing experience with human Crohn's disease provides insight into the mirrored care-giving burden and expands the conceptual framework of the blurred line between humans and animals.

A longer lifespan for humans brings with it more chronic illnesses such as arthritis, diabetes, organ failure, and some diseases often brought on by sedentary lifestyles. House-hold pets are living longer because of increases in nutrition, vaccinations, and veterinary care, but this longer life also brings an increase in some of these same chronic, rather than acute, illnesses. For pet dogs and cats, as for all companion animals, being "owned" ideally comes with reliable food sources, appropriate and clean living conditions, opti-mized social relationships (both human and animal), and effective response to illnesses and injuries. Pets are often viewed as "part of the family," a recognition of the emotional relationships between owner and pets, as well as an outcome of the marketing strength of companies that supply the accouterments of ownership: food, bedding, supplies, sup-plements, toys, and health care (American Pet). For owners, visits to the veterinarian for examination and maintenance treatments are part of the routine of a socially conscious and responsible owner. Some treatments, such as rabies vaccinations and cruelty stan-dards, are governed by law. The onset of serious illness or the occurrence of injury typ-ically results in a trip to the veterinarian for care and advice. For most pet owners, these crises and serious injury visits are episodic and unusual. Owners of chronically ill pets have a different experience.

Caring for chronically ill companion animals presents particular challenges. In acute illnesses or catastrophic injuries, the decision-making window and the treatment options are often quite narrow: without brisk decision-making and nearly immediate treatment, the lifespan of the animal is quickly shortened. By contrast, a chronic illness may present as an acute crisis, but it is only after significant investigation and testing to get to the bottom of the problem that the chronic nature is revealed. Other chronic illnesses present with more subtle symptoms that manifest and accumulate over time. Living with a chron-ically ill companion animal emerges as another commitment: choosing to care and to incorporate another set of demands into daily life.

My current experience with three chronically ill companion animals has mirrored much of my decades-long experience with Crohn's disease. My household now includes my husband who was diagnosed with Crohn's at 19; Maggie, a 13-year-old cat with long-standing frailty and kidney problems; Bela, a 9-year-old standard poodle with Addison's disease; and Russell, a 5-year-old cat with severe food allergies and chronic bladder issues. My husband and I have two adult children: a daughter and a son, who each have fami-lies.

Conventional wisdom argues that pet ownership has benefits: companionship to the lonely or house-bound, exercise to the heart-challenged or overweight, life-lessons to children, and simple joy to owners. Researchers have examined psychological, phys-iological, and social benefits of pet ownership with various research designs, populations, sample sizes, and differing definitions of "pet." Examination of a national sample by Clark Cline suggests dog ownership was more beneficial to well-being for women and for single individuals, offering that male owners may not place as much value on their relationships with their pets. For married individuals, dog ownership may contribute to role strain, just another "set of obligations that are difficult to fulfill" (126). Allen McConnell and colleagues examined elements of social support afforded owners by their pets, primarily dogs and cats, but including other species such as horses, lizards, and one goat (1242). Findings suggest companion animals provide social support resulting in higher measures of well-being and individual difference, but not at the expense of human social support, i.e., pets complement rather than supplant human social resources (McConnell et al. 1250). In a large, multinational study, pets were described as "useful" to expand social networks; pets do not offer direct support and companionship so much as they serve as a conduit to form new friendships and resultant social support (Wood et al.). Dog owners were five times more likely to form new social relationships than other pet owners, attributed to the social interaction brought about by dog-walking (8). A pet serves as an "ice-breaker" between people in a neighborhood, whether a dog, cat, chicken, rabbit, sheep, turtle, a donkey, or pet snake (9). In a broad conclusion, Wood et al. suggest that pets can help develop the well-being of a community (15).

Some pet research examines children and the elderly. For children, just the presence of their own dog buffers the child's perceived stress, more so than the presence of the parent or being alone; physiological response is unchanged, with the pet having no effect on cortisol levels in saliva (Kertes et al. 14). In a German study, Graf suggests ownership of pets by the elderly offers happiness and an incentive against passivity, but pets can be problematic since they may cause falls or overexertion. One recommendation for nursing practice was to recognize and accept elderly patients' pets as members of the family (qtd. in Tzivian, Friger, and Kushnir 110).

Barker and Wolen offer a comprehensive review of nearly thirty years of research on the benefits of pet ownership. Despite problems of weak study design, convenience samples, and small sample sizes, there is growing evidence that companion animals buffer stress for some owners and may increase health-associated behaviors such as physical activity (492). Paul and Ariella Cherniack echo the skepticism of research quality on the beneficial effects of pet ownership, suggesting that studies fail to consider potential harms. While there are implications for modest cardiovascular and mental health benefits, they contend, "For most people, however, the benefits of pet ownership remain intangible" (716).

Research also includes the influence of the animals' illness and death on owners. In a study of 213 female current and bereaved dog owners, 89 percent of the deceased dogs were euthanized because of illness. Bereaved owners showed higher levels of stress and lower levels of quality-of-life measures on physical, psychological, and relationship domains, but no effect on health domains (Tzivian et al. 11–12). For bereaved owners, lack of social support may exacerbate grief reactions; for current owners, dog ownership may be just one of many elements that influences everyday stress (12). Donna Podrazik et al. outline grief responses of those who have lost a pet, including those who have euthanized "a pet that is chronically ill, overly aggressive, or seriously injured" (364). They describe similarities between grief responses to human and companion animal loss while outlining suggestions for specific clinical psychological care. Fox offers two brief questions in decision-making about euthanasia: "1) Is the pet in pain and requiring medication to function? 2) Does the maintenance of the companion animal induce a financial hardship for the family?" (qtd. in Podrazik et al. 386). Podrazik et al. offer these as guiding questions for those who are considering euthanasia. Christiansen et al. suggest that a conflicting concern (such as balancing treatment against dog suffering or congruent family illness which demands balancing dog health against owner sacrifice) is one genesis of difficult decision-making (5–6).

Research on humans is vigorous and clear: social connections help people have longer and healthier lives. Objective, quantitative measures (few social network ties, infrequent social contact, living alone) and subjective measures (the emotional state of loneliness) predict the likelihood of premature mortality (Holt-Lunstad et al. 235–236). Yet strong social connections also come with responsibilities and demands between people. Injury or illness likely mean a change in roles for family members put in the position of caregiver. This could range from a relatively minor disruption of schedules in the short term to complete upheaval of ordinary life in the case of catastrophic illness or injuries. Somewhere in the middle is the responsibility of caring for a family member with chronic illness. In all cases, the fortunate person with robust social relationships is more likely to receive medical care and support; for the caregiver it means a greater social burden. Quality of life measures in these relationships are multidimensional and include physical, psychological, social, and spiritual elements, while expanding to burden and family function for caregivers (Lim and Zebrack). The researchers warn that "recovery from crisis" (7) may not occur for caregivers of the chronically ill, since all family systems are under continual strain and may not reach a state of adaptation. The family of the chronically ill may provide direct care while also serving as the organizer of support services and as an advocate (Griffith and Hastings 401). Caregivers expressed love for their ill family members, described the chronic stress of providing care, reported loss of identity (and occasional sense of fulfillment), while reporting that support services very often caused additional problems rather than attenuating the burden of care (416). While research on caregiving to humans is strong, with few exceptions there is a significant gap in the research on caregiving to chronically ill companion animals. A glimpse into the mirrored experiences of caregiving supports the view of a blurred line between animals and humans.

This project found its genesis in a calendar. I have kept track of all professional and personal appointments in an eighteen-month calendar for many years. While I tried to recall the dog's first seizure, the calendar revealed the seizure, notes on time, impressions of what had happened, and notes from the veterinarian appointment later that same morning. As the animals' care became more complex, the entries in the calendars grew more frequent and detailed. The data points for this project are triangulated among entries from those calendars, household records of detailed veterinarian receipts, and copies of each pet's record supplied by the veterinary practice. Recollections of events were verified and enhanced by referring to all three sets of documents. That same calendar holds the major appointments of my husband, who maintains his own calendar and notebooks.

Harry Wolcott (36) calls for qualitative researchers to specify their interest and background in a topic and my experience with companion animals and family caregiving warrants description. I have owned a cat, and typically two cats, since I finished college and began my first professional job. A dog was added as soon as I moved into a house with a yard, some years before I married. I use the term "owned"; my pets are important to me and deeply cared for, but I do not consider them to be my "family" or "children," terms used so effectively in contemporary advertising. The closest any of the animals come to "family" is when I talk about them to my adult children, describing "what your hairy sister" or "what your hairy little brother" did (typically involving a disgusting hairball or a live rodent brought into the house), or when I talk to the pets and ask whether "daddy" fed them. My cats have been obtained for free as kittens. In contrast, my three female dogs have been pedigreed, purchased as puppies at eight weeks old. My homes have been in the suburbs or farming areas, with fenced-in yards for the dogs. For forty-plus years, I have kept neutered companion animals, typically two, in my home: a cat or two and a dog. My experience for the first thirty years was straightforward and not particularly challenging. Overall, the pets had robust health until late in life when they were euthanized by a veterinarian. My husband of thirty plus years was diagnosed with Crohn's disease at nineteen, my son was diagnosed at age eleven, a typical onset pattern contrary to the aged onset that is usual for many chronic conditions. Crohn's disease is a chronic inflammatory disease of the bowels. Symptoms include pain, diarrhea, bloody stools, arthritis-like symptoms, fatigue, weight loss, and malnutrition. Initial symptoms ahead of diagnosis may be mild or fleeting, perhaps confused with a lingering flu. The complications of full-on Crohn's can be severe and life-threatening (Mayo). My personal and professional experience includes a long-standing position as an academic librarian, volunteer work and research in hospice and palliative care services, and teaching sociology coursework including gerontology and the sociology of death. These companion animal experiences, family caregiving, and professional work inform these interpretations.

Maggie arrived in August of 2005. On a late-morning walk, I heard a loud, high-pitched "mew" as a very small, black kitten emerged from a driveway culvert. It appeared someone had "dumped" a litter of kittens in my country neighborhood. The veterinarian confirmed that Maggie already had significant contact with humans, since she cried out and pursued me: a feral kitten would have been silent. In the first step of anthropomorphizing, Maggie bore the name of the friend who cared for her for a few days when she was very young. After a careful cleaning, deworming, and treatment for giardia, she joined our home with an adult female German shepherd named Kara and another cat, Crash Davis. "Sweet Maggie" settled in comfortably. She never got very large—at her first three-year rabies vaccination in 2006, she weighed seven pounds. She was athletic and small, playful and fast, often seeming to defy gravity. Generally healthy, Maggie seemed "off" her food occasionally but maintained her weight. She started to have bouts of "forgetting what food was for": she would walk away from her food as though she did not recognize it, but still drank water enthusiastically, something she had done even as a kitten.

A crisis in early March 2011, when Maggie was nearly six, was more complicated. Over the course of a couple days, she became dehydrated and weak. She continued to have bowel movements, but began to vomit her food, then refused food and water. The veterinarian ran blood work on Friday, which showed elevated liver measures and suggested those might be the result of her dehydration or something more troublesome. When the veterinarian suggested the possibility of a liver biopsy, I quickly said "no." "So no heroic measures?" We agreed on that plan of action. They would rule out pancreatitis with more blood work. She had lost nearly a pound, roughly 15 percent of her body weight. Maggie was rehydrated by a subcutaneous infusion of fluids and given steroids. I agreed to try some different food options, but over the weekend she worsened significantly. Beginning Monday, Maggie spent three days and two overnights at the veterinarian's connected to an IV fluid supply. She was described as "sweet" and "patient" and such a "cute girl." By Wednesday, she was brightened considerably, and I took her home. Friday, two days later, we had a quick checkup scheduled at the vet, where she was described as "bright" and "alert." But the bulk of that Friday appointment was devoted to a very ill Bela, described below. Maggie recovered her appetite over the next few days and gradually regained her strength. At her next wellness appointment later in the year, the veterinarian greeted Maggie and said, "I can't believe she's still here."

Maggie's health stabilized. At an annual examination two years later in September 2013, Maggie was normal and healthy at seven pounds. A week later, she was off her food again with a dry coat which called for a quick trip to the veterinarian. She had lost a half-pound in a week and was dehydrated. They gave her subcutaneous fluids and sent her home with kidney food. Two days later, she was eating and keeping food down. In mid–December 2014 and in late January 2015, there were two more veterinarian visits with a similar pattern. Throughout, her kidney function tests were mixed, with one measure slightly elevated, the other normal. In 2018, at 13 years old, she is in the early stages of kidney failure.

Bela joined the household in summer 2009. A female standard poodle, Bela was given my father's Hungarian name and I envisioned this stereotypically "fancy" dog as a country retriever. She is athletic, curious in the fields, friendly, independent, and smart. She was crate-trained on a schedule described by the Monks of New Skete (116–117). Bela only soiled the house once as a puppy, but urinary house-breaking took longer, since she had an on-again, off-again bladder infection for the first few months. With that under control, by late fall she was ringing a bell hung from the back door to signal she needed to go outside to relieve herself. At Bela's one-year exam the summer of 2010, she was doing very well. By fall, at roughly sixteen months old, she was off her food occasionally, with infrequent episodes of diarrhea and vomiting. Her weight had settled into the mid- to upper fifties. Beginning in late January through early March of 2011, Bela and I attended a local dog obedience class where we met other owners and dogs, learned a few skills, and had fun.

Unlike most dogs, poodles need to have their coats trimmed and shaped. During the winter months, I keep Bela's hair a little longer as protection against the cold Michigan weather. When I picked her up from the groomer's on a Wednesday in early March (the same day I had picked up Maggie after two days on IV fluids), I was surprised at how thin Bela looked: that shaggy winter coat was hiding a significant weight loss. By the next day she was lethargic, vomiting, and refusing all food. On Friday I took her with me to Maggie's follow-up appointment. Bela weighed 47.4 pounds. The veterinarian reminded me of our visits of the previous fall with similar symptoms and said Addison's disease was a distinct possibility. Addison's disease (or hypoadrenocorticism) is a chronic hormonal disorder that may appear suddenly or slowly (College; Klein and Peterson: Pt I 65). Bela had exhibited symptoms intermittently, but her significant deterioration and weight loss in early 2011 may have been triggered by the January to March obedience class, since circumstances that produce stress exacerbate symptoms. The grooming appointment that revealed her weight loss may have contributed as well. While Addison's chronic nature and initial vague symptoms may make it seem readily managed, an acute "Addisonian crisis" can be quickly fatal (Klein and Peterson: Pt II 181; Van Lanen and Sande). We scheduled a diagnostic test and nursed her through the weekend. With a firm diagnosis the following week, treatment began immediately, but Bela's weight continued to drop another four pounds in the next ten days. I was convinced she had crossed a physiological threshold that could not be retraced, and fearful there would be no saving her. My husband and I discussed our options for euthanasia.

Two weeks after the Addison's confirmation, armed with daily oral steroids and an injection, Bela's weight began to stabilize, then rise. Now, fall 2018, at nine years old, Bela is playful and vigorous. She weighs 65 pounds and has continued with oral steroids and a Percortin/Zycortal injection every 25–28 days. That brief description belies the reality of her care. She has had intermittent bouts of diarrhea and occasional vomiting over the years. The challenge of a dog with Addison's is discerning the severity and cause of a symptom: is the diarrhea caused by a small rodent she may have killed and eaten or is it caused by a stress reaction to out-of-town guests? The seizure described at the opening of the essay is the most dramatic event, but not the only one. On another occasion she experienced a sudden near-collapse in the field behind our home. She could barely stand, vomited violently, and took about 10 minutes to walk the 200 feet or so to the house. But her blood work that might indicate an Addisonian crisis was normal. Bela's chronic illness means each indication of illness prompts an examination of what preceded it and a decision about appropriate care. Just as in humans with complex medical histories, each medication or preventive supplement has to be assessed for interaction with her underlying Addison's treatment. Each "event" of a long car ride, a trip to the groomer, a visit from friends or relatives, or an unexpected home repairman becomes a question mark. Daily and seemingly normal events may cause enough stress that it needs to be managed by altering her steroid levels.

Russell arrived over Labor Day weekend of 2013. I had been considering another cat since having Crash euthanized in 2012. Crash and Bela had been very friendly companions, and Maggie was a poor substitute. A sign along the road for "free kittens" signaled the end of the search. Russell was named by my sister, in honor of one of her favorite actors; she kept calling him "a handsome boy." His arrival marked the beginning a new friendship and wrestling partner for Bela. Russell was born in a machine shop and at eight weeks was accustomed to humans, dogs, noise, and lots of activity. As happens to all new animals in the household, the first stop was to the vet for a checkup and parasite control. Nothing was problematic except some soft stools, readily controlled with different food. He was already litter trained and quickly made a good adjustment. By the summer of 2014, however, it was clear Russell was having some digestive issues, with many soft bowel movements every day. After cycling through a variety of food options, at his fall 2014 checkup the veterinarian suggested he may have a significant food allergy and recommended a feeding alternative. The prescription food was effective, expensive, and it solved the problem quickly.

Just before the fall holidays of 2017, my husband walked into the living room and said, "You better come look at this." It was a large puddle of cat urine on the bathroom floor, heavily streaked with blood. A urine sample showed abnormal pH levels, bladder crystals, and many blood cells. Russell received antibiotics and a recommendation for an over-the-counter dietary supplement to bring his pH levels under control. That supplement, at one-third the recommended dose, provoked a severe digestive reaction: bloody liquid stools, not contained to the litter box. There is an effective prescription diet for cats with bladder crystals, but Russell's severe food allergies make using it problematic. Russell has transitioned to another urinary care food. His bowels are normal and consistent, his bladder issues seem stable, but the resultant facial and neck scabbing and hair thinning on his front paws can only be controlled with medication. He remains friendly to humans, partial to men, will sit next to a running vacuum sweeper, and will greet strangers at the door much like a dog.

These episodes of chronic animal illness and caregiving are redolent of the decades-long experiences of caregiving within my family. A Crohn's pain or cramp may warrant a relatively mild analgesic or it could signal the beginnings of real trouble such as a bowel obstruction. A mild fever, headache, or chills could be a cold or flu, or the early signs of a perforated bowel wall and septic infection. Both the obstruction and the bowel perforation are life-threatening and demand a trip to the emergency room for immediate care. Early in our marriage, during one three-year period, my husband had seven surgeries with a cumulated six months of hospitalization and another six months away from work. I have taken my husband to the ER where we live, while on vacation, and once in a foreign country. He has found himself in the ER alone on two different trips, one time driving around the downtown area of a major Florida city in the middle of the night, trying to locate the hospital. He called home at 3:15 a.m., and our son, a graduate student at the time who was home for a few days, grabbed his backpack and drove to the airport to find a flight south. In another brush with catastrophe, a co-worker picked up my husband's car keys from the floor where he'd dropped them and said, "No, you're not driving yourself home. I'm taking you the [the ER]." He had a septic infection and was teetering on the edge of kidney failure. Travel outside the availability of Western medicine is out of the question.

Three years after his diagnosis with Crohn's, our son missed three months of his freshman year of high school with an appendectomy, a complicating infection, and a bowel resection (the first of three). At one brief period of time that fall, my husband and son were both hospitalized: same city, different hospitals a few miles from each other. This foreshadowed my experience during the spring of 2011 when both Maggie and Bela were terribly ill while I myself was preparing for surgery and trying to figure out whether to have Bela euthanized. Assessing the symptoms of Addison's disease in the dog or an off day of eating in the cats mirrors the same decision points for Crohn's disease. Is this manageable at home, worth a call to the doctor, or does it demand a high-speed drive to the ER and the swift intervention of high-level medical professionals in order to keep my husband or son or pets alive? Most months and years of Crohn's are manageable and new medical treatments can stave off surgeries, but the episodic crises are frightening and exhausting for the entire family. The same goes for my animal companions. Their health crises may be less frightening and less emotionally fraught, but exhausting nevertheless.

For my household, there are two overarching elements that revolve around chronic illness: food and scheduled doctors' visits. Maggie's eating habits are slow and precise. She is a grazer, often ignoring wet food if dry is available. Even as a kitten she sought out and enjoyed fresh water—in bowls, pans, ice-cubes floating in a cup—all were worthy of pursuit and enjoyment. The diagnosis of Maggie's kidney problems in 2017 reinforced that watery habit and introduced a wet food designed to maintain kidney function; blood work verifies its efficacy on one measure while another measure continues to indicate ongoing kidney problems. Bela has eaten a kibble diet moistened with water since she was young. With her on-again, off-again bladder infections during 2009 and 2010, cranberry extract was added at the recommendation of the veterinarian, which she takes with her food every breakfast. The Addison's diagnosis in 2011 meant medication injections plus oral steroid pills. Events that are stressful to the dog—car travel, groomer visits, houseguests—warrant adjustments to the steroid dosage and pattern. With some increasing vomiting and loose stool problems, Bela went to a digestive diet kibble in 2016. A thrice-daily feeding schedule replaced a twice-daily schedule with the addition of Russell to the household. He is a voracious and aggressive eater. He will eat his own food, then knock Maggie off her food if given the opportunity. Since any "regular" food typically prompts a bout of diarrhea and dermatitis for Russell, it is important to keep food separate and protected. A small, late evening bit of kibble for each of the cats helps keep a little weight on Maggie and keeps Russell from meowing in the night. Managing the feeding routines is a challenge because of the variety of foods, the personalities of the pets, and the medical demands of each. It involves five different foods for the three animals: one kibble for the dog, and two different wet foods, and dry foods for the cats (plus medications for all). The wet cat foods are nearly indistinguishable in can colors or in food colors and textures. There is a routine of dish colors, left and right placement of cans and dishes, labeled containers for the kibble, along with the timing and bowl locations. Meal preparation is in the kitchen. Maggie is fed in a quiet corner of the kitchen, Russell is led to the basement with a dish of food, and Bela rushes enthusiastically to the laundry room where she is confined by a gate.

While the day-to-day routine of feeding is time-consuming in its complexity, the monthly Percortin/Zycortal injections for Bela involve scheduling an appointment that is balanced against a work schedule, weekends when the veterinarian practice is not available, travel time back and forth, and predicting events that may be particularly stressful for the dog. For example, trips to the groomer are generally scheduled within a week or two after the Percortin shot, never just before a Percortin shot when she may be more vulnerable to a stress reaction. If someone comes to house-sit, Bela's schedule of medication has to be taken into account well before our departure, and the house-sitter has to be comfortable with the routine and the responsibility.

My husband's eating patterns are not ritualized, but because of long-term scarring of his intestine from Crohn's, his food choices are highly limited. Household meal shopping and preparation, vacations, and social events like a trip to a restaurant or a party all include the questions "What can I eat?" or "Will there be decent restrooms available?" Unlike the animals, though, he manages his own medications and his diet while shouldering some of the burden of care for the pets. We share the responsibility of cooking an extremely low-residue diet. "No seeds, no peels" is where we begin for him. To some degree we maintain two kitchens in our habits, one for each of us. Creamy for him, crunchy for me. My husband, too, has daily medications and periodic visits to a clinic, where every eight weeks he receives an infusion of medication. Our son's menu is more limited by grain problems rather than by food texture or residue. He self-injects his Crohn's medication every two weeks and uses daily oral medication.

Ritualization of care, both informal (daily feedings, stool examination for cats and dog, and litter and yard cleanup) and formal (veterinary visits and monthly injections), help to make the burden of caring for three chronically ill animals less so. I cover most of the hygiene tasks like litter boxes and yard cleanup, since the immunosuppression drugs to manage Crohn's make that risky for my husband (Stull et al. 736). Crohn's has been an element of our marriage relationship since its beginning and then expanded with our son's diagnosis. Three recent out-patient surgeries for our son have meant an out-of-town trip for me, my husband, and our daughter in order to accompany him to the hospital. Ritualization of human care, both informal (food selection, symptom monitoring and management) and formal (scheduled doctor visits and eight-week infusions or two-week injections), helps keep our now-expanded family in a more settled and healthy state while averting disaster. Each of the demands for responsible caregiving comes with a cost in terms of time, energy, and finances.

This complex and ongoing care regimens for animals and humans mirror each other—they look the same, but they are not the same. The blurred line of this care is narrow or wide, depending on the humans who are responsible for offering it. Both humans and animals clearly benefit by having a strong human support system. People have different resources and make varying, sometimes painful decisions about how to spend their time, energy, and monies for themselves and for their companion animals. The leading cause of personal bankruptcy in the U.S. is a family medical crisis. The specifics of the influence of caring for chronically ill animals on the average family budget is not so clearly known, and I would offer they are significant. But the option of euthanasia is the rock that breaks the mirrored glass between animal and human illness. It strips away anthropomorphism. People have the legal, moral, and cultural authority to put an animal down. Animals are treated like property and can be disposed of accordingly, as long as it is done humanely. The American Veterinary Medical Association recognizes euthanasia as an ethical act (American Veterinary, "Principles"), even publishing a table of acceptable methods and alternatives for different species ("Euthanasia"). In contrast, euthanasia of humans is a crime in all U.S. states, while legal in Canada and some countries of Europe, South America, and south-central Asia. Part of this distinction is definitive in nature: what one country labels as euthanasia another may describe as assisted suicide. Assisted suicide is legal in eight states of the U.S. (with varying regulations) and there are regular efforts to extend its reach. In almost all cases, the knowledge and/or consent of the ill person is a fundamental requirement. Legal consent or cognitive knowledge is a standard that is impossible to meet with animals, so they rely on human good will and compassionate care. In euthanizing a pet, sometimes "[h]e's had enough" is perhaps a translation of a difficult, angry, or heart-wrenching "I've had enough."

There is another blurred line in this examination that warrants mention but will not be explored here. That is the blurred line between a person who is chronically ill and the disease itself. There is a stigma attached to diseases, some more burdensome than others. People with chronic illness, particularly those with evident physical manifestations like facial or physical deformities, or those who have to shape their days differently in order to rely on bathroom availability, often become identified with the illness itself. When our son was diagnosed, I pushed back on his having to go down to the school office once a day, every day, to have his one pill dispensed to him. In my view that was a stigmatizing and isolating requirement that did more harm than good. We were firm in letting our son be a kid, not "the kid with Crohn's." My husband is a man, not "the guy with Crohn's." I am a woman who happens to care for a household full of chronically ill beings who are some days exhausting but most days hilarious. The blurred line of person/disease is one that I reject. Some of my animal experience reflects the findings of Clark Cline, who offered that pet ownership for married people, rather than a beneficial experience, may simply be another burden that is difficult to manage (126). Lillian Tzivian, M. Friger, and T Kushnir describe dog ownership as just one factor in a large number of elements that add stress (12). A marriage, a family, a house, an extended family, friendships, work, professional service, personal health, community obligations—each of these elements of adult life comes with a measure of stress. For the first time in my life, I am looking forward to having no pets. But Maggie will join me in bed tonight, purr a little, and then plop down to spend the night. No matter what trouble she causes, I will miss her terribly when she is gone. The caregiver burden of a family with two Crohn's disease sufferers is real. Food, travel, work, day-to-day recreation choices are all steered by

Crohn's. But my husband will join me in bed tonight, yawn and stretch, then fluff his pillows to spend the night. No matter what trouble he causes, I will do what it takes to keep him around.

Most families who bring an animal into a household know with certainty that the future will bring death and sadness. With compassion and generosity, we bring animals of many types (including carnivores) into our households and let them become our children's best friends, our running buddies, or our quiet companions, with certain knowledge that those pets will likely die well ahead of us. The line between human and animal is blurred as these animals burrow, leap, slink, chirp, jump, poop, pee, and sometimes vomit their way into our families—our hearts, our calendars, and our pocketbooks. Caring for chronically ill animals, just as is caring for chronically ill humans, is not for the faint of heart. That blurred line is one that many enthusiastically walk, even while challenged by the responsibility.

WORKS CITED

American Pet Products Association. "Pet Industry Market Size and Ownership Statistics." 2018. www.americanpetproducts.org/press_industrytrends.asp. Accessed 21 Mar. 2018.

American Veterinary Medical Association. "Principles of Veterinary Medical Ethics of the AVMA." *AVMA*, Apr. 2016, www.avma.org/KB/Policies/Pages/Principles-of-Veterinary-Medical-Ethics-of-the-AVMA.aspx?PF=1. Accessed 31 Dec. 2017.

American Veterinary Medical Association. "U.S. Pet Ownership Statistics." *AMVA*, 2018, www.avma.org/KB/Resources/Statistics/Pages/Market-research-statistics-US-pet-ownership.aspx. Accessed 23 Jan. 2018.

Barker, Sandra B., and Aaron R. Wolen. "The Benefits of Human-Companion Animal Interaction: A Review." *Journal of Veterinary Medical Education*, vol. 34, no. 4, 2008, pp. 487–95. *ResearchGate*, doi:10.3138/jvme.35.4.487.

Cherniack, E. Paul, and Ariella Cherniack. "Assessing the Benefits and Risks of Owning a Pet." *CMAJ*, vol. 187, no. 10, 2015, pp. 715–16, doi:10.1503/cmaj.150274.

Christiansen, Stine Billeschou, Annemarie Thuri Kristensen, Jesper Lassen, and Peter Sandøe. "Veterinarians' Role in Clients' Decision-making Regarding Seriously Ill Companion Animal Patients." *Acta Veterinaria Scandinavica*, vol. 58, no. 1, 25 May 2016, pp. 1–14. *EBSCOhost*, doi:10.1186/s13028-016-0211-x.

Clark Cline, Krista Marie. "Psychological Effects of Dog Ownership: Role Strain, Role Enhancement, and Depression." *Journal of Social Psychology*, vol. 150, no. 2, Mar.-Apr. 2010, pp. 117–131. *EBSCOhost*, monroeccc.idm.oclc.org/login?url=http://search.ebscohost.com/login.aspx?direct=true&db=aph&AN=48242199&site=ehost-live.

College of Veterinary Medicine. "Addison's Disease." Washington State U, www.vetmed.wsu.edu/outreach/Pet-Health-Topics/categories/diseases/addison's-disease. Accessed 02 Feb. 2018.

"Euthanasia." *The Merck Veterinary Manual*. Edited by Susan E. Aiello and Michael A. Moses, 11th ed., Merck, 2016, pp. 1641–43.

Griffith, G.M., and R.P. Hastings. "'He's hard work, but he's worth it.' The Experience of Caregivers of Individuals with Intellectual Disabilities and Challenging Behaviour: A Meta-Synthesis of Qualitative Research." *Journal of Applied Research in Intellectual Disabilities*, vol. 27, 2014, pp. 401–419, doi:10.1111/jar.12073.

Holt-Lunstad, Julianne T.B. Smith, M. Baker, T. Harris, and D. Stephenson. "Loneliness and Social Isolation as Risk Factors for Mortality: A Meta-Analytic Review." *Perspectives on Psychological Science*, vol. 10, no. 2, 2015, pp. 227–237, doi:10.1177/1745691614568352.

Kertes, Darlene A., Jingwen Liu, Nathan J. Hall, Natalie A. Hadad, Clive D.L. Wynne, and Samarth S. Bhatt. "Effect of Pet Dog on Children's Perceived Stress and Cortisol Stress Response." *Social Development*, vol. 26, no. 2, 2017, pp. 382–401, doi:10.1111/sode.12203.

Klein, Susan C., and Mark E. Peterson. "Canine Hypoadrenocorticism: Part I." *Canadian Veterinary Journal*, vol. 51, no.1, 2010, pp. 63–69. www.ncbi.nlm.nih.gov/pmc/articles/PMC2797351/. Accessed 3 Mar. 2018.

Klein, Susan C., and Mark E. Peterson. "Canine Hypoadrenocorticism: Part II." *Canadian Veterinary Journal*, vol. 51, no.2, 2010, pp. 179–84. www.ncbi.nlm.nih.gov/pmc/articles/PMC2808283/. Accessed 3 Mar. 2018.

Lim, Jung-won, and Brad Zebrack. "Caring for Family Members with Chronic Physical Illness: A Critical Review of Caregiver Literature." *Health and Quality of Life Outcomes*, vol. 2, no. 50, 17 Sept. 2004, pp. 1–9, doi:10.1186/1477-7525-2-50.

Mayo Clinic. "Crohn's Disease: Symptoms and Causes." 2018. https://www.mayoclinic.org/diseases-conditions/crohns-disease/symptoms-causes/syc-20353304. Accessed 15 Aug. 2018.

McConnell, Allen R., Christina M. Brown, Tonya M. Shoda, Laura F. Stayton, and Colleen E. Martin. "Friends with Benefits: On the Positive Consequences of Pet Ownership." *Journal of Personality and Social Psychology*, vol. 101, no. 6, pp. 1239–52, doi:10.1037/a0024506.

Monks of New Skete. *The Art of Raising a Puppy*. Little, Brown, 1991.

Podrazik, Donna, Shane Shackford, Louis Becker, and Troy Heckert. "The Death of a Pet: Implications for Loss and Bereavement Across the Lifespan." *Journal of Personal and Interpersonal Loss*, vol. 5, no. 4, Oct.–Dec. 2000, pp. 361–95. *EBSCOhost*, monroeccc.idm.oclc.org/login?url=http://search.ebscohost.com/login.aspx?direct=true&db=aph&AN=3696765&site=ehost-live.

Spitznagle, Mary Beth, Dana M. Jacobson, Melanie D. Cox, and Mark D. Carlson, "Caregiver Burden in Owners of a Sick Companion Animal: A Cross-sectional Observational Study." *Veterinary Record*, vol. 181, no. 12, 2017. doi.org/10.1136/vr.104295.

Spitznagle, Mary Beth, D.M. Jacobson, M.D. Cox, and M.D. Carlson, "Predicting Caregiver Burden in General Veterinary Clients: Contribution of Companion Animal Clinical Signs and Problem Behaviors." *The Veterinary Journal*, vol. 236, June 2018, pp. 23–30. doi.org/10.1016/j.tvjl.2018.04.007.

Stull, Jason W., Jason Brophy, and J.S. Weese. "Reducing the Risk of Pet-Associated Zoonotic Infections." *CMAJ*, vol. 187, no. 10, 14 July 2015, pp. 736–43, doi:10.1503/cmaj.141020.

Tzivian, Lillian, M. Friger, and T. Kushnir. "Associations Between Stress and Quality of Life: Differences Between Owners Keeping a Living Dog or Losing a Dog by Euthanasia." *PLOS One*, vol. 10, no. 3, 2015, pp. 1–15, doi:10.1371/journal.pone.0121081.

Van Lanen, Kathleen, and Allison Sande. "Canine Hypoadrenocorticism: Pathogenesis, Diagnosis, and Treatment." *Topics in Companion Animal Medicine*, vol. 29, no. 4, 2014, pp. 88–95. *PubMed.gov*, doi:10.1053/j.tcam.2014.10.001.

Wolcott, Harry F. *Ethnography Lessons: A Primer*. Left Coast Press, 2010.

Wood, Lisa, Karen Martin, Hayley Christian, Andrea Nathan, Claire Lauritsen, Steve Houghton, Ichiro Kawachi, and Sandra McCune. "The Pet Factor: Companion Animals as a Conduit for Getting to Know People, Friendship Formation and Social Support." *PLOS One*, vol. 10, no. 4, 2015, pp. 1–17, doi:10.1371/journal.pone.0122085.

I Told the Dog First

*The Delicate Relationship Between
Marginalized Youth and Animals*

JEFFREY JIN *and* KATHARINE WENOCUR

On the role of dogs in contemporary America, Okey Ndibe observed that "in a society where people are obsessed with personal space, dogs have come to serve as welcome, neo-human mediators of loneliness and solitude" (137–138). As a Nigerian national, Ndibe provides an outsider's perspective on the almost paradoxical nature of Americans' close relationships with companion animals, which stand in contrast to ideals of independence and self-sufficiency. This dynamic can be further explored through the lens of outsiders within American culture: youth whose identities are marginalized experience blurring of boundary lines between animal and human relationships. Natalie and Timmy (pseudonyms) are representative of millions of American children and adolescents experiencing isolation due to financial insecurity, homelessness, social disenfranchisement based on gender identity or sexual orientation, and social rejection. Natalie is a twenty-year-old woman sharing her experiences as a LGBT+ youth in a homophobic milieu who talked to her dog for support as his loving companionship was blurred with a lack of human acceptance. Timmy is a ten-year-old boy who received canine-assisted therapy while living in an emergency housing program for homeless families and later adopted a dog with his family. Both Natalie and Timmy shared ultimately transformative relationships with dogs and credit these relationships to helping them navigate expected challenges of coming of age, and the unique ones associated with marginalization.

Natalie grew up in a suburban home with a deeply religious foundation in Pentecostalism. At age twelve she realized that she had a sexual attraction toward other girls but was terrified to discuss this with anyone. Her family members constantly made homophobic remarks about sexual and gender minorities. Gay Pride did not exist in her household and LGBT+ activity was seen as sinful. Natalie's church and religious middle school regularly belittled those people who identified as anything other than heterosexual, and LGBT+ issues were met with hostility in this environment. No acceptance existed for sexual or gender minorities. Surrounded by negative and threatening comments, Natalie kept her lesbianism a secret from everyone as she struggled to find a way to accept herself. She was afraid to disclose anything about her own sexual orientation at school, in church, or with her family.

Timmy's family became homeless after a series of challenging experiences. Timmy's parents frequently fought, and sometimes verbal arguments escalated into violence. Fearing for her family's safety, Timmy's mother Naomi left his father, taking Timmy and his siblings with her. When Naomi struggled to find stable employment and housing, the family stayed with a series of friends and relatives for periods of several weeks at a time. During this time, Timmy, at age eight, lit papers on fire in a school bathroom trash can. Concerned for Timmy's emotional well-being, Naomi enrolled Timmy in therapy through a local juvenile justice program. After several months of treatment, Timmy's problematic behaviors subsided, and he began to perform better in school. Timmy's behavioral difficulties re-surfaced when the family entered a shelter at age nine, and Timmy began a new school. In response to physical bullying by classmates, Timmy began getting into physical altercations during the school day. He also began shoplifting small items. Timmy's mother enrolled him in therapy at the shelter, and the therapist he worked with involved a therapy dog in the treatment.

Challenges Faced by Each Population

Challenges Faced by LGBT+ Youth

Data on homophobia and its impact on LGBT+ suicide attempts further illustrate the impact of heterosexism of LGBT+ youth. In a qualitative study by McDermott et al. (815–29), LGBT+ shame is linked with self-destructive behaviors including suicide. Homophobia serves to punish LGBT+ youth as abnormal, shameful, or deviant based on their sexual orientation or sexual identity (Almeida et al. 1001–14; Bratsis, 12; Hatzenbuehler et al. 663–75). The researchers cite a statistic that LGBT+ youth attempt suicide at more than 400 percent the rate of their heterosexual counterparts (McDermott et al. 815–29). Another recent study reported that 9 percent of transgender youth have actually attempted suicide by age 15 with 30 percent attempting suicide by age 19, and a full 41 percent of transgender adults having had attempted suicide in their lifetime (Turban et al. 275–77). Societal homophobia is hypothesized as the cause for this stark difference with increased substance use, unsafe sex, and self-harm as coping strategies also being linked to this cause. Participants in the work by McDermott et al. reported severe social isolation due to family rejection and the inability to find safe places in which to form same-sex relationships. The majority of interviewees define the label of "gay" as a term of abuse that is perpetuated by homophobic behavior from others; demonstrating any characteristics associated with the opposite sex can bring even more ridicule and marginalization (815–29). Several subjects identify as having to become adults prematurely as no idealized parental figure existed. They noted that their parents were not supportive of their sexuality, as homophobia is often simply an accepted part of society.

Natalie shared a similar experience with her own parents who were not at all supportive of her sexuality. Her sexual orientation was accidentally exposed to her family when her mother discovered Natalie's diary in which she wrote about her sexual feelings. Natalie told of a confrontation with both of her parents that resulted in being sent for gay conversion "therapy" through her family church. Her father continued to argue Natalie's sexuality when she moved away to college as he stated that he would only visit her at school if she agreed to seek conversion counseling again through their church.

Natalie's entire family including her twin sister as well as another sister three years her junior all rejected her for her sexual orientation. Her mother told her aunts but forbade anyone from telling Natalie's grandmother; Natalie was told that this revelation would kill her grandmother. She felt ostracized with nowhere to turn for support as she told that she had no network of friends at that age and relied solely on her family for any kind of emotional support; she could not count on any support regarding her sexual orientation from any other person at that time. Natalie's isolation from her family as well as from human peers led her to seek support from her dogs as they were the only sources of non-judgmental love available to her.

Challenges Faced by Homeless Youth

Chronic homelessness is defined as residing in homeless shelters, living on the streets or in cars, and staying "doubled up" with a friend or extended family member for a period of at least twelve months (Bassuk et al.). Children who are part of chronically homeless families face numerous challenges beyond a lack of stable housing arrangements. Despite scoring similarly on tests of intelligence and aptitude, homeless children tend to have lower grade point averages (GPA) and higher rates of absenteeism than same-aged peers (Uretsky and Stone 91–98). Children experiencing homeless have high rates of exposure to violence and trauma (Cutuli et al.). For example, these children are three times more likely to be the victims of a substantiated child abuse case, as compared to non-homeless, low-income children (Brumley et al. 31–37). Moreover, homelessness has been identified as a leading risk factor of juvenile justice involvement, and this risk increases if the child has experiences of both homelessness and child abuse (Rodriguez 189–215). In peer relationships, homeless children may experience bullying due to their housing status, or isolation from and avoidance of classmates as result of shame and stigma (Kilmer et al. 389–401).

Timmy experienced many of the challenges for which homelessness is a risk factor. During his stay in the shelter and while he was "doubled up" with friends and family members, Timmy's school performance declined steadily. Although bright and well-spoken, he fell behind his peers in reading and mathematics. He began to fight with Naomi in the mornings before school, sharing that he "hated school" and would refuse to go. Naomi tried to get Timmy to school but, exhausted from looking for work and housing, often allowed him to stay home to avoid a fight. Timmy's academic performance continued to suffer. Socially, Timmy withdrew from his peers and began shoplifting and getting into physical altercations with his peers. This behavior escalated, culminating in Timmy entering the school bathroom, lighting a paper towel on fire, and leaving it in a trashcan. Naomi became more vigilant about Timmy's school attendance and enrolled Timmy in intensive therapy. While the family still lacked housing, Timmy began to spend more time with his peers and showed interest in attending school again.

Timmy's behavior and academic performance declined again when the family entered a homeless shelter. Knowing the impact that changes in housing status had on his behavior previously, Naomi sought out the on-site therapist to assist Timmy in coping with the changes in the family's life. Timmy's therapist conducted a trauma assessment, and Timmy reported that he had been physically hurt by his classmates, witnessed physical fighting in his neighborhood and verbal alterations between his parents, and was robbed outside of a local convenience store. Timmy reported several symptoms associated with post-traumatic stress, including difficulty regulating his emotions, hyper-vigilance, difficulty concentrating in school, and poor self-esteem. By diagnostic standards, Timmy met criteria for post-traumatic stress disorder (American Psychiatric Association 271–80). Naomi and Timmy identified several goals for therapy, including decreasing the frequency of Timmy's violent outbursts, increasing Timmy's ability to communicate about his emotions, and increasing Timmy's feelings of self- worth and competency.

Talking to Animals

While not elaborating on a causal relationship, Endenberg and Van Lith wrote of how companion animals played a significant role in the development of self-esteem, self-resiliency, and empathy among children who lived with them. Children who grew up with companion animals reported higher levels self-esteem, responsibility, and empathy with animals that transfer to empathy with other people as adults, than those children who did not (Endenberg and Van Lith 208–14). Endenberg and Van Lith examined the child's development based on human social support and the usefulness of companion animals and stated that "(h)ow a child develops is also influenced by the child's social network; the social development of a child without friends is very different from that of a child with many friends" (209). The young adolescents rated companion animals above all humans except their parents as assisting them to feel satisfied with themselves.

Natalie and Max

Natalie serves as an example of this observation as she depended upon her dogs rather than other humans to forge a healthy self-esteem. She told of how isolated she felt as an adolescent without a strong human support network, as she did not have friends in whom she could confide. She heard a constant bombardment of homophobic comments about LGBT people in her school, her church, and at home with her family. Natalie's early encounters with homophobic attitudes were not isolated, as she could not find a source of human support regarding her developing sexuality; she felt the need to keep this part of herself secret from others. Natalie found daily comfort in her dogs and told them aspects about her sexuality that she could not reveal to other humans without repercussions. She also rated her relationships with her dogs as far exceeding any human bond during her adolescence.

"Max" was a bichon frise that Natalie's family adopted two years prior to her family's discovery of her sexual orientation. Her family had another dog as well as guinea pigs and birds earlier in her childhood, but Max was different, as their relationship substituted for what Natalie lacked with other human beings. Upon mention of his name, Natalie's face lit up with a beaming smile and bright eyes:

Natalie: He's a little bichon. He's like not even two … feet, very chubby. Oh, I can show you pictures. I have a whole album of just pictures of my dog. He's so cute…. We picked Max because he was the first one who ran up to us, well specifically my dad, and started licking his face. And we were like that's it, this is the one … now I'm his favorite person in the family and he sleeps with me, and in my room. I love him. I can't wait to see him.

Natalie continued to speak about having Max stay in her room with her during her adolescence, which coincided with her family's discovery of her sexual orientation. With no one to confide in about her sexuality, Natalie felt alone and marginalized. People in her social network were not open to hearing about her sexual identity and Natalie was left alone to search for self-acceptance. Max was Natalie's only outlet for support and unconditional love, and her bond with him strengthened, blurring the relationship many youth derive from human friends and family. She described having Max stay in bed with her and unconsciously referred to him as a person at one point:

> Natalie: I feel like a lot of the reasons that I would have him come up to my room was because I didn't want to be alone at night, and I also just didn't know who to talk to. Oh, I just had a dog in my room…. A lot of it was like mostly me being silent while cuddling him, and then like processing things in my head. I tend to process things in my head before I speak them out loud…. He is very well attuned to my emotions, so he knows what I need when I need it. So like it was nice to have something living to hold onto if that makes sense. And he was also just a sweet little person who would lick my feet or lick my face if I was in a particularly bad mood.

Through middle school and into high school, Natalie continued to have Max sleep with her at night. She did not disclose her sexuality to anyone outside of her family for years due to fear and self-hatred. Natalie described a particularly poignant example of speaking to Max as she came out to him before discussing this with another person and how his non-judgmental acceptance served as needed reassurance that she could not find from another human:

> Natalie: I told my dog I was gay. I came out to my dog. I was like Max, I'm gay. He was…. He obviously didn't respond, but I was like okay, cool, I did it … because in high school every night he would sleep in my room. And I have distinct memories of crying in my room hugging my dog while I'm processing that I'm gay…. So I knew I wasn't a complete piece of shit. I was like I can't be that horrible if (he) likes me.

Max's acceptance of Natalie's sexual orientation marked the first living being in her household who accepted her. She could not find consistent support from her parents or other family members yet derived comfort from the non-judgmental comfort from Max as the distinction between dog and human was blurred for her. From her words of her disappointment, she was aware that Max could not respond to her verbally, but his physical presence was indeed lifesaving as countless numbers of LGBT+ youth contemplate suicide with no one to talk to about their feelings of isolation (McDermott et al). The relationship between Natalie and Max progressed from a companion animal bond to that of human confidant.

Timmy and Winston

Jalongo drew comparisons between the relationship that young children share with their caregivers and the bonds that children form with their companion animals, specifically their dogs. In her analysis, Jalongo discussed the uniqueness of the relationship children and dogs share and the correlation between how human and canine family members are treated. Both relationships are characterized by the "expectation of psychological and physical protection" on the part of the child (Jalongo 395–396). For a child who, like Timmy, has struggled to find safety within his family of origin and among his peers, a dog could provide a sense of stability lacking in that child's human relationships. While Jalongo wrote specifically about the relationships children have with companion animals, the notion of a close and supportive relationship could also apply to animals involved in therapy work. While therapists have invited dogs into their work for decades, formalized models of animal-assisted therapy have emerged that integrate positive inter-actions with animals into therapeutic interventions (Zilcha-Mano et al. 541). Animal-assisted therapy has been shown to enhance children's ability to heal from the impact of early life separations from parent figures through relationship building with therapy ani-mals (Parish-Plass 24). Several larger research studies have shown that for individuals with PTSD, animal-assisted therapy can facilitate decreased measures of symptoms, including the avoidance of social situations (O'Haire et al.).

While in the shelter, Timmy participated in ten therapy sessions, and worked with a therapy dog named Winston. Winston, a pug mix with a playful personality, weighed less than thirty pounds and enjoyed sitting on Timmy's lap. This was a stark contrast to Timmy's prior interactions with primarily larger dogs; often these dogs had been trained to protect their owners from physical danger in urban neighborhoods. Timmy's therapist implemented Animal Assisted Play Therapy®, a model that encourages playful interactions between nonhuman animals and therapy clients (VanFleet and Faa-Thompson 7–18). The overall goal of the model is to help children develop positive and playful connections with the therapy dog, and use skills learned in therapy to relate positively to peers and family members. Winston had a naturally playful disposition and, upon meeting the dog, Timmy almost immediately reciprocated Winston's playful demeanor. Timmy actively sought out Winston's company. Outside of his weekly therapy sessions, he often stopped by the therapist's office to visit Winston. Blurring the lines between a peer friendship and a human-animal friendship, Timmy would often share highlights and challenges he faced at school during these visits.

While working with Winston, Timmy expressed an interest in learning about dog body language, "so [he] knew how Winston [was] feeling." Timmy's therapist introduced Timmy to cartoons that illustrated common examples of postures and other non-verbal indicators of dogs' internal experiences (Chin). Timmy quickly came to identify that a wagging tail meant excitement, that a low posture signaled fear or apprehension, and that front paws stretched down and forward and rear end high communicated "I want to play!" Timmy reveled in being able to understand Winston's language, and soon became engaged in teaching Winston to understand his cues. Timmy learned the basic compo-nents of dog training and assisted the therapist in teaching the therapy dog how to jump over a small tower of blocks. Through training, Timmy established a way of "speaking" to Winston through non-verbal communication and knowledge of canine social dynam-ics. This improved Timmy's confidence in his ability to interact with his peers and family members. Timmy explained his application of this knowledge: "If I can understand what a dog is trying to say, I can figure out what my mom is trying to say."

The therapist and Timmy also played a game with Winston designed to increase Timmy's ability to communicate about his emotions. Timmy hid treats in a basket filled with small stuffed toys, each with a feeling word written on it (see Figure 1). At Timmy's cue, Winston would begin to hunt for treats in the basket. As he searched, Winston would remove toys one by one until he reached the treats. When Winston took a toy out of the basket, Timmy would generate a potential reason for the dog to have that particular emo-tion (example: "Winston is surprised because I turned into a dog"). While Timmy's dis-cussion of the dog's inner experience was mostly playful, it facilitated Timmy's ability to communicate about emotional experience. As Timmy continued playing this game, he

Fig. 1. Winston the therapy dog demonstrates the emotions identification exercise that Timmy participated in during therapy; Winston (left) looks for treats in the basket of emotion-themed toys and then poses (right) with the selected emotions that the therapy client would discuss (courtesy Katharine Wenocur).

shared his own feelings through the lens of the dog's supposed emotion (example: "Winston is confused because his parents are getting divorced").

Talking to Winston through dog training and through play preceded Timmy directly speaking to Winston about challenges his family faced. It was as though the relationship Timmy built with Winston enabled him to confide in the dog. Concurrent to Timmy receiving therapy, Timmy's father legally filed for sole custody of Timmy and his siblings. Prompted by the fear of potentially living only with his father, Timmy disclosed that his father had been physically abusive towards him. During his disclosure, Timmy was petting Winston, and spoke directly to Winston, rather than to his therapist. As result, Timmy's family was immersed not only in a courtroom custody battle, but also in a child protective services investigation. Naomi shared with the therapist that while she was glad Timmy felt comfortable enough to disclose his abuse, she feared that the stress of the investigation might damage Timmy emotionally. However, Timmy continued to make progress in therapy and learned to express and manage difficult emotions as they arose. Because Timmy lacked a consistent group of supportive peers, the closeness of his bond with Winston supported his ability to regulate his emotional experience during this challenging time.

Naomi spoke highly of Timmy's experience in therapy, specifically the relationship he formed with Winston. She shared that Timmy "really liked therapy" and, while the family resided in the shelter, he often asked, "when he could go back" to the therapist's office to visit the therapy dog. She characterized the bond that Timmy and Winston shared using language that she might use to describe a human friendship. In fact, Naomi said that Timmy "loved Winston so much" that the family adopted a dog of their own when they left the shelter. This allowed Timmy's special relationship with dogs to continue after the completion of therapy and helped him to maintain the progress he had worked toward in regulating his emotions and using coping skills that he had developed.

Benefits of Talking to Animals

Natalie and Timmy shared experiences of speaking directly to the dogs in their lives, particularly about content that might be difficult to talk about. The relationship with Max empowered Natalie to explore her sexuality and to build a support network. During her adolescence, Natalie reported that she was not able to confide anything about her LGBT+ status with any other human in her own family, school, or community. Talking with Max enabled Natalie to verbalize and thus process her thoughts about her sexual identity as she felt the need to blur Max's role with that of a human peer. An I–Poem based on Natalie's experiences of confiding in Max during her struggle with self-acceptance highlights her emotional journey.

Gilligan, et al. (259–62) first used I–Poetry to analyze spoken word from interviews. To compose an I–Poem, every "I" statement made by a person is taken along with descriptive words within an actual spoken phrase. I–Poems reveal a rhythmic yet bare quality of what each young person shared and create an intimate portrait based on what could be viewed as the skeletal framework of an interview. By using I–Poetry as a form of analysis, a person's spoken word takes on a new life and new themes are uncovered through an artistic outlet. Natalie composed an I–Poem that mirrors her struggles with sexual acceptance and coming out of the closet in a heterosexist and homophobic climate:

> *I was like ewww*
> *I ended up*
> *I was like yea*
> *I'm gay*
> *I was gay*
> *I first came*
> *I didn't exactly*
> *I sort of fell out*
> *I basically came out*
> *I was sinning*

Further excerpts of the I–Poem for Natalie reveal her adoration for her dogs and also demonstrate how she spoke to her animals. The rhythm of her I–Poem changed from a staggered staccato when she relayed her self-doubt and revelations to fluidity when she spoke about her dog and the emotional benefits that she found in him.

> *I'm his favorite person*
> *I love him*
> *I can't wait*
> *I would*
> *I told my dog*
> *I was gay*
> *I came out to my dog*
> *I was like*

I'm gay
I was like okay
I did it
I have distinct
I'm processing
I'm gay
I probably did

Natalie's words reveal how she came out of the closet to her dog, but the I–Poem prefaced her comfort level and safety that she found with Max. Concurrent to her coming-out experience with Max, Natalie relayed that she was indeed still internally processing this realization. Her revelation to Max predated that disclosure to any human being. Since the time she disclosed her sexuality to Max, Natalie expresses an increased sense of comfort with her sexuality but still finds a tremendous sense of comfort in talking to animals now as the distinction with humans is indeed blurred for her:

I distinctly recall
I'm around animals
I knew
I feel really
I always go see
I always feel better
I know

Timmy

Timmy expressed the significance of his relationship with Winston through a projective drawing of a child and a dog. Projective drawings are a form of interpretive measurement that have been used by child therapists since the 1920s (Malchiodi 2). In a projective drawing study, children are provided with basic art materials and prompted to draw specific figures such as family; a house, tree, and person; or, in this case, a child and a dog (Burns and Kaufman 12; Kaiser and Deaver 26–33). Clinicians and researchers analyze the thematic content of the drawings to learn more about the child who created the drawing. While early forms of projective drawing research relied on pre-determined schemes of analysis, contemporary projective drawing researchers seek to contextualize drawings within the literature on developmental stages of drawing, and use past studies that correlate specific aspects of the drawing to standardized measurements of psychological health. Moreover, many scholars code these drawings similarly to qualitative coding techniques for interviews (Backos and Samuelson 58–67; Singh and Roussouw 124–130). The overall goal of projective drawing research is to provide a means for communicating that is sensitive to the age and developmental level of a child.

Several months after leaving the shelter, Timmy participated in a research study designed to assess homeless children's experiences in animal-assisted therapy. In the study, Timmy was prompted to create a drawing of a child and dog, and then tell a story about the figures in his drawing. The drawing (Figure 2) depicts a monochrome stick figure, which Timmy identified as a boy wearing a crown and holding a leash. The leash is connected to a dog that has pointy ears and polka dots. Timmy's drawing is more rudimentary than would be expected for his age; it lacks detail in the human figure and does not include background or context (Malchiodi 65). However, the personalization of the

Fig. 2. The projective drawing created by Timmy (pseudonym) during a research study that occurred after his involvement in Animal Assisted Play Therapy (courtesy Katharine Wenocur and approved for use in publication by the University of Pennsylvania Institutional Review Board).

child figure as a boy and the inclusion of the crown, which resembles the toy crown Timmy often wore during therapy sessions, suggests that Timmy tapped into his own experiences when drawing this child and telling the subsequent narrative. In his story, Timmy described the dog as having been in an animal shelter and escaping. The dog ran far away from the shelter and found the boy, who welcomed him into his family and took care of him. At the end of Timmy's story, the boy's family adopted a female dog and the dog had puppies. Timmy's story, and the roles played by the dog and child figures, have many parallels with the journey Naomi and Timmy took and the progress that Timmy made in therapy. The lines between human friendships and human-canine friendships were blurred in this story, as Timmy characterized the child and dog as being "like brothers."

Timmy's story about his drawing evokes themes of rescue, of being lost and then found. In the story, the dog figure took a risk in leaving the relative safety of a shelter and found comfort with his new caretaker, the boy. The dog was uncertain of whether he would find new caretakers or a place to live but decided to leave the shelter in search of a better environment. This reflects the risk that Naomi took in leaving Timmy's father, and seeking a more stable life for her children. Timmy also took a risk in beginning therapy and, with the support of Winston's presence, was able to learn healthy coping mechanisms to replace some of the higher risk behaviors he displayed, such as shoplifting and fire-setting. Learning to take safe, appropriate risks is a core developmental task of middle childhood (Blume and Zember 232). While Timmy engaged in risk-taking behavior prior to entering therapy, working with Winston bolstered his ability to take age-appropriate risks that supported his development and overall well-being. For example, Timmy rehearsed responding to bullying at school by telling Winston (who graciously played the role of school bully) that he was hurting his feelings and asked him to stop. Here, Winston acted as a stand-in for human peer relationships, and helped Timmy to practice the kind of interactions he might have with classmates at school.

Timmy's story also highlighted the importance of second chances. The fictional dog he talked about when describing his picture, who had been living in poor conditions in an animal shelter, ultimately became a valued member of the family and created his own family through the birth of puppies. In leaving her abusive spouse, Naomi created a second chance for Timmy and his siblings. They expanded their family through the adoption of a dog and created new family routines and traditions that continued to support their healing as a family. This allowed Timmy to believe that second chances are possible. As a child with a history of fire-setting and shoplifting, Timmy might have been at risk for future acts of violence or other criminal behavior. However, through his relationships with both Winston and his new family dog, he found new ways to cope with challenging emotions and succeed in school.

Risk of Talking Only *to Animals*

Natalie and Timmy have benefited from the positive and supportive relationships with the animals of their childhoods. These relationships could have long-term implications if they remain solely human to animal bonds to the exclusion of associating with other people. Guyer et al. found in a prior study that adolescents who report increased levels of acceptance by peers demonstrate increased social competence, intimate friendships, and self-esteem (229). Their further neuroscientific work showed that for at-risk youth, regions of the brain develop in the presence of activity with peers as to opposed to a lack thereof (240–1). In a speech pathology study, Nippold et al. (876–7) conducted a measurement of narrative speaking ability of fourteen-year-old adolescents as they entered a stage of cognitive development characterized by advances in abstract thought and logical reasoning. Teenagers use narrative storytelling to develop their speech patterns and also to hone their ability to listen to others in social situations; listening to others and honing one's own ability to articulate stories though feedback suggests a benefit found only from other human contact.

In a description of the factors potentially contributing to abuse and neglect of animals, Levitt et al. introduced the concept of "pathological altruism," or the misplaced understanding of oneself as a uniquely qualified rescuer of animals (333). This altruism has been labeled "pathological" because, while it inspires one who has his quality to go to extraordinary lengths to rescue and care for animals, it may inhibit one's ability to interact with human peers. Individuals displaying this characteristic may become overwhelmed with the responsibilities they have taken on or may care for their animals at the exclusion of nurturing their relationships with humans. The concept of pathological altruism underscores the importance of marginalized youth not only developing healthy relationships with animals, but also extending their social networks to identify trustworthy and trusted adults and peers. Naomi described Timmy's relationship with the new family dog as "paternal," and reported that Timmy calls the dog his "baby." While this is not unusual for a child of his age, it does raise questions about whether Timmy might value his human-animal relationships more than those with human peers. It will be important for Timmy's family to continue providing him with opportunities to apply the lessons learned with the dogs in his life to interactions with peers. These might include sharing his dog training skills with peers or participating in an after-school activity that involves working with animals.

Natalie provides a good model for bridging the gap between human-animal and peer relationships. Natalie confided in her dogs when she had no other human beings with whom she felt comfortable to share her inner struggles and experiences with sexual development. She noted a clear difference in her support system when she left her family home and moved to a residential college. Natalie found not only supportive peers and advisers at college, but also a wealth of resources that enabled her to explore her identity. She noted that speaking to her dogs saved her sense of self-esteem as an adolescent as she felt marginalized and isolated. In a new environment, Natalie was able to build upon her animal support network to include humans and thus demonstrated talking to her animals as a bridge to building potential human support. During her adolescence when Natalie could only confide in her animals, she reported a feeling of isolation from other people, notably including no receipt of spoken encouragement. The physical and emotional comfort that she found from her dogs did not offer a permanent replacement for the human bonds that she formed once she moved away to college, but rather provided her a safe passageway to forging those eventual human relationships.

Conclusion

Several distinctions have been noted when discussing the blurred lines of human and animal support for both Natalie and for Timmy. Animals provided unconditional emotional support for each youth in the absence of human assistance while also serving as a bridge for future interactions with people. Natalie and Timmy each reported unique life experiences yet shared several key commonalities; both faced numerous obstacles in their formative years that placed them at risk for development into adulthood. As an LGBT+ youth, Natalie faced internalized and family homophobia in a heterosexist environment. Her family had a hostile reaction to learning of her sexuality, and based on this reaction she was not comfortable disclosing this aspect of herself with peers. Speaking to and confiding in her dog Max allowed her to develop a level of self-awareness and comfort about her sexual orientation. Max did not judge, scold, or reprimand her as did the humans in Natalie's life during her adolescence. Rather, she found a safe space with a living being who loved her no matter what she disclosed to him. Timmy built confidence and a sense of competence in his relationship with a therapy dog. His relationship with this dog has helped him to take safe, age-appropriate risks, and thrive in school and family life. Both turned to talking to their dogs for unconditional support and love that was not available from another human, resulting in a blurring between dog and person.

In turn, that support allowed them to build trust in family and peer relationships as they moved forward.

WORKS CITED

Almeida, Joanna, Renee M. Johnson, Heather L. Corliss, Beth E. Molnar, and Deborah Azrael "Emotional Distress Among LGBT Youth: The Influence of Perceived Discrimination Based on Sexual Orientation." *Journal of Youth and Adolescence*, vol. 38, no.7, 2009, pp. 1001–1014.

American Psychiatric Association. *Diagnostic and Statistical Manual of Mental Disorders* (5th ed.). American Psychiatric Association, 2013.

Backos, Amy, and Kristin Samuelson. "Projective Drawings of Mothers and Children Exposed to Intimate Partner Violence: A Mixed Methods Analysis." *Art Therapy*, vol. 34, no. 2, 2017, pp. 58–67.

Bassuk, Ellen, Carmela J. DeCandia, Corey Anne Beach and Fred Berman, "America's Youngest Outcasts: A Report Card on Child Homelessness." *The National Center on Family Homelessness*, Nov. 2014. www.homelesschildrenamerica.org. Accessed 15 Aug. 2017.

Blume, Libby B., and Mary Jo Zembar. *Middle Childhood to Middle Adolescence: Development from Ages 8 to 18*. Pearson Merrill/Prentice Hall, Upper Saddle River, NJ, 2007.

Bratsis, Michael. "Healthwise: Supporting Bullied LGBT Students." *The Science Teacher*, vol. 82, no. 4, 2015, pp. 247–263

Brumley, Benjamin, John Fantuzzo, Staci Perlman, and Margaret L. Zager "The Unique Relations Between Early Homelessness and Educational Well-Being: An Empirical Test of the Continuum of Risk Hypothesis." *Child and Youth Services Review*, vol. 48, 2015, pp. 31–37.

Burns, Robert C., and S. Harvard Kaufman. *Kinetic Family Drawings (K-F-D): An Introduction to Understanding Children Through Kinetic Drawings*. Brunner/Mazel, New York, 1987.

Chin, Lili. *Boogie: Doggie Language*. 2011. Doggie Drawings: Educational Graphics, https://www.doggiedrawings.net/freeposters.

Cutuli, J.J., Ann Montgomery, Michelle Evans-Chase, and Dennis Culhane. "Childhood Adversity, Adult Homelessness and the Intergenerational Transmission of Risk: A Population Representative Study of Individuals in Households with Children." *Child & Family Social Work*, vol. 20, no. 1, 2015, doi: 10.1111/cfs.12207.

Endenberg, Nienke, and Van Lith, Hein. "The Influence of Animals on the Development of Children." *The Veterinary Journal*, vol. 190, 2011, pp. 208–214.

Gilligan, Carol et al., "On the Listening Guide" Sharlene Hesse-Biber and Patricia Leavy (Eds.) *Emergent Methods in Social Research*, 2006, pp. 253–272.

Guyer, Amanda E., Brenda Benson, Victoria R. Choate, Yair Bar-Haim, Koraly Perez-Edgar, Johanna M. Jarcho Daniel S. Pine, Monique Ernst, Nathan A. Fox, and Eric E. Nelson. "Lasting Associations Between Early-Childhood Temperament and Late-Adolescent Reward—Circuitry Response to Peer Feedback." *Development and Psychopathology*, vol. 26, no. 1, 2014, pp. 229–243, doi:10.10.17/50954579413000941.

Hatzenbuehler, Mark et al., "Neighborhood Level LGBT Hate Crimes and Bullying Among Sexual Minority Youths: A Geospatial Analysis." *Violence and Victims*, vol. 30, no. 4, 2015, pp. 663–675.

Jalongo, Mary Renck. "An Attachment Perspective on the Child-Dog Bond: Interdisciplinary and International Research Findings." *Early Childhood Education Journal*, vol. 43, no. 5, 2015, pp. 395–405.

Kaiser, Donna H., and Sarah Deaver. "Assessing Attachment with the Bird's Nest Drawing: A Review of the Research." *Art Therapy: Journal of the American Art Therapy Association*, vol. 26, no. 10, 2009, pp. 26–33.

Kilmer, Ryan P., James Richard Cook, Cindy A Crusto, Katherine P Strater, and Mason Goodloe Haber. "Understanding the Ecology and Development of Children and Families Experiencing Homelessness: Implications for Practice, Supportive Services, and Policy." *Journal of Orthopsychiatry*, vol. 82, no. 3, 2012, pp. 389–401.

Levitt, Lacey, Gary Patronek, and Thomas Grisso. *Animal Maltreatment: Forensic Mental Health Issues and Evaluations*. Oxford University Press, 2016.

Malchiodi, Cathy. *Understanding Children's Drawings*. The Guildford Press, 1998.

McDermott, Elizabeth, et al. "Avoiding Shame: Young LGBT People, Homophobia, and Self-Destructive Behaviors." *Culture, Health, and Sexuality*, vol. 10, 2008, pp. 815–829.

Ndibe, Okey. *Never Look an American in the Eye: Flying Turtles, Colonial Ghosts, and the Making of a Nigerian American*. Soho Press, Inc., 2017.

Nippold, Marilyn A., Megan Frantz-Kaspar, Paige M. Cramond, Cecilia Kirk, Christine Hayward-Mayhew, and Melanie Mackinnon. "Conversational and Narrative Speaking in Adolescents: Examining the Use of Complex Syntax." *Journal of Speech, Language, and Hearing Research*, vol. 57, June 2014, pp. 876–96.

O'Haire, Marguerite E., Noémie A. Guérin, and Alison C. Kirkham. "Animal-Assisted Intervention for Trauma: A Systematic Literature Review." *Frontiers in Psychology*, vol. 6, 2015, https://www.ncbi.nlm.nih.gov/pmc/articles/PMC4528099/. Accessed 15 Aug. 2017.

Parish-Plass, Nancy. "Animal-Assisted Therapy with Children Suffering from Insecure Attachment Due to Abuse and Neglect: A Method to Lower the Risk of Intergenerational Transmission of Abuse?" *Clinical Child Psychology and Psychiatry*, vol. 13, no. 1, 2008, pp. 7–30.

Rodriguez, Nancy. "Concentrated Disadvantage and the Incarceration of Youth: Examining How Context Affects Juvenile Justice." *Journal of Research in Crime and Delinquency*, vol. 50, no. 2, 2015, pp. 189–215.

Singh, Jasmin, and Rossouw, Pieter. "Efficacy of Drawings as a Measure of Attachment Style and Emotional Disturbance." *International Journal of Neuropsychotherapy*, vol. 3, no. 2, 2015, pp. 124–130.

Turban, Jack et al., "Ten things transgender and gender non-conforming youth want their doctors to know." Journal of the American Academy of child and adolescent psychiatry, vol. 56, no. 4, 2017, pp. 275–277.

Uretsky, Mathew, and Stone, Susan. "Factors Associated with High School Exit Exam Outcomes Among Homeless High School Students. *Children and Schools*, vol. 38, no. 2, 2016, pp. 91–98.

VanFleet, Risë, and Tracie Faa-Thompson. *Animal-Assisted Play Therapy*. Professional Resource Press. 2017.

VanFleet, Risë, and Tracie Faa-Thompson. "Short-Term Animal-Assisted Play Therapy for Children." *Short-term Play Therapy for Children* (3rd Edition), edited by Heidi Gerard Kaduson, and Charles E. Shaefer, Guilford Press, 2017, pp. 175–197.

Zilcha-Mano, M. Sigal, and P.R. Shaver. "Pet in the Therapy Room: An Attachment Perspective on Animal-Assisted Therapy." *Attachment and Human Development*, vol. 13, no. 6, 2011, pp. 541–561.

Japanese People Adore
Their Animals

Jill S. Grigsby

Recently in *The New Yorker*, Matt Alt, while acknowledging the continued cultural dominance of the United States, makes a case for Japan becoming the new world leader in lifestyle culture. Americans follow Marie Kondo's rules for decluttering, and Japanese stores, like Muji and Uniqlo, now have branches in U.S. cities so that Americans and their homes can look, feel, and smell Japanese (Alt, Kondo). What is next? Perhaps Americans will begin copying the distinctive way that Japanese individuals and families have brought pets into their families. Japanese society has entered "the second demographic transition," characterized by extremely low fertility and late marriage (Rindfuss). U.S. fertility has also dropped to levels below replacement, although not as low as Japanese fertility; however, U.S. divorce rates, levels of premarital cohabitation, and extramarital childbearing, all indicators of "the second demographic transition," are higher than in Japan (Vanorman and Scommegna). Young adults in Japan typically live with their parents until they marry, and women find it difficult to combine full-time work and motherhood. Despite several policy attempts, Japanese fertility remains low, one of the lowest in the world, in part because of the work culture that encourages both long work hours and intensive efforts in the home from mothers and wives (Boling).

As of 2015, almost ten million dogs and almost ten million cats lived as part of Japanese households (Niijima), together outnumbering the 16.6 million children under the age of 15 (United Nations). Walking throughout greater Kyoto, one sees how important pets, particularly dogs and cats, have become for Japanese adults. On warm spring and autumn weekend afternoons, people walk with their dogs around suburban parks and urban gardens, and many dogs sport their finest outfits. A pair of poodles wear matching brother/sister clothes—she in a patchwork vest, trimmed in pink ruffles; he in a similar patchwork vest, trimmed in blue denim. Dogs adorned in designer T-shirts abound throughout the Kansai (Osaka-Kyoto-Kobe) region. Men and women shop at their local farmers market wearing baby carriers, but they are as likely to be carrying tiny dogs or cats as they are infant children. Alice Gordenker, writing for *The Japan Times* in 2012, reported that Japanese pet owners spent approximately $1.6 billion on food, as well as a range of other products, including special snacks, bedding, fancy clothing, floral and herbal scents, and nail polish, all of which greatly surprised one pet industry professional from Europe.

She noted, "[m]ore and more, it seems like Japanese owners want their dogs to be less like animals and more like people. They want their dogs to eat like people, dress like people and even smell like people" (Gordenker). Indeed, in many ways, Japanese people truly adore their cats and dogs, making them part of their families, and even personalizing them in human ways, thus blurring the line between human and animal. Japanese households, like those in other parts of the world, include other kinds of animals as pets, for example goldfish. However, Japanese families also consider certain types of insects (*mushi*) appropriate pets as well. Japanese people kept singing crickets in cages as early as the eighth century, and have also kept singing grasshoppers, rhinoceros beetles, and stag beetles. The insects typically live in elaborate containers such as wooden cages or terrariums, and often relate to seasons, something significant to Japanese culture (Laurent).

Even animals that are not pets have become beloved and humanized by Japanese people. At two of the most highly visited tourist sites in Japan (Nara, home of the world's largest bronze Buddha statue, and Miyajima, an island known for the orange "floating" torii gate) extremely tame deer roam the streets, approaching visitors for food and eating out of their hands. Vendors sell deer food that looks like human crackers. Many Japanese tourists enjoy this connection to the "wild" (actually, tame) animals as much or more as they appreciate seeing these most iconic spiritual and historic places. "Wild" monkey parks are also popular tourist destinations, where monkeys appear out of the forest and eat food from tourists (who are behind bars) that vendors are selling on site. Because monkeys still inhabit temperate rain forests throughout Japan, even relatively close to urban and suburban areas, it is not difficult for Japanese people and foreign visitors to encounter monkeys on a casual day hike or be advised by signs along walking paths noting that monkeys can be dangerous and should not be approached.

Another beloved animal in Japan, the tanuki, known as a raccoon dog, is neither a raccoon, nor a dog. A nocturnal wild animal, it is not widely common in highly populated areas, so relatively few people are able to get a good look at a real, live tanuki; however, tanuki ceramic statues, ranging in height from approximately one to five feet, stand in front of many Japanese stores and restaurants, and sometimes homes. The statues are highly stylized, human-like versions of the tanuki and typically depict the animal standing on hind legs (instead of walking on all fours), wearing a straw hat, and carrying a sake bottle. Most tanuki statues have large scrotums, a sign of wealth, and their faces always appear cheerful, hence, businesses find them attractive. Even though the Japanese people may never encounter an actual tanuki, they have developed a fond connection toward these animals.

One of the most famous stories in modern Japan is the one of Hachiko, aka Hachi, a dog who met his owner, a professor, at the Shibuya train station in Tokyo every afternoon. Everyone at the station came to know Hachiko—the stationmasters, other customers, store-keepers. One afternoon, Hachiko's owner was not on his usual train because he had died suddenly at work of a stroke. For years Hachiko waited at the station for his owner's return. Eventually, newspapers covered the story, and Hachiko became the symbol of loyalty and devotion. After Hachiko's death, the people of the Shibuya neighborhood wanted to donate money for a statue in honor of Hachiko in the Shibuya train station. The Hachiko statue continues to be a well-known place in Tokyo, possibly the most famous rendezvous point at Shibuya Station. Hachiko was not just a pet—he was intelligent and loyal, traits prized by Japanese culture. His story shows how a dog can be a role model for people, a true blurring of the human/animal boundary (Skabelund).

Often perceived as family members, Japanese pets receive (and often give) emotional, physical, and even economic support. A basic definition of a family provides three things according to Susan Ferguson: support to members (emotional, physical, economic); a primary group (or pack) to which members belong; and socialization of members to greater society (Ferguson 3). The pets come to learn that they are members of a primary group or pack, and their family teaches them the rules of acceptable behavior. Leslie Irvine and Laurent Cilia, in their article, "More-Than-Human-Families: Pets, People, and Practices in Multispecies Households," outline three criteria for animals to make the transition from commodities to pets or family members—the animals receive names; they are given access to the inside of the house, and they are not eaten. Eating pets is a wide taboo in contemporary Japan, and Japanese people give their pets names. Japanese households, however, still make a distinction between indoor and outdoor pets.

Over a period of five months in 2016 and 2017, I observed Japanese people with pets, and other animals (deer, monkeys, tanukis) while I walked around Kyoto and the greater Kansai area. I visited pet stores, pet grooming salons, pet cemeteries, and travel agencies that catered to people traveling with pets. The Year of Dog, 2018, began at the end of my stay, and I was able to observe even more enhanced canine celebrations in temples, shrines, and special exhibits in art museums. In addition, I interviewed twenty-five undergraduates from U.S. colleges and universities who were spending one or two semesters in Japan, living in host family households that included at least one pet.[1] Twenty of the households included at least one dog, while only three of the households included one or more cats. One of the households with cats also kept a dog at their family business, and some of the households had included both cats and dogs in the past. One household also contained a koi pond and fish tanks. Most of the dogs were relatively small and were kept inside at least some of time. The students were surprised to find that some households kept their small dogs inside all of the time, or took them outside only rarely. Some of these completely inside dogs wore diapers; others were kept in cages that had places for the dogs to urinate or defecate. A few of the dogs were allowed to "do their business" more freely inside, and the Japanese adults regularly cleaned up after them. Most dogs lived indoors and went outside for walks several times each day. One family took their cat outside occasionally on a leash. Only a few of the dogs were considered "outdoor animals," living either in the yard, front porch, or in one case, on top of the roof of the multi-story house.

Even though there may be considerable variation in how Japanese families treat their pet dogs and cats, in American terms, many Japanese families pamper, spoil, and clearly adore their pets. One of the students, Isabel, lived with a host family that rescued dogs and cats, although at the time that Isabel was there, they had only cats, but five of them. Isabel notes that her host parents do not have any children and that "maybe the pets have become a replacement for a child in their life." Isabel's host parents, an older couple, were typical of other host parents or host mothers who either never had children or whose children had grown up and left their household. Their dogs or cats had become their family. Gary, a student living in a household with a dog, says, "here dogs are given more attention and more freedom. If you were to say that the way we treat our dogs in the U.S. is normal, then you would say that a dog here is spoiled. Maybe if you were [from Japan] you would say the U.S. is strict." Leslie thinks that in Japan "they treat [a dog] almost more like a person." She goes on to say, however, that "they put them in these cute clothes, and they're … more like an accessory, or a fun thing to have for your house, or a fun thing for you to play with."

Jean, also living in a home with a dog, says "people here seem to cherish [pets] more.... In Japan I haven't heard people complain about their pets so much." She went on to say that Japanese people who do not have pets seem to consider them animals, while Japanese people with pets think of their pets as almost human, like a member of the family. Jean says about her own host family's dog, a male Pomeranian, "he is actually more of a human than an animal to them, partly because he's a pet, partly because he's a family member..." They say, "even the dog behaves not like an animal. If the dog sees other dogs, the dog will interact with more humans than he will other dogs."

Some pets in Japanese families, particularly older pets, can receive a great deal of devotion. For example, Annie's host mother doesn't travel because she does not want to leave her sixteen-year-old Shih Tzu. She says, "I'd love to go but I can't because I can't put that stress on [the dog]." The nine-year-old toy poodle in Gail's host family needed surgery on her leg, and on the day of the surgery, the family took the dog to their local shrine to pray for a successful outcome. The entire family visited the dog after the surgery at the veterinary hospital, and when they returned home, Gail's host mother prayed at home. When they brought the poodle home, both host parents slept with the dog downstairs because the dog was not able to sleep upstairs in her usual place in their bedroom.

Some of the families explicitly refer to their dog as a "baby" or themselves as "mommy" and an older dog as an older sister (Barbara). Several of the students report their host families using baby carriages or bicycle baskets to transport their dogs, something not uncommon on the streets of greater Kyoto. Japanese pet owners even give human attributes to pets that are neutered. Donna's host mother, referring to their cat, says that "Nanachan is neutered and [that] Nanachan is forever a child."

For Japanese men, pets offer an opportunity to express emotion, which may be difficult for many Japanese men (Farrer et al.). Erin reports how "[m]y host father will just hold [the dog] and rock him like a baby while watching [television]." Ji-Min's host father watches television while holding and petting the family's younger cat in the tatami room.

All of the dogs and cats had names, although some students could not remember all of them. Most of the names were Japanese (for example, Rin, Kokuchan, Chobi), but some were European (for example, Bob, Leon, Mona, Meg). Many families added the diminutive "chan" to the name, which means cute or little, as they would with a child (usually a little girl). Two of the dogs were named Momo (which means peach or peaches), and one was called Momochan, a popular dog's name in Japan. Jean's host family left their dog, Momochan, at a pet spa for a few days and when they returned to pick it up, several dogs came running after the family called out, "Momochan!"

One of the clearest signs that pets are part of the family in Japan is that collections of family photographs in public parts of the home may include pets, both living and deceased. Two students even report that their host mothers' "Line" photo (the picture that appears when they send messages or calls using the Line App) is a photo of the dog. Marta, whose host family currently has a dog, displays pictures of their former pet, which they refer to as their "Kawaii neko," or "cute cat." Neal's family, who never allow their Shiba Inu, Tonchan, inside the house (even during a typhoon!) nevertheless shows off photos of Tonchan when he was a puppy in their living room. Barbara's host sisters have a collection of baby books for their toy poodles, documenting their growth. They also display pictures of the dogs and talk about them in language the way a parent would describe a child: "[h]ere is Yuke when she was a little baby, and here's her when she's one, and here's [when] she's growing up and [another] all grown up."

It is not at all unusual for Japanese pet owners to dress their dogs, and not just to keep them warm in the winter. Pet stores sell a wide variety of clothing, from T-shirts to seasonal items to clothes linked to popular movies. Clothes are one of the best ways for owners to blur the line between humans and animals. The most significant holiday in Japan is New Year's, celebrated for three days (January 1–3). On January 1, the entire family goes together to the family shrine. In Kyoto, people dress in their best clothing, often wearing a traditional kimono, to visit the shrine. Annie reports that her host mother dresses her Shih-Tzu, Rin, in a new kimono every New Year's celebration. Each month Rin is photographed in a different seasonal outfit and the pictures are put together for the following year's calendar. For example, in December, Rin was wearing a Santa Claus sweater. Barbara's host sisters enjoy putting dresses on their toy poodles and taking pictures of them. They also put kimonos on their poodles for New Year's.

Karl reports that when his own mother came to visit him, she brought several T-shirts for his host family's dog, and according to Karl, his host mother "was way [happier] about that than even her gift." Erin describes how her family puts a bandana on their dog, "Bob," every day. Erin's host mother showed Erin a drawer with "a collection of bandanas," reflecting a range of seasons and holidays. Jean reflects on her host family's Pomeranian, Momochan, and his clothing: "When they go on walks, he usually has a different outfit every time, ... all these sweaters" (Jean).

The topic of food is one that illustrates a blurring of human and animal distinctions in Japan. Mike, a black Labrador retriever, "really likes sweet potatoes, so when the family eats sweet potatoes, the dog gets to eat some." He also gets "very nice food, like tempura sometimes when it's cooked for the family, there's a couple which are set aside for the dog" (Gary). Fred says that his host family gave their Bengal cat a treat for his birthday, a special cat cake. Charles reports that his host mother gave a birthday party for her Chihuahua, Pino. Cindy's host family gave their two poodles a special canine birthday cake for one of the dog's fifth birthday. The cake "was pink and elaborately decorated ... with lots of frosting." When the toy poodle in Gail's host family needed to have a leg amputated, the family began cooking her food to improve the dog's healing. Gail says her host mother claims, "broccoli is really good for dogs."

Families travel with their pets as well. Travel agencies continue to have a significant place in metropolitan Japan, both online and as a physical presence. Most travel agencies contain racks and racks of brochures for hotels and resorts, within Japan and internationally. Several of the Japanese resorts are now catering to pet owners, primarily dogs, although the brochures also include photos of cats, rabbits, and hamsters. In the United States, hotels and resorts invoke a language of tolerance toward pets, but in Japan, these resorts want to attract people and their pets, much like family cruise lines advertise to families with children. Photographs in the brochures show activities for humans and animals to enjoy together, such as hiking or swimming. Dogs are able to sit on chairs at the table in the dining room and enjoy the same kinds of food that people eat. Many of the resorts show the kinds of beds (both human-like and more typically dog-like) available for dogs or cats.

Companion animals in Japan are not limited to just households. Even though the phenomenon of cat cafes began in Taiwan in 1998, Japanese people have embraced it and the number of cat cafes has increased steadily since the first one opened in 2004. As of 2015, 274 cat cafes were doing business throughout Japan. Many of the customers are cat owners themselves, but many are also people who would like to have a cat, but are not able to do so because of where they live or their long commutes or long work hours. A typical cat cafe charges about 1000 yen (around $9.00) to enter and another 600–1200 yen per hour. Guests pay extra for drinks (usually coffee or tea) and snacks (for themselves or the cats). At some cafes, the cats are considered feline staff, another example of the ways that Japanese people have blurred the human-animal line (Niijima). In addition to cat cafes, cafes featuring other animals are popular in Tokyo and Osaka. While a dog cafe may not seem exotic, visitors can go to an owl cafe or a hedgehog cafe or even a cafe with snakes (Time Out Tokyo Editors).

Pet funerals, memorial services, and graves are becoming part of modern Japanese society. Elizabeth Kenney argues that both death rituals and the treatment of the corpse show a blurred line between humans and animals. When available, contemporary Japanese pet owners bury pets in their own yards, with a ceremony that includes offerings of food and lighting incense (Kenney). With less outdoor space available for individual homes, pet owners are turning to cremation and pet cemeteries (Ambros). They are providing pet funerals, including simple encoffining (laying out of the body in a box), along with cremation, and a basic Buddhist funeral, including a ceremony performed by a priest similar to a human funeral ceremony. In the Kansai area there are two large pet cemeteries (one in Takarazuka and one in Uji) and several smaller pet cemeteries. Several temples allow animals to be buried adjacent to human tombs. The dedicated pet cemeteries in Uji and Takarazuka are located on top of hills outside of town and include tombs as well as a columbarium that is like an unsealed mausoleum. Family members can bring pet cremains in an urn to the cemetery for a memorial service, often attended by friends and other relatives, followed either by burial in a tomb or placement in a columbarium or cubbies. The graves often have photos and loving words or phrases, such as "amour," "Thank you for memories," and "love hurts." The columbarium cubbies can include photos, candles, cans of pet food, toys, and silk flowers. Many of these items are available for purchase at the pet cemetery. The grieving that takes place at these pet cemeteries appears no different than that at human cemeteries.

Perhaps because Japanese fertility rates are extremely low, among the lowest in the world, Japanese society has turned to pets to supplement their family structure and become not just pet-friendly, but in the eyes of many observers, pet obsessed. Many Japanese people, with and without pets, adore animals and have created liminal spaces for some wildlife (notably deer and monkeys) to be somewhat free and tame. Not too many years ago, Japanese households were pet-free, however, in contemporary Japan, adults are treating pets—dogs, cats, and even rabbits and hamsters—as family members. After adopting pets, Japanese people name them, often endearingly and provide them with access to the inside of the family home, where pets and humans sleep together. Pet birthdays are often celebrated with special cakes, and many pets wear clothing that has little functional use other than to make a fashion statement. Japanese people treat elderly pets with devotion, providing medical treatment and special foods. When pets die, they can receive funeral ceremonies and memorials equal to that of humans.

Japanese pet culture is beginning to spread to the United States and other parts of the world. In the fall of the 2018, Netflix streamed the series "Dogs," with six episodes focusing on the relationship between canines and people around the world, including Syria, Germany, Italy, the United States, and Japan, where one episode shows a lavish canine birthday party with dogs dressed in kimonos. This episode also follows two Japanese dog groomers to an international competition in Pasadena, California, with adoring fans cheering for them, and noting the distinctive Japanese way of styling a dog. The 2018 animated film, "Isle of Dogs," set in Japan, but directed by an American, Wes Anderson, tells about a boy trying to reunite with his lost dog, further demonstrating that audiences outside of Japan connect with stories about Japanese people and their dogs. Another Japanese phenomenon that is spreading throughout the world is the cat cafe, with examples in several European countries, as well as the United States and Canada, according to The Cat Cafe in San Diego, California. Perhaps the most famous contemporary Japanese cat, "Hello Kitty," has become truly global, recognized around the world, with stores in dozens of countries and appearing on products for children and adults. In multiple ways, as Japanese people are blurring the distinctions between humans and animals, other parts of the world are adopting Japanese pet culture.

Acknowledgments

The Pomona College General Research Fund provided travel funds and funds for transcribing interviews. Elinor Aspegren helped me locate secondary literature. I am grateful to several individuals in Japan for helping me locate students who were living with host families with pets, in particular, Maki Hubbard, Tom Rohlich, Mari Kawata and Yoko Nukii of the Associated Kyoto Program; Mike Hugh and Hiromi Uehira of the Stanford University Bing Overseas Program in Kyoto; and Mark Lincicome, Fusako Shore, and Tazuko Wada of the Kyoto Consortium for Japanese Studies.

Note

1. I interviewed 18 students in 2016 and 7 in 2017. Two of the students I interviewed in 2017 were living in the same household as students I interviewed in 2016.

Works Cited

Alt, Matt. "The United States of Japan." *The New Yorker (Culture Desk)* 4 May 2018.

Ambros, Barbara. "The Necrogeography of Pet Memorial Spaces: Pets as Liminal Family Members in Contemporary Japan." *Material Religion* 6, 3: 2010. 304–335.

Boling, Patricia. "Demography, Culture, and Policy: Understanding Japan's Low Fertility." *Population and Development Review* 34, 2, 2008. 307–326.

Cat Cafe San Diego. *What's a Cat Cafe?.* 14 Jan. 2018. https://catcafesd.com/about-us/whats-a-cat-cafe/.

Farrer, James, Haruka Tsuchiya, and Bart Bagrowicz. "Emotional Expression in Tsukiau Dating Relationships in Japan." *Journal of Social and Personal Relationships* 25, 1: 2008. 169–188.

Ferguson, Susan. "Introduction." in *Shifting the Center: Understanding Contemporary Families.* Ed. by Susan Ferguson. 3rd ed. Boston: McGraw-Hill, 2007.

Gordenker, Alice. "Pampered Pets." *The Japan Times.* April 17, 2012. https://www.japantimes.co.jp/news/2012/04/17/reference/pampered-pets/#.XaXwkUZKhPY.

Irvine, Leslie, and Laurent Cilia, "More-than-human Families: Pets, People, and Practices in Multispecies Households." *Sociology Compass* 2017; 11:e12455. https://doe.org/10.1111/soc4.12455.

Isle of Dogs. Dir. Wes Anderson. Voice Perf. Bryan Cranston, Koyu Rankin, Edward Norton. 2018.

Kenney, Elizabeth. "Pet Funerals and Animal Graves in Japan." *Mortality* 9, February 2004. 142–60.

Kondo, Marie. *The Life-Changing Magic of Tidying Up: The Japanese Art of Decluttering and Organizing.* Berkeley: Ten Speed Press, 2014.

Laurent, Erick L. "Children, 'Insects' and Play in Japan." In *Companion Animals and Us: Exploring the Relationships Between People and Pets.* Ed. by A.L. Podberscek, Elizabeth S. Paul and James A. Serpell. Cambridge University Press, 2000. pp. 61–89.

Niijima, Noriko. "Chats, Cats and a Cup of Tea: A Sociological Analysis of the Neko Cafe Phenomenon in Japan." In *Companion Animals in Everyday Life: Situating Human-Animal Engagement Within Cultures.* Ed by M.P. Pregowski. Springer.com. 2016. DOI 10.1057 /978-1-137-59572-0_17. pp. 269–282

Rindfuss, Ronald, Minja Kim Choe, Larry L. Bumpass, and Noriko Tsuya. "Social Networks and Family Change in Japan." *American Sociological Review* 69 December 2004. pp. 838–861.

"Scissors Down." *Dogs*. Netflix. Dir. Roger Ross Williams. 2018.

Skabelund, Aaron Herald. *Empire of Dogs*. Ithaca, NY: Cornell. 2011.

Time Out Tokyo Editors. "Best Animal and Pet Cafes in Tokyo—Updated." *Time Out Tokyo* May 16, 2018. https://www.timeout.com/tokyo/restaurants/the-top-10-animal-cafes-in-tokyo.

United Nations. World Population Prospects 2017 Data Query. https://esa.un.org/unpd/wpp/DataQuery/.

Vanorman, Alicia G., and Paola Scommegna. "Understanding the Dynamics of Family Change in the United States." *Population Bulletin* 71, 1: July 2016. 1–24.

The "Soul" of the Circus

What Animals Under the Big Top
Continue to Teach Their Audiences

MORT GAMBLE

Animals in circuses have long performed beside humans, displaying their beauty, intelligence, and capacity to entertain—often by resembling humanlike behaviors. Because the circus generally presented unexpected twists on life, audiences delighted in seeing horses appearing to solve math problems, elephants "dancing," or bears riding motorcycles. Patrons were comfortable with seeing some of themselves cleverly reenacted in the animal kingdom. More recently, as increased concern for animal welfare has spread throughout society, questions have been raised about the propriety of such animal acts as critics point out what they see as exploitation of the creatures for cheap entertainment.

The animal rights movement has fostered a blurring of traditional human-animal relationships as advocacy has increased for rights of the sort human citizens enjoy. Whereas circus audiences once saw something of themselves in animal acts, now many in society seem to see—and demand—much more. As Kristin Henderson in *The Washington Post* wrote when Ringling Bros. and Barnum & Bailey was phasing out its elephant acts, "Americans have long viewed elephants as fellow travelers. We see ourselves in their intelligence and emotional depth" (Henderson). She posed an important question: "Now that elephants are departing from the circus that calls itself the Greatest Show on Earth … what have we learned about them? And what have we learned about ourselves?" Clearly, attitudes toward animals in circuses have begun to change, even as they serve as ambassadors of their threatened counterparts in the wild. The use of animals, especially exotic species, for amusement has led not only to bitter debate but also to questioning of long-accepted human-animal relationships. Thus, an entertainment tradition that often showed animals performing humanlike behaviors has arrived at a time when those same species are proclaimed by some no longer to qualify for public entertainment at all, indeed should have comparable legal and social standing—the same rights and freedoms—afforded to humans, further blurring the distinction between who they are and who humans are.

I was part of the colorful world of the circus myself, employed for two seasons in the 1970s with Circus Kirk, a three-ring, traveling tent show that featured many traditional circus animals, most of which were domesticated, such as dogs, ponies, and llamas. An elephant, big snakes, and monkeys were on loan to us from a zoo and another circus. In sixty years of attending circuses, I have witnessed animal acts and routines many times, and, in speaking with those who train them and care for them, have concluded that circuses are far more interesting with animals than without them. Furthermore, my observations and research indicate that, by and large, circus animals receive appropriate care, respect, and admiration for their beauty and intelligence, serving also to remind us of the fragile state of animals remaining in wilderness. My personal experience coincided with the public's expectations then that no circus was complete without animals.

Animals have defined the circus from its origins. Some of the earliest American circuses were actually traveling menageries. In the days before zoos and electronic media, these shows introduced nineteenth century audiences to strange, odd, and curious creatures from "the four corners of the Earth"—elephants, lions, tigers, rhinos, hippos, apes, and more. Dazzling posters pasted up on fences, barns, and downtown buildings promised the citizenry sights and sounds, thrills, and amusement unobtainable anywhere else. By the time many shows began to take to the rails in the 1870s, growing in size and prominence thanks to train travel which permitted them to bypass smaller towns, the wild-animal menagerie and its "educated" counterparts doing humanlike tricks on command were familiar and expected features of circuses. Wild and domestic animals—along with clowns, acrobats, aerialists, and other performers—shaped the modern circus format.

The history, contributions, and legacy of circus animals reflect over time the use of animals to entertain, educate, and inspire the public, often in ways that satisfied the audience's need to see them in a more human context. Although the circus tradition in America originated with equestrian riding, it was the exotic collections of rare and mysterious creatures housed in a separate tent adjacent to the main canvas arena—the "big top"—that for later generations captured the public's fears and fascination while often playing to audiences' tendencies to humanize chimpanzees, bears, and other animals. Circus zoology stirred the imagination, often took liberties with scientific facts, and converted some natural behaviors into delightful entertainment. From the earliest show established by John Bill Ricketts in Philadelphia in 1793, the American circus became the country's most familiar medium of popular, mass entertainment. As the nation pushed the frontier westward, troupes took to the road, often as combined circuses and menageries, notes Rodney Huey in *An Abbreviated History of the Circus in America*.

The sight of elephants shuffling down main street and gilded cage wagons filled with pacing jungle cats rolling past homes and stores offered unforgettable entertainment as the circus parade drove audiences to the show grounds to enter an exotic world "here today and gone tomorrow." With pungent odors and the trumpeting, screeches, and roaring of the denizens of the menagerie, circuses launched an assault on the senses and provided firsthand exposure to wild animals imported from their habitats and displayed amid familiar domestic settings. A town's vacant lot was transformed overnight into another realm; the menagerie that came with the circus was an exceptional contribution to popular entertainment, helping to satisfy the public's curiosity or fantasies about the natural world.

Before zoos were common, circuses brought amazing, rarely seen beasts to small-town America. A farmer might know nothing about an elephant, hippo, or rhinoceros until a poster on his barn piqued his curiosity and delivered the live specimen on circus day. By the time the ornate parade wagons appeared with their elaborate decorations recalling tales of mythology or fantasy, the customers' curiosity about what the mysterious canvas tents contained was almost feverish. Admission to the "free" menagerie tent required a ticket to the main performance in the big top where seating varied by price and, more often than not, by ushers' temperaments. Presented afternoon and night, the performance usually featured plentiful appearances of animals in assorted acts and parade spectacles along with aerialists and acrobats. The formula was basically true of large and small traveling shows.

Circus press agents made great beasts even greater. Elephants—the more pachyderms a show had, the larger and more prominent it was deemed to be—were depicted reaching with their trunks into upper-story windows. Posters showed the big cats challenging their trainers with snarling menace. Apes and monkeys delightfully mimicked humans, or were shown in advertisements wreaking havoc in the jungle. Hippos, known for a natural reddish secretion through their hides, were billed as "blood-sweating." The Ringling Bros. Circus once proclaimed that its giraffe was the only such specimen in North America, and urged the public to witness the "tallest, stateliest, grandest" creature which represented "[t]he Crowning Triumph of Zoological Research," records Charles Philip Fox in *A Ticket to the Circus*. An outlandish poster of the time depicted human visitors barely reaching to the creature's knees (Fox 123). Another advertisement claimed that the Ringling giraffe was the last of its species, and urged the public to see it now or miss it forever (Fox 71).

Importing Jumbo, a huge African elephant and a popular resident of the London Zoo, showman P.T. Barnum spurred the development of modern integrated marketing. Merchandise accompanying Barnum's publicity buildup prior to the animal's arrival fueled the Jumbo craze—as did controversy about the American's displeasing purchase of the "children's pet" of England. Thus was set up an early example of the blurring of human concern and animal "emotion." John and Alice Durant in their *Pictorial History of the American Circus* note that Jumbo did not want to move to America; he was depicted in newspaper illustrations as "weeping" with a giant handkerchief at the prospect of working for a Connecticut Yankee, Barnum. The showman, however, not only could not have cared less, but he maximized the controversy surrounding the elephant's departure. Irving Wallace in *The Fabulous Showman: The Life and Times of P.T. Barnum* recounts the animal's refusal to depart his beloved England by lying down in the street. Barnum cabled his London agent: "Let him lie there a week if he wants to. It is the best advertisement in the world" (Wallace 250). After Jumbo began touring in America, Barnum's posters claimed not only that Jumbo was "[y]he Largest Living Quadruped on Earth," but that the beast had actually "grown several inches in height and increased over a ton in weight" (Durant and Durant 88). The animal's celebrity overshadowed the rest of the attractions in the circus.

After Jumbo died in a railroad accident in 1885, Barnum installed his skeleton inside the menagerie, alongside a female elephant billed as "Jumbo's grieving widow." But first, more publicity was required about the almost-human creature. Barnum's press agents released fictional illustrations depicting the moment of the locomotive collision that killed the great pachyderm—allegedly sacrificing his own life to "save" a smaller elephant that was also threatened by the train (Durant and Durant 89).

Through the 1930s and 1940s, "Gargantua the Great," an especially fearsome gorilla that toured with Ringling Bros. and Barnum & Bailey, and other animals still played to the public's fascination, fears, and misunderstanding regarding wild creatures. As with

Jumbo, a similar blurring of animal reality and human fantasy occurred with Gargantua, the greatest single animal attraction since Jumbo, a celebrity in his own right, and a financial godsend for the Ringling circus.

Although Ringling's publicity department depicted the gorilla being captured by spear-carrying African tribesmen, the animal was actually sold to the circus by a woman in Brooklyn who had raised him as a pet. Her "Buddy" became unmanageable, and, newly promoted as the "world's most terrifying living creature," the gorilla was given a new show-business name, "Gargantua." Robert Lewis Taylor in *Center Ring: The People of the Circus* writes that the show "endowed him with near-human cunning, which gave him a permanent disposition of 'sagacious savagery'" (Taylor 88). Impossible to treat because of what all observers agreed was his perpetually hostile world view, Gargantua required his human caregivers to engage in a game of wits with him. Circus veterinarian J.Y. Henderson in his memoir *Circus Doctor* mentions one inventive treatment plan using a favorite Gargantua tonic, Coca-Cola, mixed with castor oil. He recalls that once the gorilla realized he had been tricked into taking the medicine, Henderson had "never in my life seen any animal quite so angry" (Henderson and Taplinger 178).

Beginning in 1938, the gorilla traveled in a specially constructed, "jungle-conditioned," glass-enclosed cage initially outfitted with human-styled living room furniture which Gargantua trashed (Taylor 206). The circus then bought a female gorilla, "M'Toto," and arranged a "marriage" between the two simians. As recalled by Henry Ringling North in his autobiography *The Circus Kings*, their first meeting was not auspicious: "Roaring and yelling, (Gargantua) pelted his wife with half-eaten vegetables and shook the cage in his raging efforts to tear out the bars. The congregation was hysterical between laughter and terror" (North and Hatch 226). Nonetheless, the circus printed souvenir folders about the newlyweds and sent out Christmas cards on behalf of "Mr. and Mrs. Gargantua the Great." When "Gargy" died at the end of the 1949 touring season, the circus indicated that the famous ape was such a loyal trouper that he had waited until the very last stand of the tour to expire.

Yet if nature's strangest species sparked fascination, animals performing humanlike tricks or resembling human traits offered even more pleasant amusement and comparisons to behaviors of people. Chimps walked around on stilts. Bears rode bicycles or motor bikes. "Educated" horses displayed their intelligence by performing simple mathematics, either stomping the number of times necessary for the answer or choosing a board which had the correct arithmetic solution painted on it. A popular elephant number to this day has the heavy beasts lying down to the notes of a lullaby or climbing over each other to "London Bridge Is Falling Down." In 1962, a Ringling elephant, "Big Ruth," danced her bulky version of the craze of the time, the Twist. Familiar farm animals such as pigs and goats performed simple tricks, delighting those mindful of their own barnyard versions back home. Parades of dancing poodles, dressed as Vegas showgirls, presented stunning fashion shows. Horses, dogs, and tigers were sometimes trained to refuse compliance with commands until the audience shouted out the magic word, "please!" Some of animal trainer Clyde Beatty's lions were trained to charge him on command, "refusing" to let Beatty leave the safety of a smaller, adjacent cage.

Humanlike animal routines were sometimes spectacular. In 1942, the Ringling circus hired George Balanchine of the New York City Ballet and composer Igor Stravinsky to create an elaborate "elephant ballet." Ernest Albrecht in *From Barnum & Bailey to Feld: The Creative Evolution of the Greatest Show on Earth* notes that fifty ballerinas joined fifty elephants wearing tutus made of pink canvas—"to resist the elephant's desire to pull them off and eat them" (Albrecht 136). Smaller shows created human-animal acts that played better in more intimate versions of the big top. A 1973 Circus Kirk comedy routine titled "Farmer Mike, His Wife, and Kid" featured a burly man dressed as a hayseed farmer, a female clown (his "wife"), and "Munch," a trained goat of which it was said with some accuracy that of the five tricks he knew, it was his decision at each performance to do any three of the five. On the midway of this particular circus, a menagerie tent housed llamas, boa constrictors, and monkeys from "the high mountains of Peru and the steaming jungles of the Amazon." "Come in and meet the animals," announced the ticket seller of this attraction. "They want to meet you."

In the decade prior to the debut of television, a few shows still paraded the natural world down main street. Clad in white safari uniform and armed with whip, gun with blanks, and chair, Beatty exemplified the "fighting act" in which a single man fought for survival and dominance over a steel cage full of jungle killers. Other trainers chose the "quiet" form of cat act, orchestrating the graceful tricks of lions and tigers with a whip or hand gestures. (The whip was designed to keep the big cats focused and to cue the trick, not to assault the animals physically.) In the 1980s, the Ringling circus featured a "living unicorn," promoted with tremendous publicity, and starred an 11,000-pound Asian elephant named "King Tusk"—known more commonly in show-business circles as "Tommy." Smaller shows traveling by semi-trailers stuck to their bombastic scripts that conflated the natural world with ballyhoo worthy of Barnum. In 1967, one such circus charged a separate admission to a tent to see an odd, live primate with a colorful tail. "We don't know what it is, the man who captured it doesn't know what it is, but it's alive and inside," droned a "grind tape" amid colorful banners on the midway suggesting that the unusual creature could be the result of atomic fallout (Acme).

Behind the scenes, circus animals bonded with their trainers and keepers as their counterparts have in zoos, marine attractions, and other amusements. Those who knew them best, such as Ringling Bros. veterinarian J.Y. Henderson, wrote of their charges' humanlike qualities. Following a fire that killed sixty-five animals of the Ringling circus menagerie in 1942—a day when some of the most hardened circus roustabouts wept— Henderson wrote in his autobiography of the silent, solemn dignity of the creatures caught in the disaster: "There was just a dead silence. It was one of the most touching and one of the most awful things, for that reason, that I have ever experienced…. I knew then that there is something in animal make-up akin to greatness in men." He spoke of their "inner nobility and a kinship to what is enduring in nature" (Henderson and Taplinger 138).

Circus animal handlers also maintained that their animals enjoyed the attention in the center ring, thrived on the constant travel and stimulation of circus life, and were proud of their contributions to the success of the show. For circuses with elephants, the morning raising of the big top offered a show within the show as the beasts seemed to march proudly into the rising tent and effortlessly dragged the tent's poles into position. The spectacle delighted onlookers, and it could be inferred that the elephants relished the attention and applause resulting from showing off their great strength. A longtime trainer of elephant acts went further, relating what he saw as the elephants' "pride" in doing a good morning's work. According to this trainer, the Kelly Miller Circus, a traveling truck show, one day experienced horrendous ground conditions resulting from bad weather. For their safety, the show's elephants were required to remain in their vans until the performance. The trainer, however, noticed that the animals appeared restless and depressed during their confinement—suggesting that they had concluded, mistakenly, they were being punished for some infraction, instead of being permitted to perform their normal work. They wanted to help the circus prepare, he related, but were frustrated that they could not. The story was offered as a defense of the humane care of circus elephants, an example of their sensitivity and intuition, and proof that the human-animal bond is a sacred contract that allowed the trainer to "read" the minds of those in his charge.

For some members of the public, however, of the kind whose ignorance of nature leads them to feed bears in national parks despite posted warnings, circus animals were no different than the family dog. Often shows promoted this view of "tame" wild animals by demonstrating to their audiences that the creatures were easily trained to perform human stunts and were thus "domesticated"—further blurring the line between respectful distance and dangerous familiarity. As zoos and television made the exotic more familiar, circuses found ways to "humanize" their menageries. Sea lions balanced rubber balls, played musical instruments, and "nodded" in agreement with the patrons that they should be applauded for their efforts. Tigers hopped on their hind legs or "high-fived" their trainers. Polar bears—among the most dangerous of all animals—skidded down sliding boards like children. Comedy routines featured horses or mules tossing off saddles and humiliating their cowboy riders. Elephants took up trunk painting, their slathered artistic creations fetching tidy sums at auctions. In the Kelly Miller Circus in 2015, a llama pranced around the ring costumed as Uncle Sam in a way that made it appear that the animal was walking on two legs, not four.

The author of a recent history of the Russell Bros. Circus, a World War II–era show, recounted how that show's star chimpanzee displayed "human intelligence," living alongside her trainers, eating meals with them, and babysitting circus children (Webb and Laredo). She even "authored" a regular newspaper column—courtesy of the show's press department. Clowns, however, held no illusions about how dangerous circus animals could be. It has been said that if a trained chimpanzee escapes, the human comedians dive for cover: the apes, supposedly jealous of the laughter and attention clowns receive, aggressively hunt down their "competition."

Acts featuring male lions were a study in control and discipline, even as they were presented as docile. The trainer (incorrectly referred to commonly as a "tamer") might hug and pet his subjects as if they were house cats. Yet should one of the beasts decide the human's time was up, the other cats might well join in the attack.

Despite regular pronouncements of its demise, and a 2017 announcement of the ending of the Ringling Bros. and Barnum & Bailey, the circus has persisted in popularity, offering a mix of the unusual made familiar, and the familiar made unusual (Mele). Animals remain central to the experience, performing time-honored routines that have rarely changed over decades. From Barnum's era to the present day, however, circuses have been criticized for alleged, largely unsubstantiated abuse of animals and their exploitation for entertainment. Henry Bergh, founder of the American Society for the Prevention of Cruelty to Animals, challenged Barnum on his use of animals, even objecting to the boa constrictors' being fed live mice (Wallace 221).

Opposing the use of the elephant bullhook or elephant guide, a training tool accepted in animal husbandry, as well as what they assert is general exploitation and mistreatment of animals in circuses, activists have contributed to the decline of the circus industry in the United States. Many oppose even the use of domesticated animals—horses, dogs, goats—in the center ring. On the other side are the trainers, handlers, and caregivers (including licensed veterinarians and wildlife experts) who maintain that circus animals are treated with respect, showcased for their beauty and intelligence, and provided excellent daily and on-demand veterinary care. For circus people, the animals remain the very "soul" of the big top, important to a message of environmentalism, indispensable to business viability, and vital to the maintenance of human/animal collaboration. Horses, dogs, camels, and even elephants, circuses remind their patrons, have worked alongside humans for centuries.

Shows also responded by pointing out the vital educational and conservation function of introducing people to animals. A flyer on "progressive animal care" distributed by Feld Entertainment, the parent company of Ringling Bros. and Barnum & Bailey, cited the company's commitment to saving the critically endangered Asian elephant: "Studies have shown that the public display of performing elephants contributes to heightened public awareness of the animals themselves and of man's responsibility for their well-being and protection" ("Committed to Progressive"). Two circus companies—Ringling in Florida and Carson & Barnes in Oklahoma—established breeding and research centers for Asian elephants. Nearly all circuses introduced elephant and camel rides—requiring a separate ticket, of course. Other changes were made to improve public perceptions. The crowd-pleasing spectacle of watching elephants raising the poles of the big top on circus day was discontinued. More spacious cages were carried on tour, additional awnings spread to shelter the creatures from the weather, and the animals' "tricks" redefined as natural "behaviors."

Animal act formats were updated, too. Trainers of big cats began to wear microphones so that the audience could follow their respectful, affectionate verbal cues to lions and tigers. For several seasons with Ringling Bros. and Barnum & Bailey, Sarah Houck was billed as the "Tiger Whisperer," gently interacting with creatures that circuses of yesterday would have billed as man-eating jungle killers. (Most trainers, however, never consider wild animals completely trustworthy, and reports persist of lions and tigers, suddenly and without apparent provocation, turning violent in circuses, zoos, and other settings. Seemingly mild-mannered, circus elephants are cared for—and guarded—around the clock.)

Circus animals receive more than adequate daily care (in some cases, decades ago, surpassing that of some of the human employees of the circus), and the world's largest show, Ringling Bros. and Barnum & Bailey, retained full-time veterinarians. Moreover, in modern times circus animals have no longer been captured from the wild. Although not truly domesticated, the big cats in today's acts, for example, have been bred and raised under human care—and the "fighting" displays exemplified by Clyde Beatty have long since passed into history.

But care for the animals and concern for the public's safety have not won over critics. Although smaller circuses continue to present animal acts, most of which now feature domesticated species, protests have not receded. Many activists want nothing less than the complete removal of any domestic or exotic species from the circus or any other form of entertainment.

A longtime Ringling foe, the Humane Society of the United States, joined other animal groups in suing Feld Entertainment in 2000 over alleged abuse of its elephants. Nine years later, a judge dismissed the case, citing a witness who was paid to substantiate the charges. Feld Entertainment sought recovery of its legal fees; the animal groups settled for $16 million in 2014 (Heath). Nevertheless, faced with unpredictable touring conditions resulting from widespread legislation, in 2016 Ringling Bros. and Barnum & Bailey retired its elephants from both touring units. The next year, citing resultant declines in ticket sales and other factors, Feld Entertainment shelved its entire "Greatest Show on Earth." The troupe had toured under various titles for 146 years.

One of the last, traditional, traveling tented shows, the Oklahoma-based Kelly Miller Circus, reopened under new management in 2018 with no animal acts. Its website stated: "While Kelly Miller Circus still supports circuses with exotic animals, we have chosen, this year to be exotic animal free." The different direction of that circus has drawn criticism from longtime fans and praise from activists. Other established troupes, like New York–based Big Apple Circus, have steadily retired exotic animals from their performances; the nation's youth circuses, such as Sarasota, Florida's Sailor Circus, continue to rely solely on human feats.

At issue for the protesters is not simply whether circus and other animals are treated humanely (they generally are), but rather the idea of whether animals are humans' to be used for any purpose beyond their own lives. The website for the People for the Ethical Treatment of Animals (PETA) states as follows: "Supporters of animal rights believe that animals have an inherent worth—a value completely separate from their usefulness to humans" ("Why Animal Rights?"). For its part, the nation's oldest circus-fan group, the Circus Fans Association of America (CFA),[1] supports the "humane and responsible care and exhibition of circus animals," seeking to "preserve the human-animal bond that is often expressed through respectful contact with animals and the experience of seeing them in person." The organization of active and retired circus personnel, fans, and friends, along with the Outdoor Amusement Business Association (OABA) and other groups, has fought to correct the record on circus animal care, drawing a distinction between animal "rights" and what they see as legitimate animal "welfare."

Now the circus fights to keep its animals—and audiences—by acknowledging the importance and value of its "animal performers" which are "members of the circus family." At the 2016 annual Ring of Fame ceremonies honoring circus luminaries in Sarasota, Florida, animals and the spreading controversy surrounding them took center stage as they were described as the very "soul" of the circus.

On the few animal shows surviving today, the "animal cast members" offer small towns the opportunity to ride an elephant, gawk at a camel, or handle a boa constrictor. As wilderness shrinks and the list of endangered species grows, circuses, like zoos, have embraced their animals as ambassadors of the wild. Circus narratives have moved beyond alliteration to information, advising patrons that experiencing exotic animals in person leads to greater awareness of critically threatened species like the Asian elephant and the Bengal tiger. Therefore, reevaluation of the status of circus animals has occurred along with the evolution of circus traditions. From being stars of the show—and, in some cases like Jumbo and Gargantua, true celebrities—circus animals today join humans in a common cause, as representatives of a threatened natural order.

Circus animals still attract positive press coverage in their own right, amazing those unfamiliar with, or misinformed about, their historic role in American show business. A 2018 feature in a Minnesota newspaper described how a local veterinarian was recruited to certify the health of animals traveling with the Culpepper & Merriweather Circus, a small tent show. "Although that was the first circus I've dealt with, I'd say those animals were better cared for than a lot of people are," the veterinarian was quoted. "I was a little surprised at just how well they care for their animals" (qtd. in Smith).

Several seasons ago, the Kelly Miller show offered a contrasting study of past practice and current concern. The circus's star attraction, an African elephant, was announced during the performance as the world's only "dancing elephant," a time-honored animal routine. Out of the spotlight, however, the elephant lived in relative luxury in its own air-conditioned van, like a Hollywood star, exempt from most of the customary duties of a circus pachyderm.

The vast circus menageries and some of the clever animal performers doing human-like tricks are mostly consigned to history as new production formats and social realities become ever more influential. Trained chimp and bear acts, imitating humans as acrobats or cycle riders, are rare. If circus animal performers once pleased audiences by appearing to be human, today their "humanness" has seemingly reached—even surpassed—the station of people. Better to have a circus with humans risking their lives to entertain, say the critics, than to employ animals as entertainers. Somehow, goes the logic, the animals are above that, their dignity and modern "rights" relieving them from an "unnatural" state in the center ring.

The question remains as to what may be lost without circus animals—a long show-business tradition, to be sure, but perhaps also further alienation from the natural world and appreciation for its creatures. Janet Davis of the University of Texas pointed out in a guest editorial after Ringling announced it was discontinuing elephant acts, "in its stately, lumbering way, (the circus elephant) has been a lens for how the country sees itself." Davis concluded that often circus elephants lived "long, fruitful lives, forming deep bonds with trainers…. If we lose this relationship, we lose a vital part of circus history, as well as a direct emotional tie to these magnificent animals" (Davis).

NOTE

1. The author served as an officer of the CFA.

WORKS CITED

Acme Circus Corporation, Sells & Gray Circus. Tape-recorded sideshow announcement, 1967.

Albrecht, Ernest. *From Barnum & Bailey to Feld: The Creative Evolution of the Greatest Show on Earth.* McFarland, 2014.

The Circus Fans Association of America. "We Care About Animal Welfare." Circusfans.org/animal/welfare/. Accessed 2 Jan 2019.

"Committed to Progressive Animal Care." Feld Entertainment promotional brochure, 2011.

Davis, Janet. "A Bittersweet Bow for the Elephant." *The New York Times*, 7 March 2015.

Durant, John, and Alice Durant. *Pictorial History of the American Circus.* A.S. Barnes and Company, 1957.

Elephant trainer, Kelly Miller Circus, personal interview. 2005.

Fox, Charles Philip. *A Ticket to the Circus: A Pictorial History of the Incredible Ringlings.* Bramhall House, 1959.

Heath, Thomas. "Ringling Circus Prevails in 14-year Legal Case; Collects $16m from Humane Society, Others." *The Washington Post*, 16 May 2014.

Henderson, J.Y., and Richard Taplinger. *Circus Doctor.* Bantam Books, 1952.

Henderson, Kristin. "The Big Exit," *The Washington Post*, 27 October 2016.

Huey, Rodney A. *An Abbreviated History of the Circus in America.* Unpublished manuscript, 2009.

"Kelly Miller Circus Story." *Kelly Miller Circus.* Hugo, Oklahoma. https://kellymillercircus.com/aboutus/. Accessed 28 December 2018.

Mele, Christopher. "Ringling Bros. and Barnum & Bailey Circus to End Its 146-Year Run." *The Washington Post*, 14 January 2017.

North, Henry Ringling, and Alden Hatch. *The Circus Kings.* Dell Publishing Co., 1964.

North American Operating Co., Circus Kirk. "Three Rings Under the Big Top." Personal experience as circus employee during seasonal tours, 1973–74.

Smith, Chad. "Local Vet Examines Circus Animals." *Tri-County Record* (MN), 9 August 2018.
Taylor, Robert Lewis. *Center Ring: The People of the Circus.* Doubleday & Company, 1956,
Wallace, Irving. *The Fabulous Showman: The Life and Times of P.T. Barnum.* Signet, 1962.
Webb, Keith, and Joseph F. Laredo. *The Russell Bros. Circus Scrapbook,* 2017.
"Why Animal Rights?" PETA. https://www/peta.org/about-peta/why-peta/whyanimalrights/. Accessed 28 Dec. 2018.

PART III

Reflections
Cultural Analysis of Human/Animal Blurring

From Tusk to Tail

Understanding the Animal Attraction to College Mascots

LISA LYON PAYNE

He was short, about 50 pounds, with handsome, almost sinister features: white fur, a prodigious underbite, and eyes (and snout) as black as the tinted windows of the sleek limousine from which he had just emerged. Standing on the red carpet … before the celebrity-studded premiere of *Midnight in the Garden of Good and Evil*, he appeared unfazed by the swooning fans, the paparazzi's flashbulbs and the custom-made Nonie Sutton tuxedo that adorned his frame. UGA V, English bulldog, University of Georgia mascot, SI cover boy and screen star, was ready for his close-up.
—*Sports Illustrated*'s "Show Dog" premiere story

The University of Georgia's revered English bulldog mascot—celebrated since the mid '50s—made his on-screen debut in 1997, playing his father, Uga IV, in Clint Eastwood's film adaptation of the Savannah-based, bestselling mystery *Midnight in the Garden of Good and Evil*. In preparation for filming, Eastwood flew to Savannah to assess Uga's acting ability and formed an instant connection with the canine. He wrestled and rolled around on the floor with the dog, and at one point he exclaimed, "Uga, I'm going to make you a celebrity." In response, his owner retorted confidently, "Mr. Eastwood, Uga is *already* a celebrity" (Seiler and Hannon 117). Uga is no stranger to adulation and fanfare. He is dignified and decorous compared to the throngs of wild and unrestrained fans he represents at the school's football venue, Sanford Stadium. In keeping with expectations, the film's screenwriter described the celebrity dog as a consummate ace. He noted, "Uga V is no house pet. He's quite used to performing before 80,000 rabid Georgia fans every Saturday in the fall. His bloodlines show—he's an ultimate professional, camera ready and walking and slobbering on command" (qtd. in Seiler and Hannon 120).

Perhaps one of the best-known college mascots, but certainly not the only revered collegiate animal symbol, Uga has a resume that includes both ordinary and extraordinary human achievements. He holds his own student ID card, enjoys a varsity letter and an honorary college degree, has appeared in multiple national advertising campaigns ranging from Kodak to Coca-Cola, and has even made an appearance in *Playboy* magazine. He lives the good life. In his bedroom, special Nike jerseys are hung, made from the same material as the Division I football players' jerseys. In the driveway, a custom red SUV is parked with a vanity plate boasting his name. He arrives to football games in a special golf cart before settling down in his air-conditioned doghouse on a bag of ice.

College animal mascots are an indispensable part of the pomp and pageantry of American university culture, representing a curious connection between fan and animal; these mascots range from adorable to fearsome to humble, yet as shared members of the community, fans identify with them, adore them and even dress like them. A strong, strange propinquity exists with these animals. They are elevated—even repulsive and ridiculous ones—and in so doing, they bring out the best and worst in the those they represent. Followers identify with these creatures, most of whom have never met the animals in person, in most unusual ways. Animal mascots prompt fans to snort like pigs, bark like dogs, and chomp like gators. We adore them and like to think they adore us in return; we dress like them and dress them like us. In appearing, behaving and sounding like one another, fans deliberately blur the lines between primal, frenzied behavior and anthropomorphized creatures. Mascot enthusiasts celebrate and bond with these animals by humanizing them through their attire, dwellings, care, and even death and burial rituals.

A Relationship That Defies Nature

A mascot is an identity worthy of respect. Roy Yarbrough, author of *Mascots: The History of Senior College and University Mascots/Nicknames*, notes, "Humans have always admired the grace and power of a big cat, the speed and endurance of a wolf, the cunning of a fox and the utter power of a bear" (Yarbrough 11). Yet, renowned animal expert Hal Herzog asserts in *Some We Love, Some We Hate, Some We Eat* that some creatures are inherently unlovable. Humans are hardwired to revere some and reject others based on appearances. This instinct makes some animals like the furry, wide-eyed Panda—the logo of the World Wildlife fund–appealing, and others, like the rare giant Chinese salamander, revolting. This creature, Herzog notes, is a "beady-eyed six-foot-long mass of brown slime" (38). He emphasizes "the importance of being cute" as a built-in underpinning to the human-animal relationship. Yet animal mascots have a special pull that endears some animals, transcending cuteness, when they are otherwise not endearing or even repulsive. Devotees fetishize boll weevils at the University of Arkansas at Monticello, cobras at Coker College and Virginia Intermont College, rattlesnakes at Florida Agricultural and Mechanical University, and spiders at the University of Richmond, with an emotional connection that overpowers our innate aversion to creepy or ugly. The University of Arkansas razorback, Tusk, seems to represent this phenomenon. The Russian boar, which closely resembles wild hogs known as razorbacks indigenous to the Arkansas wilderness, is known for its long, bristly hair standing high on his backbone. The *Encyclopedia of Arkansas History and Culture* described the animal this way: "Boars have long, high shoulders, a sloping rump, long, skinny legs, and small hips. The massive wedge-shaped head with short, hairy, erect ears ends in a pointed snout" ("Razorbacks"). Nevertheless, devoted fans seek kisses from the five hundred-pound creature on game day ("Animal Attraction") and celebrate him with the official "Woooo! Pig Sooie!" chant, which was granted trademark status in 2014 from the United States Patent and Trademark Office (Heitner). The University website provides detailed illustrated instructions on proper pig chanting in honor of the animal:

Raise your arms above your head during the The Hog Call, yell "Wooo" and wiggle your fingers for a few seconds. Next, bring both arms straight down with fists clinched while yelling, "Pig." Then extend your right arm with the "Sooie." Repeat these steps two more times and finish by yelling "Razor-Backs" like this: Woooooooooo. Pig. Sooie! Woooooooooo. Pig. Sooie! Woooooooooo. Pig. Sooie! Razorbacks! ["Arkansas Traditions"].

This animal-honoring ritual knits together Arkansas fans from around the country who have been observed belting out the notable pig call with fellow hogs in malls, airports, restaurants and hotels in a show of porcine kinship (Batra).

Sports Illustrated includes in its list of America's top "Jock Schools" any college or university in which sports is central to campus life; schools with culture and identity built largely on athletic status commonly create celebrity animal figureheads. However, even those who do not embrace uber-athletic traditions connect with unlikely animal champions, demonstrating strange and powerful devotion. The University of California–Santa Cruz celebrates Sammy the Banana Slug. The homely slug, described by *People* magazine as a "bright yellow gastropod mollusk that lives on fungus and debris and leaves a thick trail of slime in its slithering wake," is commonly found on campus during rainy days and on the redwood forest floor, and has been widely celebrated over the years, garnering "best mascot" awards by *ESPN* and *Reader's Digest* ("Proving That Slime Is on Their Side"). Sammy is dearly beloved by students who have long touted a kinship with the mucous-making mollusk. In the mid '80s Chancellor Robert L. Sinsheimer launched an initiative to change the mascot to a sea lion. He argued in a letter to the campus newspaper, "consider that the banana slug is: spineless (ipso facto), yellow (cowardly), sluggish (slow of foot) and slimy (enough said)" ("Slugging It Out"). The students revolted en masse to the seemingly personal insult. T-shirts sporting "Fiat Slut" (Latin for "Let there be slug") were donned, a favorite rock band named Bobby and the Slugtones belted out "The Slugs are Back," and complaints in newspapers and alumni letters groused, among other things, that "all sea lions do is fornicate on rocks and make grotesque sounds" ("Proving That Slime Is on Their Side"). Students argued impassionedly they could empathize with the slug, who embodied the characteristics that captured them, as a community of scholars.

While many schools choose lions, panthers or bears for their fierceness or physical strength, other mascots convey decidedly different qualities. Sammy denotes something special about the school, which places an emphasis on science and conservation—it offers no sororities or fraternities or athletic scholarships and grades are given only by request ("Proving That Slime Is on Their Side"). Alumnus Kevin Kittredge, who holds a Ph.D. in chemistry from the institution, described the affinity this way:

> The campus is located in the redwoods overlooking the Monterrey Bay. The slug is a native species and everyone is familiar with it in that part of the country. It's unique with respect to other mascots which typically represent something of strength, conquest, or power, and really reflects the campus culture—a Division III school not overly sports driven, but instead offers a different type of institution, one where students are encouraged to be different and their efforts to do so are strongly supported by the administration and faculty [Kittredge].

Students express allegiance to the animal by vying for a chance to dress in slug costume at sporting and other campus events. Tourists eat peanut butter-filled candy slugs and sport slug pom poms, socks, scarves, and face decorations and declare proudly, "I consider myself a slug" (White).

What They Look Like and What They Wear

Mascot enthusiasts revere and humanize conventionally lovable and unlovable animals as a means to celebrate sports teams and university cultures, with shared physical characteristics and sartorial anthropomorphization representing examples most easily apparent to the naked eye. Animal symbolism representing nonhuman aspirations of our winningest selves begins with physical features and abilities that connote awe, intimidation and respect. Eagles, tigers and bulldogs claim top rankings for most common American high school, college and university animal mascots (Fitsimons; Yarbrough). Eagles, dubbed the alpha species of the mascot kingdom, represent attributes of strength, independence, courage and freedom—ideals held dear as Americans. One estimate calculates eighty-two American colleges or universities claim the mascot (Doyle). Physically, eagles dominate the skies as the chief of the flying animal world. They symbolize predatory prowess with top speeds of almost one hundred miles per hour and a wingspan of 7.5 feet. In one of the oldest traditions of college football, Auburn University—with official mascot of tiger—rallies around the war eagle, releasing its live unofficial mascot to circle the stadium while eighty thousand fans belt out the "War Eagle" battle cry at pregame rallies.

Mike, Louisiana State University's Bengal tiger (the current mascot is a Siberian-Bengal mix), has kept residence on campus since 1934 and enjoys the top slot for the nation's most well-known live tiger mascots (Westerman). The mascot recognizes the feared Louisiana Tiger Battalion of the Confederacy, which was said to have "fought like tigers" on the battlefield (Jones). Modern-day Mike (VII), oblivious to the raging debate over whether he is a captive victim or charitable model for animal conservation efforts, is massive and intimidating. Past traditions include parading the tiger, weighing as much as 440 pounds and eating ten pounds of beef, chicken and fish daily (Lidz), through campus before football games. Cheerleaders rode atop his cage to a destination outside the opponent's locker room before the team arrived, forcing the rival players to traverse past the beast before kickoff. Fans would pound on Mike's cage and cheerleaders would poke him in the ribs with a stick to elicit a growl (Gallo), which was said to predict a touchdown at the upcoming game, before objections of cruelty changed the practice to using recorded growls ("LSU's Live Tiger Mascot").

As many as thirty-eight colleges or universities celebrate a bulldog mascot. Uga, from the University of Georgia, has appeared in Hollywood films and was flown to Washington, D.C., for a political reception; patrician Handsome Dan, who hails from Yale, was known to lunch with President Bush '48 and correspond with First Dog Millie, and Blue from Butler hosts his own blog and more than 31,000 Twitter followers. Bulldogs, with characteristic underbites and stout, pugilistic appearances, feature the physical build of a formidable linebacker: wide shoulders and big barrel chests with more narrow hips (Seiler and Hannon 84). Although the breed looks fearsome, bulldogs are characteristically quite friendly and agreeable to indulging human quirks and eccentricities, which include dressing them in human attire and accessories to represent prominent features of the university culture, namely football. For example, custom team jerseys are typical sights for Uga, Dan, and Blue, particularly on game day. Uga has also been spotted sporting sunglasses and a director's beret to mark his feature film promotions or custom-made tuxedo for more formal occasions, such as his trip to the New York Hilton Heisman banquet, accompanying Herschel Walker in 1982. For Uga III's retirement gala at the Savannah Golf Club in 1981, he appeared with signature spiked red leather collar and iconic red jersey, where he accepted the keys to the city from the mayor and dined on prime rib and hamburger—the two-legged guests were relegated to meatballs and chicken wings (Seiler and Hannon 63). Dressing our mascots is more than just fanciful frivolity; deliberately chosen garments and accessories—a varsity letter sweater, jersey, baseball cap, director's beret or tuxedo—represent an effort to underscore the meaning and importance of the occasion with a sartorial artifact, deliberately blurring the line between animal and human cultural currency.

Not all animal mascots are capable of leading pep rallies and participating in photo opportunities. Sharks, yellow jackets or spiders must energize their fans in the form of a costumed human. Most schools do offer some version of a costumed mascot, which often displays desirable but distorted or physically inaccurate characteristics, resulting in a hybrid creature that melds animal with human. Bob Marlin of Virginia Wesleyan University boasts bulging biceps and six-pack abs, strutting and swaggering on two stocky legs. The mascot, which underwent a redesign in 2014, was given a brighter complexion, bigger muscles and a more extensive wardrobe ("Bob Blog: A Mascot Makeover"). Fans celebrate the fishlike figure as a marlin and suspend disbelief because these fictitious attributes amplify the emotional connection between fan and animal. Bob is a fearless, formidable, indomitable human/animal fusion.

The art of human costumed animal is perfected with great care each year at Mascot University, sponsored by the Universal Cheerleaders Association. Students are warned that speaking or appearing in partial costume could shatter the illusion their "make-believe" character depicts (Murphy). Attendees are trained to emote properly in costume. Bears are taught to lumber, Hokie Birds learn to shake a tail feather, and mascots study pantomime skills by watching old *Looney Tunes* episodes, helping them to stay in character.

In the past decade, People for the Ethical Treatment of Animals (PETA) has ramped up pressure on all schools to retire live mascots and replace them with animatronic versions or costumed humans because they say the practice exploits, disrespects and terrifies animals. The animal rights advocates also argue that the practice of breeding purebred animals like bulldogs leads to mutations that cause health problems in some animals (Barnett). They assert that creatures like Mike, LSU's Bengal Tiger, and Bevo, University of Texas' longhorn steer, belong in the wild, and artificial habitats are inhumane, no matter how grand.

Their Dwellings and Their Care

Once ubiquitous cramped confines for large animals are becoming more uncommon and taboo as a result of a shifting tide in public opinion about treatment of captive creatures and pressure from animal rights groups like PETA. The improved dwellings, while still controversial, reflect a broader social movement extending to zoos, theme parks and circuses and are a point of pride for students and alumni. The University of North Alabama campus is home to the only live lions, Leo III and Una, living on a college campus. A streaming lion cam on the university's website shows a $1.3 million habitat that was built according to the Association of Zoos and Aquariums guidelines, featuring boulders, streams, a waterfall and a pond as part of a nearly thirteen thousand-square-foot dwelling ("George H. Carroll Lion Habitat").

Louisiana State University is seeking sanctuary accreditation for Mike's campus habitat, which could permanently alter game-day tradition and limit how fans interact with their beloved mascot. If granted, new accreditation rules could prohibit Mike from attending football games—he currently "decides" whether to attend or not (he rarely opts in). Instead, students could view him in his recently updated $2.9 million fifteen thousand-square-foot dwelling, which includes a waterfall, stream, pool downfall, logs for scratching and a one hundred-square-foot temperature adjusting rock (Morris). Chew toys shaped like rival mascot animals are also provided for his amusement.

Baylor's cinnamon-colored sister black bears, Lady and Joy, were selected as the university's mascot in 1914 over Buffalo, Antelope, Frog, Ferret, and Bookworm ("History: Baylor Bear Program"). They enjoy snacking on cherries, avocados, prunes and apricots in their one million dollar, three-thousand-square-foot habitat regulated by the United States Department of Agriculture as a Class C specialty zoo and educational exhibit. Critics condemn the size of their home, and point to the former practice of bringing Lady and Joy to games on leashes as cruel and inhumane. Lady and Joy no longer attend Baylor games; they spend their time in the one-million-dollar home with a waterfall, several pools, a stream and dead trees for the animals' entertainment (Chen).

Lions, tigers and bears housed on campus are costly and can set budget-strapped schools back up to forty thousand dollars a year per animal (Chen). Yet even with changing attitudes about animal rights and care, devotion to the large, exotic campus dwellers is stout. Thousands of support letters flooded Baylor University following an animal rights campaign pressuring the school to end the practice of live bear mascots in 2003, and the school remained steadfast in its commitment to the animals, claiming a commitment to education, conservation and display of school spirit. Large exotic animals draw scrutiny, yet University of Texas longhorn steer Bevo lives on a ranch, watched over by the former president of the Texas Longhorn Breeders Association of America, University of North Carolina Chapel Hill Dorset Horn sheep Rameses spends his days on a farm, and Ralphie, the University of Colorado's bodacious female buffalo representing the wild west, resides in a secret ranch location (McGee). These animals experience typical, if upscale versions of ordinary farm dwellers like themselves. It is the smaller animals who are treated more like kin and often reside at home with a family that treasures the tradition and long lineage of the animals, like the Seiler family who has tended to Ugas for more than sixty years. Uga X, exclusively from a long line of white males, enjoys posh digs both at home and on the road. His bedroom comes equipped with its own dog door and is decorated with framed posters of his ancestors, his own television and red and black University of Georgia tchotchkes ("A Dog's Life"). On game day, Uga travels to the stadium past fans pressed against barriers for a glimpse at the exalted one, in a specially engineered SUV that directs sixty-degree air on full blast to his seat in back of the vehicle (English bulldogs are not equipped to thrive in the Southern heat). He sleeps in a special suite in the campus hotel, and he beats the Georgia heat at the stadium by resting his squishy snout on a bag of ice in his air-conditioned doghouse next to the cheerleaders' platform, posing regularly for photos with fans.

Over the years, Uga has received special medical treatment for the breed's numerous health problems. According to Spencer Johnston, the department head of the University of Georgia's College of Veterinary Medicine Small Animal Medicine and Surgery, "The most common of which are respiratory, usually upper airway, cardiac, bone and joint, dermatologic and ophthalmologic." He also noted, "Reproductive issues are very common, with most puppies being born by cesarean section" (Peat). With special access to top veterinary care, animal mascots often receive medical treatment beyond what would be considered standard animal care. Uga III was no exception to many bulldogs, suffering from chronic dry eye problems. Unable to keep his eyes naturally moist, veterinarians tried artificial tears and lubricants to no avail. Doctors at the university's veterinary school devised an innovative solution involving an artificial tear duct from a transplanted portion of a saliva gland to the dog's eye. What resulted, to the amusement of fans, was the effect of a bulldog weeping uncontrollably at the smell of bacon (Seiler and Hannon 61).

Like humans, however, even modern medical innovations and treatments fail to keep beloved mascots alive forever. In 2016, LSU issued a press release stating that Mike VI had been diagnosed with a spindle cell sarcoma, a rare and inoperable type of cancer. In a *Today Show* segment about the ill animal, Mike can be seen wheeled down a hospital hall on a gurney, flanked by scores of physicians in white lab coats, receiving sedation and radiation in the same facility where humans are treated ("LSU Rallies Around Mascot"). Four months later, after stereotactic radiotherapy for the tumor near his snout, the cancer had spread and he was euthanized on campus in a hospice ("LSU Mascot Mike VI Dies"). The university did not hold a formal memorial service for the tiger, but thousands grieved and shared online and on-campus messages recognizing the beloved animal. Live longhorn steer Bevo XV, of the University of Texas, sent flowers (Payne).

When They Die and How They Are Remembered

Bevo XV represents the "everything is bigger in Texas" sentiment, mascot style. The steer, who has weighed in at two thousand pounds with horns measuring eighty-two inches tip to tip, was selected among four hundred to five hundred animals for his coloring, orange and white, and his disposition. Assistant coach Vance Bedford said, "I think he symbolizes what we're all about. Something that's strong and stands tall" ("Texas Mascot Bevo"). In addition to football games that he attends in his seventy-thousand-dollar air-conditioned custom trailer, Bevo XIV has attended black tie galas, weddings, funerals and both of President George W. Bush's inaugurations. *The Los Angeles Times* described the 2001 Texas Black Tie & Boots Ball, attended by celebrities including actors Chuck Norris and Bo Derek, this way:

> Bush's fellow Texans were putting on the party of the night, with 9,000 people chomping on 7,000 pounds of beef brisket, 6,000 pounds of smoked ham and 60,000 pieces of jumbo shrimp. A Texas longhorn steer named Bevo, mascot of the University of Texas at Austin, chewed hay nearby inside the Marriott Wardman Hotel as visitors posed with him for photos ["Even Bevo Came"].

The university announced in 2015 that the bovine, whose given name is Sunrise Studly, was diagnosed with bovine leukemia virus and would retire. He died peacefully in his sleep later that year and was remembered by Ricky Brennes, Executive Director of the Silver Spurs and Bevo's XIV's regular traveling partner, as a close friend:

> He loved the attention that came with being BEVO but was very cool, calm and smart. Like a dog, he would come when called by name, show up to the house looking for treats and even roll over on his side so Mrs. Baker could rub his belly. He did so much for his university and community. His last few days provided great memories, but we miss him already ["Texas Mascot Bevo"].

Descriptions of live animal mascots—both large and small—include frequent references to best friends and family members, but treatment of exotic and domesticized animals in ways traditionally reserved for humans is a newer phenomenon, growing as fans embrace their commonalities with the mascots and the hazy line between human and animal. In 1916, Bevo I's first year, students planned to brand the bovine with the (21–7) score of the school's win over rival Texas A&M, but before they could do it, the opposing team branded him with the (13–0) score of their victory the prior year. Regardless, the school's athletes celebrated him four years later by eating their mascot with beans at a banquet (Lidz).

Changing attitudes about animal treatment and animal rights have amplified animal mascot traditions and rituals and obfuscated the boundaries between human and animal. Passing of these animals, considered friends and family by many, is a somber event of collective grieving, especially with man's best friend. Texas A & M's flagship university of more than fifty thousand students is home to its Cadet Corps, the largest ROTC program in the nation (not including programs at service academies). This distinctive, high profile program is led by Reveille IX, its highest-ranking member: a female collie. To the freshmen in the corps of cadets she's "Miss Reveille, ma'am." Miss Rev, as students call her, is cared for by a Mascot Corporal, a sophomore cadet chosen each spring. Reveille accompanies the cadet to all classes, joins him on dates and goes home with him for the holidays. She is never unkempt, addressed sternly or left alone (Burson 28). This collie clearly calls the shots. The official university website describes the First Lady of Aggieland this way:

> She is the highest-ranking member in the Corps of Cadets and wears five silver diamonds (the Corps Commander only has four). That means if Miss Rev falls asleep in a cadet's bed, the cadet must find somewhere else to sleep since she outranks him. Tradition also dictates that if Reveille is in class and barks, the professor should end class because Miss Rev is bored ["Reveille"].

Honored in death as in life, Reveille—one of the few live canine mascots always chosen from adoption—was described in the most human of terms (Ladner). Explaining her significance to the campus community, Reveille's handler Ryan Kreider noted, "Reveille VIII is more than just a dog, or even a mascot. She's a lady, a former student, a loyal companion, and a perfect representation of why Texas A&M is so great" (qtd. in Ladner).

The first Reveille was given a formal military funeral at Kyle Field in 1944 (including a twenty-one-gun salute) as was Reveille IV who garnered twenty thousand mourners for the 1989 occasion. All of the collie mascots are buried outside the north end of the football stadium, where they have a special scoreboard so "they can always watch the Aggies outscore their opponents" ("Reveille"). Yet traditions like Reveille's military funeral represent more than just top-dog status; they denote the culture of respect for rank, loyalty and Southern decorum, along with a strong emphasis on athletic achievement. Where and how loved ones are buried indicate a deliberate statement about their relationships with those who loved them.

When Uga VII died in 2009, the Georgia campus mourned. *The New York Times* described the scene:

> He was buried during a private ceremony on the morning of a home game against Kentucky. The university president spoke. Fans came to the game wearing black. Players wore black dog-bone decals on their helmets. There was a moment of silence. A wreath was laid on top of the doghouse, which sat empty [Branch].

Sanford Stadium at the University of Georgia holds the deceased Ugas entombed in separate graves. They lie behind a wall of red marble, marked by a plaque honoring each one with notable information like a special nickname or accomplishment. The marriage of football and their canine representatives dates back as far as 1939 when Mississippi State's University lost its first mascot, Bully the bulldog. The funeral received a full spread of coverage in *Life* magazine, with photos picturing a half-mile procession of mourners who came to pay respects to the dog lying in state inside a glass coffin. The bulldog's burial service was conducted at the football stadium's fifty-yard line (Downey). Honoring deceased mascots with elaborate rituals or football stadium mausoleums provides an outlet for morning loved ones and a public tribute to an intimate relationship fans hold with an animal most have never met. It is with ritual, awe and respect that devotees adopt these creatures as "tribal symbols" and humanize them, suggesting that by communing with the creatures, some of their powers might magically transfer to the tribe (Yarbrough 12). Throngs salute, imitate and adorn animals in an effort to create meaning from them that translates in virtuous ways. However, in doing so, humans also celebrate primitive and nascent instincts that can draw out the worst in them.

Bringing Out the Best and Worst in Humans

Smokey IX, Tennessee's bluetick coonhound, has been accused of biting an Alabama football player in a pregame warm-up and charging into a Kentucky kicker's leg. The media reported of a chorus of howls in approval from the Tennessee fans as displays of spirit and grit to be honored (Hudson). Uga V leapt into the air in the end zone, aiming for the midsection of a showboating Auburn player who had just scored a touchdown in one of the Deep South's oldest rivalries. The crowd went "berserk"—photos of the incident appeared nationwide in newspapers. The *Montgomery Advertiser,* carrier of the original image, eventually announced reprints were unavailable because the negative had literally worn out. ESPN named the move its 1996 "Play of the Year" (Seiler and Hannon 110).

Displays of unchecked aggression and lack of restraint, however, are celebrated even when they turn violent or lewd, and costumed humans who portray the mascots also give way to undignified, animalistic behavior that is permitted and even encouraged by fans. University of Oregon's human costumed duck mascot—Oregon uses the Donald Duck character as its mascot under a special agreement with Disney—was suspended in 2007 after he attacked the University of Houston's Shasta the cougar during the season opener. The two tangled for a bit before the duck repeatedly punched the cougar and performed simulated lewd acts on him as he lay on the ground ("Oregon Duck Suspended"). Fans can be seen cheering and screaming during the brawl, available on YouTube with more than two million views, rewarding the pugilistic duck with high fives after the incident.

Mascot believers amplify animal attributes that underscore how they see themselves: as a scholarly slug of the redwoods or a feisty Southern charmer with some bite. In turn, fans permit primitive, unchecked animal behavior in the name of feverish allegiance. These relationships buck conventional wisdom that we are hard wired to prefer cuddly relationships with Labrador puppies or fuzzy bunnies. Loyalty defaults to the tribe and its symbols are elevated to celebrity status that transcends customary human animal boundaries. Revered as more than animals, mascots are luminaries celebrated as superstars often treated like humans. Academy Award-winning actor Kevin Spacey plays Jim Williams, a Savannah antique dealer accused of murdering his friend, in *Midnight in the Garden of Good and Evil,* a cinematic tribute to the culture of Southern peculiarities and eccentricities. Shortly after opening credits, Spacey strolls with actor John Cusack in a Savannah park, walking Uga who wears his iconic red leather, studded collar. The dog is nonplussed when approached and admired by unfamiliar fans. Spacey remarks, "Neither one of us will ever be as famous as that dog." "Who's the dog?" Cusack inquires. "Why, that's Uga, the University of Georgia mascot. He's better known than we'll ever be."

Works Cited

"Animal Attraction: Live Mascots of the SEC." *ESPN* n.d. http://www.espn.com/espn/photos/gallery/_/id/8252260/image/21/tusk-mascots-southeastern-conference. Accessed 26 Jul 2018.

"Arkansas Receives Trademark for 'Wooo! Pig! Sooie' Chant." *Sports Illustrated*, 18 July 2014 https://www.si.com/college-football/2014/07/18/arkansas-woo-pig-sooie-receives-trademark-hog-call-razorbacks. Accessed 23 July 2018.

"Arkansas Traditions." *University of Arkansas.* https://www.uark.edu/athletics/traditions.php. Accessed 26 July 2018.

Barnett, Lindsay. "After the Death of Uga VII, PETA Asks University of Georgia to Stop Using Bulldog Mascots." *Los Angeles Times,* 24 November 2009. http://latimesblogs.latimes.com/unleashed/page/160/. Accessed 26 July 2018.

Batra, Amy. "Arkansas Football: 5 Best Razorback Traditions Every Fan Should Experience." *Bleacher Report,* 18 July 2012. https://bleacherreport.com/articles/1262470-arkansas-football-5-best-razorback-traditions-every-fan-should-experience. Accessed 23 July 2018.

"Bob Blog: A Mascot Makeover." *Virginia Wesleyan University*, 17 February 2014. http://www.vwu.edu/news-a-events/news-releases/bob-blog-a-mascot-makeover. Accessed 26 July 2018.

Branch, John "Long Live the Mascot, Uga VIII" *The New York Times*, 16 October 2010. https://www.nytimes.com/2010/10/17/sports/ncaafootball/17bulldog.html. Accessed 24 July 2018.

Burson, Rusty. *Reveille: First Lady of Texas A&M,* Texas A&M University Press, 2004.

Chen, Stephanie. "Animal House: College Mascots Get Luxury Digs: Habitats Replace Cages but PETA Still Objects." *The Wall Street Journal*, 15 August 2007, A1.

"The Cutest Live College Mascots" *People Magazine*, 15 October 2010. https://people.com/pets/the-cutest-live-college-mascots/. Accessed 23 July 2018.

Dixon, Schuyler. "New Bevo, Ill Mike Reminds Us How Attached We Are to Mascots." *USA Today,* 28 May 2016. https://www.usatoday.com/story/sports/ncaaf/2016/05/28/new-bevo-ill-mike-remind-us-how-attached-we-are-to-mascots/85085098/. Accessed 26 July 2018.

"A Dog's Life." *CBS News*, 16 November 2014. https://www.cbsnews.com/news/a-dogs-life-meet-university-of-georgia-mascot-uga/. Accessed 26 July 2018.

Doyle, Brian. "Go-o-o-o Lemmings: Stomp those Stormy Petrels!" *American Scholar* 79:1 (2010) 18–19.

"Even Bevo Came to This Shindig." *The Los Angeles Times*, 20 January 2001. http://articles.latimes.com/2001/jan/20/news/mn-14799. Accessed 26 July 2018.

Fitsimons, Patrick. "Animal Magnetism." *Texas Monthly* 43:9 (2006), 150.

Gallo, Andrea. "With Mike VII, Here's How LSU Could Potentially Become an Accredited Tiger Sanctuary." *The Advocate*, 19 January 2017. https://www.theadvocate.com/baton_rouge/news/article_9b3859aa-de7a-11e6-b0d6-d718de3bf9aa.html. Accessed 23 July 2018.

Gamard, Sarah. "The Case For and Against the Tiger Living on Campus." *Salon*, 1 January 2018. https://www.salon.com/2018/01/01/the-case-for-and-against-the-tiger-living-on-lsus-campus/. Accessed 23 July 2018.

"George H. Carroll Lion Habitat." *History of Our Live Mascots*, n.d. https://www.una.edu/lioncam/history-of-our-live-mascots.html/#habitat. Accessed 26 July 2018.

Heitner, Darren. "University of Arkansas Trademarks the Hog Call." *Forbes*, 18 July 2014. https://www.forbes.com/sites/darrenheitner/2014/07/18/university-of-arkansas-trademarks-the-hog-call/#70c8c5564c66. Accessed 26 July 2018.

Herzog, Hal. *Some We Love, Some We Hate, Some We Eat.* Harper Perennial, 2011.

"History." *Baylor Bear Program*, nd. https://www.baylor.edu/bear/index.php?id=947807. Accessed 26 July 2018.

Hruby, Patrick. "Endangered Species." *Insight on the News*, 17:28 (2001) 28.

Hudson, Daniel. "Tennessee Volunteers Football: Smokey IX Is Definitely a Vol for Life." *Bleacher Report*, 25 November 2012. https://bleacherreport.com/articles/1421603-tennessee-volunteers-football-smokey-ix-is-definitely-a-vol-for-life. Accessed 25 July 2018.

Jones, Terry. "The Terrifying Tigers." *The New York Times*, 13 September 2011. https://opinionator.blogs.nytimes.com/2011/09/13/the-terrifying-tigers/. Accessed 23 Jul 2018.

Kelly, Mary Louise, and Rachel Martin. "The LSU Tigers' New Tiger Makes His Debut." *Morning Edition,* National Public Radio 1, September 2017. Transcript. Accessed 23 July 2018.

Kennedy, Kostya. "Georgia Mascot Steals the Show." *Sports Illustrated,* 1 December 1997, p. 49.

Kittridge, Kevin. "Slug 411." Received by Lisa Lyon Payne 21 June 2018.

Ladner, Ben. "Texas A&M Mascot Reveille V Passes Away at Age 12." *Sports Illustrated,* 26 June 2018. https://www.si.com/college-football/2018/06/26/texas-am-mascot-reveille-viii-dies-age-12. Accessed 24 July 2018.

Lidz, Franz. "Woofers and Tweeters." *Sports Illustrated,* 29 October 1991, pp.88–98.

"LSU Mascot Mike VI Dies After Cancer Battle." *ESPN,* 11 October 2016. http://www.espn.com/college-football/story/_/id/17771750/lsu-tigers-mascot-mike-vi-dies-cancer-battle. Accessed 24 July 2018.

"LSU Rallies Around Mascot 'Mike the Tiger,' Who Is Battling Cancer" *Today Show,* 10 September 2016. https://www.today.com/video/lsu-rallies-around-mascot-mike-the-tiger-who-is-battling-cancer-762182723724. Accessed 26 July 2018.

"LSU's Live Tiger Mascot, Mike VII." 23 March 2018. http://www.lsusports.net/ViewArticle.dbml?DB_OEM_ID=5200&ATCLID=177271. Accessed 23 July 2018.

Lyndsey, Lewis, and Elizabeth Quill. "Mascot Watch." *Chronicle of Higher Education* 53:43 (2007) A4.

Malaronte, Chip. "Yale Mascot Handsome Dan an American Sports Pioneer." *New Haven Register,* 25 September 2015.

McGee, Ryan. "The Secret Life of Mascots." *ESPN,* 8 November 2017. http://www.espn.com/espn/feature/story/_/id/21187100/the-secret-life-live-mascots. Accessed 25 July 2018.

Midnight in the Garden of Good and Evil, directed by Clint Eastwood, Warner Bros., 1997.

Morris, George. "LSU's Renovated Tiger Habitat Features 'Above and Beyond' Comforts for New Mike VII." *The Advocate,* 15 August 2017. https://www.theadvocate.com/baton_rouge/entertainment_life/article_4fa430da-7bab-11e7-922c-6767396b028e.html. Accessed 23 July 2018.

Murphy, Austin. "At Mascot U's Animal Fair, All the Birds and Beasts Are There to Learn." *Sports Illustrated,* 4 November 1985, pp. 9–15.

"Oregon Duck Suspended for Mascot Melee." *Associated Press,* 13 September 2007. https://www.cbsnews.com/news/oregon-duck-suspended-for-mascot-melee/. Accessed 25 July 2018.

Payne, Marissa. "LSU's Tiger Mascot Mike VI Dies After Battle with Cancer." *The Washington Post,* 11 October 2016. https://www.washingtonpost.com/news/early-lead/wp/2016/10/11/lsus-tiger-mascot-mike-vi-dies-after-battle-with-cancer/?noredirect=on&utm_term=.05c83633a834. Accessed 24 July 2018.

Peat, Savannah. "A More Resilient Uga: Seiler Family Making Changes to Breed Healthier Georgia Bulldog." *The Red & Black,* 31 August 2016. https://www.redandblack.com/sports/a-more-resilient-uga-seiler-family-making-changes-to-breed/article_4bb13132-6f43-11e6-9b36-6f2311e9d059.html. Accessed 24 July 2018.

"Proving That Slime Is on Their Side, Santa Cruz Students Make the Slug Their Mascot." *People Magazine,* 16 June 1986. https://people.com/archive/proving-that-slime-is-on-their-side-santa-cruz-students-make-the-slug-their-mascot-vol-25-no-24/. Accessed 23 July 2018.

"Razorbacks." *The Encyclopedia of Arkansas History and Culture,* 1 January 2018. http://www.encyclopedia ofarkansas.net/encyclopedia/entry-detail.aspx?entryID=2125. Accessed 26 July 2018.

"Reveille." *Aggie Culture.* https://www.tamu.edu/traditions/aggie-culture/reveille/. Accessed 26 July 2018.

Seiler, Sonny, and Kent Hannon. "Damn Good Dogs! The Real Story of Uga, The University of Georgia's Bulldog Mascot." The University of Georgia Press, 2011.

"Slugging It Out: UC Santa Cruz Students Try Again to Adopt Slimy Local Creatures as Mascot." *Los Angeles Times,* 25 April 1986. http://articles.latimes.com/1986-04-25/news/mn-1468_1_santa-cruz. Accessed 26 July 2018.

"Smokey Accused of Biting Alabama Player." *Associated Press,* 26 October 2006. http://www.espn.com/college-football/news/story?id=2639328. Accessed 25 July 2018.

"Texas Mascot Bevo Retiring to Ranch After Cancer Diagnosis." *USA Today,* 13 October 2015. https://www.usatoday.com/story/sports/ncaaf/2015/10/13/texas-mascot-bevo-retiring-to-ranch-after-cancer-diagnosis/73890704/. Accessed 24 July 2018.

Troop, Don. "A Dog's Life … and Death." *Chronicle of Higher Education* 54:45 (2008) A5.

Warren, Lydia. "Meet Georgia's Mascot Uga the Dog Who Has His Own SUV, License Plates and a Personalized Wardrobe." *Daily Mail,* 17 November 2014. http://www.dailymail.co.uk/news/article-2837856/Meet-Georgia-s-mascot-Uga-dog-SUV-license-plates-personalized-Nike-wardrobe.html. Accessed 23 July 2018.

Westerman, Ashley. "The LSU Tigers' New Tiger Makes His Debut." *Morning Edition,* National Public Radio 1 September 2017. Transcript. Accessed 23 July 2018.

White, Dan. "As the Slug Rises: Once Subversive, UCSC's Beloved Mascot Turns 25." UC Santa Cruz News Center, 10 June 2011. https://news.ucsc.edu/2011/06/banana-slug-25th-anniversary.html. Accessed 23 July 2018.

Willdorf, Nina "Stop the Hunt." *Chronicle of Higher Education* 46:29 (2000) 12.

Yarbrough, Roy. *Mascots: The History of Senior College and University Mascots/Nicknames.* Bluff University Communications, 1998.

Body Boundaries

Animal Body Adornment, Lifestyle Holism and Cosmetic Surgeries

Kathy Shepherd Stolley

Speaking as President of the American Pet Products Manufacturers Association, Bob Vetere opined that pets are increasingly treated like human members of the family: "We have to reward them as humans. That's what makes us happy. Pets are happy. I could throw an old tennis ball to my golden retriever and he'd be thrilled. But *we* need more" (qtd. in Schaffer 19; italics in original). That "more" increasingly translates into modifying and "improving" pet lives and pet bodies in many of the ways humans seek to modify and "improve" human lives and bodies. Animal bodies, like human bodies, are increasingly being adorned, targeted by the lifestyle product industry, and surgically enhanced for cosmetic purposes.

"The very act of body modification is a centrally human act. No other animal can change its body in the ways that we can, and there is no evidence to suggest that animals want to change the appearance of their bodies. Yet, since the dawn of animal domestication, humans have been changing, sometimes radically, animal bodies through both temporary, but usually permanent, modifications," says Margo DeMello ("Modification" 345), an expert in both the fields of Body Studies and Human-Animal Studies. Animal bodies have long been modified, surgically and otherwise, to meet human aesthetics and uses. Tail docking and ear cropping for "breed conformity" to win show awards, de-beaking and de-horning farmed poultry and livestock, de-clawing cats so they will not scratch upholstery, and de-barking dogs so they will not make too much noise demonstrate the ubiquity of practices that surgically modify animal bodies for human purposes. Artificial insemination, spaying, and neutering control their fertility. Animals are branded, tattooed, ear-tagged, and microchipped for identification and as property. They are dyed colors for special events (think pastel blue chicks at Easter). Selective breeding for specific traits has created not only designer pets like Labradoodles that were "invented" by crossing-breeding a Labrador retriever with a standard poodle to be non-allergenic companions to otherwise allergic humans (Anthes 20–21; Canales), but also fifty different colors of canaries, neon fish that make sushi glow in the dark (Anthes; "Glowing Sushi"), and beefier cattle and plumper chickens for the dinner table. Animal bodies are routinely modified and commodified in puppy mills and factory farming, in laboratories to test products from shampoo to pharmaceuticals, and in entertainment. Such practices make animal bodies less natural and wild, and more under human control, while demarcating boundaries between human and animal (DeMello, "Modification" 350). However, modifications of animal bodies in ways previously relegated for humans are more and more blurring these human-animal boundaries in new ways.

Adorning Animals Bodies: Extreme Grooming

Model Gisele Bündchen's Yorkshire and P. Diddy's miniature Maltese have both received "Asian fusion" styling from Jorge Bendersky, celebrity dog groomer at Manhattan's PlanetJorge. Bendersky described the look, which originated in Japan, as "trending" and "very short on the body and very long on the legs, like big bell bottoms, which gives the opportunity to wear a dress or a sweater and necklace without messing up the hairstyle" (qtd. in Haldeman). The style was so on trend that PetQuest, a trade Expo featuring a variety of grooming competitions such as the World Cup Grooming Games, added an Asian fusion contest to its 2018 line-up ("PetQuest 2018").

According to Bendersky, current grooming styles have evolved from function into an art form reflecting fashion and popular culture. The iconic poodle clip, now associated with show rings and chic pompom coifs originated to enhance the performance of the breed as hunters. Grooming intentionally left thick balls of fur to protect the dogs' joints and lungs from cold while strategically shaving parts of the body made maintenance easier (Bendersky). The distinctive cut became so associated with the breed that it has persisted, entrenched in popular culture long after widespread use of the breed for hunting has passed. "If it's true that 'the bigger the hair, the closer to God,' well then let's just say that 1950's [*sic*] and 1960's [*sic*] hair was at Heaven's Gate with the help of lots of hairspray and teasing," Bendersky observes. "The beehive hairdos popular with women found their parallel with even bigger and better poodle topknots" (Bendersky 5). To Bendersky, dog grooming has become a harmonious art form that, in its optimal expression, relies on trust, cooperation, and bonding between dog and groomer. The pair "perform a dance where they move together like dancers on a ballroom floor" with the groomer taking the lead (Bendersky 4).

As spa customers increasingly request many of the same services for their animals that they request for themselves including "pawdicures," color highlights, and glitter tattoos "for that extra rock 'n' roll edge" (Haldeman), extreme dog grooming is also growing in popularity. Dogs are clipped, shaved, dyed, decorated, used as art canvases, and styled with hair extensions and adornments (Stern). They sport looks that ostensibly reflect their personalities, but that almost certainly say much more about their human's politics and interests than those of the dog and risk making the animal's body itself a human accessory (Gladwell). A short-lived Animal Planet series, "Groomer Has It," even brought the world of extreme grooming competitions to reality television (Dunne). At Intergroom, an international grooming conference held in New Jersey that features a wildly popular extreme grooming competition, dogs are "clipped and dyed to look like flamingoes, clowns, leopards, and parrots, among other un-dogly things" (Dunne). Photo collections in books and shared widely online document these fancifully coiffed canines with commentators often attributing a human-like self-awareness to the dogs.

Extreme dog grooming has evolved into a subculture comparable to child beauty pageants. Groomers note that some dogs, like child stars, have the temperament to remain patient through lengthy pageant preparation processes and others less so (Dunne). Writing for *dogster*, Chris Hall ponders the implications of this child pageant: "The comparison with child stars is unfortunate, because it just kind of plays into the suspicion that the process isn't great for the dog. Bring up child stars, and you evoke Jackie Coogan's exploitation by his parents, Judy Garland's descent into drug addiction and early death, and the conflicts between Macauly [*sic*] Culkin's parents" (Hall).

If, or when, a line is crossed between extreme grooming practices and exploitation, harm, or cruelty remains a point of contention as does the question of whether the dog's (or their human's) dignity is a causality of these practices. (Groomers sometimes dress like their dogs, or wear costumes that complement the dog's theme.) One writer observed that a collection of extreme grooming photos shows dogs that "look understandably embarrassed or confused, but others just look smug, convinced their new fur is super fly" (Dunne). Such attributions are "human psyche, not canine psyche," according to Amy Bullet Brown, founder and president of the National Association of Professional Creative Groomers LLC. She adds that dogs who crave attention will love the extreme grooming experience without embarrassment ("Extreme Pet Grooming: Cute or Cruel?"). Defending extreme grooming practices on a United Kingdom television interview, Daniela Forshaw stated simply, "It's not cruel. My dog is the best kept in country, just pink" (qtd. in "Extreme Pet Grooming: Cute or Cruel?").

Animal rights advocates at PETA disagree, as do "Dog Whisperer" Cesar Millan and others. Critics take issue with the lack of agency on the part of dogs subjected to confinement and processes outside of their control ("Extreme Pet Grooming: Cute or Cruel?"). In a tragic case of extreme grooming, Russian actress, model, and writer Elena Lenina had a kitten dyed pink for a "pretty in pink" party and publicity stunt. The hairdresser who dyed the animal did not use pet-safe dye and the cat succumbed to toxic poisoning from ingesting too much of the color (Willgress). Responding to concerns that extreme grooming practices in general could cross the line into abuse, the National Association of Professional Creative Groomers stated, "We at the NAPCG believe that animals are not embarrassed by their appearance…. If we tell our pets that they are beautiful and treat them as such, they will respond positively to this type of positive feedback" (qtd. in AFP Relaxnews). Whether that is totally human projection, or if our pets do actually recognize beauty or are satisfied with their own appearance remains a question for researchers (Hogenboom).

Living the Best Life: Lifestyle Products and Health and Wellness Holism

"Lifestyle" products, or as Alyssa Giaccobe writing for *DuJour* dubs them, "practically everything that makes people-life worth living," are now offered for pets, mirroring items marketed to their humans to improve and beautify both their lives and their bodies. Among these posh pet offerings are high-end spa services like facials and detox wraps, resorts and boutique hotels branding their own amenities, designer labeling on formalwear to casual hoodies, and their own social media fans (Ginsberg; Haldeman; Pogash). The pet product industry drives an economic engine worth $69.51 billion in 2017 (APPA).

For body and mind health and wellness, pets can exercise with dog yoga ("doga") and build their core muscles with PuPilates, tracking progress on their Fitbits; they can end their days by dining on personalized, organic diet foods complemented by pet-friendly beer and wine (Bonnington; Ginsberg; Haldeman; Pogash). Life-coaches and motivational methods such as those presumably benefiting Oprah's golden retrievers empower a pet to "be all that she can be" (Haldeman). Peter Haldeman writing for *The New York Times* was advised about his extremely active dog that "[c]hances are he has a lot more to offer, like a gifted child…. That takes a different level of you showing up as a parent" (Haldeman). Even after animals die, pet psychics keep them in touch with their humans as demonstrated by actress and producer Paula Killen's dead cat who conveyed to Killen through a psychic that her demise had been due to an altercation with a coyote (Ginsberg). Cloning dead animals allows creation of another "them," at least sort of. After having her dog cloned, Barbra Streisand lamented, "You can clone the look of a dog, but you can't clone the soul. Still, every time I look at their faces, I think of my Samantha … and smile" ("Barbra Streisand Explains").

Veterinary services regularly reflect medical care offered in human hospitals—surgeries, cancer treatment, obesity programs—and offer an ever-widening menu of options including acupuncture, chiropractic, aromatherapy, Ayurvedic herbs, massage, and energy work (Ginsberg; Haldeman). Psychopharmacological approaches address diagnosed conditions ranging from depression, to autism, to Tourette's Syndrome, to stress and trauma-related problems attributed to animal's early lives (Haldeman). As Tufts University animal behaviorist and author Nicholas Dodman says of animals, "When they find themselves in the pressure cooker of life, animals' emotions can erupt into psychological problems that in many ways are similar to the ones we get" (qtd. in Haldeman). Animals are even in on the medical marijuana trend. Specially formulated "pot for pets" marijuana and hemp products are growing in popularity among pet owners (Associated Press; Ginsberg; Haldeman; Seales). Faced with increasing questions about therapeutic use in animals and more pets managing to get into their humans' stash (especially edibles), the American Veterinary Medical Association published a special document on *Cannabis: What Veterinarians Need to Know.*

Surgical Enhancements: Cosmetic Surgery and Blurred Boundaries

Pets are also getting in on the trend in cosmetic surgery. According to International Society of Aesthetic Plastic Surgery (ISAPS) data, the U.S. leads the world in cosmetic procedures with more than 4 million procedures being performed in 2016 (or approximately 18 percent of procedures globally). Perhaps it comes as no surprise then that Beverly Hills cosmetic surgeon Toby Mayer says that he "frequently fields requests from patients who inquire whether he might take a look at their dog too?" (Giacobbe). As another writer covering this phenomenon ponders, "In a nation of surgically enhanced human breasts, teeth and skin, perhaps it was just a matter of time before the beauty stakes were raised for pooches and cats" (AFP Relaxnews).

Practices like ear-cropping, tail docking, or de-clawing are long-standing and common, but increasingly controversial, examples of surgical modifications made largely to meet human preference. Most cosmetic procedures on animals are, however, for medical reasons, not purely aesthetics. Entropion surgery that lifts the eyelid to keep eyelashes or fur from rubbing against the cornea can avoid permanent damage to the eye of numerous breeds susceptible to the condition. Brachycephalic dogs with "flat" faces like pugs or Shih Tzus often benefit from surgery to improve restricted breathing. Shar-Pei wrinkles that may make that breed vulnerable to skin infections are reducible by skin fold surgery (Castillo). Applying human terms—an eye lift, a nose job, a little nip/tuck—dismisses these procedures as purely cosmetic, when they have actual medical benefit for the animal.

Medical care for animals, as for humans, can also be pricey. Americans spent $62 million on cosmetic surgery for pets in 2011 (Castillo), but what is too much for the health of a family member? Pet owner Christy and Trevor Gale finally sought a surgical fix for a regurgitation problem experienced by their one-year-old French bulldog, Tonka, after spending between $15,000 and $20,000 on other approaches. The successful surgery cost an additional $1,500. The Gales justified the cost and the procedure: "It's not just a dog." "It's our family" (qtd. in Kent and Stump).

Perceptions of Gender

Pets are even undergoing transgender surgery, although not for gender identity purposes. Peter Haldeman reports in *The New York Times*, "Transgender pets usually fall into one of two categories: animals whose birth sex poses health issues (like Bishop, a German shepherd from Chicago who became Bishy to get rid of the stones lodged in his bladder and penis) or those with risks tied to being born intersex (Red, a California Pomeranian whose male organs were removed to reduce the chance of cancer)" (Haldeman).

Pets and their bodies do, however, reflect societal stereotypes and norms surrounding gender. The "crazy cat lady" provides a familiar and well-worn example of a pet-related gender stereotype. Pets also serve as "gender props," supporting owners' gender identities and serving as an outlet for the humans "doing gender," reflecting cultural notions of masculinity or femininity (Ramirez; West and Zimmerman). Particularly large dog breeds, and by extension their owners, may be perceived as more masculine. Sentiment expressed by the male owners of large-breed dogs include embarrassment at the thought of having to walk "a small foo-foo dog like a poodle or a Westie… [That] sort of violates my manhood" and the perception that "[a] bigger dog is more human. It's like your pal, in comparison to a smaller dog that has a tendency to yap" (qtd. in Bashinsky).

Perhaps no other example better illustrates the impact of human gender stereotypes on animals than Neuticles. Described as "part of a trend of anthropomorphism gone wild" (AFP Relaxnews), Neuticles are synthetic testicular implants for pets. The product was invented by Gregg Miller to help owners who are hesitant to neuter their pets "overcome the trauma of altering and allowing their beloved pet to retain its natural look and self esteem" ("Crafted with Integrity"). In 1995, Max, Independence, Missouri, police officer Mike Pyle's Rottweiler puppy, received the first Neuticles implants. Max's surgery was celebrated by *Parade Magazine* as one of the Top 10 news events of that year ("Neuticles"). Since then, Neuticles have gone global. Half a million animals across the U.S. and in 49 countries, including dogs, cats, prairie dogs, an elephant, a monkey, water buffalo, and "a colony of rats for the University of Louisiana," have received Neuticles (Haldeman; "Neuticles"). Miller's CTU corporation, billed on the corporate website as "the only company of its kind on Earth," has expanded into other product areas such as surgical mesh, ear stays, and eye implants for animals ("Crafted with Integrity"). Miller, himself, has been awarded the Ig Nobel Peace Prize for Medicine. Ig Nobel awards "honor achievements that first make people **laugh**, and then make them **think**. The prizes are intended to celebrate the unusual, honor the imaginative—and spur people's interest in science, medicine, and technology" ("About the Ig Nobel Prizes"; emphasis in original). Buck, Miller's bloodhound who was his original inspiration for creating Neuticles because "Buck would no longer be Buck!" ("Neuticles"), died of liver cancer before ever receiving his implants, leaving Miller to make this observation: "Even though [Buck] never got Neuticles, he changed the world" (Anthes 132 footnote).

Many commentators have pondered whether Neuticles are actually for dogs or for humans, while some advocacy groups have endorsed Neuticles as a way to encourage owners (particularly men) to have their dogs neutered (Anthes 134–135). Having heard that then–President Bill Clinton was indecisive about getting First Dog, Buddy, neutered, Miller "did something that required both literal and figurative *cojones*; he asked the leader of the free world to give some thought to a prosthetic package" (Anthes 135; italics in original). *Hustler* magazine publisher Larry Flynt got Neuticles for his two Doberman pinschers (Bashinsky). Kim Kardashian, reality television celebrity of *Keeping Up with the Kardashians*, got Neuticles for her boxer, Rocky (Tyrrel). Tamara Ecclestone, the Formula 1 heiress with her own British reality show, *Tamara's World*, who found herself accused of including her long-haired Chihuahua, Duke, in a campaign to "rebrand herself as anything but the British answer to Paris Hilton" (Tyrrel), was quoted as saying, "I need to cut Duke's balls off, but you can now get fake balls for dogs…. I'm going to get him those so he doesn't feel emasculated" (qtd. in Tyrrel). When she treated her dogs to a trip to the canine spa at Harrods, one commentator observed, "To the eager reality-TV audience, that must have been absolutely the dog's Neuticles" (Tyrrel).

Perceptions of Beauty

Considering cosmetic procedures more broadly, some animal welfare advocates feel that their use may result in fewer dogs being dumped by owners, or help those in need of a new home find one more quickly. Referring to Pickle, a Chihuahua with "ranky teeth" and a large mass on her side, veterinarian Jennifer Cole observed, "[t]hat's an animal who may have a hard time getting someone to take her home … But for me, it's a 15-minute fix. If we can get more shelters to do that, it means fewer pets are getting euthanized. Hangy boobs and lumps and bumps make people uncomfortable" (qtd. in Carlos). Kate Comfort, the owner of Bonnie, a collie mix dubbed Britain's ugliest dog, turned to a crowd-funding campaign to afford surgery for Bonnie. Comfort rescued Bonnie after the dog was found in Romania with her nose, leg, and tail missing, injuries that her veterinarian attributed to possible human abuse. Comfort felt Bonnie was a happy dog, but sought the surgery to improve Bonnie's life because "[p]eople and children think she looks aggressive. One time this guy said to me 'get her away from me, she's ugly'" (qtd. in Stroud). Other animal advocates feel that less attractive pets tug at the heartstrings and get adopted first (Giacobbe).

Reflecting a thriving and lucrative Korean cultural obsession with cosmetic surgery on humans (Jang), Korean popular culture website Koreaboo noted that reports of controversial surgeries to make pets "more pleasing to the eye" had gone viral ("Netizen"). One widely shared procedure was eye widening, a procedure popular in Korea for humans. The procedures are supported by some veterinarians, such as an anonymous veterinarian who stated the following to a Korean publication: "Plastic surgery for pets in the past were [*sic*] for medical reasons but the result also brought better looking dogs, so there is a growing customer base getting a plastic surgery for cosmetic reasons on their dogs" (qtd. in Ashcraft). Another, Dr. Yoon Sin Geun, argued that it is "*the owner's right for wanting to make their pets pretty and it is too much to criticize procedures that are proven to be safe*" (qtd. in "Netizen," italics in original). A poster identified as Miss Lim, referring to her dog, stated, "After looking at his face closely, the veterinarian pointed out the gap between her mouth and asked, 'Isn't that a little uncomfortable to see from a cosmetic perspective?'" (qtd. in "Netizen"). However, support for cosmetic surgery for dogs was far from universal in that country, with one opinion poll finding almost two-thirds (63 percent) of dog owners were against the practice (Ashcraft). Animal welfare groups and others criticized these procedures as abusive, not chosen by the animal, or treating the animal as an ornament. Among the responses, one questioned, "Did the dogs say they want plastic surgery?" and another asked, "What is the difference between this and forcing your own children to get plastic surgery?" (qtd. in "Netizen").

While dogs and cats get much of the press, fish are having a little cosmetic work done in the name of beauty as well. In Singapore, having an Asian arowana fish in one's aquarium is a status symbol. Selling for hundreds of thousands of dollars, the large, brightly colored fish are targeted by thieves and sold on the black market. Because their whiskers and aggressiveness suggest mythical dragons, folklore considers them to be especially good luck and holds that they have been known to "sacrifice their lives by jumping out of tanks to warn owners about a bad business investment or other potential dangers" (Qin). To become even more alluring, the fish have Eugene Ng, described in *The New York Times* as one of Singapore's "premier cosmetic surgeons for Asian arowana" who regularly gives them eyelifts. Responding to critics who see the practice as cruel, Ng says that, "I'm doing it a favor. Because now the fish looks better and its owner will love it even more" (qtd. in Qin). As one top breeder explains, "It's like a beauty pageant. The fish cannot be fat. It must look strong and have personality. It must swim confidently and be firm, stern and fierce. It cannot be timid" (qtd. in Qin).

São Paulo, Brazil, veterinarian Edgard Brito gained global notoriety for advocating cosmetic surgery on pets solely for aesthetics, arguing that the interaction between the animal and its humans will be better, resulting in a more cuddled, well fed, and walked dog that is less likely to be euthanized (Carlos). "Why shouldn't a dog be beautiful?" Brito asked. "Beauty is desirable. We all like talking to someone who looks good and smells nice. It's the same with dogs" (qtd. in Kingstone). Serving "a who's-who of Brazilian models, actors and television presenters, all of whom have asked the Sao Paulo vet to beautify their favourite pooch," Brito's clients also included show dogs (Kingstone). Brutus, an Argentinian miniature schnauzer, won several prestigious top-in-show awards after Brito straightened one of his ears (Kingstone). And although Brito advocated support for surgery solely in the name of dog beauty, he expressed his limits: "Here at my clinic I would never attach an artificial testicle" (qtd. in Kingstone). Since then, Brazil— a country with a culture that holds humans have a "right to beauty" and cosmetic surgery is often government subsidized at no or low cost (Jarrin)—has remarkably put legal restrictions in place addressing cosmetic surgery on pets (van Hees).

Ethical Concerns: Motivations and Agency

Cosmetic procedures performed for attention, commodification, show, or breeding are often suspect, raising ethical questions particularly surrounding medically unnecessary surgeries and concealing defects (e.g., Kingstone). As Margo DeMello recalls, tattooed families, complete with tattooed dog, were once popular sideshow attractions ("Modification" 349). Modification of animal bodies still remains a "family" event in some cases. Members of the human body modification subculture—those who get extensive tattoos, piercings, skin implants, and other alterations that deliberately and purposefully permanently alter one's physical appearance—sometimes also have their pets tattooed or pierced. Having animal's bodies modified in these ways, DeMello observes, is "like people tattooing or piercing themselves ... ostensibly marks of individuality (although they likely reflect the owner's personality more than the dogs's), and, like branding, marks ... ownership as well" (DeMello, "Modification" 349). Pictures of animal modifications are a small part of the collection of photos uploaded to BMEzine.com, the Body Modification Ezine, on which people post shots of their body modifications; those practices are not widely supported by tattooists and piercers, and the website contains a disclaimer about them as noted by DeMello ("Animal Tattooing" 16).

Marina Esmat and her family took a very different approach to the attention their Jack Russell terrier puppy might generate for their family. Wanting the puppy to look more like Milo (played by animal actor Max McCarte), the dog in Jim Carrey's *The Mask*, they used weights and glue to try to make the pup's ears lay flat like the dog in the movie. That process did not work so they sought out a veterinarian in Esmat's home Russia who reluctantly performed the surgery. Afterward, Esmat was pleased that the dog would be more competitive in shows and better appeal to potential breeders, enthusing "[n]ow everything is great" (qtd. in Hartley-Parkinson). Online response called the procedure cruel and the family torturers and bullies (Hartley-Parkinson).

When a Tibetan mastiff in China died during cosmetic surgery for a forehead skin lift and the owner sued for compensation in the dog's death, the case generated international attention and criticism. The expensive breed is valued by the Chinese elite as a luxury and a status symbol (Wen). The dog's owner, a breeder, explained that he sought the surgery to increase stud fees. "The skin of my dog's head was very flabby, so I wanted to cut part of his forehead and straighten the skin. And also in this way, his hair would look longer as the rear part of the head will have more hair.... If my dog looks better, female dog owners will pay a higher price when they want to mate their dog with mine" (qtd. in Wen). Animal activists and others took issue with what they deemed a misleading business practice as well as disregard for the animal. As one pet owner commented, "I would never let my pet undergo plastic surgery like that. It treats the animal like a toy instead of a living being" (qtd. in Wen).

Acting on the belief that breeders had resorted to cosmetic enhancement of cow udders to better their odds of winning awards, Tasmania's Agricultural Show Council banned cows that had undergone any such procedures in the early 2000s ("Rural News Week"). In 2017, twelve camels were disqualified from the King Abdulaziz Camel Festival held annually in Saudi Arabia. The camels had each been given Botox-like injections in their lips to make them more competitive in the beauty portion of the competitions. Aside from being disqualified from sharing in the lucrative financial prizes, owners were also fined (Wamsley). In a horrific example of cruel modification of animal bodies for profit, camels were also featured in other international headlines when photographs circulated from Fuzhou, China, of a legless camel being used by street beggars to solicit sympathy and money. Police responded that the tactic of mutilating people had seemingly become less profitable, so beggars had undertaken new tactics of mutilating animals. Authorities found themselves at a loss to prosecute, however, due to weak animal abuse laws (Hughes).

Reactions: Evolving Perspectives and Blurred Boundaries

Although many modifications to animal bodies raise concerns surrounding intent and motivation, prosthetic modifications to animal bodies generally garner widespread support. Technological advances that have provided prosthetics to replace human veterans' limbs lost in combat, or to restore functionality to human victims of injury, disease, or other misfortunes, or cosmeses for disfigurements are also providing the same benefits to animals. Among the range of applications, prosthetics have provided reconstructed duck bills, a replacement dolphin tail, and legs for wounded military dogs. These prosthetic limbs have been as delicate as a crane's leg and as substantial as an elephant's foot (Anthes; Arnold; Griffin; Vaughan). A rockfish at the Vancouver Aquarium received surgery to replace an eye lost to cataracts. The "first of its kind surgery was … partly cosmetic, and partly for the fish's safety" so that other fish would not attack or bully what they perceived to be a weak or injured fish because of the missing eye (Buzz:60). One writer said of his own dog who had received a prosthetic eye after losing his real eye to diabetes: "No one mistook it for the real thing, but it did lend him a raffish Sammy Davis Jr.-like charm" (Haldeman).

Writing for *American Veterinarian*, Don Vaughan notes, "As with other aspects of medicine, many advances in human prosthetics have trickled down to the veterinary side." Conversely, in the promising area of transdermal osseointegration—a procedure in which a titanium rod is anchored directly into the bone to form a permanent prosthesis—veterinary medicine is leading the field (Vaughan). The growing use of 3-D printers has meant more accessible and affordable use of prostheses as well (Anthes; Arnold; Griffin; Vaughan). Veterinary use of prosthetics is not without its critics, however, as evidenced by the upset some members of the equestrian community expressed when a pony that also had hind leg problems was fitted with a prosthetic front leg lost to an injury. Some felt that euthanasia would have been a better solution. *Horse & Hound* veterinary adviser Karen Coumbe MRCVS questioned the pony's quality of life, saying: "Horses are designed to be able to run away from danger and it will be stressful for this little individual who would be unable run anywhere" (qtd. in Radford).

Surgery on animals for solely cosmetic purposes is banned, highly restricted, or opposed by veterinary organizations in many countries (e.g., Bennett and Perini; Canadian Veterinary Medical Association; Crook; Hamity; Lefebvre, Lips, and Giffroy; Quartarone et al.). After providing an explanation of accepted, ethical veterinary surgeries that have a cosmetic aspect such as eye lifts to prevent ocular damage, procedures to assist with breathing, and skin fold reduction for health reasons, one veterinary practice points out that these types are procedures have medical benefit and improve quality of life "when applied intelligently and with discretion" ("The Medical and Legal Implications"). The statement closes with this sentiment, strongly differentiating these approaches from other requests: "I have been asked to perform botox, collagen, and restylane injections as well as testicular implant surgery. My answer, whenever I have been asked, is a resounding 'No!!' In my opinion, these procedures serve no known medical benefit for the patient. The pet owners that ask for such procedures to be performed on their pets would be better off spending their money on psychotherapy in order to understand why anthropomorphization of their pets is flat out crazy" ("The Medical and Legal Implications").

Although animal cosmetic surgery is a serious matter, popular culture has sometimes treated it a novelty. Billboards spotted in Los Angeles, California, and New York City subway signage in 2013 asked in large letters "Is Your Dog a Total 'Dog'?" followed by "Canine Plastic Surgery by Dr. Armond." Graphics of a man holding a "happy-looking" dog advertised a "Free Consultation" beside "before" and "after" photos and a website URL linking to a skit video promoting Comedy Central's *Kroll Show* starring Nick Kroll (Nudd).

News stories and headlines that frame animal body modification as if the animal is a decision-maker or willing participant can also confound deeper considerations surrounding modification of animal bodies, the human-animal boundary, and human treatment of, and responsibilities to, other living beings, whether human or not. Taking issue with the implication of animal agency in a headline that proclaimed "Even Dogs Have Gotten Into the Plastic Surgery Craze with Botox, Nose Jobs and More," Marc Bekoff, professor emeritus of ecology and evolutionary biology at the University of Colorado, Boulder, writes, "let's be very clear, it's not dogs who have gotten into the cosmetic surgery craze, it's humans." Such articles do, however, force humans "to rethink why we choose to live with other animals and what is acceptable behavior on our part. After all, we can do whatever we want to them, whether they like it or not. And," Bekoff concludes, "it's essential to honor that this imbalance in power is not a license to do whatever we choose."

WORKS CITED

"About the Ig Nobel Prizes." *Improbable Research*. n.d. https://www.improbable.com/ig/.

AFP Relaxnews. "Fake Testicles, Facemasks, the New Level of Pet Pampering." *Daily News*. 21 May 2012. http://www.nydailynews.com/life-style/health/fake-testicles-facemasks-new-level-pet-pampering-cruelty-beauty-article-1.1081872.

American Pet Products Association (APPA). "Pet Industry Market Size & Ownership Statistics: 2017–2018 APPA National Pet Owners Survey. APPA. n.d. https://www.americanpetproducts.org/press_industry trends.asp.

American Veterinary Medical Association. *Cannabis: What Veterinarians Need to Know*. January 2018. American Veterinary Medical Association.

Anthes, Emily. *Frankenstein's Cat: Cuddling Up to Biotech's Brave New Beasts*. Scientific American/Farrar, Straus and Giroux, 2013.

Arnold, Carrie. "Injured Animals Get Second Chance with 3-D Printed Limbs." *National Geographic*. 19 August 2016. https://news.nationalgeographic.com/2016/08/prosthetics-animals-rescued-3d-dogs-cats/.

Ashcraft, Brian. "In South Korea, Dogs Are Getting Plastic Surgery." *Kotaku*. 3 August 2015. https://kotaku.com/in-south-korea-dogs-are-getting-plastic-surgery-1721711793.

Associated Press. "Medical Marijuana for Animals Is a Pet Project for Scientists." *New York Post*. 7 December 2017. https://nypost.com/2017/12/07/medical-marijuana-for-animals-is-a-pet-project-for-scientists/.

Bashinsky, Ruth. "Doggone It, Size Matters: Many Men Say for Hounds, Bigger Is Better." *Daily News*. 29 July 2010. http://www.nydailynews.com/doggone-size-matters-men-hounds-bigger-better-article-1.887573.

Bekoff, Marc. "Bowsers on Botox: Dogs Get Eye Lifts, Tummy Tucks, and More." *Psychology Today*. 23 March 2017. https://www.psychologytoday.com/us/blog/animal-emotions/201703/bowsers-botox-dogs-get-eye-lifts-tummy-tucks-and-more.

Bendersky, Jorge. "Foreword." *Groomed*, by Nathan, Paul. Pelluceo Publishing, 2014, pp. 4–5.

Bennett, P.C., and E. Perini. "Tail Docking in Dogs: Can Attitude Change Be Achieved?" *Australian Veterinary Journal.* 2003 (81): pp. 277–82.

Bonnington, Christina. "Go Ahead, Quantify Your Pet." *Slate.* 1 November 2017. http://www.slate.com/articles/technology/technology/2017/11/go_ahead_put_a_fitness_tracker_on_your_pet.html.

Buzz:60. "Fish Gets Cosmetic Surgery to Stop Other Fish from Bullying It." MSN Video. 30 December 2014. https://www.msn.com/en-us/video/tv/fish-gets-cosmetic-surgery-to-stop-other-fish-from-bullying-it/vp-BBhmbCA.

Canadian Veterinary Medical Association. "Cosmetic Alteration—Position Statement." Canadian Veterinary Medical Association. 27 January 2014. https://www.canadianveterinarians.net/documents/cosmetic-alteration.

Canales, Molly-Marie. "Labradoodle Creator Now Regrets Cross-Breeding." *GlobalAnimal.org.* 2 December 2010. https://www.globalanimal.org/2010/12/02/man-who-created-labradoodles-regrets-the-cross-breed/.

Carlos, Naia. "Even Dogs Have Gotten into the Plastic Surgery Craze with Botox, Nose Jobs and More." *Nature World News.* 22 March 2017. https://www.natureworldnews.com/articles/36610/20170322/even-dogs-gotten-plastic-surgery-craze-botox-nose-jobs-more.htm.

Castillo, Michelle. "Implants and Facelifts for Your Pet? Inside the Pet Plastic Surgery Industry." *CBS News.* 27 January 2015. https://www.cbsnews.com/news/implants-and-facelifts-for-your-pet-inside-the-pet-plastic-surgery-industry/.

"Crafted with Integrity—A History of Trust." Neuticles. n.d. https://www.neuticles.com/index.php.

Crook A. "Cosmetic Surgery in North America and Latin America." *Proceedings of World Small Animal Veterinary Association.* 2001: 54–55. https://www.vin.com/apputil/content/defaultadv1.aspx?id=3843659&pid=8708&print=1.

DeMello, Margo. "Animal Tattooing." *Encyclopedia of Body Adornment.* Greenwood: 2007, pp. 15–16.

DeMello, Margo. "Modification. Blurring the Divide: Human and Animal Body Modifications." *A Companion to the Anthropology of the Body and Embodiment*, 1st ed., edited by Frances E. Mascia-Lees, Blackwell, 2011, pp. 338–352.

Dunne, Carey. "The Deeply Weird World of Extreme Dog Grooming." *Fast Company.* March 20, 2014. https://www.fastcompany.com/3027906/the-deeply-weird-world-of-extreme-dog-grooming.

"Extreme Pet Grooming: Cute or Cruel?" *Lifestyle.* n.d. https://www.lifestyle.com.au/pets/extreme-pet-grooming-cute-or-cruel.aspx.

Giacobbe, Alyssa. "Fido Gets a Facelift." *DuJour.* n.d. http://staging.dujour.com/lifestyle/pet-plastic-surgery/.

Ginsberg, Merle. "The Secret Life of the 1 Percent Pet." *Yahoo!* 9 August 2013. https://www.yahoo.com/entertainment/news/animal-plastic-surgeons-pot-presicing-vets-secret-life-050000619.html.

Gladwell, Amy. "Extreme Dog Grooming: Harmless Fun or Threat to Pets?" *BBC News.* 9 April 2018. https://www.bbc.com/news/uk-england-43416967.

"Glowing Sushi." n.d. http://www.glowingsushi.com/.

Griffin, Julia. "Brace Yourself: This Prosthetic Engineer Is Giving Animals a Leg Up." *PBS News Hour.* 24 May 2017. https://www.pbs.org/newshour/science/brace-prosthetic-engineer-giving-animals-leg.

Haldeman, Peter. "The Secret Price of Pets." *The New York Times.* 4 July 2018. https://www.nytimes.com/2018/07/04/style/how-to-pamper-your-pet.html.

Hall, Chris. "How Much Extreme Dog Grooming Is Too Extreme?" *dogster.* March 25, 2015. https://www.dogster.com/dog-grooming/extreme-dog-grooming-pictures-photos-too-much.

Hamity, Matthew. "Cosmetic and Convenience Surgeries on Companion Animals: The Case for Laws with Bite to Protect a Dog's Bark." *Contemporary Justice Review.* 19 (2): pp. 210–220.

Hartley-Parkinson, Richard. "Family Gave Pet Plastic Surgery to Look Like Dog from The Mask." *Metro News.* 17 February 2017. https://metro.co.uk/2017/02/17/family-gave-pet-plastic-surgery-to-look-like-dog-from-the-mask-6453868/.

Hogenboom, Melissa. "Why Have Animals Evolved a Sense of Beauty?" *BBC.* 11 May 2015. http://www.bbc.com/earth/story/20150511-why-are-animals-so-beautiful.

Hughes, Ian. "Homeless Men 'Deliberately Mutilated Camel' to Get People to Feel Sympathetic and Donate Money." *Mirror.* 20 October 2014. https://www.mirror.co.uk/news/world-news/homeless-men-deliberately-mutilated-camel-4468355.

International Society of Aesthetic Plastic Surgery (ISAPS). "ISAPS Global Statistics." ISAPS. n.d. https://www.isaps.org/medical-professionals/isaps-global-statistics/.

Jang, Ho Kyeong. "Why Is Plastic Surgery So Popular in South Korea?" *Korea Exposé.* 9 January 2018. https://www.koreaexpose.com/plastic-surgery-popular-south-korea-history/.

Jarrin, Alvaro. "In Brazil, Patients Risk Everything for the 'Right to Beauty.'" *The Conversation.* 2 May 2018. https://theconversation.com/in-brazil-patients-risk-everything-for-the-right-to-beauty-94159.

Kent, Jo Ling, and Scott Stump. "Puppy Plastic Surgery on Pets Is a Booming Business." *Today.* 13 July 2017. https://www.today.com/pets/puppy-plastic-surgery-pets-booming-business-t113801.

Kingstone, Steve. "Brazilian Dogs Go Under the Knife." *BBC News.* 16 August 2004. http://news.bbc.co.uk/2/hi/americas/3923099.stm.

Lefebvre, D., D. Lips, and J.M. Giffroy. "The European Convention for the Protection of Pet Animals and Tail Docking in Dogs." *Scientific and Technical Review*. 2007, 26 (3): pp. 619–628.

"The Medical and Legal Implications of Veterinary Cosmetic Surgical Procedures." The Animal Medical Center of Southern California. n.d. https://animalmedcenter.com/cosmetic-surgical-procedures/.

"Netizen Sickened by People Getting Plastic Surgery on Their Pets." Koreaboowww. 18 October 2017. https://www.koreaboo.com/news/netizens-sickened-plastic-surgery-pets/.

"Neuticles." Neuticles. n.d. https://www.neuticles.com/inventor.php.

Nudd, Tim. "Canine Plastic Surgery Advertised on Billboard in Los Angeles." *Adweek*. 9 January 2013. https://www.adweek.com/adfreak/canine-plastic-surgery-advertised-billboard-los-angeles-146404/.

"PetQuest 2018." *Groomer to Groomer*. 8 February 2018. https://www.groomertogroomer.com/petquest-2018/.

Pogash, Carol. "Something Else to Enjoy with Your Cat: Happy Hour." *The New York Times*. 15 February 2017. https://www.nytimes.com/2017/02/15/business/smallbusiness/wine-products-for-cats-and-dogs.html.

Qin, Amy. "Cosmetic Surgery for a Pet Fish? In Asia, This One Is King of the Tank." *The New York Times*. 27 March 2018. https://www.nytimes.com/2018/03/27/world/asia/singapore-fish-plastic-surgery.html?smid=fb-nytimes&smtyp=cur.

Quartarone, Valeria, et al. "A Comparison of Laws Preventing Unnecessary Canine Cosmetic Surgery in Italy and in the Czech Republic." *Acta veterinaria Brno (Acta Vet)*. 81(1): pp. 83–88.

Radford, Sarah. "Outcry Over Three-legged Pony Fitted with Prosthetic Limb." *Horse & Hound*. 7 April 2017. https://www.horseandhound.co.uk/news/outcry-three-legged-pony-fitted-prosthetic-limb-617161.

Ramirez, Michael. "Dog Ownership as a Gender Display." *Between the Species: Readings in Human-Animal Relations*. Eds. Arnold Arluke and Clinton Sanders. Boston: Pearson, pp. 53–60.

"Rural News Week." *ABC Rural*. 7 August 2004. http://www.abc.net.au/site-archive/rural/breakfast/stories/s1170782.htm.

Schaffer, Michael. *One Nation Under Dog: America's Love Affair with Our Dogs*. Holt, 2009.

Seales, Rebecca. "Pot for Pets: Could Medical Marijuana Help Your Dog?" *BBC News*. 23 December 2017. https://www.bbc.com/news/world-us-canada-42222187.

Stern, Rebecca. "The Weird, Wondrous World of Competitive Dog Grooming." *The Atlantic*. Video. https://www.theatlantic.com/video/index/549953/competitive-dog-grooming/.

Streisand, Barbra. "Barbra Streisand Explains: Why I Cloned My Dog." *The New York Times*. 2 March 2018. https://www.nytimes.com/2018/03/02/style/barbra-streisand-cloned-her-dog.html.

Stroud, Carl. "My Dog's Got No Nose... Britain's Ugliest Dog That Has NO Nose to Get Plastic Surgery After Owner Sets Up Fundraising Drive." *The Sun*. 8 March 2017. https://www.thesun.co.uk/news/3039311/britains-ugliest-dog-that-has-no-nose-to-get-plastic-surgery-after-owner-sets-up-fundraising-drive/.

Tyrrel, Rebecca. "When Kim Kardashian Had Her Dog Castrated, She Replaced the Orbs with Fakes." *The Independent*. 6 October 2012. https://www.independent.co.uk/voices/commentators/when-kim-kardashian-had-her-dog-castrated-she-replaced-the-orbs-with-fakes-8198365.html.

van Hees, Frans. "Ban on Plastic Surgery to [*sic*] Animals in Brazil." *About Brazil*. April 2014. http://www.aboutbrasil.com/modules/brazil-brasil/news_brazil_news_brasil.php?hoofd=5&sub=27&art=1179.

Vaughan, Don. "Pets and Prosthetics: Growing Interest, Advancing Technology." *American Veterinarian*. 29 June 2017. https://www.americanveterinarian.com/journals/amvet/2017/june2017/pets-and-prosthetics-growing-interest-advancing-technology.

Wamsley, Laurel. "A Dozen Camels Disqualified from Saudi Beauty Pageant Over Botox Injections." *NPR*. 24 January 2018. https://www.npr.org/sections/thetwo-way/2018/01/24/580228837/a-dozen-camels-disqualified-from-saudi-beauty-pageant-over-botox-injections.

Wen, Zhang. "Man Sues Over Dog's Fatal Face-lift." *Global Times*. 2 July 2013. http://www.globaltimes.cn/content/760673.shtml.

West, Candace, and Don H. Zimmerman. "Doing Gender." *Gender and Society*. 1, 1987: 125–151.

Willgress, Lydia. "I Meant DYE Not Die! Writer Paints Her Cat Pink for Party—and the Cat Is Later Found DEAD from Toxic Blood Poisoning." DailyMail.com. 28 February 2015. http://www.dailymail.co.uk/news/article-2973430/Elena-Lenina-paints-cat-pink-party-cat-later-DEAD-toxic-blood-poisoning.html.

Farewell, Flipper

Sending Dolphins Back to the Sea

Jay Alabaster

"Do you love me?"

The tan, sandy-haired boy rests his hands on his cutoff jeans, leans forward, and peers into the blue waters of the Florida Keys. Up from the ocean rises *Tursiops truncatus*, the common bottlenose dolphin.

"Do you love me, Flipper?"

The boy looks into the animal's eyes and asks again, but there is no need. Even before he finishes, the cheerful grey creature pops half out of the water, nods vigorously, and blasts out a happy, guttural yelp.

Of course I love you!

—*Flipper* (1963) 1:00:44

The original *Flipper* (1963) was a Hollywood success. It also marked the beginning of the dolphin's grand ascension into our world, across that sacred line which separates person and animal. Those watching the dolphin on screen as it talks and laughs—and loves!—got a first glimpse of just how *human* the animal could be. Over the half century since, we have gradually lifted the dolphin out of the depths and adopted it as one of our own.

Today the dolphin has exalted status. Its flagship species, the bottlenose, is an acknowledged member of the "charismatic megafauna," that collection of animals who receive special treatment from humans for their charm and mass appeal. Like other members of the group—humpback whales, red wolves, koalas, eastern grey kangaroos—bottlenose are not endangered, but are protected by laws and societal norms to a degree that far exceeds the protections given to more precarious species (Barney and Mintzes 41–42). But our gifts to dolphins exceed simple protections. A new generation of researcher-activists have anointed dolphins as self-aware, with their own dolphin cultures, languages, and tools, while an increasingly vocal cadre of environmentalists and lawyers has pushed for dolphin rights on par with humans, under the same legal arguments used to free the slaves. The final step is emancipation—we are now in the process of setting dolphins free, evacuating them from aquariums and pools across much of the world.

When *Flipper* was released in 1963, the idea of a boy-meets-dolphin story was not an obvious one at all. Dolphins were still relatively mysterious, even to those who worked and lived around the sea. Western fishermen knew the animals mainly as clever bandits, plucking fish from their nets and lines. In the U.S., dolphins had long been disparaged as "herring hogs" for their thieving ways (Burnett). Ricou Browning, who co-wrote *Flipper* with his brother-in-law, was an experienced diver who had played the underwater monster role in *Creature from the Black Lagoon*. Inspired by his children's fascination with *Lassie*, the famous tale of friendship between boy and collie, Browning set out to make an oceanic version (Gonzalez). But Lassie, and dogs in general, had long been known as friends of man—they had been bred for this purpose for millennia, and socially the connection was clear. The year *Flipper* was released, *Lassie* was on its sixth sequel and had been appearing in theaters for two decades. Dolphins would need to be completely recast in order to compete.

There was historical precedent. Many who have seen the animals cavorting at sea have been beguiled, as when Melville celebrates the dolphin's antics in *Moby Dick*:

> Huzza porpoise—I call him thus, because he always swims in hilarious shoals, which upon the broad sea keep tossing themselves to heaven like caps in a Fourth of July crowd. If you yourself can withstand the cheers at beholding these vivacious fish, then heaven help ye; the spirit of godly gamesomeness is not in ye [140].

Melville stopped short of casting the animals as friend or equal to human. He reported that the animals yield good oil, albeit in small quantities compared to whales, and advised that the "meat is good eating, you know" (141). In England, among all sea life, whales and dolphins, along with sturgeon, have been considered "Royal Fish" since the fourteenth century, and any that are caught or found in local waters must be offered to the Crown. The statute still stands today, although in practice the animals are protected from harm by environmental regulations (Roman 49). Numbers of the early Christian saints were rescued at sea by dolphins, and earlier still dolphins were strongly linked to the god Apollo. In ancient Greece they were largely viewed as friendly to people and featured heavily in murals, sculptures and pottery; hunting them was considered a crime by many during the era (Catton 11–17).

The creators of *Flipper* wanted to render the animals as more than huzza entertainers—key to the story was that dolphins could bond with humans and share our emotions. Subtle but important tweaks were necessary to portray them this way. Like all of her species, Mitzi, who played *Flipper* in the original film, could not actually "speak" through her mouth, as she had no vocal cords. She could only produce sonar clicks from inside her forehead or blast high-pitched whistles and squawks through her blowhole. For the original movie, Mel Blanc, who had voiced cartoon characters like Bugs Bunny, was hired to create a more appealing dolphin voice, which was dubbed over scenes when the animal had its mouth open (O'Barry and Coulbourn 30). In the subsequent television series, a recording of the Australian kookaburra bird was used (the same sound was later recycled as the voice of a gopher in the 1980 golf comedy *Caddyshack*) (Arthur; Nashawaty). *Flipper*'s signature "tailwalk," a sort of dance move where he rises up almost completely out of the water and scoots backwards with just his tail submerged, is not a natural behavior. Ric O'Barry, an activist who was formerly a dolphin trainer for the franchise, describes how dolphins have to prepare by "building up the muscles in their tails. Like any other athletes, they must condition themselves and practice" (150). So dolphins had to be groomed and trained in preparation for crossing the human-animal line.

The viewing public had to be prepared as well. In 1963, dolphins were still a mystery to most, and the movie took advantage, introducing the animals in a decidedly human light. After Flipper first appears in the film, a young girl questions whether dolphins are "animals" that are different from other sea life. Sandy, the boy protagonist, patiently explains: "A dolphin isn't a fish. They breathe air and have eyelids, and have babies, just like people" (*Flipper* [1963] 24:18). A preview for the movie begins with the assertion that the dolphin has been "found" in the manner of a previously unknown human actor:

> Now for the first time a glamorous new star has been discovered in the middle of the Atlantic Ocean. It's Flipper the fabulous dolphin. What kind of a movie is this? It's a brand new entertainment experience, like a fresh ocean breeze.... Yes, *Flipper* is a story with a new kind of hero. You may not understand everything he says. But he will steal your heart without saying a word [Movieclips].

The preview, set to jaunty music and filled with scenes of the dolphin cheerfully interacting with Sandy, make clear MGM's efforts to introduce the idea of the cetacean as friend and peer to people.

Flipper has no real human antagonist. The boy's fisherman father and community struggle with natural challenges including a lack of fish to catch, severe storms, and shark attacks. While the movie goes to great lengths to portray the dolphin as friendly and even kind, it also shows the traditional fishermen's point of view. At one point Flipper eats fish caught by Sandy's father, drawing his rage, and he later informs Sandy that "if the dolphins come they tear our nets, they eat our fish, they chase the rest away. Now they may be your friends, but when the fish are scarce they're a deadly enemy. If they come, we'll kill them. We have no choice" (1:22:20). This conflict is resolved in the movie when Flipper leads the boy and his father to a new fishing ground, with plenty of food to go around. But it leaves open the question of what happens when fish become scarce again.

In the film reviews of the day, one can see the news media beginning to wrestle with the idea of a dolphin as an almost human-like actor, blurring the line between the two species. A *New York Times* review from 1963 reports that Flipper "clearly enjoys the limelight. It registers pathos and joy in its own way, and manages to upstage anything less than eight feet long." The review highlights the tricks the soon-to-be-famous dolphin can do, including fetching objects and dancing above the water, and gives the real-life dolphin Mitzi a credit as the "actor" that plays Flipper in the film (Shepherd).

Flipper was a box-office hit. It grossed over $23 million on a reported $500,000 budget and inspired multiple sequels and long-running television series (Parent and Govern; Gonzalez). A small number of dolphin attractions had existed in the U.S. since at least 1938 at locations such as the Marine Studios in Florida ("A History of Adventure"). After the film demand exploded, tourists flocked to dolphin attractions, eager to meet the clever, friendly animals up close, and the number of aquariums with dolphin attractions rose sharply (Wiener 149).

The dolphin became known as a charismatic, friendly animal, even in nations where cetaceans are a food source. The *Flipper* television series was shown in Japan from 1966 to 1968, under the name *Mischievous Flipper*. Ironically, it was sponsored by Nippon Suisan Kaisha, a massive marine products conglomerate known as Nissui that operated one of Japan's Antarctic whaling fleets at the time.

This cultural love affair of dolphins, marked by the popularity of Flipper, coincided with a parallel increase in scientific interest in the animals. The massive naval battles of World War II had established the importance of submarines to the modern navy, and as the Cold War intensified, the underwater vessels began to carry nuclear missiles. Improving sonar was a priority, and funded by military grants, U.S. scientists focused in on the natural abilities of whales and dolphins, although for obvious reasons only the latter could be kept in captivity and studied up close. The same year *Flipper* launched in the U.S., for instance, the *Los Angeles Times* ran a series of articles on dolphins titled "Our Flippered Friends." One article in December of 1963 focused on the sonar abilities of the animals, the workings of which were still largely a mystery. The article cited experiments by scientists from military contractor Lockheed and local aquariums to conclude that dolphin research into the "wonderful secrets these gentle, friendly creatures possess" could "revolutionize man's activities underwater" (Bengelsdorf).

Also in 1963, the First International Symposium on Cetacean Research took place in Washington, D.C., sponsored by the American Institute of Biological Sciences. A summary of the articles and discussion from the symposium published three years later noted the old way of studying such animals was passing:

> Until rather recently the whaler, who made his observations from the vantage point of the masthead or a seat in a whaleboat, told us most of what we knew about whales. His observations were centered on the chase: a frightened whale or a stricken one, men avoiding flailing flukes, or the line snaking from the amidships tub. [Norris v].

Increasing attention was given to the social nature of cetaceans. Such research naturally focused more on dolphins, which could be observed closely in captivity. Several articles from the symposium focused on dolphin behavior and communication, such as "Behavior of the Bottlenose Dolphin: Social Interactions in a Captive Colony" and "Information in the Human Whistled Language and Sea Mammal Whistling" (Norris xiv).

The burgeoning field of cetacean studies examined the animals' underwater abilities, social lives, and physiology, but unlike *Flipper* they stopped short of erasing the line between animal and human, of comparing the mental abilities of dolphins directly to those of man. In the scientific world, the first steps across that line were taken by John C. Lilly, a renowned neuroscientist. He became convinced that dolphins had intelligence on par with humans, mainly due to their large, developed brains. In his opinion, interspecies communication, true conversations between people and dolphins, was a strong possibility. In 1960, after an accomplished career at the National Institute of Mental Health, Lilly assembled a collection of grants from sources such as the Office of Naval Research, NASA, and the Department of Defense to build a dolphin research laboratory in the Virgin Islands. Equipped with multiple dolphin pools and advanced video and audio recorders, the facility was designed to facilitate direct communication between dolphin and man (Burnett). One of Lilly's experiments at the lab involved locking a young woman, Margaret Lovatt, in a shallow pool with a bottlenose dolphin named Peter for six days a week. Video footage from the experiment shows Lovatt plying Peter with fish and attempting to teach him to count to three, or trying to overcome the lack of lips on his blowhole to say her first name: "'M' is just impossible. But he eventually rolled over, so that he could kind of … bubble it into the water" (Riley). The two bonded, and even became physically intimate, but ultimately failed to achieve meaningful conversation.

Despite his failures in the lab, Lilly had already taken his ideas to the general public with his 1961 book *Man and Dolphin*. "We must strip ourselves, as far as possible, of our preconceptions," he wrote (13), emphasizing that communication with dolphins was close, and once established would require that we adopt the animals into human society:

If they achieve a bilateral conversational level, corresponding, say, to a low-grade human moron and well above a human imbecile or idiot, then they become an ethical, legal, and social problem. They have reached the threshold of humanness, as it were.... If the means of their further education in humanity is available, there probably will be an explosive development of such education [124].

Lilly felt that the scientific proof of the dolphin's humanity would come from its ability to communicate on equal terms with people, just as moviegoers had been convinced when they saw boy and dolphin bond in *Flipper* (for which he served as an advisor).

The book, and Lilly's increasingly eccentric experiments, were widely panned by the scientific community, but captured the imagination of the general public. While a cadre of top scientists criticized Lilly's conclusions as fanciful conjecture (Casey 44), *Man and Dolphin* received glowing reviews from the mainstream press, and he was treated to national television interviews and a spread in *Life* magazine (Burnett). His work inspired fictional depictions of what he had hoped to prove in the lab—intelligent dolphins, fully capable of conversing with people. These included the 1967 French novel *The Day of the Dolphin* about military dolphins that try to communicate with humans, which was translated and turned into a feature film in 1973, and *Flipper* itself.

The emergence of the dolphin as friend and potential cognitive equal to people occurred both in the mainstream public and in science. Dolphins were then elevated to our peers in a third realm—environmental activism. As public interest in and sympathy for dolphins increased, they were increasingly adopted as symbols of the emerging environmental movement. Concern over the plight of dolphins caught as by-product in industrial tuna fishing led to the "dolphin safe" movement that began in the late 1980s. The U.S. passed official standards for labeling tuna in 1990 with the Dolphin Protection Consumer Information Act. Environmental group Earth Trust instituted a "Flipper Seal of Approval" program with strict requirements and a laughing dolphin insignia:

The "Flipper" name and image were chosen after extensive research revealed that "Flipper" is known throughout Asia, North and South America, Europe, Scandinavia, and many other nations as a "happy friendly dolphin" ... and is in fact the only such universal dolphin image. Cans labeled with Flipper are thus instantly recognizable throughout the world as "dolphin saving" tuna ["Flipper Seal of Approval"].

Such programs gave dolphins special protections, in line with their elevated status as friend and peer to humans. But they did nothing to protect the tuna, stuck firmly in the animal kingdom, which have been overfished for decades and are now on the brink of collapse in many parts of the world.

This singular focus also had dire effects on other sea species. To avoid entrapping dolphins in their nets, fishermen often turned to fish aggregation devices, or FADs, floats or rafts that attract a myriad of marine life on the open sea. The use of FADs allowed fishermen to gain the coveted Flipper logo and placate consumers, but also greatly increased the bycatch of endangered species of sharks, rays, marlins and sea turtles (Eaves). Human adoption of dolphins as environmental ambassadors, which awarded them special protections and generated interest in environmental issues, came at a steep cost.

All three of the dolphin's new roles were present in the remake of *Flipper*, which came to theaters thirty-three years after the original. By 1996, the dolphin as friend to man—playful, intelligent, loving—no longer needed special introduction or explanation. The movie was backed by MCA Universal, which had watched rival Warner Brothers score a lucrative surprise with its own tale of boy-dolphin friendship—the *Free Willy* franchise. *Free Willy* had one-upped *Flipper* with the tale of a young boy that bonded with a bus-sized killer whale (technically a member of the dolphin family). The first *Free Willy* in 1993 generated strong returns and even triggered a successful campaign to free Keiko, the animal used in the movie (although it died soon after). *Free Willy 2* was released in 1995, the year before the *Flipper* redux, with a third version to come in 1997.

The new *Flipper*, like the original, emphasized the communicative abilities of dolphins, and once again the dolphins were enhanced to make them more human. But this time the technology was far more advanced. In animated scenes Flipper is shown holding ocean "meetings" with dolphin friends and family, where the animals float vertically as if they are standing underwater, heads up and fins down. They face each other and squeak back and forth to organize ocean rescues and shark defense. The second *Flipper* relies much more heavily on digital editing and computer graphics, along with the extended use of full-sized robot dolphins (Kopecky). Close shots of Flipper's (often animatronic) eyes and face show the animal's almost human emotions, and throughout the film animated versions of the dolphin leap and swim perfectly into frame.

These creative liberties were noted and applauded by movie reviewers, many of whom focused on the treatment of the animals as the movie was made. "Working with captive dolphins is more complicated now than it was in the 1960's, when little was known about these big-brained mammals and their family structure," wrote the *New York Times,* describing how the movie's producers made costly changes to placate dolphin activists when they shifted filming to the Bahamas, a process that involved a "substantial reinvestment" in training local dolphins and rebuilding their dolphin robots to match. The director is quoted as saying, "In the future, I would love to not use a live animal" (Kopecky).

The plot of the remake is more traditional than the original, with easily distinguishable "good" and "bad" characters. Gone are the well-meaning fishermen who must occasionally eliminate their ocean competitors. Any thoughts of killing dolphins are assigned to a designated antagonist, an ill-tempered local fisherman who is later found to be polluting the local waters by secretly dumping drums of "hazardous waste" from his boat. A strong anti-aquarium theme also runs throughout the film. When a local policeman sets a deadline for releasing Flipper out of a local harbor, he states that if the dolphin remains, "I will personally see to it that he's jumping through flaming hoops at SeaWorld" (Flipper [1996] 1:07:36).

The concern for dolphins connected to the film had a real-world component as well. Prior to general screening, Universal canceled a promotion involving swimming with captive dolphins after complaints from the Humane Society. Partially to placate activists, concerned viewers are instructed on screen to dial "1-800-FLIPPER" to learn about "marine mammal issues" (Kopecky).

The *Flipper* remake wasn't nearly as successful as the original, but it remains a clear demonstration of how far the dolphin had come since first appearing on screen as a "glamorous new star" in 1963. Dolphins were now established as humans' cheerful companions, scientifically capable of thought and communication, and our willing partners in battling the world's broader environmental woes.

Dolphins are now ranked among the most charismatic animals on the planet, despite their lack of fur and somewhat remote marine habitat (Albert, Luque, and Courchamp; Barney and Mintzes). A series of research publications has continued to push the limits of how humans perceive the animals, assigning them consciousness, culture, and even distinct, pod-based "languages" and individual names (Casey). Dolphins are still a major touchstone species for environmentalists and animal rights activists. Since the movie *The Cove*, a scathing documentary on the Japanese practice of hunting the animals, won an Academy Award in 2010, activists gather each year at international "Dolphin Day" events that take place in dozens of countries worldwide ("World Love for Dolphins Day 2017"; "World to Japan"). Efforts also continue to elevate dolphins into a distinct category of animals, separate and above less charismatic species. A group of prominent lawyers and scholars is now working to legally reclassify dolphins and whales, along with great apes and elephants, "from mere 'things,' which lack the capacity to possess any legal right, to 'legal persons,' who possess such fundamental rights as bodily liberty and bodily integrity" ("Who We Are").

It is hard to imagine an animal being brought any further across that increasingly hazy line that separates animal from human. The irony is that humans were only able to know dolphins—to put them in our blockbuster movies, to endow them with human traits and empathy, to grant them a persona and free will—by keeping them at close quarters, in small, glass-walled aquariums to be studied, trained, and interrogated. The next stage in our relationship with dolphins is the process of setting them free again.

While a handful of individual activists have protested dolphin captivity for half a century ("About Ric O'Barry"), in recent years a full-fledged international movement has developed. The crusade to free the dolphins coalesced around the 2013 documentary *Blackfish*, a scathing critique of SeaWorld and its use of captive killer whales for entertainment. The documentary, produced in part by cable network CNN, is based on "The Killer in the Pool," an article by reporter Tim Zimmerman that appeared three years earlier in *Outside* magazine. Zimmerman details multiple incidents in which trainers were harmed by captive killer whales, focusing in on one episode in which an experienced SeaWorld trainer was repeatedly dragged underwater and killed by a male named "Tilikum" that had been captured at sea. He argues that keeping killer whales, the largest member of the dolphin family, in captivity is dangerous—but not because the animals are inherently wild or monstrous. Rather they are too human to be locked up. His article cites scientists, trainers, and activists that use distinctly human terms to describe the mental state of orcas in captivity, such as "mentally disturbed," "pathological," and "psychotic," a line of argument also emphasized strongly in *Blackfish*.

The article and documentary coincided with a surge in activism aimed at ending dolphin captivity, advanced by global campaigns such as "Empty the Tanks," which labels dolphin shows "animal slavery" and each year organizes dozens of protest events at aquariums around the world ("About Us"). SeaWorld, which had long been an industry leader for dolphin and killer whale encounters, with a franchise reportedly worth billions (Zimmermann), became a major target. The company had for decades used killer whale imagery in its logo and advertising, and initially tried adapting its shows and policies to placate activists. But then the political tide turned against the park, with local and national lawmakers calling for an end to orca captivity. In March 2016, Joel Manby, the president and CEO of SeaWorld Parks and Entertainment, penned a *Los Angeles Times* article in which he announced that the company would phase out its training and breeding programs, stating "we need to respond to the attitudinal change that we helped to create" ("SeaWorld CEO"). Three months later, Baltimore's National Aquarium announced it would build a new dolphin sanctuary and move its dolphins there, ending its captive dolphin program ("National Aquarium to Build First Dolphin Sanctuary"). In Canada, the CEO of the Vancouver Aquarium initially fought a government ban against keeping the animals in captivity, but after pressure from activists and even the Vancouver mayor, he announced in 2018 it would end its dolphin program (Wells; Lindsay).

Dolphins are also disappearing from aquariums from other parts of the world. Fishermen in the Japanese town of Taiji, featured in *The Cove*, once supplied dolphins to aquariums across Japan and Asia. An increasing number of facilities both in and outside of the country have now stopped buying dolphins captured in the town, to avoid negative media attention and the threat of being thrown out of the World Association of Zoos and Aquariums, which banned the use of Taiji-caught dolphins after pressure from foreign activists at its headquarters in Switzerland. Prior to the protests, several dozen dolphins from the hunt had been purchased by Japanese aquariums annually (Whiteman). Similar protests have sprung up in locations as diverse as Singapore, India, and Australia. Many European countries have moved to ban or strictly regulate commercial dolphin shows, with various activist groups teaming up to form cross-border coalitions to press for further change, such as Dolphinaria-Free Europe (*EU Law*).

Those dolphins that do remain in captivity may soon have a new avenue to freedom, once an option for humans alone—the courts. Activists are teaming up with like-minded lawyers to give dolphins and other animals judged to be of sufficient intelligence the same fundamental rights given to people. The Nonhuman Rights Project, made up of activists, scientists, and legal experts, is seeking to apply the writ of habeas corpus to dolphins, along with whales, apes, and elephants. The project seeks to use the law, which traditionally allows one individual to challenge the unlawful imprisonment of another, in order to "secure legal personhood and rights for nonhuman animals" ("Litigation").

As the dolphins that are currently in captivity fade away or are set free, the average person will have little or no opportunity to meet one in person. But it may not matter. The modern version of the movie *Flipper* ends with a ship full of passengers who cheer for a wild dolphin that isn't really there. It has been digitally added so that it appears to be cheerfully jumping alongside the human vessel as the screen fades to black. Presumably the actors were instructed to gaze at the empty ocean and imagine a friendly dolphin, one that can communicate and love. Recently in Times Square in New York, National Geographic sponsored a virtual aquarium, where visitors walked through dark rooms with giant screens, packed with sea life "animated by the team that brought *Game of Thrones*' dragons to life, with authentic nature sounds and original compositions" ("National Geographic's Aquarium of the Future Opens in Times Square"). Over the last half century we have invited dolphins into our world, adding tricks and sounds and special effects to make them more human. Ultimately, this was not enough. The ultimate culmination of our bringing the dolphin across the human-animal line is to expel it back into the animal kingdom, replaced with a virtual version of our own making.

WORKS CITED

"About Ric O'Barry." *Dolphin Project*, www.dolphinproject.com/about-us/about-ric-obarry/. Accessed 4 Apr. 2019.

"About Us." *Empty the Tanks*, www.emptythetanks.org/about-us/. Accessed 3 Mar. 2019.

Albert, Céline, Gloria M. Luque, and Franck Courchamp. "The twenty most charismatic species." *PloS One*, vol. 13, no. 7, 2018, p. e0199149.

Arthur, Nicole. "Day of the Dolphin." *Washington Post*, 31 Jan. 2003. www.washingtonpost.com, www.washingtonpost.com/archive/lifestyle/2003/01/31/day-of-the-dolphin/493063d2-ef69-42d5-952a-73e7a8b4c20b/.

Barney, Erin C., and Mintzes, Joel J. "Assessing Knowledge, Attitudes, and Behavior Toward Charismatic

Megafauna: The Case of Dolphins." *The Journal of Environmental Education*, vol. 36, no. 2, Jan. 2005, pp. 41–55. *Taylor and Francis*, doi:10.3200/JOEE.36.2.41-55.

Bengelsdorf, Irving S. *Dolphins May "Listen" with Jaws and "Speak" with Their Foreheads*. 1963.

Burnett, D. Graham. "Orion Magazine | A Mind in the Water." *Orion Magazine*, Apr. 2010, www.orionmagazine.org/article/a-mind-in-the-water/.

Casey, Susan. *Voices in the Ocean: A Journey into the Wild and Haunting World of Dolphins*. New York, Doubleday, 2015.

Catton, Chris. *Dolphins*. New York, St Martin's Press, 1990.

Eaves, Elisabeth. "Dolphin-Safe but Not Ocean-Safe." *Forbes*, 24 July 2008, www.forbes.com/2008/07/24/dolphin-safe-tuna-tech-paperplastic08-cx_ee_0724fishing.html#2b1bd9f01d67.

EU Law. dfe.ngo/eu-law/. Accessed 7 Mar. 2019.

Flipper. Directed by Alan Shapiro, Universal Pictures, 1996.

Flipper. Directed by James B. Clark, Metro-Goldwyn-Mayer, 1963.

"Flipper Seal of Approval." *EarthTrust*, earthtrust.org/flipperfund/homepage/flipper-seal-of-approval/. Accessed 8 Aug. 2017.

Gonzalez, Gaspar. "The House That Flipper Built." *Biscayne Times*, Mar. 2012.

"A History of Adventure." *Marineland*, www.marineland.net/our-history/. Accessed 7 Mar. 2019.

Kopecky, Gini. "Dolphin Advocates Persuaded 'Flipper' to Change Course." *The New York Times*, 19 May 1996.

Lilly, John Cunningham. *Man and Dolphin*. New York, Doubleday, 1961.

Lindsay, Bethany. "Vancouver Aquarium Will No Longer Keep Whales, Dolphins in Captivity." *CBC/Radio-Canada*, 18 Jan. 2018, www.cbc.ca/news/canada/british-columbia/vancouver-aquarium-will-no-longer-keep-whales-dolphins-in-captivity-1.4492316.

"Litigation." *Nonhuman Rights Project*, https://www.nonhumanrights.org/litigation/. Accessed 7 Mar. 2019.

Melville, Herman. *Moby-Dick*. London: Richard Bently, 1851, *Princeton*, etcweb.princeton.edu/batke/moby/moby-1.html.

Movieclips Trailer Vault. *Flipper (1963) Official Trailer*. 2014. *YouTube*, youtu.be/-c1-Y6YWS1w.

Nashawaty, Chris. *Caddyshack: The Making of a Hollywood Cinderella Story*. Flatiron Books, 2018.

National Aquarium to Build First Dolphin Sanctuary in North America. National Aquarium, 14 June 2016, aqua.org/press/news/2016/16-06-14-dolphin-sanctuary.

"National Geographic's Aquarium of the Future Opens in Times Square." *Metro US*, 5 Oct. 2017, www.metro.us/things-to-do/new-york/national-geographic-encounter-ocean-odyssey-aquarium-of-the-future-times-square.

Norris, Kenneth Stafford. *Whales, Dolphins, and Porpoises*. Berkeley, University of California Press, 1966. *Trove*, trove.nla.gov.au/version/20845944.

O'Barry, Richard, and Keith Coulbourn. "Behind the Dolphin Smile." Chapel Hill, NC: Algonquin, 1989.

Parent, Mary Pergola, and Kevin Hugh Govern. "Florida and the Film Industry: An Epic Tale of Talent, Landscape, and the Law." *Nova Law Review*, vol. 38, 2013, p. 39.

Riley, Christopher. "The Dolphin Who Loved Me: The Nasa-Funded Project That Went Wrong." *The Observer*, 8 June 2014. www.theguardian.com, www.theguardian.com/environment/2014/jun/08/the-dolphin-who-loved-me.

Roman, Joe. *Whale*. London, Reaktion Books, 2006.

"SeaWorld CEO: We're Ending Our Orca Breeding Program. Here's Why." *Los Angeles Times*, 17 Mar. 2016. *LA Times*, www.latimes.com/opinion/op-ed/la-oe-0317-manby-sea-world-orca-breeding-20160317-story.html.

Shepherd, Richard. "Flipper, the Educated Dolphin, Cavorts in a Seascape Drama." *New York Times (1923-Current File)*, 1963, search.proquest.com/docview/116438496/.

Wells, Nick. "Vancouver Mayor Calls for Aquarium to Stop Holding Whales, Dolphins." *CTV News Vancouver*, 10 Apr. 2014, bc.ctvnews.ca/vancouver-mayor-wants-aquarium-to-stop-holding-whales-dolphins-1.1769248.

Whiteman, Hilary. "Japan Aquariums to Stop Taking Dolphins Hunted at Taiji." *CNN*, www.cnn.com/2015/05/21/asia/japan-aquariums-taiji-dolphins/index.html. Accessed 7 Mar. 2019.

"Who We Are." *Nonhuman Rights Project*, www.nonhumanrights.org/who-we-are/. Accessed 3 Mar. 2019.

Wiener, Carlie S. "Dolphin Tourism and Human Perceptions: Social Considerations to Assessing the Human-Dolphin Interface." *Animals and Tourism: Understanding Diverse Relationships*, edited by Kevin Markwell, 1 edition, Channel View Publications, 2015, pp. 146–62.

"World Love for Dolphins Day 2017." *Sea Shepherd*, 6 Feb. 2017, seashepherd.org/news/world-love-for-dolphins-day-2017/.

"World to Japan: Stop the War on Dolphins!" *Dolphin Project*, 4 Sept. 2018, www.dolphinproject.com/blog/world-to-japan-stop-the-war-on-dolphins/.

Zimmermann, Tim. "The Killer in the Pool: A Story That Started a Movement." *Outside Online*, 30 July 2010, www.outsideonline.com/1924946/killer-pool.

Horses in Hats, Frogs in Frocks

Elizabeth A. Larsen

When humans put a hat on a horse, a Halloween costume on a hound, or Elizabethan ruffles on a guinea pig, what does it mean, socially and culturally? And why, on a carousel with a menagerie of animal figures, is the frog wearing a modest frock coat and pants? What are the implications of these practices? Dressing nonhuman animals in human clothing is one piece of the larger phenomenon of blurring the boundaries between human and nonhuman. Adorning animal companions—horses, dogs, guinea pigs—in human clothing may represent a human desire for a closer emotional bond with them by blurring the inter-species boundaries. Humans want to feel more connected with these loved creatures but cannot and do not want to fully embrace their nonhuman ways of life. They do not want to eat hay or live in ponds like frogs, for instance. One alternative is for humans to welcome animals into their social worlds—dressed accordingly.

Safety

Warmth and safety are fundamental human needs, among the most basic in Maslow's hierarchy (Maslow). Humans dress their children for warmth and safety, making sure before they leave for the bus stop that they have donned coats, hats, and shoes appropriate to the weather, and reflective wear so they can be seen by early morning traffic. For pet parents, their nonhuman children deserve the same love and care, and use the same criteria, e.g., if one needs a sweater today, so does one's dog.

Humans judge that dogs need to wear sweaters to beat the cold, and reflective wear for visibility in dim light, and sometimes even shoes to protect their paw pads from excessive wear and the irritation from winter road and sidewalk salt. A United Kingdom publication, *Express*, which publishes daily and Sunday editions, says that veterinarians recommend that most dog breeds not wear clothes. In addition to being unnecessary, human clothing is known to cause or irritate skin in dogs, such as through atopic dermatitis from the rubbing of clothing fabric on their skin, and overheating. Dogs also do not need to be clothed to stay warm and dry. Their fur does a great job. Still, 78 percent of those who dress their dogs do so to protect them from bad weather and keep them warm, according to a survey issued by *K9 Magazine* ("Dog Owners Blasted").

Humans may not always know what is best for their animals. Urban work horses in the late-nineteenth and early-twentieth centuries often wore peaked straw hats with red tassels, their tall ears poking through holes on either side (McGraw). By the time studies emerged showing that hats made horses hotter and bareheaded horses had lower body temperatures, horses were already yielding to automobiles on city streets, and urban workhorse numbers were plummeting.

Horses today may stay warm and clean wearing a product called a sleazy. Sleezy Barb Horsewear, based in Michigan, is one place to go online for "custom clothing for your special horse" ("Custom Clothing"). The site sells a few variations of a product called a sleazy. Described on the website as "the ultimate in protection," a sleazy is made of Lycra and covers all or parts of the horse's head, neck, chest, and abdomen. Claims for this equine garment are that it reduces rubbing, protects the coat from sun bleaching, reduces hair growth and polishes the coat, and is non-restrictive and comfortable, with large holes for the eyes. Sleazys can be full-body, faceless, for mane or face only (think equine balaclava), polar-fleece lined, and sized smaller for ponies and young horses. These can be custom- or ready-made and can be easily stored in a Sleazy Sack Storage Bag.

Reflective clothing and accessories, such as bridles, neckbands, hoof bands and sheets fitted over the hindquarters, are recommended and sold by this company for horses in low-light conditions or on wooded trails in hunting season. Suburban dogs must be seen by cars, and rural horses by hunters. And for the much-loved horse, there are luxury items such as fleece bit warmers for owners who do not want to put cold metal in their horses' mouths. As with dogs, horses are also dressed for what humans deem to be cold or inclement weather. In addition, sleazys appear to benefit humans who wish to keep a neat appearance for horses they groom and show.

Art and Entertainment

Beyond warmth and safety, humans also dress animals for the social worlds of art and entertainment. William Wegman is the owner of those dogs in human clothing on *Sesame Street*. Whether they are demonstrating how make homemade bread (Statz), forming the letter H with their bodies (four dogs required here), or waiting tables at a restaurant, these large hunting dogs are of the Weimaraner breed and are owned by their painter/photographer/filmmaker owner, Wegman. Dubbed with human voices and augmented with human hands, generations of these dogs have been performing with Wegman for over forty years. In the summer of 2017, dogs Flo and Topper even appeared in *French Vogue*, modeling clothing by designers like Gucci (Thompson).

Early in his career, Wegman did not want to persist in photographing his dogs, as he thought it might be perceived as gimmicky and a little lazy for an artist, but a Weimaraner named Man Ray "kept giving him ideas" (Thompson). Wegman clearly enjoys working with his dogs and appears to view them as collaborators in the creation of his art. He says these dogs are well suited to their work, which sometimes requires standing still, because they are a type of pointer, bred to freeze and point to an animal being hunted. Wegman says the dogs love to work; they "love to be picked … they wanna be the one that you're looking at and talking to" (Thompson).

If Wegman is primarily working with one of his dogs, the other must also be included in some way: "I have to pretend—if I'm working with Topper, I have to put Flo nearby on a pedestal, so she thinks she's working" (Thompson). Wegman credits Flo with probably knowing that she is "just a stand-in" but also with knowing that is acceptable in this circumstance. Wegman states that his dogs are "in on everything" and that he is never without them (Thompson). This close contact with his often-clothed dogs appears to have contributed to Wegman's sense of respect and responsibility for these animals. He tries to avoid clichéd poses and scenarios, like dogs in sunglasses or poker playing dogs. He is fine with the dogs being funny, but they must also be beautiful and mysterious, even when portraying people (Thompson).

Some dressed animals do not exist in the flesh but appear only as artwork on canvas or print. Even more can be done with these animals in the way of stature, clothing, and costumery since these creatures can never bite, resist, or run away. If family members want to add an adorable photo of their dog wearing a Santa hat to their holiday cards, this can be done even if the dog will not cooperate. Robert Baldwin shows how to accomplish this. His process utilizes a hatless photo of a dog and photoshop techniques involving the Santa hat and a stuffed animal with fur of a shade similar to the live dog. Humans want to put clothes on our animals badly enough to do it behind their backs with the latest technology. The website Art.com sells a large selection of anthropomorphic animal prints ("Anthropomorphic Animals"). Now the possibilities expand to skirt-wearing rabbits sitting cross-legged as they chat over a cup of tea, a moose dressed in a three-piece suit standing upright on two legs, and a fox outfitted as The Mad Hatter.

The boredpanda.com site highlights the photographic work of a Barcelona-based photographer, Yago Partal, who spent three years dressing zoo animals like humans ("This Artist Spent"). His series also expanded to include baby zoo animals. The animals are posed as young humans for school pictures with front-facing head and chest shots. There may be an arctic wolf wearing a tie under a sweater, a leopard cub outfitted as a pilot, complete with flying goggles resting on the forehead, and a lion in a denim jacket. Toxel.com has a similar section on its site called "Animals in Human Clothing," where deer wear raincoats and polar bears sport infinity scarves. A disturbing comment from a site visitor follows one image of a sable-furred bull wearing a dark-hued leather jacket and facing the camera with narrowed eyes: "ha ha, he looks like a gangster!" ("Animals in Human Clothing"). Also, as one might imagine, these and other photos of dressed animals show up on Pinterest boards ("Dressing Animals").

In the worlds of art and entertainment, animals both real and imagined appear in human clothing. The animals that only exist as painted or photoshopped images are spared the experience of wearing fabrics that may be hot and uncomfortable, but clearly the potential meanings and consequences are not always innocent, as when black animals may function as a source of amusement as racial stereotypes.

Fun and Recreation

In the Customers' Horse Costumes page of Sleezy Barb Horsewear, the Web surfer is greeted by Ernie, the CEO of the company. He shares some photos of his friends wearing Halloween costumes and hopes this page will inspire others to create their own costumes and send photos to him for posting on the site. He wears a wide-brimmed straw hat and a coat with southwestern print. And he is a horse. So is Mindy Sue, the executive assistant, a miniature horse sporting a she-devil Halloween costume, which she says is easy to make by adding embellishments to an existing sleazy, like 99-cent devil horns from a dollar store. And Mindy Sue, also the official website model, recently represented the company as the event mascot at The Great Sleepy Hollow Treasure Hunt, where human participants engaged in a treasure hunt on horseback, with humans and horses dressed in pirate garb as they searched for hidden treasure.

The Sleezy Barb website encourages visitors to expand Halloween beyond human-only trick-or-treating and costume parties. Take it out to the barn "and let your horse join in" (Sleezy Barb Horsewear). Horses should not miss out on this holiday fun. Photos of humans and horses in Halloween costumes abound on the site, with brief explanatory blurbs from customers all over the United States. Wonder Woman, Disney characters, a zebra, Pokémon characters (including a family dog dressed as the Poké ball), a human Statue of Liberty riding an equine American flag, a racecar, and a Minion all appear. The site encourages unbridled creativity with a costume and reminds visitors that they can even turn their horses into other animals, such as sheep or spiders.

At the culmination of one exhibition of twenty-five top equine Halloween costumes, humans are invited to laugh at themselves: "Most of all, be thankful that your horse is willing to put up with your silliness!" ("25 Horse and Rider Halloween Costume Ideas"). Left unstated is the fact that the horse does not have much say in the matter except possibly to resist the human putting the costume on. Still, the costume sleazys and the treasure hunt activities appear to be reflective of humans' authentic desires to socialize and spend even more time with their horses, including them in fun activities that appear to engage the horse socially and to do no harm.

Decency

Given the fun outfits and Halloween costumes sported by horses today, it is curious that in the menagerie of carved wooden carousel animals in America, the only one wearing human clothing is a frog. Although mostly populated by horses, our old-time carousels sometimes include other animals, such as lions, tigers, camels, rabbits, ostriches, cheetahs, dogs, deer, and even imaginary creatures like dragons and the hippocampus—a mythical horse/fish hybrid sea horse. Although most are carved with some sort of saddle or decorative cloth, the only American carousel animal wearing human clothing is Herschell-Spillman's whimsical frog, or hop-toad (1910–1914), on exhibit at the Henry Ford Museum in Dearborn, Michigan ("Carousel Figure").

The "hop-toad" wears blue form-fitting short pants with a yellow stripe at the waist and a multi-colored sleeveless frock coat of blue with red trim, and some accents of white, yellow, and crosshatch patterns. His white shirt collar is accented by a red bow tie. It is curious that the artist created this frog figure in human clothing, rather than with a saddle of some sort. Perhaps the view of a frog's rear end, with no tail to cover it modestly, might have been off-putting to the human amusement park goers of the early twentieth century, dressed in their Sunday best? As in the social worlds of art and entertainment, this recreational wooden frog experiences no discomfort from its representation in human clothing but does still reflect some cultural meanings, sensibilities, and consequences.

The idea of some "indecent" animals needing to be clothed is not new, and re-emerged in 1957 with a man named Alan Abel, the master of a number of unusual media hoaxes around that time (Crockett). Under his alias, G. Clifford Prout, Abel claimed to be president of an organization called the Society for Indecency to Naked Animals (S.I.N.A.), whose mission was to clothe naked animals for the sake of decency. Purportedly, the inspiration for this organization came to Prout when he was stuck in a traffic jam caused by a loose (in every sense) bull and cow who were mating in the middle of a road, thereby acting as if the world was their bedroom. He noticed the discomfort of other drivers at the sight, especially ladies, and determined that something needed to be done.

Among Prout's mantras were that animals without clothing were "destroying the moral integrity of our great nation" and "a nude horse is a rude horse" (Crockett). Even though his organization was completely fake, Prout attracted 50,000 dues-paying members, appeared on the *Today Show,* and even fooled television news anchorman, Walter Cronkite (who was reportedly very angry when the hoax was exposed). Clearly Prout/Abel had tapped into some cultural sentiment that the public was ready to embrace, with one woman contributing a $40,000 check, which Abel returned.

American sensibilities up to the mid-twentieth century included a discomfort with naked, even if fur-covered, bodies. Animals who displayed, and even utilized, their private parts in public were characterized as shameless and immoral. Clothing them was a form of social control by humans, to add to our comfort, if not to theirs.

Fashion

Knowing that pets are already dressed for warmth and safety, shelter pet ads and billboards extend pet clothes into the human social world of fashion ("Shelter Pet Project"). A black bulldog with an adorably cocked head and wearing a smart yellow bow tie is not just a shelter pet, but also the life of the party. A dignified orange shelter cat in a blue shirt sitting at a keyboard is a globally recognized pianist, and a shelter spaniel with long glamorous fur and oversized pink eyeglasses is a fashion icon. Building on what pet owners are already doing—dressing them—and kicking it up a notch or two in intensity, the Humane Society wants prospective adopters to know that these hidden gems, these animals with a real spark of fun and personality, are out there ("Shelter Pet Project"). These kooky characters, foolishly unwanted by someone else, are available for adoption into loving homes. Pet owners are following the lead of these unique, hip shelter animals. One in ten dog owners in the *K9 Magazine* survey from the U.K. say they dress their dog simply because it looks nice and seven percent say they do it as a fashion accessory ("Dog Owners Blasted").

Cats and dogs are not the only shelter pets that are dressed to impress. A series of three books by Alex Goodwin and Tess Gammell/Newell adapt the well-known stories of the Christian nativity, Jane Austen's *Pride and Prejudice*, and Charles Dickens' *Oliver Twist* with beautiful full-color photos zoomed in on guinea pigs dressed for their parts wearing custom-made costumes created by a seamstress. In *A Guinea Pig Nativity*, rich glossy fur, huge dark button eyes, and sweet little pink noses and lips are center-stage, and furry bodies are embellished with angels' wings, shepherd's cloaks, wise men's colorful, satiny hats, and even Herod, in the form of a guinea pig, wearing a gold crown (*A Guinea Pig Nativity*). The fact that the second wise man appears to be nearly asleep seated between his colleagues adds to the charm.

Elaborate period costumes, including top hats and miniature stage sets transport *A*

Guinea Pig Pride and Prejudice readers through the familiar Austen tale with a cast of nine shelter guinea pigs. Midway through, a lovely head-on shot of Elizabeth in rose-pink ruffles is captioned, "What painter could do justice to those beautiful eyes?" (Goodwin and Gammell 11). Perhaps the most poignant, and unapologetically transparent in terms of encouraging support of shelters is the Dickens tale of a lost boy and his perilous adventures before his adoption by a kind man. The hero in *A Guinea Pig Oliver Twist* is a white and black guinea pig, Oreo, who wears a shabby green newsboy hat and totes a red and white gingham hobo bindle, thereby easily capturing both the sweet and the scrappy aspects of his role, Oliver Twist (Goodwin and Newell).

All three guinea pig books include brief statements at the end, after the authors' and seamstresses' biographies, about small pets being abandoned every day and the lucky ones finding their way to shelters where they can be rehomed. *A Guinea Pig Oliver Twist* ends with direction on what humans can do next: "If little Oliver Twist has melted your heart over the course of his adventures, perhaps think of supporting your local rescue centre!" (Goodwin and Newell 63).

Adorable, fashionable shelter animals, portrayed on billboards, websites, and books, encourage humans to consider bringing one of these sweet, dignified, or sassy characters into their homes and lives. The human clothing and accessories serve to capture attention while driving and highlighting the character, fun, and individuality of these diamonds in the rough. Perhaps in this age of visual and information overload, highly stylized images of shelter pets compete best for human attention.

Control

Do horses really enjoy their Halloween costumes, as one human customer on the Sleezy Barb website proclaimed? Maybe they do, particularly if the costume is comfortable and provides a scenario for these social animals to spend more time with their humans. Still, Samantha Hurn claims that the act of clothing animals can be viewed as a way of exerting control over the "animality" of the nonhuman. Certainly, clothes are not neutral; human clothing communicates multiple messages about sex, style, status, and power. Within the bounds of cultural expectations and budget, humans choose what to wear. Left to their own devices, animals do not wear or seek out clothing. When humans choose clothing for animals, they are making decisions about the bodies, comfort, and even health of those who have no input.

People dress their animals for reasons of safety and warmth, perceived aesthetics, and as a sort of symbolic capital for their humans, similar to material accessories like cars, jewelry, smart phones, and so on. The jury is still out on anthropomorphism as showing respect for nonhuman animals by treating them as if they were quasi-human or as a distancing device that reinforces the divide between humans and nonhumans. When animals are dressed in human clothing for comedic effect, such as the zoo animals photographed in human clothing, it emphasizes difference.

In the colonial past, non–Western people were often viewed in an anthropomorphic manner (Hurn). Eighteenth- and nineteenth-century Christian missionaries often began their work by dressing "savage" people in Western clothing, humanizing them through concealment, and as a way of asserting dominance and control. Perhaps that is what humans are sometimes doing when clothing animals.

Treating animals with respect and the recognition that they are active, nonhuman subjects is related to a post-domestic worldview that enables people to engage with their animals in a more empathetic way. Instead of assuming that horses prefer to wear rugs and sleazys in foul weather based on what humans would prefer, a shift in emphasis that encourages trying to see the world from the horse's perspective can be good for both humans and nonhumans. It is a common practice in horse racing, when feasible, to allow a horse who normally spends time either on the track or in a barn stall to be turned out in field for at least a few hours. Horses are often turned out in pairs based on trainers' knowledge of the horses' friendships so that the time off will be fun and relaxing for both animals. Sans harness and other equipment, horses exemplify the beauty and grace of their bodies, and their movements can be described as breathtaking. The change of space and place refreshes these hard-working animals and helps them race better when they return, which makes good business sense, too.

Dressing animals in human clothing is by and large unnecessary. Humans do it because of their perceptions of the need for warmth and safety and comfort, which are well-intended and sometimes valid, but at other times harmful to the nonhuman. The love with which a human mother regularly dresses a child in a windbreaker on 75-degree days she deems a bit breezy is charming and harmless because the child can, and often does, remove the jacket once out of her sight. But animals are usually not able to express their wills in this way. Humans make these decisions for them, rather than being guided by more animal-centric recommendations provided by their veterinarians.

Although dressing animals for warmth and safety can connote concern and affection for animals, dressing them for "decency" is transparently self-serving on the part of humans. In the social worlds of art, entertainment, and recreation, dressing animals as humans is more nuanced in social meanings and consequences. Dressing and photographing shelter dogs, cats, and guinea pigs briefly in light clothing in the context of finding them good "fur-ever" homes is probably harmless, but does reflect our cultural desire for pets represented as more unique and special given their implied fashionable tastes, life of the party personalities, and musical abilities.

Dressing horses and dogs in Halloween costumes is short term and the animals may benefit from the increased social and tactile contact with their humans. Images of animals wearing clothing may appear more humane when created artificially by computer-aided means, but the tendency to personify these animals may sometimes seep into the territory of race or gender stereotypes. Are non-white animals to be considered "animals of color"? Do humans really want to bring animals into the realm of some of the most intractable human problems and stereotypes?

Making clothing decisions for animals, even when based on authentic love and concern for their comfort and welfare, has its pitfalls. Humans need to move past the mindset of "I'm cold so my dog needs a sweater" to a more empathetic frame of mind where the primary focus becomes trying to understand what human choices would best maintain the animal's agency and dignity. This approach would afford animals both the opportunity to enjoy human company and to maintain the unique wills and natures of their species.

WORKS CITED

"Animals in Human Clothing." Toxel.com RSS, 19 Mar. 2013, www.toxel.com/inspiration/2013/03/29/animals-in-human-clothing/.

"Anthropomorphic Animals." Art.com, 2018, www.art.com/gallery/id-b453628/anthropomorphic-animals-posters.htm.

Baldwin, Robert. "Dog Wearing Santa Hat—Photoshop Tutorial." YouTube, 18 Dec. 2013, www.youtube.com/watch?v=n_eIQAG-Gw0.

"Carousel Figure of a Frog or 'Hop-Toad,' 1910–1914." Henry Ford Museum. 2018, www.thehenryford.org/collections-and-research/digital-collections/artifact/167422/.

Crockett, Zachary. "The Campaign to Make 'Indecent' Animals Wear Clothing." Priceonomics, 3 Mar. 2016, www.priceonomics.com/the-hoaxster-who-revealed-sad-truths-about-america/.

"Custom Clothing for Your Special Horse!" Sleezy Barb Horsewear, www.sleezybarbhorsewear.com/.

"Dog Owners Blasted for Putting Clothes on Their Pets." Express.co.uk, 16 Mar. 2017, www.express.co.uk/news/nature/779453/Dog-owners-blasted-putting-cloths-on-pets-animals.

"Dressing Animals in Human Clothing Seems to Be a Trend These Days. In This Series, Entitled Segundas Pieles (Second Skins), Madrid-Based... | Photography | Pinterest | Portraits, Sci Fi and Illustrations." Pinterest, www.pinterest.com/pin/278801033155247867/.

Goodwin, Alex, and Tess Gammell. *A Guinea Pig Pride and Prejudice*, Bloomsbury Publishing, 2015.

Goodwin, Alex, and Tess Newell. *A Guinea Pig Oliver Twist,* Bloomsbury Publishing, 2016.

A Guinea Pig Nativity. n.a. Bloomsbury Publishing, 2013.

Hurn, Samantha. "Dressing Down." *Civilisations*, vol. 59, no. 2, Feb. 2011, pp. 109–124.

Larsen, Elizabeth Anne. *Gender, Work, and Harness Racing: Fast Horses and Strong Women in Southwestern Pennsylvania.* Lexington, 2015.

Maslow, A.H. "A Theory of Human Motivation." *Psychological Review.* 50 (4): 1943: 370–96.

McGraw, Eliza. "Why Horses Used to Wear Bonnets, Caps and Peaked Straw Hats." *The Washington Post*, WP Company, 1 Aug. 2017, www.washingtonpost.com/news/animalia/wp/2017/08/01/why-horses-used-to-wear-bonnets-caps-and-peaked-straw-hats/?noredirect=on&utm_term=.5f8ad196b42d.

"The Shelter Pet Project." *Animal Sheltering Online by The Humane Society of the United States*, The Humane Society of the United States, 2018, www.animalsheltering.org/programs/shelter-pet-project.

Statz, M. "Sesame Street—Dogs Bake Homemade Bread." YouTube, 14 June 2007, www.youtube.com/watch?v=wgQNx_aRZgk.

"This Artist Spent 3 Years 'Dressing' Zoo Animals Like Humans and The Clothes Fit Unbelievably Well." Bored Panda, 2017, www.boredpanda.com/animals-dressed-like-humans-zoo-porraits-yago-partal/?utm_source=google&utm_medium=organic&utm_campaign=organic.

Thompson, Megan. "Artist William Wegman and His Weimaraner Muses." Public Broadcasting Service, 15 Oct. 2017, www.pbs.org/newshour/show/artist-william-wegman-weimaraner-muses.

"25 Horse and Rider Halloween Costume Ideas You Won't Believe!" Double D Trailers, Blog, 8 June 2019. https://www.doubledtrailers.com/25-horse-rider-halloween-costume-ideas-you-wont-believe/.

Animals and the Law

Persons or Property?

GEORGE S. JACKSON

Introduction

What does it mean to be a person? Is a person an animal? Is an animal a person? Are these mutually exclusive domains? What is property? Can a person be property? Can property own property? Questions regarding the boundaries between humans and animals continue to vex legal theorists, moral philosophers, and scientists, as legal precedents create evolving, sometimes surprising, interpretations that blur the lines. Casually speaking, the word "person" is usually assumed to mean a human being, and property typically refers to "things," such as land or vehicles. Despite, or perhaps due to, the repeated judicial scrutiny afforded both terms, their legal definitions continually evolve, sometimes in surprising ways. For example, at law, inanimate entities such as corporations, which are owned by human beings, are recognized as persons, and, as such, possess constitutional rights.

The arguments to be made here are as follows: (1) For living creatures, cognition is a critical element in determining legal status; (2) Human beings are animals, and, at least in terms of rights under the Constitution of the United States, certain sentient nonhuman animals should be deemed persons; and (3) Nonhuman animals are subject to being property, and despite being property, they are entitled to possess certain property rights.

Human Distinctiveness: Varying Notions from Religion and Science

The law, when it works best, reflects humankind's knowledge and values. One might say that law, which sets out mandatory rules, is the ultimate arbiter of human culture, with many of its provisions emanating from religion, science, and philosophy. If so, before delving into the law's treatment of nonhuman animals (hereinafter, for simplicity referred to as "animals"), it is worthwhile to review how these disciplines have addressed the nature of humanity and its relationship to animals since these perspectives underlie the law's perspectives.

The nature of humankind is a fundamental issue in religion. Christianity and Islam, which together include more than half the world's population, maintain that humans differ from all other life by the endowment of "immortal, God-given souls" (Barash). From that point forward, however, there is considerable disagreement on what this means. Within Christianity, Genesis, the Biblical story of earth's creation, is unequivocal:

> And God made the beasts of the earth according to their kinds and the cattle according to their kinds, and everything that creeps upon the ground according to its kind. And God saw that it was good. Then God said, "Let us make man in our image, after our likeness; and let them have dominion over the fish of the sea, and over the birds of the air, and over the cattle, and over all the earth, and over every creeping thing that creeps upon the earth" [Genesis].

"Evangelical rationalists" accept the teachings of the Bible, but not necessarily its text, as "without error" (Gier). For example, Pope Francis, head of the Roman Catholic Church, the world's largest Christian denomination (Guinness World Records), recently declared that "paradise is open to all of God's creatures" (Gladstone).

In contrast, defenders of inerrancy believe the Bible is "God-breathed and thus free from error in all its statements and affirmations" (Hindson 208). Robert Smith, a leading Biblical literalist, argues that "To insist that the Bible is factually correct in all respects is to impose a scientific worldview on a prescientific document… [I]t is not to be taken as an encyclopedia of empirical facts." Smith describes the Bible as "perfect," but not "perfect the way a mathematician or scientist would define it" (qtd. in Gier). He accuses Christian rationalists of obfuscation in wanting to judge the Bible's accuracy using a standard that cannot be met by "even the best scientific documents" (Gier).

The scientific definition of "human being" is as muddled as the religious one. Humanists argue that human knowledge and rationality are ever advancing, fueled by a human mind that "reflects the order of the cosmos," and so it is appropriate for humankind to dominate other life forms (Nagel). The closely related speciesist view is that humankind's "superior intelligence, language and self-awareness" justify the exploitation of nonhuman animals (Shermer).

Other scientists disagree, describing viewpoints such as those set out above as no more than a "secular faith," built upon a "delusional self-flattery" (Nagel). Jeff Sebo, director of the animal studies graduate program at New York University, argues that "There is nothing special about species in and of themselves…. They are morally arbitrary taxonomic categories" (Sebo).

The conflicting perspectives within the religious and science communities give rise to the question, "How smart are animals?" In addition to being an important scientific issue, cognition is, or at least should be, a critical determinant of an animal's legal dignity since the law is concerned with justice. Justice anticipates that those governed should be able to expect fairness, and, as best now understood, a sensation of fairness requires awareness.

Many scientists look to the brain's cerebral cortex as the key to intelligence (Herculano-Houzel). It serves as a processing center that "integrates all kinds of information, makes decisions, interprets emotions, solves problems, and creates complex behavior" (Fischman). Within the cerebral cortex, its neurons "act a bit like tiny information processors to form thoughts" (Fischman).

As evidenced by Figure 1, if that standard is applied, pilot whales are nearly twice as intelligent as humans. More recent studies point to other critical factors such as brain organization (Blackmore 53) and brain size relative to body mass (Sherwood 63).

SOME ESTIMATES OF BRAIN NEUROANATOMY
(all numbers reflect averages)

SPECIES	BRAIN SIZE * (Weight in Grams)	CEREBRAL CORTEX NEURONS	
		(numbers in billions)	(source of estimate)
Long-finned Pilot Whale	2670	37	****
Adult Human	1350	16	*
Elephant	4783	11	***
False Killer Whale	5620	10	***
Chimpanzees	420	6.2	****
Rhesus Monkey (Old World)	420	4.8	***
Dog	72	0.5	*
Cat	30	0.25	*

Sources:
*Brain Facts & Figures, https://faculty.washington.edu/chudler/facts.html
**Adding Up Animal Neurons, Scientific American (July 2018) p. 59
***Neuronal Factors Determining Higher Intelligence (2016),
     https://www.ncbi.nlm.nih.gov/pmc/articles/PMC4685590/ (2016)
****Mortenson, Quantitative Relationships in Delphinid Neocortex, Frontiers in Neuroantomy (2014)

Fig. 1. Estimating the average brain size is relatively straightforward. Measuring neurons is considerably more difficult. Accordingly, different studies yield different results, and researchers often disagree on how closely neuron count predicts intelligence. This table utilizes the higher range of estimates.

Repeated studies demonstrate that chimpanzees, whose neuron counts fall far below that of the average human being, can "communicate through sign language, pursue goals creatively, and form long-lasting friendships" (Sebo). Similarly, in tests conducted at Kyoto University, a chimpanzee repeatedly bested university students in recalling a random series of nine numbers (de Waal).

On specific tests of human senses affecting cognition, animals sometimes demonstrate superior abilities. Dolphins, for example, have a hearing range of 200 to 150,000 Hz, compared to humankind's average range of 20–20,000 Hz (Herculano-Houzel). Dogs, who fare poorly on the cerebrum neurons scoring scale, have a sense of smell estimated to be at least 10,000 times more powerful than that of humans (Millar 32). In studies focusing on nonhuman communication skills, researchers have determined that many species "talk" with one another. A 2018 test off the coast of Maryland recorded seventy-seven different marine species using their voice to distinguish themselves (Guarino).

Neuroscientist Suzanna Herculano-Houzel, who heads the Laboratory of Comparative Anatomy at the Federal University of Rio De Janeiro, subscribes to the cerebral cortex neurons/intelligence quotient theory. However, she observes, "If we are the ones putting other animals under the microscope, and not the other way around, then the human brain must have something that no other brain has" (Herculano-Houzel).

Thomas Suddendorf, writing in *Scientific American*'s special 2018 issue, "The Science of Being Human," contends that two differences distinguish human cognition from animal cognition: first, humans' ability to envision several different possible future scenarios, and second, the human desire to exchange one's knowledge with other humans (Suddendorf 43). Another contributor, Kevin Laland, takes a similar tack: "The emerging consensus is that humanity's accomplishments derive from an ability to acquire knowledge and skills from other people. Individuals then build iteratively on that reservoir of pooled knowledge over long periods. It was not our large brains, intelligence or language that gave us culture but rather our culture that gave us large brains, intelligence and language" (Laland 34). He acknowledges that the same is true for "perhaps a small number of other species" (Laland 35).

As well as the matter of calculative intelligence and culture, cognition includes emotional elements. Animal behavior researcher Marc Bekoff argues, "[T]here is compelling evidence that at least some animals likely feel a full range of emotions, including fear, joy, happiness, shame, embarrassment, resentment, jealousy, rage, anger, love, pleasure, compassion, respect, relief, disgust, sadness, despair, and grief" (Bekoff 861). Michael Shermer, a onetime animal researcher turned animal rights activist, refers to the task of gassing lab rats following their use in experiments as "one of the most dreadful things I ever had to do" (Shermer). He argues that "mammals are sentient beings that want to live and are afraid to die." To illustrate the point, Shermer writes about a slaughterhouse video showing a bull in line for slaughter: "[H]e hears his mates in front of him being killed, backs up into the rear wall … seeking an escape. He looks scared."

Many animals mourn. Biological anthropologist Barbara King describes mourning as what occurs when at least two living creatures have chosen to be together for purposes other than mating and foraging; and, following the death of one animal, the survivor behaves differently, "perhaps reducing the amount of time devoted to eating or sleeping, adopting a body posture or facial expression indicative of depression or agitation, or generally failing to thrive" (King 64). Her research focuses on the bottlenose dolphin's mourning behavior, but she points out that it is common in several species, including elephants and giraffes.

Scientists now recognize that attempts to demonstrate human intellectual superiority frequently yield inaccurate results because of the experimenters' anthropomorphic approach. Frans de Waal, director of the Living Links Center at the Yerkes National Primate Research Center, relates the story of how experimenters tried to determine whether elephants lacked the intelligence of primates, a category that includes humans and other animals with hands and forward-facing eyes (de Waal).

In repeated tests, the elephants failed to successfully retrieve food placed outside their cages, despite having within their cage a stick that could be used to reach the food. The experimenters did not consider that, unlike primates, an elephant's trunk, often used to pick up objects, is also its smelling organ. When an elephant picks up a stick, it blocks its nose, which, with an elephant, is its primary sense, vision being a secondary one. Moreover, using the trunk to hold a stick makes it quite difficult for the elephant to use its mouth, an essential tool in eating. Sometime later the experimenters tried a different test. When given both the stick, and a box, the elephant quickly analyzed how it could use the box to climb high enough to reach the food without using the stick.

de Waal also criticizes a typical approach of experimenters: "[T]he children are held by their parents and talked to ('Watch this! Where is the bunny?'), and they are dealing with members of their own kind. The animals, in contrast, sit behind bars, don't benefit from language or a nearby parent who knows the answers, and are facing members of a different species" (de Waal). Then there is "the problem of negative evidence," when researchers conclude there is a lack of animal cognition because they didn't find evidence supporting its presence. de Waal contends "absence of evidence is not evidence of absence."

Putting aside its attempts to distinguish humans from other animals, the entire scientific discovery process is not without critics. The *Stanford Encyclopedia of Philosophy* refers to Thomas Kuhn's *The Structure of Scientific Revolutions* as "one of the most cited academic books of all times." In it, Kuhn addresses the strengths and shortcomings of scientific research, pointing to the unexpected prevalence of "error, myth, and superstition" (Kuhn 2), and to the scientific method's propensity for reaching incompatible conclusions from the same inquiry (Kuhn 3). He argues that "normal science" often impedes new discoveries because it is "predicated on the assumption that the scientific community knows what the world is like." Consequently, it typically focuses on discrediting any view that contradicts what is currently deemed to be the truth, i.e., its current paradigm (Kuhn 5). Notwithstanding its shortcomings, science appears to be moving toward a recognition that humankind is not so unique and special as once thought.

Individual Morality as Protector of Animal Rights

If religion and science leave us short in terms of better understanding the relationship of humans to the surrounding world, and the legal dignity of animals, then perhaps these issues are outside the realm of knowledge, and can be best approached as values that differ from person to person. Reinhold Niebuhr, hailed by many as the most influential Christian philosopher of the twentieth century (Swaim), questions the wisdom of relying on individual morality alone to solve societal problems.

Niebuhr argues that individuals may be "endowed with a measure of sympathy" that leads them to consider the interests of others, at least in small groups. This measure of concern, however, dissipates as the group becomes larger and more complex. Niebuhr writes, "[T]here is less reason to guide and check impulse, less capacity for transcendence, less ability to comprehend the needs of others and therefore more egoism than the individuals, who comprise the group, reveal in their personal relationships" (Niebuhr xi). This is particularly true when there is a dominant group, since its members enjoy more special privileges (Niebuhr xiv). If true, this does not bode well for animals in their relationship with human beings.

Niebuhr was not the first to question the limits of over-reliance on individual morality. Moral philosopher Adam Smith, writing in the early eighteenth century, made the following observation:

> [T]he rules of justice are the only rules of morality which are precise and accurate... [A]ll the other virtues are loose, vague, and indeterminate; ... [T]he first may be compared to the rules of grammar; the others to those which critics lay down for the attainment of what is sublime ... and which present us rather with a general idea of the perfection we ought to aim at, than afford us any certain and infallible directions for acquiring it [Smith, A.].

Niebuhr recognizes unselfishness as the highest human moral value (Niebuhr 257). However, when carried to its logical extreme, unselfishness ends in a conundrum. Where does concern for others rightfully give way to concern for self? Although ethical theory might support the generalized statement that there is a dignity residing in all living creatures, it provides little specific guidance on how much legal dignity the law of humankind should afford to nonhumans. Consider the recurring decision confronting many homeowners. Is it appropriate to stomp the palmetto bug that skirts across the kitchen floor?

The spider? The snake? What about plant life? More generally, where is the boundary between rightfully protecting oneself and respecting the rights of others?

Others take a more optimistic view. In *The Moral Arc*, Michael Shermer makes the case that humankind's moral awareness continues to advance, albeit slowly, and perhaps in uneven fashion. He recommends several measures for best assuring that the trend continues, and pinpoints the human/animal interface as the single most important issue, saying, "If by fiat I had to reduce these ... principles to just one it would be this: Try to expand the moral sphere and to push the arc of the moral universe just a bit farther toward truth, justice, and freedom for more sentient beings in more places more of the time" (Satel).

Law as the Arbiter of Last Resort

The rules of law do not rest upon supposed certain truths as does science or religion (Baggini). Instead they exist because knowledge is imperfect, and humans are imperfect. To use a statement attributed to President James Madison, "If men were angels, no government would be necessary" (Madison). The same is true for law, both as applied to humans, and to the human-animal boundaries.

Balancing relationships is one of the primary concerns of law, and the lawsuit is one of its primary vehicles. Judge Thomas Stephens describes the process: "[The lawsuit] is the grand stage on which lawyers strut, and fret, and perform to an audience of 12 disinterested strangers, selected randomly, who represent the moral conscience of their community, as they engage in a search for justice" (Stephens 22).

James Fishkin, director of the Center for Deliberative Polling at Stanford University, contends that societal issues can best be resolved if average citizens, selected at random, first deliberate, and then recommend solutions. He writes, "Under the right conditions, ordinary persons are perfectly capable of making complicated policy choices" (Fishkin). Or, as William Buckley famously put it, "I would rather be governed by the first 2000 people in the Boston telephone directory than by the 2000 people on the faculty of Harvard University" (Buckley).

Despite its many imperfections and contradictions, law is the *quid pro quod* that meshes together the varying perspectives and viewpoints of individuals comprising the societal unit. It is the social contract, and like any contract, there is a *this for that*. It addresses what one can do and what one cannot not do, thereby enforcing prevailing social norms (Brooks).

Like Adam Smith, Niebuhr acknowledges the necessity of laws, saying, "The selfishness of human communities must be regarded as an inevitability. Where it is inordinate it can be checked only if coercive methods are added to moral and rational persuasion" (Niebuhr 272).

In addition to its enforceability, there is another reason it is an effective mechanism for exploring the proper relationship between humans and animals. As set out earlier, for individuals, the highest moral value is unselfishness, which is limited by the need to survive. For society, however, "the highest moral ideal is justice" (Niebuhr 257), and there is no limitation on that quest. As Niebuhr puts it, "The supposition is that the government is impartial with reference to any disputes between citizens, and will therefore be able to use its power for moral ends" (Niebuhr 238).

The Law's Evolving Definition of Person

Court decisions are notoriously obscure, and depending on circumstances, the words employed have a variety of meanings. Defining what the law means by the term *person* has been a longstanding issue. The word appears numerous times in the Constitution. At the outset it apparently refers to human beings. Article I, Section 2, for example, reads, "No person shall be a Representative who shall not have attained to the age of twenty-five years, and been seven years a citizen of the United States, and who shall not, when elected, be an inhabitant of that state in which he shall be chosen."

Moreover, under the Constitution a person was initially deemed to infer men, primarily white men of European descent. Later it came to embrace persons of color, indigenous Americans, and women. Surprisingly, even before constitutional personhood included all natural persons born in United States, it was expanded to include certain non-living, intangible entities, i.e., corporations.

In *Bank of the United States v. Deveaux*, an 1809 Supreme Court decision, Chief Justice John Marshall, searching for some rationalization to allow a bank to be a citizen, turned to the English common law: "As our ideas of a corporation, its privileges and its disabilities, are derived entirely from the English books, we resort to them for aid, in ascertaining its character. It is defined as a mere creature of the law, invisible, intangible and incorporeal. Yet, when we examine the subject further, we find that corporations have been included within terms of description appropriated to real persons" (*Bank*). Apparently this was adequate pedigree, since, in 1898, the Court, referring to the Fourteenth Amendment's due process rights, declared, "That corporations are persons within the meaning of this amendment is now settled" (*Smyth* 522).

A few years later, Professor Bryant Smith, referring to *legal personality*—a term that signifies having legal rights, noted, "most of the confusion of thought with respect to the subject comes from the disposition to read into legal personality the qualities of natural human personality" (Smith, B. 291). Instead, he opined, "To confer legal rights or to impose legal ... is to confer legal personality" (Smith, B. 283).

Smith pointed out that words and definitions are often more figurative than exact. The wind does not really howl, and, to use legal terminology, negotiations do not actually ripen. The law's tendency to borrow from old words for new concepts "serves the double purpose of supplying a word where one is needed, and of obtaining a welcome for a new idea by introducing it under a familiar name" (Smith, B. 286).

The law's refusal to be burdened by strict wordsmithing continues as a centerpiece of jurisprudence. Supreme Court Justice Potter Steward, concurring in the Court's 1964 *Jacobellis v. Ohio* decision, made clear his lack of concern for words: "I shall not today attempt further to define the kinds of material I understand to be embraced within that shorthand description ['hard-core pornography'], and perhaps I could never succeed in intelligibly doing so. But I know it when I see it, and the motion picture involved in this case is not that" (*Jacobellis* 184).

Similarly, Supreme Court Justice William Douglas's 1965 opinion in *Griswold v. Connecticut*, illustrates how the law works around words. In a decision denying to states the power to forbid the use of contraceptives, the Court refused to be bound by the literal wording of the Constitution: "...[S]pecific guarantees in the Bill of Rights have penumbras, formed by emanations from those guarantees that help give them life and substance..." (*Griswold* 479).

The wording of the Constitution's Fourteenth Amendment evidences the close relationship between person and citizen. "All persons born or naturalized in the United States, and subject to the jurisdiction thereof, are citizens of the United States and of the state wherein they reside. No state shall make or enforce any law which shall abridge the privileges or immunities of citizens of the United States; nor shall any state deprive any person of life, liberty, or property, without due process of law; nor deny to any person within its jurisdiction the equal protection of the laws..." The Constitution is silent towards nonhuman animate creatures. However, interpretive court decisions evidence a clear trend in extending citizenship and legal personality to previously excluded human beings, and even to inanimate entities.

A critical issue in defining legal personality is whether cognition of a right, and a willingness to be regulated are prerequisites, a controversy long recognized by some to be "the most difficult in the whole domain of Jurisprudence" (Smith, B. 284). Bryant Smith answered in the negative:

> [T]hough the function of legal personality ... is to regulate behavior, it is not alone to regulate the conduct of the subject on which it is conferred; it is to regulate also the conduct of human beings toward the subject or toward each other.... The broad purpose of legal personality, whether of a ship, an idol, a molecule, or a man, and upon whomever or whatever conferred, is to facilitate by regulation, by organized society, of human conduct and intercourse [Smith, B. 296].

The issues are complex, and there is good cause for concern about unintended consequences. As Smith observed, "Legal personality is a good servant, but it may be a bad master" (Smith, B. 299). Nonetheless, there is a growing awareness among jurists and others that the issue of legal personality for animals must be addressed. Judge Eugene Faley's concurring opinion in *Nonhuman Rights Project v. Lavery* dated 2018, a case discussed below, succinctly frames the issue: "[The issue] speaks to our relationship with all the life around us. Ultimately, we will not be able to ignore it. While it may be arguable that a chimpanzee is not a 'person,' there is no doubt that it is not merely a thing" (*Nonhuman Rights Project v. Lavery*, Motion 2).

Leading Cases on Animals as Persons

No doubt, human beings are distinctly different from other living creatures, but does that mean animals are no more than property? Or, are they entitled to some degree of legal personality? That is the question being put before the courts with increasing frequency. Court decisions addressing animal rights typically focus on both legal personality and *standing*. In order to seek relief from the courts, one must be a person in the eyes of the law—the legal personality test. Then, one must demonstrate that court action is necessary to protect a "substantive legally protected interest" (Black 1577)—the standing test. For example, one might be a person in the eyes of the law, but the relief sought is either not one available under any law, or not one available under the particular law at issue in the case.

The following four cases, appearing in chronological order, evidence commonly used avenues to seek judicial protection for sentient animals. The first two cases were filed in federal courts, and the latter two are state court cases. In the United States, federal courts typically have a limited jurisdiction, addressing claims that arise from federal statutes. In contrast, state courts have a broader jurisdictional range, covering the common law and claims arising under state statutes. The term "common law" refers to the body of law arising from the deference given by later courts to the decisions of earlier courts.

Cetacean Community v. Bush (2004)

The Cetacean Community, a "name chosen by the self-appointed attorney for all of the world's whales, porpoises, and dolphins" (*Cetacean* 1171), brought this federal lawsuit, alleging that the U.S. Navy had violated the Endangered Species Act, the Marine Mammal Protection Act, the National Environmental Protection Act, and the Administrative Procedure Act, by repeatedly emitting low-frequency "pings" designed to identify submarines. The "Cetaceans contend that SURTASS LFAS harms them by causing tissue damage and other serious injuries, and by disrupting biologically important behaviors including feeding and mating" (*Cetacean* 1172).

The trial court dismissed the lawsuit without a trial, holding that cetaceans, the biological name for members of the order Cetacea, including whales and porpoises, lacked standing under the listed statutes to bring the lawsuit. The Cetacean Community appealed the decision to the Ninth Circuit Court of Appeals.

The appeals court decision is significant for two reasons. First, it addresses legal personality. The court acknowledged that in an earlier case, "we wrote that an endangered member of the honeycreeper family, the Hawaiian Palila bird, has legal status and wings its way into federal court as a plaintiff in its own right." However, the court ruled that its language in the earlier case was nonbinding dicta. As the court explained, "a statement is dictum when it is made during the course of delivering a judicial opinion, but … is unnecessary to the decision in the case and [is] therefore not precedential" (*Cetacean* 1173).

Second, the decision addresses the standing issue. The three-judge appellate panel wrote that the Constitution "does not compel the conclusion that a statutorily authorized suit in the name of an animal is not a 'case or controversy'" (*Cetacean* 1175–76). Later federal appellate courts, criticizing *Cetacean* as a fluke, have determined that this phrase, when shed of its double negatives, must be construed to provide that, at least in some instances, animals do have standing to sue under the U.S. Constitution.

However, as the *Cetacean* panel concluded, to sue under a specific federal statute (such as any of the ones relied on in this lawsuit), the statute must also "plainly state" that animals have standing in order for animals to rely upon it. What does this mean? Although the statutes named in this lawsuit do not grant standing for animals, it would not be unconstitutional for Congress to pass a statute and include in it standing for animals. Moreover, it opens the door for a future plaintiff to argue that a particular federal statute implies standing for animals even though it is not expressly stated.

Tilikum v. Sea World Parks & Entertainment (2011)

This federal lawsuit was filed by People for the Ethical Treatment of Animals (PETA), and others, as *next friends* for Tilikum and five other orcas (killer whales) captured and kept in tanks at two Sea World entertainment parks. Next friends is a doctrine that allows someone to represent an incompetent person (Cornell "Next friend"). In order to have next friend status, one must demonstrate that (1) the real party in interest is unable to bring the action without someone's assistance, and (2) the next friend is dedicated to serving the best interest of the real party (*Tilikum*).

The lawsuit alleged that the orcas' "captivity violates the slavery and involuntary servitude provision of the Thirteenth Amendment" (*Tilikum* 1261). The court dismissed the action on a preliminary motion before trial, holding that, unlike the Fourteenth Amendment, the Thirteenth Amendment is to be narrowly interpreted. It "applies to persons, and not to non-persons such as orcas" (*Tilikum* 1263). The court did acknowledge, however, that the equal rights and due process protections of the Fourteenth Amendment are "fundamental constitutional rights subject to changing conditions and evolving norms" (*Tilikum* 1264). Perhaps recognizing it would fare better under a Fourteenth Amendment case, PETA did not appeal the decision.

Nonhuman Rights Project (NHRP) v. Lavery (2017 and 2018)

These state court decisions relate to several lawsuits, beginning in 2013, that were filed in New York courts under next friends petitions, all virtually identical in terms of legal theory (Cupp 474), and several of which involved the same animals. The lawsuits were based on the common law's *habeas corpus* doctrine that, when successful, results in a court order mandating release of someone in custody or being held against their will.

In each instance, the petition sought the transfer to a sanctuary of several chimpanzees being held in small cages. According to NHRP, "chimpanzees are entitled to legal personhood under a New York statute allowing humans to create trusts for the care of the animals" (Cupp 475). In each instance, the trial courts dismissed the petitions. NHRP chose to appeal a 2015 trial court decision dismissing its claim.

In New York state courts, appeals from trial court (known as "Supreme Courts") decisions go to the Appeals Division. The Appeals Division upheld the Trial Court, citing two reasons. First, the court noted that the 2015 trial court dismissal was proper because the petitions "were not supported or warranted by any changed circumstances" relative to NHRP's earlier petitions, which NHRP had not appealed (*Nonhuman Rights Project v. Lavery*, 152 A.D 1). Then, although not required based on its first holding, the Appeals Division opinion addressed the merits of the *habeas corpus* petition:

> The asserted cognitive and linguistic capabilities of chimpanzees do not translate to a chimpanzee's capacity or ability, like humans, to bear legal duties, or to be held legally accountable for their actions.
> Petitioner argues that the ability to acknowledge a legal duty or legal responsibility should not be determinative of entitlement to habeas relief, since, for example, infants cannot comprehend that they owe duties or responsibilities and a comatose person lacks sentience, yet both have legal rights. This argument ignores the fact that these are still human beings, members of the human community [*Nonhuman Rights Project v. Lavery*, 152 A.D 4].

NHRP filed an appeal with the state's highest appellate court, the "Court of Appeals," which agreed to review the lower appellate court decision. Without discussion, it upheld the decision; however, Judge Fahey, one of the five judges reviewing the petition, wrote a concurring opinion, which took issue with the Appeals Division's decision regarding the merits of NHRP's lawsuit:

> Even if it is correct, however, that nonhuman animals cannot bear duties, the same is true of human infants or comatose human adults, yet no one would suppose that it is improper to seek a writ of

habeas corpus on behalf of one's infant child, or a parent suffering from dementia. In short, being a "moral agent" who can freely choose to act as morality requires is not a necessary condition of being a "moral patient" who can be wronged and may have the right to seek redress.

The better approach in my view is to ask not whether a chimpanzee fits the definition of a person, or whether a chimpanzee has the same rights as a human being, but instead whether he or she has the right to liberty, protected by habeas corpus. That question, one of precise moral and legal status is the one that matters here [*Nonhuman Rights Project v. Lavery*, Motion 2].

Despite the court's denial of relief, and the fact that Justice Fahey's opinion was not signed by the majority of justices, his comments appear to have significantly impacted subsequent rulings in the New York courts. For example, in November 2018, a trial court responding to another NHRP petition regarding an elephant named Happy, issued a "show cause" order, requiring a Bronx zoo to appear and demonstrate why the court should not order "her immediate release … to an appropriate sanctuary" (*Nonhuman Rights Project v. Breheny*). The case is still pending as of January 2019. In another 2018 decision, a New York appellate division court judge upheld a trial court's criminal conviction for vandalizing a corporation's automobiles, ruling that "it is common knowledge that personhood can and sometimes does attach to nonhuman entities like corporations or animals" (*People*).

Justice v. Vercher (2018)

Kim Mosiman, Guardian for "Justice," an American Quarter Horse, filed this negligence lawsuit in the Oregon state courts. Negligence is a common law doctrine that falls within tort law, which allows persons who are wronged by another individual to recover damages. A tort is "an act or omission that gives rise to injury or harm to another" (Cornell "Tort"). The essence of a negligence claim is that the defendant has either acted, or failed to act, in a reasonable manner.

The complaint alleged that the individual who had custody and control of the horse negligently "denied Justice adequate food and shelter for months, abandoning him to starve and freeze" (*Justice* Complaint 1). The defendant voluntarily surrendered control of the horse, and veterinarians determined that the animal's near-starvation and exposure to weather resulted in permanent penile paralysis, which required castration, and is expected to require repeated surgeries. The complaint sought at least $100,000 to cover the future costs of the special care the horse will require (*Justice* Complaint 13).

The court dismissed the complaint prior to trial, holding that "a nonhuman animal such as Justice lacks the legal status or qualifications necessary for the assertion of legal rights and duties in a court of law." The opinion acknowledged the court's concern that allowing the lawsuit to move forward "would likely lead to a flood of lawsuits" on behalf of animals. It also cited the court's concern that "animals are incapable of accepting legal responsibilities." Despite its decision, the court recognized that an appellate court might "come to a different conclusion if it wades into this public policy debate"; "however, as a trial court, it was 'unable to take that leap'" (*Justice* Opinion 1).

Evolution of the Legal Definition of Property

Humans tend to think of animals as *property* more so than as citizens. The term "property" has a variety of meanings. To the layman, it usually relates to things that are owned, such as real estate or automobiles. At law, property is often defined as the bundle of rights that one has in relation to an object. Moreover, one may own things that are not objects, such as a patent or a copyright. Property rights are usually matters of state law, and rather than statutory law, they are usually based on the common law. Professor Lee Reed summarizes some of the "varied connotations" associated with property:

> It connotes theft, murder, and slaver to some but security and liberty to others. Anthropologists have identified property with social relationships of power, but philosophers have called it a myth. It either exploits the poor or protects them most of all. Some view property as a matter of natural right while others see it as an artificial creation of the state. Its institution may lead to environmental degradation or the principal hope for preventing ecological disaster in the world's rainforests. Legal scholars assert that property is in rem as opposed to in personam, but to many of them the characteristics that define property are still as ambiguous as a Rorschach inkblot (Reed 459).[1]

Although not attempting to define the term, the Supreme Court's 1856 ruling in *Scott v. Sanford* demonstrates the impact of property: "[Slaves] are not included, and were not intended to be included, under the word 'citizens' in the Constitution…. The Constitution … recognizes slaves as property…. And Congress cannot exercise any more authority over property of that description than it may constitutionally exercise over property of any other kind" (*Scott*).

The decision, derided from the outset, was overridden in 1865 by the Thirteenth Amendment, which outlaws slavery: "Neither slavery nor involuntary servitude, except as a punishment for crime whereof the party shall have been duly convicted, shall exist within the United States, or any place subject to their jurisdiction." The Fourteenth Amendment, passed in 1868, reinforces the ban on slavery. It provides, "All persons born or naturalized in the United States, and subject to the jurisdiction thereof, are citizens of the United States."

When read in concert, the two amendments seem to imply that persons cannot also be property. However, subsequent court decisions can lead to a different conclusion. As evidenced by the cases set out above, some courts are beginning to regard certain animals as persons, at least in the legal sense. Innumerable courts have recognized that animals are property. Indeed, the right of humans to own animals is so widely acknowledged, there is little appellate authority on the issue, other than who is the owner.

But, there is the other question: If animals are property, can property own property? Professor Frances Foster, a leading critic of the common law's typical disdain for pet's inheritance rights, argues the common law is still "trapped in an outdated family paradigm" that assumes "the decedent's closest relatives by blood, adoption, or marriage are the most deserving recipients" (Foster 803).

Foster argues that the "family paradigm" gives virtually no credence to interpersonal relationships and "excludes the very people a particular decedent may have valued most—those connected by affection and support" (Foster 804). Citing surveys and examples, she argues that most pet owners consider their pets to be family members, and notes roughly one-fourth of pet owners include them in their wills (Foster 811). Nonetheless, she points out, trial courts still tend to follow the common law rule that "just as the refrigerator cannot inherit the stove and kitchen sink, a pet cannot inherit. Property cannot own property."

However, common law rules can be overridden by subsequent court decisions, or, as is more often the case, by state legislatures, who enact statutory law. According to the Animal Legal and Historical Center at Michigan State University, all fifty states now have some type of statutory scheme that permits individuals to create trusts for the benefit of pets (Map). When property is put into trust, ownership is split, with the management responsibility going to a trustee, and the enjoyment right going to one or more beneficiaries (Cornell "Trusts"). So, at least under state law, pets are entitled to own property, albeit in a limited fashion.

Leading Cases on Animals and Property

Animals are property, and there have been no legal challenges to that rule as of May 2019. Moreover, as set out above, state laws recognize that animals can own property indirectly as trust beneficiaries. The two following cases focus on other property issues. The first case tackles the question of determining the value attached to animals as property. The second case, arising under federal law, addresses animal property rights under the more limited federal property law, which relies almost exclusively on specific legislative grants.

Strickland v. Medlen (2013). This state law case arose when owners of a dog that was mistakenly euthanized at an animal shelter sued the shelter for emotional damages, claiming that the animal was unreplaceable, and despite minimal economic value, had considerable "sentimental or intrinsic" value (*Strickland* 186). The trial court dismissed the lawsuit prior to trial. The owners filed an appeal, and the Court of Appeals determined that since recent Texas cases had allowed sentimental value for items such as old family photographs, the claim for emotional damages should be allowed to go to trial. The shelter appealed to the Texas Supreme Court, which reversed the lower appellate court decision, opting instead to stand fast by its 1891 decision that animals, at least for purposes of calculating losses, are no more than property (*Strickland* 184). However, the Court's opinion acknowledged the special relationship between humans and dogs:

> Texans love their dogs. Throughout the Lone Star State, canine companions are treated—and treasured—not as mere personal property but as beloved friends and confidants, even family members. Given the richness that companion animals add to our everyday lives, losing "man's best friend" is undoubtedly sorrowful. Even the gruffest among us tears up (every time) at the end of Old Yeller [*Strickland* 184].

Nonetheless, it refused to overrule the longstanding common law rule recognized in most states, that at law one can only recover the economic value associated with property (*Strickland* 185). Despite its decision, the court acknowledged that its ruling might be out of step with today's values:

> We recognize that the benefit of most family dogs like Avery is not financial but relational, and springs entirely from the pet's closeness with its human companions. Measuring the worth of a beloved pet is unquestionably an emotional determination—what the animal means to you and your family—but measuring a pet's value is a legal determination. We are focused on the latter, and as a matter of law an owner's affection for a dog (or ferret, or parakeet, or tarantula) is not compensable [*Strickland* 193].

Moreover, like the concurring opinion in New York's highest court, Texas's highest court noted that it may be time for a change in the law:

> Societal attitudes inexorably change, and shifting public views may persuade the Legislature to extend wrongful-death actions to pets. Amid competing policy interests, including the inherent subjectivity

(and inflatability) of emotion-based damages, lawmakers are best positioned to decide if such a potentially costly expansion of tort law is in the State's best interest, and if so, to structure an appropriate remedy [*Strickland* 195].

Despite the court's refusal to allow special damages for the loss of a pet, the decision has potential to serve as a needed wedge for animal rights activists. First, it upholds the principle that animals are property. As such, they can be owned, which is necessary for an orderly society. Second, it upholds the principle that recoverable damages for injury to animals are limited to economic value, thereby minimizing the attractiveness of spurious litigation by owners aimed at securing money damages for injury to animals. Recall that the fear of a surge in litigation is what worried the Oregon court in the *Justice* case. Third, it does not suggest that animals should be denied legal personality. If anything, animal rights activists should be encouraged by the court's acknowledgment that animals are not "mere personal property," but are better viewed as "beloved friends and confidants, even family members."

Naruto v. Slater (2018)

This property rights lawsuit was filed in federal court by People for the Ethical Treatment of Animals (PETA), as next friends for Naruto, a monkey, living in an Indonesian animal reserve. *Naruto* focuses on the particular ownership rights created by federal copyright statutes. The lawsuit alleges that Naruto is the copyright owner for several "selfie" photographs that became part of book created by wildlife photographer, David Slater.

The trial court dismissed the action on a preliminary motion before trial, holding that a monkey lacked standing under the Federal Copyright Act (*Naruto* 6). PETA appealed, and the Ninth Circuit Court of Appeals upheld the trial court decision, but with an abundance of criticism both for its own 2004 *Cetacean* decision (discussed earlier), and for PETA's claim of "next friend" standing.

The three-judges hearing the *Naruto* appeal acknowledged that the *Cetacean* decision, rendered by a different panel of Ninth Circuit judges, until overridden by either a Supreme Court decision or an *en-banc* panel (participation by all judges of the Ninth Circuit), established legal precedent that animals have standing to sue under the Constitution. Nonetheless, in line with *Cetacean*, the court concluded that the instant dismissal was proper because the Federal copyright statute relied upon did not explicitly extend its privileges or protections to animals (*Naruto* 6).

Moreover, the judges pointed out that any organization or individual attempting to bring a best friend's lawsuit on behalf of animals should be prepared to prove both its significant relationship with the animal it represents and its true dedication to the best interests of the animal, rather than a generalized common interest in some outcome. In this instance, PETA did not meet that standard, and in a footnote to the decision, the court derided PETA for "employ[ing] Naruto as an unwitting pawn in its ideological goals" (*Naruto* 8). A close reading of the decision leads one to wonder whether its decision might have been different had there been a different best friend representing Naruto.

Other Avenues for Protecting Rights of Nonhuman Animals

Public Trust Doctrine

Cornell Law School's Legal Information Institute defines the Public Trust Doctrine as "The principle that certain natural and cultural resources are preserved for public use, and that the government owns and must protect and maintain these resources for the public's use" (Cornell "Public Trust"). It places a limitation of private property rights. Attorneys at the National Wildlife Federation's Northern Rockies Resource Center argue that under the public trust doctrine, "states have not only the authority to regulate and conserve wildlife, but also an affirmative duty to do so" (Musiker, France, and Hallenbeck 88). They note that the states' police power is also available for matters such as regulating hunting, however, unlike the public trust responsibility, the police power does not mandate protection (Musiker et al. 95). The public trust doctrine's protection for animals is important, but limited. Its purpose is to "protect the corpus of its wildlife from substantial impairment" (Musiker et al. 95), rather than address the dignity of living creatures.

Patriae Doctrine

This rule is closely related to the public trust doctrine, but differs in two respects. First, the *parens patria* doctrine does not burden the state; instead, it recognizes the state's privilege to intervene on behalf of animals. Second, the potential shortcoming that it protects against is different. *Parens patriae* protects against the risk that the "judiciary may fail to provide for entities incapable of protecting themselves, while the public trust doctrine protects against the potential shortcomings of democracy" (Musiker et al. 101). Under the *parens patriae* doctrine, the "sovereign owner" of wildlife—the state, via its executive branch, if it chooses, has *standing* to sue, demanding legal relief from the courts for injury to wildlife.

Conclusion

What can be gleaned from the foregoing? Arguably, it demonstrates the following: (1) Religion and science fall short in providing satisfactory explanations for how humankind should relate to other living creatures; (2) Individual morality, due to its unenforceability, uncertainty, and humankind's inherent frailties, cannot alone provide a societal solution; and (3) The law, which exists to resolve conflicts, is an appropriate tool for addressing the animal rights issue. That leaves the bigger question: What, if anything, happens next?

Fundamental fairness, a cornerstone legal principle, suggests that if one is affected by the law, especially one who is sentient, then, he, she, or it should have some means of influencing the law, as opposed to relying solely upon legislative grace or executive branch action. If so, certain animals should enjoy some degree of legal personality, thereby allowing human intermediaries to represent their interests in human courts.

This is not akin to declaring there are no differences between human and animals. Moreover, it does not mean that rights and privileges of animals should mirror the rights of humans. Just as with non-animate persons and non-sentient humans, the extent of legal dignity should be based on what is deemed reasonable, given humankind's knowledge. Since the law is a creation of humankind intended to affect human behavior, the determination of reasonableness is made by human beings. It is a balancing act.

Cetacean recognizes an ephemeral constitutional right for animals to seek redress in the federal courts, at least in the Ninth Circuit. However, that circuit's decisions, riddled by internal contradictions, obscure language, and apparent disagreement among its various panels, may provide little more than a mirage of legal personality for animals. State courts, by their very nature, better reflect local values, and have broader jurisdictional powers. Moreover, in the few reported cases, they appear to be sympathetic to the need to address the present-day legal status of animals. Although the court decisions routinely point to the issue as a public policy debate that is best resolved by legislative action, they demonstrate there is sufficient plasticity and precedent for juries and judges, applying present-day legal principles, to move "the arc of the moral universe just a bit farther..." (Satel).

But those seeking change bear the burden of persuasion in legal proceedings, and opponents of the animal rights movement make important points. Despite the many similarities between animals and humans, there are also many differences. For example, merely telling an animal to do something, or refrain from it, is fraught with difficulty, if not approaching the impossible. Many unrestrained animals are dangerous. Accordingly, the law, if it is to serve both humankind and animals, must include some measure of control over the actions of animals. The difficult question is how much.

Control is a continuum, not a point. As among humans, the extent of humans' control over animals depends in part on the risk of danger to others or their property. But troublesome personhood questions arise when the degree of control approaches involuntary servitude, such as horse racing, elephant rides, or still further along the continuum, the slaughter of animals for food. The property issues are similarly challenging. From an unvarnished legal perspective it is constitutionally appropriate to categorize animals as both persons and property, assuming, as appellate courts have ruled, they enjoy certain protections afforded by the Fourteenth Amendment, but none from the Thirteenth Amendment. But how does society structure rules that accept the use of animals to satisfy humankind's needs, all the while appropriately protecting the rights they enjoy as persons? That challenge remains.

Aside from the question of the treatment of animals, assuming they are both persons and property, there is another property issue—the property rights of animals. Among the privileges associated with legal personality is the right of ownership. In addition to being controlled as property, animals, if persons, should have some right, to own property, again via human intermediaries. Statutes in every state already provide equitable ownership rights for animals. Is there good reason why animals should not enjoy limited ownership privileges under federal law?

There are as many questions as answers. As these issues work their way through the courts and legislatures, it is worthwhile to remember both Judge Faley's observation in his 2018 opinion, "Ultimately we will not be able to ignore our relationship with all the life around us" (*Nonhuman Rights Project v. Lavery*, 152 A.D 2); as well as Jeff Sebo's argument: "The fact that a question is unsettling is not a justification for avoiding it. We should not ignore injustice out of fear of what it might mean to recognize it" (Sebo). Indeed, if law is to fulfill its purpose, it must be responsive to issues that wear hard on the fabric of society, and few questions are more central to mankind's evolving morality than the relationship between humans and animals.

Note

1. The Latin terms *in rem* and *in personam* relate to who is the appropriate defendant in a lawsuit. With an *in personam* proceeding, a person, typically the owner of the property, is the defendant. With an *in rem* proceeding, ascertaining or suing the owner is not necessary; the property itself is deemed to be the defendant.

Works Cited

Baggini, Julian. "Beyond A Reasonable Doubt." Rev. of *On Truth*, by Simon Blackman. *Wall Street Journal* 25 July 2018: A17.

Bank of the United States v. Deveaux, 5 Cranch 61 (1809) http://press-pubs.uchicago.edu/founders/documents/a3_2_1s50.html 3 Aug. 2018.

Barash, David. "The Leap from Beast to Man." Rev. of *The Gap*, by Thomas Suddendorf. *Wall Street Journal* 16–17 Nov. 2013: C5.

Bekoff, Marc. "Animal Emotions: Exploring Passionate Natures." *BioScience* Oct. 2000: 861–870.

Black, Henry. *Black's Law Dictionary*, 4th Ed. (1951): 1577.

Blackmore, Susan. "Decoding the Puzzle of Human Consciouness." *Scientific American* Sept. 2018: 49–53.

Brooks, Kim. "Motherhood in the Age of Fear." *New York Times* 29 July 2018: SR1.

Buckley, William. Interview. <https://www.youtube.com/watch?reload=9&v=2nf_bu-kBr4> 24 July 2018.

Cetacean Community v. Bush, 386 F.3d 1169 (9th Cir.2004).

Cornell Legal Information Institute. WEX Legal Dictionary. <https://www.law.cornell.edu/wex/next_friend> 4 Aug. 2018.

Cupp, Richard. "Cognitively Impaired Humans, Intelligent Animals, and Legal Personhood." *Florida Law Review* 69 (2017): 469–517.

de Waal, Frans. "The Brains of the Animal Kingdom." *Wall Street Journal* 23–24 Mar. 2013: C1.

Fischman, Josh. "Adding Up Animal Neurons." *Scientific American* July 2018: 59.

Fishkin, James. "Yes, Ordinary Citizens Can Decide Complex Issues." *Wall Street Journal* 4–5 Aug. 2018: C3.

Foster, Frances. "Should Pets Inherit." *Florida Law Review* 63 (2011) 801–855.

Genesis. *Holy Bible*, Rev. Std. Ver. (1962): Ch. 1, verses 25–26.

Gier, N.F. "Inspiration and Inerrancy." *God, Reason and the Evangelicals* Ch. 6 (1987). <http://www.webpages.uidaho.edu/ngier/gre6.htm> 24 July 2018.

Gladstone, Rick. "Dogs in Heaven? Pope Leaves the Pearly Gate Open." *New York Times* 12 December 2014: A1.

Griswold v. Connecticut, 381 U.S. 479 (1965).

Guarino, Ben. "Whales Go Quiet and Dolphins Shout in loud Oceans, New Studies Show," *Washington Post.* <https://www.washingtonpost.com/science/2018/10/26/whales-go-quiet-dolphins-shout-loud-oceans-new-studies-show/?noredirect=on&utm_term=.9936e361b7b9> 27 Oct. 2018.

Guiness World Records—Christian Denominations. <http://www.guinnessworldrecords.com/world-records/largest-christian-denomination> 24 July 2018.

Herculano-Houzel, Suzana. "The Paradox of the Elephant Brian" *Nautilus* 7 Apr. 2016 <http://nautil.us/issue/35/boundaries/the-paradox-of-the-elephant-brain> 26 July 26 2018.

Hindson, Edward. "The Inerrancy Debate and the Use of Scripture in Counseling." *Grace Theological Journal* 3–2 (1982): 207–219.

Jacobellis v. Ohio, 378 U.S. 184 (1964).

Justice v. Vercher. Complaint filed in Washington County Circuit Court, Oregon. 1 May 2018. <http://media.oregonlive.com/washingtoncounty_impact/other/horse%20lawsuit.pdf> 16 Aug. 2018.

Justice v. Vercher. Opinion Letter filed in Washington County Circuit Court, Oregon. 17 Sept. 2018. <https://www.portlandmercury.com/images/blogimages/2018/09/17/1537229464-documentfragment_66832151.pdf> 12 Nov. 2018.

King, Barbara. "When Animals Mourn." *Scientific American*, July 2013: 63–67.

Kuhn, Thomas. *The Structure of Scientific Revolutions*. 2nd ed., University of Chicago, 1970.

Laland, Kevin. "How We Became a Different Kind of Animal." *Scientific American*, Sept. 2018: 33–39.

Madison, James. Federalist No. 51. <http://avalon.law.yale.edu/18th_century/fed51.asp> 17 Aug. 2018.

Map of States with Companion Animal (Pet) Trust Laws. <https://www.animallaw.info/content/map-states-companion-animal-pet-trust-laws> 6 Aug. 2018.

Millar, Heather. "The Nose Knows." *Cure* Spring 2017: 31–35.

Musiker, Deborah, Tom France, and Lisa Hallenbeck. "The Public Trust and Parens Patriae Doctrines: Protecting Wildlife in Uncertain Political Times." *Public Land and Resources Law Review* Vol. 16 (1995): 87–116.

Nagel, Thomas. "Pecking Order." Rev. of *The Silence of Animals*, by John Gray. *New York Times Book Review* 7 July 2013: 19.

Naruto v. Slater, No. 16-15469, OR Ct. of Appeals (9th Cir., 2018).

Niebuhr, Reinhold. *Moral Man and Immoral Society*, Charles Scribner 1932. Preface Copyright 1960.

Nonhuman Rights Project v. Lavery, 152 A.D. 3d 73 (N.Y. App. Div. 2017).

Nonhuman Rights Project v. Lavery, Motion No. 2018–28, N.Y. Ct. of Appeals (8 May 2018).

Nonhuman Rights Project v. Breheny, Order of Supreme Court, County of Orleans, NY (2018) <https://www.nonhumanrights.org/content/uploads/Order-to-Show-Cause-Happy.pdf> (26 Nov.2018).

People v. Graves, N.Y.S.3d 613, 2018 N.Y. Slip Op. 04503 <https://www.nonhumanrights.org/content/uploads/People-v-Graves.pdf> 26 Nov. 2018.

Reed, Lee. "What Is Property?" 41 *American Business Law Journal* Summer 2004: 459–501.

Satel, Sally. "Getting Better All the Time." Rev. of *The Moral Arc*, by Michael Shermer. *Wall Street Journal* 19 Jan. 2015 <https://www.wsj.com/articles/book-review-the-moral-arc-by-michael-shermer-1421711530> 21 Nov. 2018.

Scott v. Sandford, 60 U.S. 393 (1856).

Sebo, Jeff. "Are Chimpanzees 'Persons?" *New York Times* 8 Apr. 8 2018: SR10.

Shermer, Michael. "Confessions of a Speciesist." *Scientific American* Jan. 2014: 79.

Sherwood, Chet. "Are We Wired Differently?" *Scientific American* Sept. 2018: 60–63.

Smith, Adam. *The Theory of Moral Sentiments*. Editors D.D. Raphel, and A.L. MAcfie. (Liberty Fund, 1984) Part VII, Sec. IV, pp. 1 & 36 (orig. pub. 1723).

Smith, Bryant. "Legal Personality." *Yale Law Journal* 37.3 (1928): 283–299.

Smyth v. Ames, 169 U.S. 466, 522 (1898)

Stanford Encyclopedia of Philosophy. <https://plato.stanford.edu/entries/thomas-kuhn/> 27 Oct. 2018.

Stephens, Donald. "As I Leave the Bench, What Troubles Me About Trial Lawyers," *North Carolina State Bar Journal* Fall 2018: 22–23.

Strickland v. Medlen, 397 S.W.3d 184 (Texas Sup. Ct) (2013).

Suddendorf, Thomas. "Two Key Features Created the Human Mind: Inside our Head." *Scientific American* Sept. 2018: 43–47.

Swaim, Barton. "Sifting the Wheat from the Chaff." Rev. of *Reinhold Niebuhr: Major Works on Religion and Politics*, by Elizabeth Sifton. *Wall Street Journal* 27–28 June 2015: C8.

Tilikum v. Sea World Parks & Entertainment, 842 F.Supp.2d 1259 (2012) <https://www.leagle.com/decision/inadvfdco120926000315> 4 Aug. 2018.

The Cross-Cultural Animal

*Human-Animal Interactions in
American Study Abroad Marketing*

Jennifer R. Auerbach *and*
Jonathan Z. Friedman

Introduction

A young woman kisses a towering giraffe in Kenya, which is leaning forward to reach her face. Another woman befriends a camel in Jordan, while a third cuddles with a koala bear in Australia. These moments of human-animal interaction have been memorialized in a set of photographs taken on the spot, which are by turns fun, exciting, and unexpected. Though snapped in vastly different locales, these images—these moments—are interconnected. They each exhibit a young American tourist abroad, interacting with an "exotic" animal, in a way deemed worthy of photographing. These individuals strike engaging poses with these animals, and these pictures, in turn, have become a common feature on the websites of leading American universities, as a means to advertise their study abroad programming.

It is perhaps curious that such a motif can be found so commonly in this marketing domain. After all, study abroad programs at American universities are commonly offered for academic credit, many are led by expert faculty, and most promise their participants unique opportunities to learn about foreign cultures, histories, languages and environments. What do animals have to do with any of these aims? The recurring presence of exotic animals in these digital spaces, rather than reflecting these explicit goals, arguably represent something different. Among the giraffes, camels, and koalas, there is instead an *implicit* message about how these travel experiences should be understood and consumed by American students, and about how cross-cultural interactions are best navigated, experienced, and enjoyed. The animals serve, in a sense, as a proxy, effectively communicating ideas about cross-cultural interactions between Americans and people from other countries. At first blush, such creatures certainly appear benign; yet close attention to their usage in this marketing domain can raise important questions about the way they come to represent ideas about foreign peoples or "other" cultures. These pictures blur the boundary between humans and animals, while simultaneously diminishing the boundary between Americans and other peoples of the world. Their implicit message is that foreign peoples, as represented in these animals, are unthreatening and welcoming, ready to be friendly and act tamely for American visitors. In so doing, these pictures present an objectified and subjugated depiction of cross-cultural interactions, with peoples from around the world happily partaking in the consumption of their culture by young American travelers.

Higher Education and American Study Abroad

To examine the content of these images and the blurring of this human-animal line, it is helpful to first offer some context about study abroad programs in American higher education. First, it is worth noting that the past two decades have seen a widespread shift toward focusing on internationalization and "the global" in higher education. Colleges and universities of all stripes have invested efforts in recruiting more foreign students, developing their study abroad programs, highlighting their international partnerships and engagements, and dedicating attention to branding, marketing and articulating institutional missions around *being* global. Many of these developments have been observed in universities around the world (Wildavsky; Baker; Mittelman), but they are also to a certain degree shrouded in ambiguity. There is, after all, no obvious or undisputed definition of what these institutional reforms should entail, despite the efforts of some universities to position themselves at the forefront of these changes. Regardless of the broader sweep of these reforms, they have no doubt impacted the proliferation of study abroad programs, and the growth in the number of American college students traveling abroad for academic credit.

The term "study abroad" is not new, and it can refer to various programs—the range of which has expanded in the past two decades. College students today can study abroad for a semester by taking a course at a foreign university, or participate in a shorter faculty-led program, lasting usually between ten days to three weeks. They can opt to assist with research abroad, volunteer or engage in service projects, or even complete a professional internship in contexts outside the U.S. According to data compiled by the Institute of International Education (IIE), more than 325,000 students studied abroad for academic credit in the academic year 2015/16, up from 200,000 a decade earlier, and fewer than 100,000 the decade before that (Open Doors). Increasing student participation is both reflected in and propelled by more abundant marketing of these programs, in both college viewbooks and on university websites. The latter has become the most convenient source for information on these programs for students, but faculty, academic advisers, parents, and even peers can all also influence whether a student chooses to pursue these opportunities as part of their college experience.

As the availability of different programs has mushroomed, more American students now study abroad than ever before, but for shorter durations of time on average (Chieffo and Griffiths). Jonathan Friedman and Cynthia Miller-Idriss argue that whereas many students in the past tended to travel abroad to obtain deep linguistic and cultural knowledge of foreign places, today many are more likely to go abroad in search of cultivating a greater cosmopolitan openness to the world. Certainly, the increasing mobility of students has often been hailed as an important means of facilitating broader attitudes or global citizenship, but there remain significant questions about exactly what students get out of these programs. For their part, students have reported developing not just a better sense of other cultures, but a better sense of their own national background (Dolby). A survey conducted by Calvert Jones revealed that American students were not necessarily prone to feeling less patriotic from studying abroad, but to feeling less afraid of individuals from other backgrounds.

Such debate over the benefits and effects of studying abroad is far from settled. However, today one is quite likely to encounter the idea that traveling abroad at the college level is important and beneficial for young Americans, even if it is difficult to pinpoint these programs' direct effects. International travel is part of the zeitgeist of the American upper and middle classes, often seen as something generally good to do, beneficial for developing a moral compass, a sense of civic duty, or a charitable disposition toward the world and its different peoples. A basic knowledge of foreign cultures and of foreign places has generally been viewed as at a premium for ordinary Americans to acquire. This perhaps reflects domestic efforts to celebrate multiculturalism, diversity, and the varied backgrounds of the country's many waves of immigrants. These cultural trends in the U.S. have played a significant role in the popularization of study abroad programs in college in the past two decades, as greater numbers of students have expressed interest in these opportunities, and likewise, colleges and universities have seen financial benefits to expanding these programs to cater to growing demand.

As they have grown in popularity, a chorus of voices has also criticized the way study abroad programs have tended to present international experiences as a commercial product for American students to purchase (Zemach-Bersin). Mell Bolen pinpointed this shift at the turn of the century, noting how study abroad marketing began utilizing "hip" images reflecting popular forms of "cool" advertising. One extension of this work is to consider possible effects of these marketing approaches on the way students imagine foreign peoples and locales and make sense of the purposes of studying abroad overall. For example, Ifeyinwa Onyenekwu, et al. have expressed concern for the way some marketing imagery reifies negative stereotypes about people in African countries and societies. Others have taken issue with the way foreign people might be shown as backward, misguided, or in need of American intervention (Caton and Santos; Bishop). By the same token, just what do contemporary marketing materials suggest about foreign peoples when they utilize images of animal-human interaction? What do such images suggest to students about what they should anticipate when they enroll in a study abroad program?

Animals and the "Other" in Study Abroad Marketing

Images and imagery can play a major role in how products, including tourist destinations, are perceived (Dichter). This is well known in marketing circles, where there is great primacy on assembling the *right* photograph, with the *right* words, to convey the messages that sellers are most interested in popularizing. The resulting images can have multiple meanings, and their meanings can be subjective, but they can also do more than just reflect existing understandings about reality. Images, as analysts of visual material can attest, also work to shape understandings about reality, about interesting products— or in some cases, about entire groups of people (Pieterse). Marketing images deployed in study abroad advertising arguably are no different, conveying consequential ideas to American student audiences.

Indeed, an entire line of scholarship has been developed along these lines, interrogating the visual materials utilized in the marketing of foreign locales. Scholars have previously written about the need for more critical research into the privileged nature of tourism (Higgins-Desbiolles and Powys Whyte; Echtner; Echtner and Prasad; Larsen) and study abroad, along with it. These writers call for more examinations of the inequity inherent in the "tourist's gaze" which involves a visual practice of commodifying and consuming other cultures (Larsen 304). The representations offered in touristic marketing, they argue, exacerbate polarizing divisions between the global North and South and reinforce inequality in the distribution of global power (Echtner and Prasad). These scholars raise important questions about the history of imperial relations in the world and the way that old motifs about exoticized cultures remain a part of the way the rest of the world is popularly imagined in the U.S. today.

For example, nature and natural environments have come to be regarded as sites for tourist consumption and pleasure-seeking activities globally (Saarinen). As an extension of nature, animals have thus increasingly become the focal point of humans' touristic experiences and part of tourism as a consumptive process (Carr). This may explain the presence of animals in study abroad marketing, reflecting broader touristic trends with animals appearing in a broad range of modern advertising, embodying particular ideals, identities, and cultures (Carr). Cultural attitudes toward particular animals often suggest that they have certain human characteristics and are thus anthropomorphized in the popular imagination, too (Clark; Tanner). As Stephen Lloyd and Arch G. Woodside argue, an animal can act as a symbol in advertising that activates a "cultural schema," or deeply held belief, which consumers connect with and respond to in an automatic way (5). Lions and tigers, for example, are often employed in automobile advertising to communicate strength and pride (Lloyd and Woodside). Moreover, there are multifaceted ways in which the meaning of animals in popular culture can be interpreted in advertising. Animals may signify particular human groups including racial, ethnic or gendered constructs symbolically reinforcing out-group boundaries and perpetuating inequality (Lerner and Kalof). In this sense, the presence of animals in study abroad marketing may similarly be predicated on cultural meanings—calling upon widespread associations people may have with a giraffe, a camel, or a koala bear.

These animals are all present *together*, almost interchangeably, on the study abroad websites of leading American universities. Arguably, a more general kind of messaging is underway than the particular associations one may have with one animal or another. Just what then are the marketers of these programs trying to *communicate* in this media? What perceptions are they trying to *promote* or conversely, to *negate*, in their use of so many varied animals, placed alongside American students? While there may be messages conveyed about particular foreign peoples or cultures, the broad sweep of these images suggests that they are speaking to something more common, namely, the relationship between Americans and peoples of other cultures, and the process of cross-cultural interaction. The general messaging these images convey is therefore central to communicating ideas about the cross-cultural experiences of students on American study abroad programs. At the same time, they may in fact also help to delineate and reinforce the power differential between citizens of the U.S. and the peoples in the many of the destinations they visit.

The Cross-Cultural Animal

Among the thirty-nine leading research universities' websites surveyed in the development of this project,[1] one of the most recurring images used to represent study abroad included images of animals. Thirty universities contained at least one image of an animal, and these were all animals that a typical American college student would not likely encounter in daily life outside of a zoo. While there was a great deal of variety in the types of animals featured, there were a few animals that could be found across several universities. The most popular animal was the camel, but others commonly pictured included elephants and kangaroos, as well as monkeys, pandas, lizards, oxen and tortoises.

While there was sharp variation in the types of animals pictured, what they have in common is how they were presented and what they symbolize in the context of marketing the study abroad experience. A camel, an elephant or a kangaroo seems distinctly foreign to the American context and emblematic of particular faraway peoples and places. Moreover, the most commonly displayed exotic animals are particularly endearing in terms of their representation in popular culture. Elephants, as well as whales, have certain significance as cultural symbols in that they are widely considered friendly to humans despite evidence to the contrary (Peterson). Moreover, the image of a mother kangaroo with a baby in her pouch hopping about is an iconic and endearing figure in childhood popular imagination. It is noteworthy that there were relatively few images of exotic animals known to be stereotypically threatening to humans. For example, there was just one image of a shark and one of a tiger, across the thirty university websites, compared with a preponderance of what are perceived as friendlier creatures like a deer, giraffe, zebra, ostrich, iguana, sheep, frog, peacock or dove. Notably, this image of a seemingly young tiger found on the University of California–Los Angeles (UCLA) website shows it sitting docile next to a smiling student who has his arm around the animal as if posing for a photograph with a friend. As such, the otherwise threatening animal is made to appear as a gentle, approachable companion. Moreover, on the Global Education page of the Carnegie Mellon University website, there was a close-up photograph of a female student receiving a slobbery kiss on the mouth from a friendly giraffe. Though the student's expression reflects aversion to the kiss, the image nevertheless communicates the gentleness and affectionate nature of the animal with an unexpected yet endearing gesture. Though one can certainly imagine ferocious animals bearing their sharp teeth or devouring weaker creatures, these are definitely not the kinds of images used on these sites where cute and snuggly creatures abound.

There were notable patterns to the contextual depictions of animals across webpages. These include two distinct categories of depictions that we term "in the wild" and "tame with a human." The most common depiction was to display the animal in its natural habitat or "in the wild." Displayed in its natural environment, the animal is exoticized and the viewer is invited to imagine encountering the creature roaming free. Unlike one's experience coming across such an animal at a zoo, the imagined encounter is free from the restraint and protection of a controlled environment. In one image on Purdue University's website, for example, an elephant roams on a grassy plain with a group of seemingly Caucasian tourists looking on from a van in the foreground. In this case, the viewer could imagine encountering this creature in the wild. Meeting this creature may be a fearsome yet exciting prospect, certainly worthy of capturing in a photograph. But it is not simply this distinct encounter with an elephant being symbolized. Rather, the picture is showing the kind of unique opportunity that such an organized study abroad program can facilitate, and the wild animal, in this image, is shown to be beautiful, non-threatening and accessible. As such, study abroad programs communicate that they provide the prospect of encountering the unknown, peaceful other. Remarkably though, no images show animals engaging in their full range of carnivorous or devious behavior. The viewer is shown curated images of animals looking harmless and even dull, ready to be photographed.

The second type of image—"tame with a human"—is notable precisely because the animals are not shown in the wild or in the distance, but in close proximity to what are presumably American student travelers. These depictions ranged in intimacy and action, showing humans riding animals, posing alongside them like friends, or even hugging or kissing them warmly, as described in the aforementioned image of a giraffe. A range of different species was shown in each position. Elephants and camels, among the most common animals displayed on these webpages, were often shown being ridden by humans. These photographs demonstrate how the animal can be at once enjoyed and dominated by the human traveler. In a cozier image, a young female on the website of Columbia University was pictured smiling while kneeling beside a camel draped in colorful hand-knit fabric along with a saddle. Another similarly adorned camel was in the background of the image. These adornments draw attention to the camels' connection to a foreign culture, and the saddle indicates the animals' utility as a vehicle for human transportation and enjoyment. Moreover, the camels' large eyes, gentle expression, and seated position make them appear child-like, non-threatening, and tame. The camel in this way appears as a stand-in for the cultural "other," demonstrating that like a tamed animal, the people from another culture can be friendly, unintimidating and encountered in a controlled manner. Likewise, in the previously mentioned image of a tiger, an animal that can be particularly dangerous to humans, it is happily embraced by a UCLA student, which demonstrates that the animal/cultural other need not be feared.

Similarly, displaying the animal next to a person who appears to be a local in the typically non–Western environment in which the animal resides was also common. These images draw a more direct connection between the exotic animal and the cultural other it symbolizes. Drawing on historical prejudice and stereotypes of non–Western peoples, the viewer is invited to equate the tameness of a typically wild animal with the civility of a cultural other, which an American student might otherwise stereotype as a fearsome or threatening figure. The line between human and animal blurs, as the tone of the images is not confined to actual interactions between humans and animals, but situated within a broader set of expectations about study abroad as a cross-cultural experience. In this way, prospective study abroad participants may perceive cross-cultural experiences in which they can approach the unfamiliar with a sense of ease, control and even superiority, as if cultural interaction is largely meant for the students' enjoyment, and with the expectation that they will be welcomed. Friendly, unthreatening animals, in other words, stand in for notions of friendly, unthreatening people.

This is evident, too, in images displaying an animal being fed, being embraced or being kissed. These images provide examples of how an American student may imagine having a pleasant, even affectionate interaction with the animal/cultural other. As demonstrated in one image from the website of the University of Michigan, a student is seen affectionately nuzzling a water buffalo, an animal that can certainly be threatening, though in this case the viewer is meant to assume that the animal has been tamed and is safe for the cuddling. By highlighting this image on the website of a study abroad program in which the academic subject (in this case, sustainable business) has no direct relationship to the wildlife presented, the symbolism inherent in the encounter between the student and the animal is clear. In this case, the water buffalo can be seen as representing the people of another culture, who might seem foreign and even intimidating; however, the study abroad message is that they can be readily embraced. This image and others like it not only make cultural contact on study abroad seem more accessible, but they communicate the notion that other cultures can be approached, tamed, befriended, and even cuddled up to, in the same way that this student traveler engages with the water buffalo.

A Tame World?

The animals in these images are not just examples of the myriad of interesting opportunities to experience on study abroad. Rather, they play a particularly symbolic role in their ubiquitous use on study abroad webpages. They are not just animals, but stand-ins, proxies for the foreign places, peoples and cultures that American students can experience on study abroad. Their ubiquity serves to communicate a set of consistent messages about these cultures, peoples and the study abroad experience itself.

Meaning, in visual analysis, has long been understood as in the eye of the beholder (Hall), and these messages are undoubtedly ambiguous, multi-faceted, and to a degree, subjective. However, what is arguably consistent in them is the way they position American students alongside animal subjects as close peers, cuddly toys, and unthreatening creatures.

The line between human and animal in these images is thus blurred in multiple ways, producing different effects. On one hand, there is a physical blurring, as the animals are pictured much as fellow humans might be, as friends, lovers, or companions. The animals are humanized, attributed great significance as arbiters of the study abroad experience. After all, these images are not taken from students' complete photographic rolls. Rather, they are consistently selected as worthy of being used in study abroad advertising, precisely because they seem to reflect an implicit set of meanings and expectations about these programs. To be sure, these pictures have been taken mostly by students or faculty on these programs, most likely with smart phones, and thus have an onus to be worthy for social media. But just as individuals often tend to take the same pictures of the same historic landmarks (Cole), so too are these students opting for the same kinds of poses with animals, relating to, and re-creating, the same overall narrative.

Why does this blurring occur? Why do animals become humanized in these photographs? One answer may be that it is both easier—and more socially acceptable—in today's politically-minded context, to capture selfies with posed animals, than with cultural others directly. Such playful engagements with animals simplify and de-politicize intercultural contact and suggest that the international world is a welcoming zoo-like playground awaiting Americans, in which they can act child-like, celebrate their openness to non–U.S. cultures, and garner cosmopolitan status. Images of student encounters with exotic animals, for example, are likely meant to be less offensive to critics of cultural domination and the objectification of non–Western cultures. Representing an animal as a stand-in for the cultural other rather than an actual human being may, in fact, be read as less offensive than displaying a photograph of an American student arm in arm with a "happy native." With the longstanding critique of displaying predominantly white upper/middle class students with impoverished people of color, these images are likely meant to provide more palatable, less offensive cultural representations. Nevertheless, these representations can be read as highly problematic, for in blurring the line between exotic animals and foreign peoples, these images still reinforce a binary cultural construct which positions an empowered American alongside a world of others presented as tame, infantilized, and unthreatening.

These programs deliberately market themselves as a means of facilitating cross-cultural interaction. Such visual media may indeed be consequential for the kind of impressions students get about the world beyond their borders. Much like young children visiting a zoo, American students are being sold the idea that they can experience the adventure and excitement of international travel and intercultural experience within the safety and comfort of a study abroad program. The animals in these images are thus central to the messages they convey—demonstrating a clear deliverable experience that signifies the acquisition of cultural competence in a seemingly politically correct manner. Whether it is a tiger in Asia, a koala in Australia, or a camel in the Middle East, the petting, cozying up or riding upon of these animals by American students provide messages about what they can expect of these programs, and of cross-cultural interactions more broadly. These images may ease the fears of parents or anxious new travelers by making the unknown appear friendlier and more approachable. However, the images also show Americans as dominant in a world that is simultaneously friendly and ready to receive them. This focus on the American student's control and comfort is incongruent with most writing about the goals of study abroad, indicating these programs seek to promote respect and under-standing of other cultures and encourage notions like global citizenship (Streitwieser and Light). However, this is hardly what these images of human-animal interaction convey.

This raises important questions. First, what happens if the world does not turn out as tamable and friendly to American visitors? Second, what if there is hostility, anger, resentment or even disrespect for these student travelers in search of the supposedly exotic and unknown? Such outcomes are not portrayed in the predominant ways in which study abroad programs are marketed. This begs the question of where the responsibility lies if American students on these programs act disrespectfully toward people from their host countries, or treat foreign locales as a kind of zoo or playground. Unfortunately, the way these images market the study abroad experience, and arguably, shape students' expectations—if not behaviors—has been given short shrift by existing scholarship on the subject. That these images blur the line between human and animal may in fact be directly linked to the way these students can lose sight of the line between learning about foreign cultures and taking advantage of them, opting to snap a selfie rather than engage deeply with the shared challenges facing humanity today.

A Paradoxical Animal

Prospective students or consumers understand that study abroad is a readily available method for engaging in cross-cultural contact and gaining a cosmopolitan experience. Images used to market these programs help viewers imagine these programs in action. By commonly displaying American students cozying up to tame yet exotic animals, these images may communicate many messages, but chief among them is the expectation that these cross-cultural interactions will be positive and playful. They will also allow American students to engage with the animals, and by proxy, cultural others, from a position of relative power. These images thus objectify and subjugate foreign peoples in a distinctly disempowering manner consistent with the consumptive and polarizing nature of touristic marketing discussed above (Higgins-Desbiolles and Powys Whyte; Echtner; Echtner and Prasad; Larsen). The underlying message in these images is that the cultural other is like a friendly animal, a notion which rests upon a biased and paternalistic construct that pits the civilized "us" against the uncivilized "them."

The cross-cultural animals in these images are thus rife with paradoxes. Much like hugging a panda or riding a camel, encountering people from a foreign culture can be intimidating and uncomfortable, yet exciting, fun and a pleasant way to acquire an expanded outlook. But like visiting a zoo, these images present study abroad as a safe way to have a somewhat superficial encounter with the foreign. While the impetus behind these images may be that they show how these programs can be exciting and non-threatening, their implicit messages about cross-cultural interaction are potentially problematic. As currently practiced, these images allow for the marketing of cross-cultural interaction as an essential facet of what study abroad programs provide. Administrators in universities and colleges responsible for these image choices should think more about their ramifications, for they may largely inadvertently be communicating ideas about study abroad that are in fact counter to the ideals surrounding cross-cultural exchange, which usually seek to promote mutual respect and understanding. The fact that this practice is widely found in study abroad marketing is arguably one challenging aspect of this visual domain, as the symbolic blurring of the line between human and animal creates a vision of the cultural other as tame and subjugated. This is hardly the image that most universities and colleges have of themselves, nor of the missions they purport to support in bettering the global world of tomorrow.

Appendix

Top U.S. Universities in *Times Higher Education* World University Rankings 2012–13

1. Boston University
2. Brown University
3. California Institute of Technology
4. Carnegie Mellon University
5. Columbia University
6. Cornell University
7. Duke University
8. Emory University
9. Georgia Institute of Technology
10. Harvard University
11. Johns Hopkins University
12. Massachusetts Institute of Technology
13. Northwestern University
14. New York University
15. Ohio State University
16. Pennsylvania State University
17. Princeton University
18. Purdue University
19. Rice University
20. Stanford University
21. University of California, Berkeley
22. University of California, Davis
23. University of California, Los Angeles
24. University of California, San Diego
25. University of California, Santa Barbara
26. University of Chicago

27. University of Illinois at Urbana-
    Champaign
28. University of Massachusetts
29. University of Michigan
30. University of Minnesota
31. University of North Carolina at
    Chapel Hill
32. University of Pennsylvania

33. University of Pittsburgh
34. University of Southern California
35. University of Texas at Austin
36. University of Washington
37. University of Wisconsin–Madison
38. Washington University in St. Louis
39. Yale University

NOTE

This project is part of a multi-faceted study of the imagery used on the websites of leading universities in the U.S. and in 15 other countries around the world. Data were collected in 2013 by systematically capturing all the images used on these websites, and it was thereafter analyzed using content coding (Saldaña). The 39 U.S. universities surveyed are the highest-ranked universities listed in the *Times Higher Education* World University Ranking, for 2012–2013, a list of which is included as an appendix. We discuss in this essay only a small portion of the data and analysis completed as part of the larger project. Thanks to Cynthia Miller-Idriss for her leadership and support of this project.

WORKS CITED

Baker, David. *The Schooled Society: The Educational Transformation of Global Culture*. Stanford, CA: Stanford University Press, 2014. Print.

Bishop, S.C. "The Rhetoric of Study Abroad: Perpetuating Expectations and Results through Technological Enframing." *Journal of Studies In International Education* 17.4 (2013): 398–413. Print.

Bolen, Mell. "Consumerism and U.S. Study Abroad." *Journal of Studies in International Education* 5.3 (2001): 182–200. Print.

Carr, Neil. "Animals in the Tourism and Leisure Experience." *Current Issues in Tourism*, vol. 12, no. 5–6, 2009, pp. 409–411, doi:10.1080/13683500903132575.

Caton, Kellee, and Carla A. Santos. "Images of the Other: Selling Study Abroad in a Postcolonial World." *Journal of Travel Research* 48.2 (2009): 191–204. Print.

Chieffo, Lisa, and Lesa Griffiths. "Here to Stay: Increasing Acceptance of Short-Term Study Abroad Programs." *The Handbook of Practice and Research in Study Abroad: Higher Education and the Quest for Global Citizenship*. Ed. Lewin, Ross. New York: Routledge, 2009. 365–79. Print.

Clark, Stephen R.L. "Is Humanity a Natural Kind?" *What Is an Animal?*, edited by Tim Ingold, Routledge, 1988, pp. 17–34.

Cole, Teju. "Take a Photo Here." *New York Times*, June 27, 2018. https://www.nytimes.com/2018/06/27/magazine/take-a-photo-here.html.

Dichter, Ernest. "What's in An Image." *Journal of Consumer Marketing*, vol. 2, no. 1, 1985, pp. 75–81, doi:10.1108/eb038824.

Dolby, Nadine. "Encountering an American Self: Study Abroad and National Identity." *Comparative Education Review* 48.2 (2004): 150–73. Print.

Echtner, Charlotte M. "The Content of Third World Tourism Marketing: a 4A Approach." *International Journal of Tourism Research*, vol. 4, no. 6, 2002, pp. 413–434, doi:10.1002/jtr.401.

Echtner, Charlotte M., and Pushkala Prasad. "The Context of Third World Tourism Marketing." *Annals of Tourism Research*, vol. 30, no. 3, 2003, pp. 660–682, doi:10.1016/s0160-7383(03)00045-8.

Friedman, Jonathan Z., and Cynthia Miller-Idriss. "The Dual Logics of International Education in the Global University: The Case of Middle East Studies at New York University." *Middle East Studies for the New Millenium: Infrastructures of Knowledge*. Eds. Shami, Seteney and Cynthia Miller-Idriss. New York: New York University Press, 2016. 189–224. Print.

Hall, Stuart. "Introduction." *Representation: Cultural Representations and Signifying Practices*. Ed. Hall, Stuart. London: Sage, 1997. Print.

Higgins-Desbiolles, Freya, and Kyle Powys Whyte. "Critical Perspectives on Tourism." *The Wiley Blackwell Companion to Tourism*, edited by Alan A. Lew et al., First ed., John Wiley & Sons, Ltd., 2014, pp. 88–97.

Jones, Calvert W. "Exploring the Microfoundations of International Community: Toward a Theory of Enlightened Nationalism." *International Studies Quarterly* 58.4 (2014): 682–705. Print.

Larsen, Jonas. "The Tourist Gaze 1.0, 2.0, and 3.0." *The Wiley Blackwell Companion to Tourism*, edited by Alan A. Lew et al., First ed., John Wiley & Sons, Ltd., 2014, pp. 304–313.

Lerner, Jennifer E., and Linda Kalof. "The Animal Text: Message and Meaning in Television Advertisements." *The Sociological Quarterly*, vol. 40, no. 4, 1999, pp. 565–586, doi:10.1111/j.1533-8525.1999.tb00568.x.

Lloyd, Stephen, and Arch G. Woodside. "Animals, Archetypes, and Advertising (A3): The Theory and the

Practice of Customer Brand Symbolism." *Journal of Marketing Management*, vol. 29, no. 1–2, 2013, pp. 5–25, doi:10.1080/0267257x.2013.765498.

Mittelman, James H. *Implausible Dream: The World-Class University and Repurposing Higher Education.* Princeton, NJ: Princeton University Press, 2018. Print.

Onyenekwu, Ifeyinwa, et al. "(Mis)Representation Among U.S. Study Abroad Programs Traveling to the African Continent: A Critical Content Analysis of a Teach Abroad Program." *Frontiers: The Interdisciplinary Journal of Study Abroad* 29.1 (2017): 68–84. Print.

Open Doors. *"Fast Facts."* New York: Institute of International Education, 2017. Print.

Peterson, John H. "Epilogue: Whales and Elephants as Cultural Symbols." *Arctic*, vol. 46, no. 2, 1993, pp. 172–174. *JSTOR*, www.jstor.org/stable/40511509.

Pieterse, Jan Nederveen. *White on Black: Images of Africa and Blacks in Western Popular Culture.* New Haven: Yale University Press, 1995. Print.

Saarinen, Jarkko. "Tourism and Tourists in Nature, National Parks, and Wilderness." *The Wiley Blackwell Companion to Tourism*, 2014, pp. 500–512, doi:10.1002/9781118474648.ch40.

Saldaña, Johnny. *The Coding Manual for Qualitative Researchers.* London, UK: Sage, 2009. Print.

Streitwieser, Bernhard T., and G. Light. "The Grand Promise of Global Citizenship through Study Abroad: The Student View." *Global and Local Internationalization.* Eds. Jones, Elspeth, et al. Rotterdam: Sense Publishers, 2016. 67–73. Print.

Tanner, Nancy. "Becoming Human, Our Links with Our Past" *What Is an Animal?*, edited by Tim Ingold, Routledge, 1988, pp. 127–140.

Wildavsky, Ben. *The Great Brain Race: How Global Universities Are Reshaping the World.* Princeton, NJ: Princeton University Press, 2010. Print.

Zemach-Bersin, Talya. "Selling the World: Study Abroad Marketing and the Privatization of Global Citizenship." *The Handbook of Research and Practice in Study Abroad: Higher Education and the Quest for Global Citizenship.* Ed. Lewin, Ross. New York: Routledge, 2009. 303–20. Print.

Presenting One's Self as a Furry

What Does This Mean?

JACKIE ELLER, JACOB LAX *and*
MARY DE LA TORRE

Introduction

A furry is loosely defined as "someone … expressing an interest in anthropomorphic animals and/or creatures (and perhaps some affiliation to the furry fandom)" (Wikifur). Being a furry involves being intentional about appearances, which signal attitudes as well as behaviors. It may include embracing a fursona (a furry identity) and potentially queering the gender binary. It is, most importantly, a social construct. The furry phenomenon has spawned a lively fandom that communicates online to establish identity and connections.

The Furries (Sometimes Otherkin or Therians)

If someone claims to be a furry and is therefore blurring the line between the human and nonhuman animal (NHA from now on), what does this mean in terms of appearances, attitudes, and social presentation? One such blurring occurs in those who claim identities as otherkin, another in therians, and also the blurring found in being a furry and/or committing to the furry fandom. It is important to explore briefly these otherkin and therian "blurred" identities (both of which may include furries) prior to a discussion of furries, as these three groups are often linked both appropriately and inappropriately.

While recognizing the difficulty in clearly identifying who is or is not an otherkin, Joseph P. Laycock works from qualitative interviews of self-identified otherkin to make the argument that these individuals "believe they are not completely human" (68). Based on these interviews and those from Lupa, who published *A Field Guide to Otherkin*, Laycock points out a diversity of identities: faeries, elves, vampires, angels, and demons to mention a few (69). These identities are made meaningful within the otherkin community, which exists primarily online and "is regarded as an alternative nomos—a socially constructed worldview—that sustains alternate ontologies" (Laycock 65). A significant distinction for those who identify as otherkin is that their "not completely humanness" tends to be more other worldly, so to speak, than NHA. Those who identify as being a furry may also claim to be otherkin, but only sometimes.

Therianthropes identify in a biological and metaphysical or spiritual sense as both human and NHA. Thinking as a human and as an NHA necessitates walking between the two worlds of existence. Based on her study of therianthropy websites and interviews with therians, Venetia Laura Delano Robertson argues that these NHA shape-shifting individuals emphasize they are defined as having "a beast within" ("The Beast Within" 17), are "born, not made" ("The Beast Within" 18), and have looked into themselves in a kind of awakening to find remnants of their animal existence, something most humans do not do ("The Law of the Jungle" 265). Canid and feline theriotypes are most common, but therians are also born as hawks, ravens, and even earwigs. The point is not so much the particular beast, but that one exists in the liminal space between human and NHA. Sometimes those who identify as being a furry also claim to be therian, but only sometimes. Many would argue that the two groups exist in different subcultures where the frivolity of furry fandom is to be separated from the solemnity of those who claim fursonas (an animal identity) and the spirituality of therianthropes (Robertson, "The Beast Within" 13).

The official brochure for Anthrocon 2016 (reproduced on the Anthrocon 2018 website) describes the furry fandom as "a distinct artistic and literary genre" characterized by "enthusiasm for anthropomorphic animals" (Anthrocon). It claims that as a diverse group, furries are linked by "mutual admiration for these creatures of myth and legend who, by simple reflection, grant us a better window into understanding our own natures" (Anthrocon). The exact boundaries of the "fandom" definition are unclear, as is the meaning of furriness itself. While members of the fandom seem to use "fandom" in a formal capacity explicitly to describe particular interest in forms of art, it is also used less formally to refer to all members of the furry community regardless of artistic involvement and commitment to a furry identity or fursona.

Furries are more likely to be male (but this does depend somewhat on level of commitment to a fursona), self-identify as white, and are sexually and gender diverse (Eller, Eller, and Santoni-Sanchez 234–235; Roberts et al.; Gerbasi et al.). This diversity implies they are not tightly constrained by gender or sexual binaries. Furries might claim to be heterosexual, homosexual, bisexual, pansexual, or non-sexual, for example. Further, these studies find that furries may claim one sexuality and/or gender in his/her fursona and another in "real life."

Whether in fursuit, wearing tails or ears, or claiming a fursona without furry accouterments, furries' NHA "choices" range broadly with canines, big cats (lions not as common as others), cervidae, bovidae, and ursidae being the most common. Rarely, whether in artistic presentation or in human-animal form are NHA identities primates. Reasons given for these identity "choices" may be about gender ideologies, striving for innocence, giving voice to a forgotten or overlooked animal, embracing the NHA assumed characteristics, or even challenging social norms such as found in plushie love (sexual intimacy with stuffed animals) or predator/prey anthropomorphization. Whatever the "choice," the range reflects a wished-for self, a spiritual self, or a presentation of the actual self identity (Eller et al. 238–239).

The meaning of furriness, then, varies among groups and individuals within the furry community, which itself is loosely defined. Individual levels of furriness seem to fall somewhere along a continuum ranging from enjoyment of furry art to feelings of species dystopias, more akin to therianthropes, even if not so identified. In addition, individual commitments to fursonas (NHA identity) and the degree of kindred association vary as well. Some furries speak of their fursonas simply as avatars or characters and make clear distinctions between these and their human lives. Others identify deeply with their fursonas and view themselves or their avatars as inseparable from their "true," authentic selves. It is here, through fursonas, that furries play with social constructions of identity, appearance, gender, and sexuality.

It is generally assumed in the larger society that NHAs do not perceive, or perhaps are incapable of perceiving, the norms of human societies. Moreover, NHAs are not expected to hold humans accountable to normative structures of human behavior. Perhaps herein lies where furries find a particular freedom to play with and blur these constructions of identity, gender and sexuality. Through the blending of NHA characters with human characteristics (i.e., the anthropomorphizing of NHAs), furries loosen the rigidity of accountability structures firmly rooted with constructions of human experience. This may at first seem contradictory because a central contention of the furry community is that the boundary between human and NHAs is socially constructed, but to recognize this point is to embrace that same sense of freedom.

Presentation of Self and Impression Management

In *The Presentation of Self in Everyday Life*, Erving Goffman lays a groundwork for the study of self and impression management proposing a dramaturgical approach to studying interactions in society. For Goffman, social interactions are essentially theatrical: actors tailor their behaviors to engage in particular performances, which are designed with specific audiences in mind. These performances are "scripted" and depend on an actor's definition of the situation, any roles she or he may occupy, and how audiences respond. By comporting one's self according to social expectations, one's interactions take on a dramatic effect: "good" or "competent" people become so when evaluated positively by others. Thus, Goffman emphasizes that the process of interacting in society is characterized by individuals actively managing their impressions to be viewed favorably by others, based on perceived feedback.

Writing in 1959, Goffman could not have predicted how the rise of social media might influence particular types of impression management decades later. In certain cyberspaces, however, the synchronicity of individual performances and others' reactions to them may be called into question. On this note, Bernie Hogan argues that there is an ontological distinction to be made between Goffman's concepts of performances, which take place in synchronous situations, bounded to specific times and places, and the type of impression management which may occur on social media. Hogan contends that online presentations of self which are more static in nature, such as a personal profile on a social networking website, may be more aptly understood as artifacts, which take place in asynchronous exhibitions. In these settings, impression management is still deliberate, but there are some important differences—for instance, interactions do not necessarily take place in real time, social actors may never fully know their audiences, and presentations of self are recorded and easily reproduced in other contexts. These contextual transformations exert new, different pressures on individuals to manage their impressions accordingly.

The present study analyzes furries' presentations of self on online dating profiles, which may be better understood as artifacts rather than performances. Here, the furry community shapes furries' presentations of self, including expressions of furry identity, by exploring communications on a large, online furry discussion forum. Here, too, posts on this online discussion forum may be understood as artifacts—however, given the purpose of discussion boards to promote ongoing communication about certain topics, the extent to which online discussion boards are an "exhibition space" is debatable and beyond the scope of this study. Nonetheless, these concepts provide a foundation for understanding the research methods and analysis.

The proposed research questions examine how furries present themselves on online dating websites as well as within a larger online community, with attention to gender and sexuality. It is important to consider what being a furry means in the online furry community and how interactions with members of the online furry community help to shape others' identities as furries.

Data were collected from two online furry dating websites and one large online furry discussion forum. A total of 115 dating profiles were collected and coded for themes. On the forum, discussion threads were selected to be viewed largely based on the relevance of their title to the research questions. Individual posts within the selected discussion threads were then read and significant statements were identified. Significant statements about similar topics were grouped together and analyzed for dominant themes.

Certain precautions were taken as well. If any user identified as under the age of eighteen, their posts were excluded from the study. However, if the age could not be identified, the posts were included. Pseudonyms were used for all users. In addition, the grammar of certain quotes was corrected to enhance readability, but care was taken not to change meaning.

Safe Spaces, Supportive Communities: Pushing the Boundaries of Gender and Sexuality

The first broad theme revealed by the research indicates that furries interact within online communities that are widely perceived to be safe, supportive spaces for exploring alternative constructions of gender and sexuality. Though not all furries present themselves in ways that challenge traditional gender and sexuality norms, many do—and the community is characterized by widespread acceptance of this.

An Open-Minded Community

Many furries describe the fandom as welcoming and more tolerant than some other fandoms. On the discussion boards, some users state that they joined the furry community after interacting with other members because of how welcome they felt. Laughing-Dog, for example, says, "I can't pinpoint how I discovered the fandom, but what drew me to it was the personalities of the people and the friendships." It is clear from LaughingDog's statement that he enjoys the sense of community the online furry fandom provides, as do many other furries.

In addition to this general sense of community, the furry fandom welcomes the participation of gender and sexual minorities in particular. SmaugTheDragon describes feeling comfortable among furries as a gay person:

I've always liked furry-type characters, and when a childhood friend became absolutely toxic about them, I got curious and did a bit of research…. I focused on the people side. I found that most of the ones who caught my interest were pretty cool. When I started to have suspicions that I was gay, I tried to find a place that I could be myself.

SmaugTheDragon not only finds the furry fandom to be a source of for entertaining his anthropomorphic interests, he also finds the furry fandom to be a comfortable setting for expressing an alternative sexuality in the presence of others. He is not alone.

On the discussion boards, there are numerous threads established by members raising concerns about "being a furry" and asking questions about fursonas, such as which NHA one should choose for their fursona, if one could have multiple fursonas, or whether a fursona could be multiple genders. Most of the responders address these concerns in a supportive way that suggests a general sense of openness toward individual presentations of furriness. GrayWolf, for example, states that "You should choose whichever sona feels right for you." For Blackbear, "The fandom is many things to many people … do what you want." According to MangoTree, another member of the discussion board, "You're the only one who can decide whether you want to consider yourself a furry, and if you do, you are perfectly welcome to do furry your own way."

Together, these examples reflect the loose definition of furriness described earlier. Individuals are given considerable latitude to define the meaning of furriness to them. Such flexibility seems to be discussed in a way that helps to support new furries and integrate them into the community across whichever experiences they bring with them to the fandom, including diversity of gender and sexuality categories. Although many furries may find the community to be open-minded toward gender and sexuality generally, it is through fursonas in particular that furries frequently challenge traditional constructions of gender and sexuality.

Gender, Sexuality and Furry Selves

The furry community appears to be quite open to diverse presentations of furriness, especially in terms of gender and sexuality. Our analysis of presentations of self on dating websites helps to lend more specific insight into how gender and sexuality may play out in relation to fursonas and furry identities. Many furries openly address their nonconformity to traditional gender norms. Francois, for example, a dog with multiple self-described genders, writes,

I'm genderfluid, meaning some days I feel masculine, some days feminine, some days neither, some days both. Basically I don't mind if you call me he, she, they, or pup! I don't like being called a trap, femboy, shemale, or other trans slurs though. Zero tolerance for transphobia, racism, homophobia, and slurs. If none of those apply to you, we'll get along fine!

It is common for gender nonconforming furries like Francois not only to make this clear on their profile but also to go so far as to demand acceptance of this from others. It is also common for transgender furries to share information, sometimes very detailed, about transitioning. These particularly forward expressions of gender nonconformity suggest that gender fluidity, or non-traditional gender expression, may not be seen as transgressive in the furry community as they may be in other contexts. These diverse presentations of self further indicate that the furry community offers a safe space for exploring alternative constructions of gender and sexuality.

Especially interesting in this regard are furries with more than one fursona. Consider, for instance, how Muse describes his two fursonas:

> My two current sonas are a bat and a rabbit. I tend to think of them as just different states of mind that I shift between. The bat … is the craftsman, activist, musician, the kinkster. The bunny … is the Buddhist, the spiritualist, the mediator, martial artist and tea connoisseur. [The bat] is mostly male. [The rabbit] however is fairly androgynous. Part of [the rabbit's] basis for being so is founded in the balance of male and female in Tao, the gender fluid representations of the Bodhisattva Avalokiteshvara and my own somewhat NB [non-binary] traits. My fursonas represent who I am. I have deep connections with a number of other animals as well: wolves, foxes, hyenas, among others.

For Muse, the bat is "mostly male" but the rabbit is "fairly androgynous." One may infer from Muse's description that his association with the androgynous rabbit reflects something of a spiritual journey, and there is a sense of personal connection with this in terms of Muse's self-described "NB" characteristics. Speculation remains as to whether Muse's choices of NHA species are motivated by perceptions of one species (in this case, rabbits) as possessing a more "androgynous" quality over the other.

On another profile, ZestySkunk, who indicates his gender as "male," shares, "I also have another character who is a curvy, bovine taur. She has long brown hair and expresses my sexual side of me." In real life, and in his primary fursona, ZestySkunk identifies as male, but at the same time, he finds a more feminine character better suited to express his "sexual side," suggesting that he does not identify with traditional ideas of masculinity and sexuality. It is difficult to imagine such outward disruptions of traditional gender and sexuality norms in other settings, but within the furry community, it is fairly commonplace.

Even among cisgendered furries on the dating profiles, many indicate an attraction to socially constructed characteristics of gender rather than to specific types of gendered bodies. Thad, for instance, states, "I am mostly into females, but I also like girly guys and trans." PurplePuppy notes that he is looking for "a woman or girly male who can understand me." As Harper explains, "I don't care much if you're a guy, girl, or trans, as long as we get along." And in closed-ended questions, a large number of furries indicate on their dating profiles that they are looking for "trans" in addition to at least one other gender.

Overall, it appears that the furries enjoy interacting within what they perceive to be a supportive, open-minded community. To this end, they often approach gender and sexuality in ways that suggest recognition of these concepts as socially constructed. However, there are limits to this openness—when constructions of furriness push the boundaries of humanness, the community pushes back. On the discussion boards in particular, furries are sanctioned when they take their identities "too seriously"—in other words, when their identities or presentations as furries threaten to supersede their identities or presentations as humans. On the dating sites, however, this does not appear to be an issue, as expressed by the following differences.

Coming Out vs. Going Out: Sexuality and Humanness in the Furry Community

The second broad theme revealed by our findings indicates a stark contrast between permissible expressions of identity on the discussion forums and permissible expressions of identity on the dating sites. Whereas blurring the line between humans and NHAs is problematic on the discussion boards, this does not appear to be the case on the dating sites.

Community Policing of Identity Intensity

There are many threads on the discussion forum related to "coming out" as furry. Despite this preoccupation with the topic, most users do not consider disclosing one's status as a furry to be a serious matter. In response to those furries seeking guidance for coming out, many users offer a simple, curt reply: "Don't." Some users joke about coming out as furry while dressed in a fursuit or during a yiffing party (i.e., a furry sex party). Others seem exasperated by the topic.

Concern with disclosing one's furry status to others is so common that the forum administration created a "Public Service Announcement" (PSA) on the topic of "coming out" as furry. Permanently pinned to the top of the forum, an indication of this thread's importance, the PSA clearly communicates that coming out is something no furry should do: "We can debate until the end of time about whether or not furry is a hobby or lifestyle," the post begins. "However, it is certainly not a sexuality. As a result, there is no need to treat it as such. It only makes things weird." The PSA continues, noting, "People seem to act like being a furry is this massive taboo that will get you disowned, like being homosexual in a homophobic family. However, this is not the case. Not only do the majority of people not even know what a furry is, nobody really cares." The post then warns that coming out as furry "will only make things awkward. If you're worried your parents or friends will think you're a weirdo because you're a furry and its negative stereotypes, then coming out will only make it worse. That just makes it seem like you have something to hide, and that furry is a bigger deal than it really is."

Thus, the forum administration takes the position that "coming out" as furry not only exaggerates the intensity of being furry but rejects the idea that furriness is a sexuality. Furthermore, coming out as furry is expected only to worsen one's relationships with others because it is likely to add unnecessary tension, or awkwardness, to interactions with friends and family. The post concludes with what appears to be a somewhat contradictory point, explaining that coming out as furry "makes it seem like you have something to hide" and suggesting that furries instead should withhold disclosing their status to others to avoid the appearance of deliberately concealing additional information about their participation in the fandom. The PSA almost implies that to consider one's furriness seriously enough to "come out" about it is so nonsensical and bizarre that to do so is to invite suspicion about something that is deservedly stigmatizing (perhaps bestiality or zoophilia), because furriness in itself most certainly is not.

In addition to the PSA, there is also an unofficial "rules board" on the forums, a post replete with guidelines for acceptable furry behavior. Not surprisingly, the board proclaims that "Furry is not a sexuality" and then instructs readers, "Do not 'come out' as a furry." Another rule on the board advises, "Don't flaunt your furry pride in real life or online," which is then followed by "If you wear ears, tails, collars, leashes, etc., in public people will make fun of you. We will make fun of you if you whine about it because you definitely should have seen that coming." In this example, the condemnation of "furry pride" is telling. Whereas gay pride festivals are designed to combat the stigma of homosexuality with group visibility, the meaning of furriness presented here suggests that no such spectacle would ever be appropriate or useful for furries. From this dominant view, furriness is characterized as so insignificant or inconsequential to life outside the fandom that public expressions of furriness actually warrant derision from within the fandom.

Together, the rules and community pushback on the discussion forums appear to deviantize those who identify or present themselves "too intensely" as furries. In so doing, the boundary between furriness and humanness is maintained by sanctioning an overlapping or "crossing" of statuses—humans should never experience furriness as strongly as they do their sexual identities, and presentations of furriness should never enter the public, predominantly human, sphere.

Furry Dating

The status and stigma of furriness are approached quite differently on the dating profiles. Several users actually draw on the metaphor of "the closet" to indicate their level of status disclosure to the larger society. JungleJoe, for example, first describes himself as "very much a closet furry" who has not "gotten around to publicly expressing my interests in [the furry fandom]." Describing how he would like to connect with other furries, he writes, "As a friend, we could talk about what it meant for you to create your fursona, share some of our favorite artists or styles, and other activities that would kind of let me come out of the closet some more." Here, JungleJoe uses the metaphor of the closet to describe his current level of status disclosure as well as to suggest a desire to "come out of the closet" over time, to continue to share his furriness with others. In a different vein, FlyFox writes, "I'm a furry. I don't go around trying to convince people to accept me, but I am not closeted. I am looking for someone who isn't ashamed of who they are and is not afraid to be themselves." FlyFox invokes language of being "closeted" to contrast with the security he feels with his furry identity—a sense of security he seeks to find in a potential romantic partner, as well. Insofar as these and other furries use language of "the closet" on their dating profiles, they do not appear to be bothered by—or even aware of—any comparisons that may be drawn between a furry identity and a sexual identity. They do, however, appear to express a level of commitment to a furry identity not typically seen on the discussion forums.

Even if they do not use the metaphor of the closet to describe their level of status disclosure, many users of the dating sites still feel compelled to share something about the extent to which others are aware of their furriness. As Thunderhoof explains, "I've been drawing furry stuff for years, but I've never told anyone I am a furry, or met any other furries." On another profile, Gilbert describes himself as "a furry, but not an out there furry. Some friends know I am and they're cool with it. Coworkers know and they're cool with it. They ask questions to get to know the fandom a bit better, which I appreciate." Although Gilbert feels comfortable enough to share his furriness with certain others, he indicates that he is not an "out there furry," making it a point to express that there are other furries more deviant than he in what appears to be an attempt to neutralize and thus normalize his actions. Of course, other groups in society may consider Gilbert to be "out there" simply by virtue of being furry in the first place. It is likely that many members of the discussion forum would view Gilbert's disclosure as furry to friends and coworkers as foolish, if not harmful.

Nevertheless, there is the sense that most users of the dating sites are able to embrace their furriness in a way not typically seen on the discussion boards. Many profiles suggest that users identify deeply with their fursonas and do not mind if someone else takes their identity as furry seriously; in fact, many users indicate a desire to share their furriness with a romantic partner in a serious way. They speak of the close associations they feel with NHAs and/or their fursonas and wish to share this experience with similar others. Dreamer describes his ideal romantic partner, saying, "I am looking for the other half to my furry self ... someone that loves food as I do, loves to cuddle, loves to read, has a brain for conversations, likes animals or is one themselves inside, has their faults, likes massages, and likes the idea of actually having children." Dreamer, who may also be therian, suggests that furriness is an important part of his identity which he would like to share with a romantic partner on an intimate level.

Vincent echoes Dreamer's desires: "I know what I want and I'm not afraid to say it. I want to date my own kind. I need to date a furry like me. I want a mate that understands this. I will not settle for anything less. I am furry and proud of it. I am here to meet others like me for a relationship." Vincent suggests that furriness is an important part of his identity, and he wishes to share his furriness with a romantic partner. In so doing, the extent to which he maintains a boundary between a human and nonhuman self is unclear. Vincent also goes so far as to express his pride as a furry, an action specifically prohibited by the informal rules board on the discussion forums. In the context of furry dating, however, this open expression of commitment to a furry identity seems more welcome. After all, it is reasonable to expect that those furries who experience their furriness more intensely would be more committed to a furry identity and thus most interested in finding another furry to date.

Implications of Identity

Our research demonstrates that furriness exists along a continuum ranging from simple admiration of anthropomorphic art to a deeply rooted identity which expands or blurs the line between humans and NHAs. Regardless of the extent to which one embraces a furry identity, a common denominator of all furries includes enjoyment of the anthropomorphization of NHAs as a process in which many furries participate in a deliberate, intentional way. To this end, furriness extends, and thereby blurs, the meaning of humanness. Through the anthropomorphization of NHAs, furries entertain themselves and, to various extents, make sense of themselves.

This is not unique to the furry community. In the larger society, humans frequently anthropomorphize NHAs to entertain (for example, the University Georgia bulldog or fursuited sport mascots). Further, humans anthropomorphize pets as friends and family members. For example, someone living with a dog might construe that the animal "knows" when the person is sad, in need of a hug, or wants to have a conversation, and that the dog accepts and depends on them. Through the dog, the human makes sense of their own self as a loving person. Because the human is not a dog, this connection is due to the human's interpretation of the dog's behavior. What appears to distinguish furries from non-furries in this regard is the extent to which the anthropomorphization of NHAs is consciously meaningful, intentional, deliberate, and about an NHA identification.

Whether in the larger society or in the furry community, the process of anthropomorphizing NHAs frequently includes ascribing gendered meanings to them. Numerous examples exist of species with separate names based on perceived biological sex differences and then by implication, gendered differences (e.g., peafowl and peacock, goose and gander). In many of these anthropomorphizing cases, humans continue to entertain and make sense of themselves, perhaps even legitimating certain beliefs about gender. But in the furry community, this gendering process looks quite different in its openness and freedom.

One need not blur the lines of humanness to blur the lines of gender. Throughout human history and in various contemporary non–Western cultures, nonbinary genders have been institutionalized and considered normal. Indian society has long recognized hijra, a third gender perceived to be neither man nor woman. Although hijras occupy unique roles in Indian society—for example, blessing families during weddings and childbirth on behalf of their androgynous goddess, the Bahuchara Mata—they are often treated with ambivalence, as their social positioning invokes anxieties about gender and caste despite the necessity of their contributions to the Hindu religion (McNabb). Although Eastern and indigenous cultures have especially rich histories of nonbinary genders, nonbinary gender identities are becoming increasingly visible in contemporary Western societies. The presence of transgender celebrities such as Caitlyn Jenner, Laverne Cox, and Chaz Bono helps to normalize the existence of nonbinary individuals in the United States. Nevertheless, transgressing the traditional gender binary continues to remain deviant in wider culture. With this in mind, one wonders the extent to which such transgressions may push the limits of humanness, if at all.

Even if a hobby or artistic pursuit, furriness exists as a place in which traditional and binary meanings of gender are to be expanded and challenged. Perhaps one may begin to understand gender in the furry community by again focusing on how the anthropomorphization of NHAs is consciously meaningful, intentional, and deliberate. If meanings of humanness are to be expanded and challenged, then it quite reasonably follows that so too will be meanings of gender. Indeed, a key point to consider is that gender is intimately tied to our conceptions of what it means to be human. To meet dominant expectations of gender is to meet the standards of successful humanness. To be a "strong man," for example—whether this includes building muscles, lacking emotional expression, or some other culturally defined characteristic of masculinity as strength—is to be a successful human, as defined by society. Furriness may disrupt the linkage between gender and humanness by projecting human characteristics onto other species; it seems likely that somewhere in the process of anthropomorphizing NHAs, furries destabilize human constructions of gender, making them visible and vulnerable to challenge.

In addition to anthropomorphization, furries also integrate characteristics of NHAs into their fursonas. Whether the choice of being a furry is consciously made or is perceived as an understanding of what exists within (partially NHA, maybe otherkin or therian), being a furry is about meanings of self and of the NHA. To the extent that a fursona is constructed, a furry embraces both the perceptions of personality and human characteristics as well as those perceived "personalities" and characteristics of the NHA. One might claim, "I am or want to be sly as the fox," for example. This fluctuation between anthropomorphization and zoomorphization also blurs the line between humans and NHAs in the furry community.

Against the backdrop of sexuality, however, the line between humans and NHAs can be fiercely maintained, particularly as evidenced by discussions on the forums. Anxiety about furriness as sexuality seems to operate in this regard. There is a general aversion to the idea that a furry identity would be experienced as deeply and internally as one would experience sexual orientation. To "come out" as furry, therefore, is to exaggerate the furry experience and create a potentially controversial comparison between furriness and sexuality. One may ask, why is this the dominant view? It is possible that to "come out" as furry is to present oneself in a way that may confirm dominant stereotypes of furries as sexual deviants, as people who may be perceived to engage in bestiality and are equated with zoophiles.

There appears to be some inclination on the discussion boards to deny that stereotypes or stigma surrounding furriness even exist, but the existence of the PSA and unofficial rules board implies otherwise. Consider, for example, another rule on the unofficial rules board that reads, "NEVER mention that *CSI* episode or anything on the media that has 'mocked' furries. They are irrelevant, old, and just stupid." In an episode of *CSI*, the popular crime series, furries were portrayed primarily as sexual deviants, partaking in various deviant activities including group sex in fursuits. This *CSI* episode appears to have been influential in introducing many outsiders to the furry community and perpetuating incorrect and harmful stereotypes, which in turn appears to impact the community, as members express a clear desire to move past this.

Thus, it appears that diverse presentations of sexuality are welcome by the furry community insofar as such presentations are of human sexuality. Presentations of sexuality that decouple sexual attraction from binary constructions of gender may be warmly received. However, presentations of sexuality that suggest an attraction to NHAs in themselves (e.g., bestiality, zoophilia) are hotly deviantized (see Eller et al. for more information). Humanness appears to impose limitations to sexuality and sexual interactions that are strongly upheld by furries. For this and other reasons, it appears possible for one to take his or her furriness "too far."

The very human challenges of acceptance into a community of like-minded others, where all struggle for appreciation and support, exists for those who claim degrees of NHA fursonas. Whether in the communities made available via the Internet or through expressions of desire on the online dating sites, furries, after all, are humans seeking to find friends, lovers, colleagues, and communities that support and accept who they are or perceive themselves to be.

WORKS CITED

Anthrocon. *"Anthrocon 2016."* Cary, NC: Anthrocon, Inc., 2016. https://www.anthrocon.org/what-is-furry/ Accessed 4 June 2019.

Eller, Jackie L., Andrea Eller, and Zachary Santoni-Sanchez. "Furries and Their Communities." *Deviance Today,* edited by Alex Thio, Thomas Calhoun, and Addrain Conyers, Pearson Education, 2012, pp. 233–242.

Gerbasi, Kathleen C., et al. "Furries from A to Z (Anthropomorphism to Zoomorphism)." *Society and Animals,* vol. 16, pp. 197–222. doi:10.1163/156853008X323376.

Goffman, Erving. *The Presentation of Self in Everyday Life.* New York, Anchor Books, 1959.

Hogan, Bernie. "The Presentation of Self in the Age of Social Media: Distinguishing Performances and Exhibitions Online." *Bulletin of Science, Technology & Society,* vol. 30, no.6, 2010, pp. 377–86.

Laycock, Joseph P. "'We Are Spirits of Another Sort': Ontological Rebellion and Religious Dimensions of the Otherkin Community." *Nova Religio: The Journal of Alternative and Emergent Religions,* vol. 15, no. 3, 2012, pp. 65–90. DOI:10.1525/nr.2012.15.3.65.

Lupa. *A Field Guide to Otherkin.* Baltimore, Megalithica Books, 2007.

McNabb, Charlie. *Nonbinary Gender Identities: History, Culture, Resources.* Rowman and Littlefield, 2018.

Roberts, Sharon E., et al. "The Anthrozoomorphic Identity: Furry Fandom Members' Connections to Non-human Animals." *Anthrozoos,* vol. 28, no. 4, 2015, pp. 533–548. DOI:10.1080/08927936.2015.1069993.

Robertson, Venetia Laura Delano. "The Beast Within: Anthrozoomorphic Identity and Alternative Spirituality in the Online Therianthropy Movement." Nova Religio: *The Journal of Alternative and Emergent Religions*, vol. 16, no. 3, 2013, pp. 7–30. DOI: 10.1525/nr.2013.16.3.7.

_____. "The Law of the Jungle: Self and Community in the Online Therianthropy Movement." *The Pomegranate*, vol. 14, no. 2, 2012, pp. 256–280. DOI: 10.1558/pome.vl4i2.280.

Wikifur. https://en.wikifur.com/wiki/Furry. Accessed 2 July 2018.

The Story of PARO,
a Robotic Harp Seal Pup

Yoko Sakuma Crume

PARO is a robot that "looks and acts" like a harp seal pup. Many readers may immediately think that they have no idea what a harp seal pup looks like, let alone its robotic clone. But the cute little creature covered with snow-white fur and adorable coal-black eyes is immediately recognizable to most people from nature-themed calendars, books, or television programs. In reality, few people have ever seen the real pups because harp seals live in the icy waters of the remote Northern Atlantic and Arctic oceans, and also because their adorable pup stage lasts only a few weeks (Lavigne 455). As it turns out, this balance between the familiar and yet unknowable aspects of the harp seal pups was important to PARO's success as a zoomorphic robot, having an animal-like appearance and demeanor.

The robot's brand name PARO came from Japanese pronunciation of the English *personal robot*, and as the name suggests, it was created in Japan. Today, PARO is considered one of the most talked-about zoomorphic robots in the world (Weir). In spite of its price tag of $4,000 or more, over 5,000 units have been sold in more than 30 countries around the world (Steinberg). One can find a PARO in the living room of a nursing home in Tokyo, a therapy room at a VA hospital in the United States, and the car of a Danish therapist making home visits. PARO even appeared in temporary housing in the aftermath of the devastating 2011 Fukushima earthquake and tsunami (Shibata, "Developing Paro" 5). As these examples indicate, PARO is a robot with a health care mission, and its zoomorphic appearance is by no means a coincidence. PARO looks and acts like an animal because its developer planned PARO to serve as a live animal replacement in animal therapy, primarily for older adults with dementia who would not have access to the therapy otherwise (Shibata and Wada 379).

The prospect of the proliferation of zoomorphic robots should be of great interest to everyone because they are likely to impact the nature of long-cherished relationships between humans and animals in some fundamental ways, and that, in turn, may further blur the line between the two. Traditional relationships, especially between humans and pets like dogs and cats, were built upon the notion of bonding between two independent, if not equal, partners. As people learn more about the complex intellectual and emotional lives of pets and begin to question human superiority, love and respect for these animals have been growing and the distinction between humans and animals is already becoming less clear.

A typical zoomorphic robot is a man-made machine packed with desirable animal qualities, as perceived by humans. The field of zoomorphic robots is still in the early stages of development, and its ultimate impact on the human society is unclear. What is clear is their proliferation in the near future. How will zoomorphic robots impact the traditional relationships between the humans and the animals? Will they find a niche of their own and serve as useful tools to enhance the human experience, as "good" robots are expected to? As we look into the future, will robots like PARO replace live pet animals, except in zoos, because these zoomorphic replacements will offer all companionship and entertainment people expect from their pets without the inconvenience of caring for live animals?

Zoomorphic robots are still a novelty in the marketplace today. Even so, the different approaches in building one are already evident. Some developers are focusing on making their robots look like a real dog or cat so that one might mistake it for the real thing, until observing its movements. Other developers have adopted more of a cartoonish appearance, but with poses and movements remarkably close to the real animals they are modeled after. Still other developers, like the creator of PARO, are incorporating a composite of desirable characteristics taken from different animals, and this is the type of robots that may be the most interesting, but also the most confounding, to humans.

PARO stands out today as an example of an early zoomorphic robot that may remain popular for a long time, thanks to its developer's strategy to secure a niche in the marketplace as a therapeutic robot for older adults with dementia. The story of its development is fascinating because it illustrates how many of the robot development projects today are not mere technological exercises done in isolation. Instead, these developmental projects often require many different factors (e.g., technology, social condition and need, policy development, and understanding of human psychology) coming together in a complex way before the developer can visualize what it will be and how it will be used (Crume 6–17). PARO is, in many ways, a unique robot, but its history is highly instructive in learning how zoomorphic robots are being developed in several countries having a strong focus on robotics, not only in the United States and Japan, but also in Europa, Russia, China, South Korea, Australia, New Zealand, and elsewhere.

Profile of PARO

Externally, PARO looks like a well-made stuffed animal resembling a harp seal pup. It is around 24 inches tall and weighs 5.5 pounds, and by design, it "feels soft and has the weight and size of an easy-to-hold baby" (Wada et al. 1781–1783). Internally, it is a robot that fits the common robot definition: an intelligent machine with sensing, thinking, and acting functions. Sensing is performed by several types of sensors that simulate common animal senses, such as seeing, hearing, smelling, touching, and light-sensitivity. The installed computer, having twice the capacity of a common laptop, serves as the command center and performs thinking and controlling duties that include recognizing incoming information from the sensors, developing an action plan, and coordinating actions. Quiet-type actuators move seven parts of the body in accordance with commands given from the computer. The source of energy that enables all of these activities is a rechargeable battery that lasts about five hours. In PARO, these machine components are integrated and programmed to approximate how a real harp seal pup might respond to a human, or more precisely, how people might imagine how it responds.

PARO "responds" when it is called or touched, as people expect a real animal might. Also, like a living creature, PARO has a demeanor that changes from daytime to night-time: perkier during daylight hours and less so at night. Further, because people expect their pets to respond favorably to affectionate touches, PARO does the same, and when handled roughly, PARO acts displeased. PARO also has the limited capacity "to learn" (or act like it has learned, to be more precise) from experience so that the owner can feel that a "personal relationship" is being built with PARO. For example, PARO will learn to respond to the name given it by the user. These features create a situation where PARO becomes more responsive to the owner's preferences, such as responding to a particular name given by the owner (Shibata, "Non-Pharmaceutical Treatment for Dementia" 219).

Important Context Surrounding PARO's Development

PARO was developed in the mid–1990s to the early 2000s as a part of the beginning phase of developing these types of robots. As expected of many new technology developments, this was an expensive proposition requiring many technological, social, and policy elements coming together to back the development effort. The development of PARO has taken place in Japan, one of the leading centers of robotics in the world, and its engineering took into account a wide range of factors, such as the ongoing commercialization and diversification of the robotics field, major demographic shifts taking place in Japan accompanied by a rise in new social needs, and the explosion of interest toward animals in popular culture.

Commercialization of Robots

Although interest in man-made humans and animals can be traced back to the Middle Ages, it was not until 1921 when the word *robot* was coined from the Czech word *robota* (hard work) and introduced by Karel Capek in his play *R.U.R.*, which is about a factory making artificial people (Margolius 3). Today, people worldwide commonly associate the word robot with a humanoid, a machine with the human-like body structure of a head, a torso, and limbs. Of course, robots do not have to look like humans at all. As noted earlier, they are defined by what they do and not so much by how they look (although some experts point out the importance of physical attractiveness for people accepting one robot over another [Steinberg]).

After years of trials and failures in cutting-edge research laboratories as well as the small workshops of inventors, the idea of a commercially viable robot became a reality in the early 1960s, when the General Motors company introduced the first industrial robots into their car-manufacturing assembly lines in the United States. Outwardly, the industrial robots looked like anything but what people had imagined as a robot, and to a casual visitor, they appeared just like any other machine. They were, however, distinctly different from the ordinary machines because of their ability to function "intelligently" using artificial intelligence (AI) and engage in their defined production activities autonomously or semi-autonomously. This new capability was brought on by technological breakthroughs that enabled the cost-effective integration of three key functions (information gathering, action planning, and execution) for practical uses in production facilities. In other words, these industrial robots were machines that, by design, were capable of functioning like assembly line workers (albeit much faster and stronger).

Diversification of Robots

Building upon the success of industrial robots, the robotics industry's attention shifted to the next frontier in the 1980s: development of service robots. The International Federation of Robotics (IFR) defines a service robot as any robot, other than an industrial robot, that provides useful services to people autonomously or semi-autonomously. As this definition suggests, service robots are not inherently different from industrial robots. Rather, the emergence of service robots expanded the context under which a robot could be used. The robots were no longer just big utilitarian machines tucked away in the factories. The first group of service robots to emerge fell under the category of professional robots. These professional robots were designed to be used by trained professionals to perform highly specialized tasks, such as space exploration, mining, explosive handling, wide-area surveillance, and surgery and rehabilitation in hospitals.

More recently, an increasing emphasis has been placed on commercializing service robots for personal and domestic use in the areas of housekeeping, home security, education, and entertainment. One of the most successful examples of robots in this group is Roomba, a vacuum cleaning robot developed in the United States. Roomba and similar products are marketed worldwide today. Another commercialized example is RT-2, a robotic walker developed in Japan for older adults to assist with walking outside of their homes. The biggest innovation in this category, and a source of considerable excitement, is the self-driving car, some models of which are already being road-tested in several countries. None of these robotic examples, which are beginning to transform the way people live, fit the classical image of the robot.

Emergence of Socially Assistive Robots

In the early 1990s, a group of robot engineers and scientists embarked on developing a new type of service robot called Socially Assistive Robots (SARs). SARs are intended to assist their human users through social interactions (Feil-Seifer and Mataric 265), which makes them distinct from the other robots developed to that point in time. Specifically, these robots encourage development, learning, or behavioral change in their human users through their ability to provide appropriate cognitive, emotional, and social cues. In other words, the goal of SARs was to serve people and enhance their well-being through direct interactions, both mentally and emotionally.

Two of the leading SAR pioneers are Cynthia Breazeal at the Massachusetts Institute of Technology's (MIT's) Media Lab and Maja Mataric at the University of Southern California's Interaction Lab. Kismet (meaning "fate" in Turkish), a mechanical-looking robot head that recognizes and simulates emotions, was developed by Breazeal and is considered the mother of all SARs (Menzel and D'Aluisio 66). Maja Mataric's zoomorphic robot, Spritebot, is a one-foot-tall green owl robot designed to assists older adults in playing games with their children and grandchildren (Caruso).

In the United States, SAR development has been focused on assisting youth with disabilities in educational and therapeutic settings. The importance of the landmark legislation commonly known as the Tech Act of 1988 cannot be overemphasized in this respect. The goal of the Tech Act was to promote the application of advanced technology to assistive devices and services so as to support the daily functioning and learning of people with disabilities. This Act, combined with other legislation, galvanized efforts to apply advanced technology (especially robotics) to improve assistive devices and services for children with disabilities in educational settings (Crume 4). The Tech Act was vital, not only for the development of SARs in the United States, but also in how it encouraged other nations, including Japan, to follow suit.

Care Robot Innovation in Japan

PARO is a SAR developed in Japan, but unlike many SAR projects in the United States, its primary aim has always been to serve older adults (although applications in working with youth have also been reported). This focus is not surprising for the nation known as the most aged society, with the highest proportion of older adults anywhere in the world. In 2016, 35.5 million people, or 27.7 percent of the total Japanese population, were already age 65 and older (Cabinet Office, *2018 White Paper*). The enormity of this demographic profile may be easier to comprehend when one learns that in the United States, a country with a large older population, the percentage of older adults is 15 percent (Mather et al. 15).

Rapid societal aging, especially in places like Japan, often takes place not only because people are living longer (as expressed in longer average life expectancies), but also because the number of children born to reproductive-age women (reported as fertility rates) is declining. The result is that Japan finds itself facing the prospect of an increasing number of older adults who need care and a dwindling number of younger people to care for them. While Japan is not alone in this predicament, many agree that the situation is most intense in Japan (Foreman et al. 2086).

The concern over this demographic shift was the driving force behind the Japanese legislation commonly known as the Assistive Device Law of 1993. This law, in part, was designed to encourage the application of robotics and other cutting-edge technology to improve assistive devices for use by the older population and people who care for them. Initially, some were skeptical about using robotic assistive devices (i.e., robot-assisted care), pointing out that the essence of caregiving is human-to-human, tender-loving interaction, according to information compiled by Kanafuku (17). The majority of the public, however, is positive toward the prospects of robot-assisted care, according to a 2014 national survey on care robots (Cabinet Office, *Care Robot Survey* 5). The survey indicates that one of the most popular reasons for robotic assistance is the expectation of and hope for a decreased sense of guilt and burden among both older adults and their likely caregivers.

Dementia Care Focus

The term "dementia" covers a wide range of symptoms associated with a decline in memory and other cognitive skills in later life (often in the 60s and older) severe enough to lower a person's ability to perform daily activities. The Alzheimer's type of dementia is the best known and most common type of dementia. In severe cases, people with dementia suffer from many difficulties, such as losing the ability to move around and even swallow food, and these conditions often lead to death. Even before reaching the end-stage of the disease, caring for people with dementia is notoriously challenging, often requiring specialized care to address "problem behaviors," such as agitation, wandering, and withdrawal. Today, these problem behaviors are considered among the most challenging aspects of caregiving.

In Japan, it is predicted that by 2025, seven million, or one in five, older adults age 65 and older will suffer from dementia (MHLW), partially due to the high proportion of very old people in Japan. For this reason, a governmental policy commonly known as the New Orange Plan was introduced to define how Japan will address the dementia challenge, with the application of robotics prominently discussed as an important vehicle in dealing with this challenge. The global prevalence of dementia has been estimated to be as high as 24 million, and is predicted to double every 20 years until at least 2040. As the population worldwide continues to age, the number of individuals at risk will also increase, particularly among the very old.

Development of Animated Robots

The first step toward a robot that looks and acts like a human was WABOT-1, the world's first full-scale humanoid, developed by a robotic engineering team at Waseda University in Tokyo in the early 1970s (Geere). Since then, these robotics engineers have continued their work in this area, helping Japan become an international powerhouse both in production and use of the industrial robots. The experience and confidence built up during this period formed the foundation for furthering the development of animated robots.

In 1999, Sony Corporation commercialized a zoomorphic robot named AIBO, the name taken from the English phrase *Artificial Intelligence roBOt*. The name's double-meaning in Japanese is "a companion." AIBO was billed as the first consumer robot designed to entertain and learn through interactions with its owners (Hatano 212). In spite of its high price for a consumer entertainment item, at around 2,500 dollars or more, the initial 3,000 units offered in Japan were sold in just twenty minutes, and an additional 2,000 units sold in the United States in only four days (AIBO). The original AIBO (Model ERS-110) looked like a little mechanical toy dog, with a silver-colored hard surface and a helmet-like design that covered the face. It was clear to anyone that it was modeled after a beagle, and it was also clear that no one could mistake it for a real dog. AIBO became a cult item, with a group of small but highly enthusiastic followers. Although Sony halted production in 2006 as a part of the company's reorganization, a new-generation AIBO has been back on the market since early 2018. Today, other zoomorphic robots are also available in both Japan and the United States, as well as elsewhere in the world.

Human Psychology

In developing an animated robot, there are two psychological aspects that are highly relevant. One is that users have a history of close emotional relationships with nonhumans, including non-animated objects. The other concerns a peculiar sensation that takes place when people see a robot that looks like a living creature, but is not.

It has long been known that having strong relationships with other humans is very important for a person's psychological well-being. It has been pointed out, however, that people are accustomed to having strong relationships, not only with other humans, but also with nonhumans. Especially, the relationships people have with their favorite pets, such as dogs, cats, and horses, are often strong enough to be termed as quasi-human relationships. In addition, people are known to treat technological devices, such as computers (today) and automata (before the advent of computers), like their best friends, to the point where the line between animate and inanimate objects becomes blurred (Coeckelbergh 199). Coeckelbergh observed that humans today sometimes view and treat computers and smart phones like other human beings, giving them names, talking to them, and cursing at them when they do something wrong or malfunction. Based on these observations, Coeckelbergh argued that people would easily warm up to the idea of zoomorphic robots and humanoids as companions, especially because of their ability to be animated, and that the distinction between living creatures (natural and biological) and robots (artificial and technological) will become less and less important (200). Finally, Coeckelbergh predicted that the successful development of zoomorphic robots will come before humanoids because they are easier to develop technically and face fewer ethical problems (197).

Developers, however, will face a major challenge in overcoming the phenomenon known as the *Uncanny Valley* effect when they try to make their robots life-like. The Uncanny Valley hypothesis was proposed by Masahiro Mori in 1970 as the sense of eeriness or creepiness people feel toward humanoids when they look very much like real people but are clearly not (33). This phenomenon occurs because people know each other intimately, and therefore, they consciously or subconsciously can detect any "unhumanness" in life-like robots, causing a creepy or eerie feeling. Pet owners and animal lovers may also experience this phenomenon when encountering life-like animal robots because of their intimate knowledge of pets (Steinberg).

Finding a Niche

It is hard to imagine today, but PARO and other similar robots were nowhere to be found just twenty years ago, except in research and developmental laboratories, and people did not even recognize a need for them. Therefore, the challenge for the robot engineers and developers was not only technological (designing all of the components and putting them together as a functioning robot), but also sociocultural (creating a scenario that convinces people that they need one). Roomba's success, for example, is partially due to convincing many consumers that it is worth the money to let a robot clean the floors in their houses, perhaps not too high a hurdle to jump over!

As described earlier, many factors (e.g., capabilities of the robotics industry, clarification of social needs and development of governmental policies, and understanding of human psychology toward robots and other technological innovations) were converging in the mid- to late-1990s in Japan, creating a favorable condition for developing care robots to assist older adults and their caregivers. Takanori Shibata, a robotics engineer at the National Institute of Advanced Industrial Science and Technology (AIST), developed the PARO project in this environment. What was unique about this project was that Shibata had a clear idea early on about how PARO would be used, as alternative to live animals in therapeutic sessions with older adults with dementia, targeting certain difficult behavioral issues such as agitation and social isolation. He noted that animal therapy was effective in dealing with these symptoms, but many people, especially older adults with dementia, were not benefiting from this type of therapy because many hospitals and residential facilities limit the entry of live animals onto their premises due to health concerns. Another reason for low utilization of animal therapy was the high cost of training and caring for the animals in a therapy setting. Further, transporting a live animal can be a logistical nightmare, especially when long-distance travel is required. For those reasons, he found a niche for a zoomorphic robot-like PARO.

Animal therapy is based on the idea that interactions between animals and humans are beneficial to humans physically, physiologically, and mentally. In animal therapy, a therapist uses an animal as the primary tool for engaging and working with clients to address the issues confronting them. Dogs are the most frequently used animals in animal therapy, but the use of other animals, such as cats, horses, and birds, has also been reported.

The term *animal therapy* was first introduced by Boris Levinson in his seminal book *Pet-oriented Child Psychotherapy* in 1969, and since then, numerous clinical data have been published to support the therapy's benefits. The reported benefits, for example, include the psychological effects of increased motivation and relaxation, the physiological effects of improved vital signs, and social benefits through better communication and interaction with other people. Today, animal therapy is popular in the United States and European countries, and it is also gaining a foothold in Japan and elsewhere. With the ever-increasing popularity of pet animals today, it is hard to imagine the popularity of pet therapy declining anytime soon.

Animal therapy is known to be especially effective in working with people with Alzheimer's dementia (Richeson 357). As popular as animal therapy is in working with this population, however, there are barriers that prevent it from becoming more widely used (Vann). Shibata identified these barriers, as discussed earlier, as reasons for developing a therapy robot. Shibata spotted a perfect opportunity for PARO in such therapy, where PARO would be an essential component of the therapy (replacing the live animal), but the therapy itself would be conducted by a human. This arrangement is perfectly suited for SAR-type devices still in the early stages of development and experimentation. Also under this arrangement, the extent of ethical questioning will be limited because a vulnerable older adult with compromised cognition will not be left alone with a robot. Eventually, Shibata named his PARO-centered therapy *robot therapy* to distinguish it from animal therapy with a live animal.

Line Between Real and Imagined

Shibata chose a harp seal pup as the model for his robot to be used in therapy. His original thought was to pattern his robot after a dog, or possibly a cat, as they are the most common and practical choices for animal therapy, but he was concerned about psychological experiments suggesting a potential problem using a robot that is modeled after an animal people are very familiar with. This is because people would be more likely to be bothered by any differences that exist between real animals they know well (e.g., dogs or cats) and their robotic copies. Thus, modeling PARO after a seal pup was considered a safer choice. At the time of PARO's development and even today, technology has not yet overcome the Uncanny Valley effect and other detectable gaps that exist between humans and robots both in terms of physical appearance and action, although there are indications that this day will come.

The selection of a harp seal pup as the model was brilliant in several ways. First, the pup is relentlessly adorable, and cuteness matters in popular culture. That was why the MIT Media Lab consulted animators when they created Tega, a learning companion robot for children (Steinberg). The common practice of people routinely decorating and personalizing their technology possessions, such as smartphones and computers, with cute stickers and personalized covers also confirms the relevance of cuteness. These machines interact with humans, and they feel even closer to them when they look visually attractive.

In the case of PARO, the creator captured the harp seal pup's cuteness by incorporating white fur, a rounded body, coal-black eyes, and hand-sewn eyelashes, and by including the recorded voice of a real harp seal pup, PARO seems even more realistic. Further, PARO's head moves so adoringly, and research shows that a robot's head movement and facial expression are important to attract human attention and initiate human-robot interaction (Bartneck et al. 202). At the stage when PARO was developed, creating a convincing facial expression would have been difficult, but this did not matter because the harp seal pup's face is dominated by its eyes, and the remainder of the face is practically covered by fur.

Most important to Shibata's selection of the seal pup for PARO is that most people hardly know what harp seal pups are really like, and this fact gave Shibata and his team a creative license to align PARO with their goal of creating a therapeutic robot for older adults with dementia. An obvious creative license adaptation is evident in PARO's size. In reality, a harp seal pup weighs around 24 pounds and is 31 to 33 inches long at birth, more than four times heavier than PARO at 5.5 pounds and around 24 inches in length. This sizing modification fits the scenario of how PARO would be used in therapy, being similar to the size of an easily held human baby. It is also the size of small dogs trained to be held comfortably in the arms of the therapy clients. Further, as discussed earlier, PARO's responses to humans and the environment are patterned after pet behaviors and human expectations. All of these features are geared toward creating a therapeutic tool that is useful in giving therapy recipients a sense that they are in a real relationship, taking advantage of the fact that most people have little idea how a real harp seal pup might respond when it is held in their arms.

Effectiveness of PARO as a Therapeutic Robot

PARO was initially introduced into the marketplace in 2004 as a companion robot for people who do not have access to real pet animals because they cannot take care of them or they live in facilities where pets are not allowed. Shibata explained that this marketing decision was made largely because animal therapy was not well known at the time in Japan even though it was popular in other countries (*Developer's View*). The idea of using PARO in a setting similar to animal therapy, however, quickly inspired the imagination of international researchers and practitioners in the field of dementia care, especially in Denmark. Soon after PARO entered the marketplace, the Dementia Center in Copenhagen offered PARO a spot in its care robot evaluation project, which received funding from a Danish national project called Be Safe. The Danish expectation for PARO was high because, in spite of animal therapy's popularity in the country, there have been concerns about the high costs and risks associated with using live animals in therapeutic settings for older adults with dementia. PARO was thought to have the potential to address these concerns, and the findings from clinical studies conducted at the Center (along with other studies that had already conducted in Japan) were very encouraging, if not conclusive.

The successful experience at the Dementia Center led to a contract with the highly respected Danish Technological Institute (DTI) under the condition that DTI would work closely with Danish dementia care experts and Shibata's team at AIST to ensure the proper use of PARO. In addition to marketing PARO in Europe, DTI initiated a set of activities, such as convening user conferences, developing training programs for PARO-based therapeutic activities, and building a network of PARO-using therapists and advocates. DTI named these activities "the PARO model" and attempted to apply the model to help promote other care robots, but these efforts were largely unsuccessful, according to a communication from Shibata in August 2018.

The success in Denmark and other European countries enhanced PARO's marketing potential. Under Shibata's leadership, AIST has hosted nine annual international symposia in Japan so far, attended by professionals and practitioners interested in PARO and robot therapy, and they have expanded the target population for therapy to include children with learning disabilities and disaster survivors.

In the field of care robots and assistive devices, safety and practicality factors are just as important as the use of cutting-edge technology and eye-catching newness. From this perspective, it is interesting to note that the level of AI used in PARO is considered "appropriate" rather than cutting-edge. The Danish Council of Ethics in 2016 has noted that high-powered AI is not necessarily required to create an emotional bond between human and robot, using MIT's Kismet and PARO as examples (Yamauchi 5). Further, the Council has recommended that PARO be used under the guidance of a responsible individual (care provider or caregiver) who is capable of protecting the dignity of the user (8). As noted earlier, the use of PARO in robot therapy patterned after animal therapy is in line with this recommendation.

Acceptance of PARO as a therapeutic robot for older adults with dementia is spreading today, as mentioned earlier, and research activities continue to further verify the reported benefits, such as reducing the need for medication to control agitation and increasing social engagement. For example, the findings from a randomized controlled trial (RCT) using PARO at the University of Texas concluded that PARO was effective in the management of problem behaviors among patients with dementia. The same study also reported that PARO was effective in reducing the use of pain medications (Peterson et al. 573). Further, the cluster–RCT by Jones et al. (625) found PARO effective in controlling low to moderate agitation episodes, and another cluster–RCT by Jøranson et al. (3020) reported a decreased need for using psychotropic medication. Lane et al. (298) also found less need for medication in an eighteen-month study conducted among twenty-three veterans in a United States Veterans Admiration long-term care facility. Currently, the Chinese University in Hong Kong is conducting an RCT on PARO-based symptom management in cases of older adults with dementia (Yu et al.).

In addition, PARO has received approvals for therapeutic use in non-dementia areas as well. For example, the U.S. Food and Drug Administration (FDA) has approved PARO as a Class II medical device for symptom-management for treating depression and pain, in addition to use in dementia care. The FDA also approved PARO for use in rehabilitation of stroke victims. Medicare and some private insurance plans in the United States cover biofeedback therapy with PARO, with a doctor's prescription. (In biofeedback therapy, the patients learn how to utilize their mind to alleviate headaches, pain, and other physiological and physical problems, a technique that has been gaining popularity in the United States.)

Considering all of the research conducted to date, PARO is one of the most studied zoomorphic robots in the world today. This is a testament to the expectation and hope for PARO and other devices like it. Indeed, PARO has been approved for use as a therapeutic tool by many health insurance programs, including programs in Japan, Europe, and the United States. Thus, one can safely conclude that PARO has achieved the general goal set for all robots: to serve a useful purpose and enhance the quality of life.

What Does PARO's Success Mean to Humans and Animals?

The positive outlook for PARO's therapeutic use and effectiveness clearly demonstrates the impact of PARO on the relationship between humans and animals. The irony of PARO is that it enhances the overall success of animal therapy (by virtue of creating robot therapy patterned after animal therapy), but it does so by replacing the animal with a robot. PARO has demonstrated that a zoomorphic robot may be good enough to replace a live, warm-blooded animal in certain carefully designed therapeutic settings, and it has further demonstrated that the robot does not even have to look like the animal a person feels closest to, such as a dog or cat. In fact, the wisdom gained in developing PARO suggests it may be more expedient to design zoomorphic robots based on unfamiliar animals, at least until the technology becomes more exacting in replicating animal appearance and movement. PARO's example illustrates that a better strategy for now appears to be designing zoomorphic robots around the qualities and features people value and want, possibly resulting in the robot being a composite of features and qualities taken from different sources.

In the case of PARO, it is a composite of the physical likeness and cuteness of a harp seal pup, the behavior patterns of a well-trained therapeutic dog, and the expectations of humans for comfort and companionship. It is not far-fetched to imagine a future world full of these robots that look like one animal but behave like another. In this regard, the blurred line between humans and animals could not be more evident.

Epilogue

There is an inclination to assume that PARO works because its intended users are cognitively compromised older adults with dementia. There may be some truth to that, but my personal experience visiting an upscale care robot exhibit hall in Tokyo makes me think differently. The exhibit hall showcased some of the most talked about care robots today in Japan, such as HAL, a cyborg robot that helps caregivers lift and transport a heavy person, and a self-cleaning diaper robot incorporated into a bed. Many of the businessmen I accompanied to the exhibit drifted toward the robotic assistive devices that looked high-tech, but one man walked directly toward PARO, appearing somewhat less sophisticated than the high-tech devices, and picked it up tenderly as he might do with his grandchild. PARO, in response, looked up at the man adoringly with its coal-black eyes. The impression was that as PARO expressed pleasure at being picked up and held, the businessman also felt pleasure, somehow finding the experience meaningful. Fully aware that he was handling a robot, the man said he plans to buy PARO for himself, even though the price is a bit high, explaining he is fascinated by his feeling of connectedness with this animal-like device!

WORKS CITED

AIBO. *AIBOs History*. AIBO, Nov. 2, 2018, www.sony-aibo.com/aibos-history/.

Bartneck, Cristoph, et al. "Does the Design of a Robot Influence Its Animacy and Perceived Intelligence?" *International Journal of Social Robotics*, vol. 1, 2009, pp. 195–204.

Cabinet Office of Japan. *Heisei 30-nen-do-ban kourei hakusho* [*2018 White Paper*]. Naikakufu, https://www8.cao.go.jp/kourei/whitepaper/w-2018/zenbun/30pdf_index.html.

Cabinet Office of Japan. *Kaigo robot ni kansuru tokubetsu yoron-chosa no gaiyo* [*Care Robot Survey*]. Sept. 12, 2014. Naikakufu, https://survey.gov-online.go.jp/tokubetu/h25/h25-kaigo.pdf.

Caruso, Catherine. "Engineering Grandma's Little Robot." *Scientific American*, May 30, 2017, pp. 1–8. www.scientificamerican.com/article/grandma-rsquo-s-little-robot/.

Coeckelbergh, Mark. "Humans, Animals, and Robots: A Phenomenological Approach to Human-Robot Relations." *International Journal of Social Robotics*, vol. 3, no. 2, Apr. 2011, pp. 197–204. DBLP, doi:10.1007/s12369-010-0075-6.

Crume, Yoko. "Assistive Device Revolution for the Independence of Older Adults in Japan." *ILC-Japan*, Nov. 2018, www.ilcjapan.org/studyE/doc/2018_1.pdf.

Feil-Seifer, David, and Maya J. Mataric. "Defining Socially Assistive Robotics." *IEEE International Conference on Rehabilitation Robotics Proceedings*, 2005, pp. 265. IEEE Xplore, doi: 10.1109/ICORR.2005.1501143.

Foreman, Kyle J., et al. "Forecasting Life Expectancy, Years of Life Lost, and All-Cause and Cause-Specific Mortality for 250 Causes of Death: Reference and Alternative Scenarios for 2016–40 for 195 Countries and Territories." *The Lancet*, Vol. 392, Issue 10159, Oct. 16, 2018, pp. 2052–2090.

Geere, Duncan. "A History of Humanoids." *Medium*, 1 Sept. 2015, www.howwegettonext.com/watch-a-history-of-humanoids-9708a4a0d42.

Hatano, Aiko. "Zaitaku hitori-gurashi no koreisha no nichijo-seikatsu ni okeru ningyo robot no yakuwari [The Roles of Animated Robots in Daily Life of Older Adults Living Alone]." *Core Ethics*, vol. 14, 2018, pp. 211–222.

IFR (International Federation of Robotics). "1.2.1 Definition Service Robotics." *IFR*, 2016, ifr.org/img/office/Service_Robots_2016_Chapter_1_2.pdf.

Jones, Cindy, et al. "Does Cognitive Impairment and Agitation in Dementia Influence Intervention Effectiveness? Findings from a Cluster-RCT with the Therapeutic Robot, Paro." *Journal of American Medical Directors Association*, vol. 19, no. 7, 2018, pp. 623–626.

Jøranson, Nina, et al. "Change in Quality of Life in Older People with Dementia Participating in Paro-activity: A Cluster-randomized Control Trial." *Journal of Advanced Nursing*, vol. 72, no. 12, 2018, pp. 3020–3033.

Kanafuku [Kanagawa Fukushi Service Shinko-kai]. *Heisei-23-nendo kaigo iryo bunya robot fukyu suishin model-jigyo hokokusho* [*2011 Report on Long-term Care and Medical Robots*]. *Kabafuku*, March 15, 2012, pp. 1–173. www.kaigo-robot-kanafuku.jp/image/CBDCCAD4_merged.pdf.

Lane, Geoffrey W., et al. "Effectiveness of A Social Robot, Paro, in a VA long-term care setting." *Psychological Services*, vol. 13, no. 3, 2016, pp. 292–299.

Lavigne, David L.M. "Harp Seal: Pagophilus Groenlandicus." *Encyclopedia of Marine Mammals*. 3rd ed., Academic Press 2018, pp. 455–457.

Levinson, B.M. *Pet-oriented Child Psychotherapy*. C.C. Thomas, 1969.

Margolius, Ivan. "The Robot of Prague." *The Friends of Czech Heritage Newsletter*, no. 17, 2017.

Mather, Mark, Linda A. Jacobsen, and Kelvin M. Pollard. "Aging in the United States." *Population Bulletin*, Vol. 70, No. 2, Dec. 2015, pp. 1–19.

Menzel, Peter, and Faith D'Aluisio. *Robosapiens*. The MIT Press, 2000.

MHLW (Ministry of Health, Labor and Welfare). *Ninchisho shisaku suishin sogo senryaku-ninchisho-koreisha nado ni yasashii chiiku-zukuri ni muke te (Shin Orange Plan)* [*New Orange Plan*]. MHLW, www.mhlw.go.jp/stf/houdou/0000072246.html.

Mori, Masahiro. "Bukimi no tani [Uncanny Valley]." *Energy*, vol. 7, no. 4, 1970, pp. 33–35.

Peterson, Sandra, et al. "The Utilization of Robotic Pets in Dementia Care." *Journal of Alzheimer's Disease*, vol. 52, no. 2, 2017, pp. 569–574.

Richeson, Nancy E. "Effects of Animal-Assisted Therapy on Agitated Behaviors and Social Interactions of Older Adults with Dementia." *American Journal of Alzheimer's Disease and Related Dementias*, vol. 18, no. 6, 2003, pp. 353–358.

Shibata, Takanori. "Azarashi-gata robotto paro no kenkyu kaihatsu to kokunaigai no doko [Developing Paro]." *Azarashi-gata robotto Paro ni yoru robotto serapi- kenkyukai shoroku.* no.1, Sept. 29, 2012, pp. 4–17.

Shibata, Takanori. "Mental Commit Robot PARO no kaihatsu to fukyu: Ninchisho nado no hi-yakubutsu-ryoho no innovation [Non-Pharmaceutical Treatment for Dementia]." *Joho Kanri,* vol. 60, no. 4, 2017, pp. 217–228.

Shibata, Takanori. *PARO: Kaihatsusha no koe* [*Developer's View*]. Daiwa House, Nov. 2, 2018, https://www.daiwahouse.co.jp/robot/paro/products/developer.html.

Shibata, Takanori. Personal e-mail communication. August 27, 2018.

Shibata, Takanori, and Kazuyoshi Wada. "A New Approach for Mental Healthcare of the Elderly—A Mini-Review." *Gerontology,* vol. 57, 2011, pp. 378–386.

Steinberg, Neil. "Why Some Robots Are Created Cute." *Mosaic,* 13 Jul. 2016, mosaicscience.com/story/why-some-robots-are-created-cute.

Vann, Madeline. "How Animal Therapy Helps Dementia Patients." *Everyday Health*, Nov. 2, 2018, https://www.everydayhealth.com/alzheimers/how-animal-therapy-helps-dementia-patients.aspx.Wada, Kazuyoshi, et al, "Effects of Robot-Assisted Activity for Elderly People and Nurses at a Day Service Center." *IEEE Proceedings of the IEEE*, vol. 92, no. 11, Nov. 2004, pp. 1781–1783.

Weir, Kirsten. "Robo Therapy." *Monitor on Psychology,* vol. 16, no. 6, 2015. www.apa.org/monitor/2015/06/robo-therapy.aspx.

Yamauchi, Shigeru. "Social Robot ni kansuru kankoku [Recommendations on Social Robots]." *Waseda*, March 2016, http://www.f.waseda.jp/s_yamauchi/Robot/Danish_Gov.html.

Yu, Ruby, et al. "Use of A Therapeutic Socially Assistive Pet robot (PARO) in improving Mood and Stimulating Social Interaction and Communication for People with Dementia: Study Protocol for A Randomized Controlled Trial." *JMIR Research Protocols* Vol. 4, no. 2, 2015, e45.

Selective Bibliography

CAMILLE MCCUTCHEON

Books

Anderson, P. Elizabeth. *The Powerful Bond Between People and Pets: Our Boundless Connections to Companion Animals*. Praeger, 2008.

Baker, Steve. *Picturing the Beast: Animals, Identity, and Representation*. University of Illinois Press, 2001.

Beck, Alan M., and Aaron Honori Katcher. *Between Pets and People: The Importance of Animal Companionship*. Revised ed., Purdue University Press, 1996.

Becker, Marty, with Danelle Morton. *The Healing Power of Pets: Harnessing the Amazing Ability of Pets to Make and Keep People Happy and Healthy*. Hyperion, 2002.

Boehrer, Bruce Thomas. *Animal Characters: Nonhuman Beings in Early Modern Literature*. University of Pennsylvania Press, 2010.

Bovenkerk, Bernice, and Jozef Keulartz, editors. *Animal Ethics in the Age of Humans: Blurring Boundaries in Human-Animal Relationships*. Springer, 2016.

Bradley, Carol. *Last Chain on Billie: How One Extraordinary Elephant Escaped the Big Top*. St. Martin's Press, 2014.

Bradshaw, John. *The Animals Among Us: How Pets Make Us Human*. Basic Books, 2017.

Brown, Stephen, and Sharon Ponsonby-McCabe, editors. *Brand Mascots: And Other Marketing Animals*. Routledge, 2014.

Burt, Jonathan. *Animals in Film*. Reaktion, 2002.

Cosslett, Tess. *Talking Animals in British Children's Fiction, 1786–1914*. Ashgate, 2006.

Daston, Lorraine, and Gregg Mitman, editors. *Thinking with Animals: New Perspectives on Anthropomorphism*. Columbia University Press, 2005.

DeMello, Margo. *Animals and Society: An Introduction to Human-Animal Studies*. Columbia University Press, 2012.

Elick, Catherine L. *Talking Animals in Children's Fiction: A Critical Study*. McFarland, 2015.

Feuerstein, Anna, and Carmen Nolte-Odhiambo, editors. *Childhood and Pethood in Literature and Culture: New Perspectives in Childhood Studies and Animal Studies*. Routledge, 2017.

Freund, Lisa. S., et al., editors. *The Social Neuroscience of Human-Animal Interaction*. American Psychological Association, 2016.

George, Amber E., and J.L. Schatz, editors. *Screening the Nonhuman: Representations of Animal Others in the Media*. Lexington Books, 2016.

Grier, Katherine C. *Pets in America: A History*. University of North Carolina Press, 2006.

Grimm, David. *Citizen Canine: Our Evolving Relationships with Cats and Dogs*. PublicAffairs, 2014.

Haraway, Donna Jeanne. *When Species Meet*. University of Minnesota Press, 2008.

Hauser, Marc D., et al., editors. *People, Property, or Pets?* Purdue University Press, 2006.

Herman, David, editor. *Animal Comics: Multispecies Storyworlds in Graphic Narratives*. Bloombury Academic, 2018.

Hogan, Walter. *Animals in Young Adult Fiction*. Scarecrow Press, 2009.

Homans, John. *What's a Dog For?: The Surprising History, Science, Philosophy, and Politics of Man's Best Friend*. Penguin Press, 2012.

Howl, Thurston, editor. *Furries Among Us: Essays on Furries by the Most Prominent Members of Fandom*. Thurston Howl Publications, 2015.

Hunter, Susan, and Richard A. Brisbin. *Pet Politics: The Political and Legal Lives of Cats, Dogs, and Horses in Canada and the United States*. Purdue University Press, 2016.

Irvine, Leslie. *Filling the Ark: Animal Welfare in Disasters*. Temple University Press, 2009.

Kalof, Linda, editor. *The Oxford Handbook of Animal Studies*. Oxford University Press, 2017.

Malamud, Randy. *An Introduction to Animals and Visual Culture.* Palgrave Macmillan, 2012.

Mazis, Glen A. *Humans, Animals, Machines: Blurring Boundaries.* SUNY Press, 2008.

McCardle, Peggy D., et al., editors. *How Animals Affect Us: Examining the Influence of Human-Animal Inter-action on Child Development and Human Health.* American Psychological Association, 2011.

Melson, L. Gail. *Why the Wild Things Are: Animals in the Lives of Children.* Harvard University Press, 2001.

Mitman, Gregg. *Reel Nature: America's Romance with Wildlife on Films.* Harvard University Press, 1999.

Nance, Susan. *Entertaining Elephants: Animal Agency and the Business of the American Circus.* Johns Hopkins University Press, 2013.

Oerlemans, Onno. *Poetry and Animals: Blurring the Boundaries with the Human.* Columbia University Press, 2018.

Ortiz-Robles, Mario. *Literature and Animal Studies.* Routledge, 2016.

Overall, Christine, editor. *Pets and People: The Ethics of Our Relationships with Companion Animals.* Oxford University Press, 2017.

Patten, Fred. *Furry Fandom Conventions, 1989–2015.* McFarland, 2017.

Podberscek, Anthony L., et al., editors. *Companion Animals and Us: Exploring the Relationship between People and Pets.* Cambridge University Press, 2000.

Ratelle, Amy. *Animality and Children's Literature and Film.* Palgrave Macmillan, 2015.

Rudy, Kathy. *Loving Animals: Toward a New Animal Advocacy.* University of Minnesota Press, 2011.

Schaffner, Joan. *An Introduction to Animals and the Law.* Palgrave Macmillan, 2011.

Serpell, James. *In the Company of Animals: A Study of Human-Animal Relationships.* Cambridge University Press, 1996.

Strike, Joe. *Furry Nation: The True Story of America's Most Misunderstood Subculture.* Cleis Press, 2017.

Tait, Peta. *Wild and Dangerous Performances: Animals, Emotions, Circus.* Palgrave Macmillan, 2012.

Virga, Vint. *The Soul of All Living Creatures: What Animals Can Teach Us About Being Human.* Crown, 2013.

Wells, Paul. *The Animated Bestiary: Animals, Cartoons, and Culture.* Rutgers University Press, 2009.

Williams, Marta. *My Animal, My Self: A Breakthrough Way to Understand How You and Your Reflect Each Other.* New World Library, 2013.

Journal Articles

Baranko, Jessica. "Hear Me Roar: Should Universities Use Live Animals as Mascots?" *Marquette Sports Law Review,* vol. 21, no. 2, 2011, pp. 599–619.

Brown, Stephen. "Where the Wild Brands Are: Some Thoughts on Anthropomorphic Marketing." *Marketing Review,* vol. 10, no. 3, 2010, pp. 209–224.

Carr, Eloise C.J., et al. "Exploring the Meaning and Experience of Chronic Pain with People Who Live with a Dog: A Qualitative Study." *Anthrozoös,* vol. 31, no. 5, 2018, pp. 551–565.

Chadwin, Robin. "Evacuation of Pets During Disasters: A Public Health Intervention to Increase Resilience." *American Journal of Public Health,* vol. 107, no. 9, 2017, pp. 1413–1417.

Christiansen, Stine B., et al. "Looking After Chronically Ill Dogs: Impacts on the Caregiver's Life." *Anthrozoös,* vol. 26, no. 4, 2013, pp. 519–533.

Gerbasi, Kathleen C., et al. "Furries From A to Z (Anthropomorphism to Zoomorphism)." *Society & Animals,* vol. 16, no. 3, 2008, pp. 197–222.

Hamity, Matthew. "Cosmetic and Convenience Surgeries on Companion Animals: The Case for Laws with Bite to Protect a Dog's Bark." *Contemporary Justice Review,* vol. 19, no. 2, 2016, pp. 210–220.

Hansen, Paul. "Urban Japan's 'Fuzzy' New Families: Affect and Embodiment in Dog-Human Relationships." *Asian Anthropology,* vol. 12, no. 2, 2013, pp. 83–103.

King, Margaret J. "The Audience in the Wilderness: The Disney Nature Films." *Journal of Popular Film & Television,* vol. 24, no. 2, 1996, pp. 60–68.

Lerner, Jennifer E., and Linda Kalof. "The Animal Text: Message and Meaning in Television Advertisements." *Sociological Quarterly,* vol. 40, no. 4, 1999, p. 565–586.

Malia, Linsey M., et al. "The Effects of Age and Sex on Saving Pets Over Humans." *Psi Chi Journal of Psychological Research,* vol. 23, no. 4, 2018, pp. 306–310.

McGlynn, Sean A., et al. "Understanding the Potential of PARO for Healthy Older Adults." *International Journal of Human-Computer Studies,* vol. 100, Apr. 2017, pp. 33–47.

Pierson, David P. "'Hey, They're Just Like Us!': Representations of the Animal World in the Discovery Channel's Nature Programming." *The Journal of Popular Culture,* vol. 38, no. 4, 2005, pp. 698–712.

Porter, Pete. "Engaging the Animal in the Moving Image." *Society & Animals,* vol. 14, no. 4, 2006, pp. 399–416.

Roberts, Sharon E., et al. "The Anthrozoomorphic Identity: Furry Fandom Members' Connections to Non-human Animals." *Anthrozoös,* vol. 28, no. 4, 2015, pp. 533–548.

Serpell, James A. "Anthropomorphism and Anthropomorphic Selection—Beyond the 'Cute Response.'" *Society & Animals,* vol. 11, no. 1, 2003, pp. 83–100.

Takanori, Shibata. "Mentally Soothing Robot 'Paro.'" *Economy, Culture & History Japan Spotlight Bimonthly,* vol. 26, no. 1, 2007, pp. 21–23.

Vänskä, Annamari. "New Kids on the Mall: Babyfied Dogs as Fashionable Co-Consumers." *Young Consumers,* vol. 15, no. 3, 2014, pp. 263–272.

Yampell, Cat. "When Science Blurs the Boundaries: The Commodification of the Animal in Young Adult Science Fiction." *Science Fiction Studies,* vol. 35, no. 2, 2008, pp. 207–222.

About the Contributors

Jay **Alabaster** is a Ph.D. student at the Walter Cronkite School of Journalism at Arizona State University. He is conducting fieldwork for his dissertation in Taiji, Japan. He previously worked as a reporter in the Tokyo bureaus of the Associated Press and Dow Jones.

Jennifer R. **Auerbach** is an international education specialist at the City University of New York. She received a Ph.D. in international education from New York University specializing in near Eastern studies and global education. Her research interests include higher education, cultural symbols and cultural conflict, and Islam, secularism, and collective identity in Turkey.

Tammy **Bar-Joseph** is pursuing an MA in cultural studies at the Open University and belongs to the human-animal bond research forum at Tel Aviv University. She studies dog culture in Israel, and focuses on the human-canine relationship, particularly in terms of the Holocaust and collective memory. She has published an article for a journal about Holocaust documentation and research.

Yoko Sakuma **Crume** is an aging-service consultant and advocate specializing in the health and well-being of older adults. She has taught graduate school social work classes and conducted international research on wide-ranging topics affecting quality of life in later years. Her research on robotics and artificial intelligence has been published in both English and Japanese.

Mary **De La Torre** is an adjunct professor of sociology at Tennessee Wesleyan University. She earned an MA in sociology from Middle Tennessee State University. Her research interests include deviance, identity, stigmatized groups, and motherhood/non-motherhood with a specific focus on how these concepts relate to and affect women who are incarcerated.

Jackie **Eller** is a professor of sociology at Middle Tennessee State University. She specializes in research and teaching related to social deviance, sociology of emotions, gender and feminism, as well as drugs in society. Her work blends these perspectives as she addresses aspects of nonhuman animals within society.

Jonathan Z. **Friedman** is the project director for campus free speech at PEN America, where he oversees advocacy, analysis, and outreach concerning free speech, diversity, and inclusion in higher education. He has a Ph.D. in international education from New York University and has been an adjunct professor at New York University and Columbia University. His research focuses on American and international higher education.

Mort **Gamble** earned an Ed.D. in higher education leadership, MA in English, and BA in English from West Virginia University. He served in various positions in higher education before becoming senior vice president for Virginia Wesleyan University. Although he made his living in academe, Gamble held a life-long passion for the circus. He died on January 29, 2020.

Jill S. **Grigsby** is a professor of social sciences and sociology at Pomona College in Claremont, California, where her teaching and research include animal studies, family, and population. In 2017 she taught "Japanese Families in a Globalizing World" for undergraduates studying at the

Associated Kyoto Program at Doshisha University in Japan and continued her research on families and pets.

Stacy **Hoult-Saros** is an associate professor of Spanish at Valparaiso University, where she teaches courses on Spanish language and on Latin American and Latinx cultures and cultural production. She also serves as chair of the board of directors for the Institute for Humane Education. Her research focuses on Latin American and Latinx poetry and Latinx popular culture through the lens of humane education.

George S. **Jackson** is a professor of management, business, and economics at Virginia Wesleyan University and the 2019–2020 J. Robert Beyster Fellow at Rutgers University. He holds law degrees from the University of North Carolina and Georgetown University. His published writings typically address tax or property law matters.

Kathy Merlock **Jackson** is a professor of communication at Virginia Wesleyan University, where she teaches courses in media studies and children's culture. She has published over a hundred articles, chapters, and reviews and has written or edited ten books, four of them on Disney-related topics. Her most recent titles include *Revisiting* Mister Rogers' Neighborhood and *Shapers of American Childhood*. She is the former editor of *The Journal of American Culture* and the 2019–2021 president of the Popular Culture Association.

Jeffrey **Jin** is an adjunct professor and medical social worker. He earned his undergraduate degree in anthropology and both his MA and Ph.D. in social work from the University of Pennsylvania. His research focuses on minority access to mental and physical health services with a recent qualitative study examining the clinical significance of companion animals for LGBT+ youth.

Candace **Korasick** earned a Ph.D. in sociology, with a certificate in women's and gender studies, from the University of Missouri–Columbia. As a Mizzou Advantage Postdoctoral Teaching Fellow, she shifted the focus of her teaching and research to human-animal relationships. She teaches for the MU Department of Sociology and the MU Honors College.

Terri **Kovach** is a sociologist and academic librarian who has been a volunteer and researcher in hospice and palliative care, with publications related to services for the terminally ill and PTSD in the community. She is a professor and librarian at Monroe County Community College in Michigan. She holds a Ph.D. in sociology from Wayne State University and an MA in library science from the University of Michigan.

Amy J. **Lantinga** is a teaching professor at Northeastern University. Her research focuses on outcomes in first-year programs for underserved populations, service-learning, and American popular culture in the area of disasters and discourse. She received the Excellence in Teaching Award in 2012. She holds a BA from the University of Michigan–Ann Arbor and an Ed.D. in curriculum and instruction from the University of Tennessee–Knoxville

Elizabeth A. **Larsen** is the director of sociology at California University of Pennsylvania. Her research is published in *Journal of Contemporary Ethnography, Gender, Work and Organization*, and *Journal of Women and Minorities in Science and Engineering*. She served as president for the Pennsylvania Sociological Society, and the Association for Applied and Clinical Sociology. She is the author of *Gender, Work and Harness Racing: Fast Horses and Strong Women in Southwestern Pennsylvania* (2015).

Jacob **Lax** received an MA in sociology from Middle Tennessee State University in 2018. His areas of interest include gender, deviance, and nonhuman animals in society. His work in sociology is motivated by his desire to transform the social world in ways that are more equitable and just, not just for humans but for all the animals among us.

Terry **Lindvall** occupies the C.S. Lewis Chair of Communication at Virginia Wesleyan University. He is the author of ten books, including *God Mocks: A History of Religious Satire* (NYU Press, 2015), *Divine Film Comedies* (Routledge, 2016), and *God on the Big Screen: A History of Cinematic*

Prayers (NYU Press, 2019). He previously taught at Duke University and the College of William and Mary.

Hadas **Marcus** teaches English for Academic Purposes (EAP), focusing on environmental studies, the arts, and biology at Tel Aviv University and Oranim College of Education, Israel. She belongs to a research forum on the human-animal bond at Tel Aviv University and is an associate fellow of the Oxford Centre for Animal Ethics. She has written a nature book, many articles and book chapters, and presented numerous talks at conferences worldwide, particularly about animal welfare, ecocriticism, environmental topics, and popular culture.

Kristi **Maxwell** is an assistant professor of English at the University of Louisville. Her research interests include the body, poetic form and performance, and theories of representation and difference. She is the author of six books, including *Bright and Hurtless* (Ahsahta Press, 2018), *That Our Eyes Be Rigged* (Saturnalia, 2014), and *Hush Sessions* (Saturnalia, 2009).

Camille **McCutcheon** is the coordinator of Collection Management and Administrative Services at the University of South Carolina Upstate Library. She is a past president of the Southeastern Library Association and a former book review editor for *The Journal of American Culture*. She has published articles in *CHOICE: Current Reviews for Academic Libraries*, *Against the Grain*, and *Research Strategies*. Her research interests include children's literature, film history, and film star biographies.

Lisa Lyon **Payne** is a professor of communication at Virginia Wesleyan University. She obtained a Ph.D. from the University of Georgia's Grady College of Journalism and Mass Communication. In addition to a book co-authored with Kathy Shepherd Stolley and Kathy Merlock Jackson, she has authored or co-authored more than twenty book chapters or journal articles in the areas of college media, popular culture, crisis communication, reputation management and public relations theory development.

Lynnette **Porter** is a professor of humanities and communication at Embry-Riddle Aeronautical University in Daytona Beach, Florida, and the editor of the journal *Studies in Popular Culture*. She frequently writes books or chapters about popular culture, especially television series (e.g., *Sherlock*, *Doctor Who*, *LOST*) or famous people (e.g., Benedict Cumberbatch, Johnny Weir).

Kathy Shepherd **Stolley** is a professor of sociology at Virginia Wesleyan University. In addition to developing and teaching classes on "Animals and Society" and "Animals in Criminal Justice," she specializes in applied sociology and sociological practice. Including this collection, she has written or edited six books.

Katharine **Wenocur** works as an adjunct professor and in private practice, focusing on the provision of animal assisted therapy and play therapy to children and families. She holds an MA and a Ph.D. in social work from the University of Pennsylvania. Her research has focused on canine assisted therapy, play therapy, and the treatment of childhood trauma.

Mark I. **West** is a professor of English at the University of North Carolina at Charlotte, where he teaches courses on children's and young adult literature and holds the title of Bonnie E. Cone Professor of Civic Engagement. He has written or edited sixteen books, the most recent of which is *Shapers of American Childhood*, which he co-edited with Kathy Merlock Jackson.

Martin **Woodside** is a writer, educator, and founding member of Calypso Editions. He earned a certificate of specialization in children's literature from San Diego State University and a Ph.D. in childhood studies from Rutgers University–Camden in 2015. He is the author of *Frontiers of Boyhood: Imagining America Past and Future* (2020).

Index